MIGRATION CRISES AND THE STRUCTURE OF INTERNATIONAL COOPERATION

STUDIES IN SECURITY
AND INTERNATIONAL AFFAIRS

Migration Crises and the Structure of International Cooperation

Jeannette Money
Sarah P. Lockhart

The University of Georgia Press
Athens

Paperback edition, 2023
© 2018 by the University of Georgia Press
Athens, Georgia 30602
www.ugapress.org
Set in Minion Pro by Graphic Composition, Inc., Bogart, Georgia

Most University of Georgia Press titles are
available from popular e-book vendors.

Printed digitally

Library of Congress Cataloging-in-Publication Data

Names: Money, Jeannette, author. | Lockhart, Sarah P., 1980–, author.
Title: Migration crises and the structure of international cooperation /
    Jeannette Money, Sarah P. Lockhart.
Description: Athens, Georgia : University of Georgia Press, [2018] |
    Series: Studies in security and international aff airs | Includes
    bibliographical references and index.
Identifiers: LCCN 2018008699 | ISBN 9780820354057 (hardback : alk. paper) |
    ISBN 9780820354064 (ebook)
Subjects: LCSH: Emigration and immigration—International cooperation. |
    Sovereignty. | Immigrants—Political activity.
Classifi cation: LCC JV6035 .M65 2018 | DDC 304.8—dc23
LC record available at https://lccn.loc.gov/2018008699

Paperback ISBN 978-0-8203-6490-2

For our children:
Justine and Connor
Leah and Benjamin

CONTENTS

ACKNOWLEDGMENTS

The *Economist* reminds us that "the starting point of science is collecting [data].... Then, once the collection is large enough, patterns begin to emerge" ("Exoplanets" 2017). This book is testament to the collection of data — patterns of state behavior on international migration — sufficiently large to begin to see patterns emerge. In the process, we taxed the comity of several colleagues who read meandering conference papers and draft articles, until we uncovered the patterns that we describe in this volume. Even then, we received extraordinarily useful comments on the first draft of this book so that our theoretical focus and presentation of empirical evidence are now more concise and coherently presented. In particular, we thank Gary Freeman, Audie Klotz, Jeroen Doomernik, and Eiko Thielemann, as well as two anonymous reviewers, who understood our goals and helped us better achieve them. We have benefited from the research of many scholars in our own discipline of political science as well as in economics, history, sociology, law, and demography, as the study of migration is multidisciplinary and insights from these fields are critical to understanding the politics of migration. Our debt is acknowledged in the extensive citations in the text. We cannot forget Randall Hansen and Jobst Koehler, who originally invited us to participate in a collaborative project on international cooperation on migration; without that initial invitation, our research agenda would have taken other paths. Other colleagues have provided moral support along what turned out to be a much longer road than anticipated, including Scott Gartner, Gabriella Montinola, Jo Andrews, Heather McKibben, and Shaina Western, among others. Finally, our families remained an arena of refuge throughout the process of research and writing. Although the remaining errors of commission and omission are ours, we offer our warmest thanks to those who supported us along the way.

TABLES AND FIGURES

ABBREVIATIONS

AMU	Arab Maghreb Union
APEC	Asia-Pacific Economic Cooperation
APTA	Asia-Pacific Trade Agreement
ASEAN	Association of South East Asian Nations
Benelux	Belgium-Netherlands-Luxembourg
BLA	bilateral labor agreement
BLEU	Belgium-Luxembourg Economic Union
CAIS	Central American Integration System
CARICOM	Caribbean Community
CCPCJ	Commission on Crime Prevention and Criminal Justice
CEDAW	Convention on the Elimination of All Forms of Discrimination Against Women
CEFTA	Central European Free Trade Agreement
CEMAC	Communauté Economique et Monetaire de l'Afrique Centrale/ Economic and Monetary Union of Central Africa
CEPGL	Communauté Economique des Pays des Grands Lacs/Economic Community of the Great Lakes Region
CES	Conseil Économique et Social/Economic and Social Council
COMESA	Common Market for Eastern and Southern Africa
CPED	International Convention for the Protection of All Persons from Enforced Disappearance
CRC	Convention on the Rights of the Child
CRPD	Convention on the Rights of Persons with Disabilities
EAC	Eastern African Community
ECCAS	Economic Community of Central African States
ECO	Economic Cooperation Organization
ECOWAS	Economic Community of West African States
ECSC	European Coal and Steel Community
EEA	European Economic Area
EEC	European Economic Community
EEU	Eurasian Economic Union
EFTA	European Free Trade Association
EU	European Union
FDI	foreign direct investment

GATS	General Agreement on Trade in Services
GATT	General Agreement on Tariffs and Trade
GCC	Gulf Cooperation Council
GFMD	Global Forum on Migration and Development
ICCPR	International Covenant on Civil and Political Rights
ICE	US Immigration and Customs Enforcement
ICEM	Intergovernmental Committee for European Migration
ICERD	International Convention on the Elimination of all forms of Racial Discrimination
ICESCR	International Covenant on Economic, Social and Cultural Rights
ICMPD	International Center for Migration Policy Development
ICRG	International Country Risk Guide
ICRMW	International Convention on the Protection of the Rights of All Migrant Workers and Members of Their Families
IGC	Intergovernmental Consultations on Migration, Asylum and Refugees
IGO	intergovernmental organization
ILO	International Labor Organization
IMF	International Monetary Fund
IMO	International Maritime Organization
IOC	Indian Ocean Commission
IOM	International Organization for Migration
LAIA	Latin American Integration Association
Mercosur	Common Market of the South
MIREM	Migration de Retour au Maghreb
MOA	memorandum of agreement
MOU	memorandum of understanding
MRU	Mano River Union
NAFTA	North American Free Trade Agreement
NGO	nongovernmental organization
OAS	Organization of American States
OECD	Organisation for Economic Co-operation and Development
OECS	Organization of Eastern Caribbean States
OHCHR	Office of the High Commissioner for Human Rights
ONI	Office national d'immigration/National Immigration Office
OPCAT	Optional Protocol to the UNCAT
OPEC	Organization of Petroleum Exporting Countries
PICMME	Provisional Intergovernmental Committee for the Movement of Migrants from Europe
PICW	President's Interagency Council on Women

POEA	Philippine Overseas Employment Administration
RCM	Regional Conference on Migration
RCP	regional consultative process
REO	regional economic organization
SAARC	South Asian Association for Regional Cooperation
SACU	Southern African Customs Union
SADC	Southern African Development Community
SOPEMI	Système d'observation permanente des migrations
TTTA	Trans-Tasman Travel Arrangement
TVPA	Trafficking Victims Protection Act
UN	United Nations
UNCAT	United Nations Convention against Torture and Other Cruel, Inhuman, or Degrading Treatment or Punishment
UNCTAD	United Nations Commission on Trade and Development
UNDP	United Nations Development Program
UNECA	United Nations Economic Commission for Africa
UNHCR	United Nations High Commissioner for Refugees
UNICEF	United Nations Children's Fund
UNODC	United Nations Office of Drugs and Crime
WAEMU	West African Economic and Monetary Union
WTO	World Trade Organization

MIGRATION CRISES AND THE STRUCTURE OF
INTERNATIONAL COOPERATION

Migration Crises as a Lens into International Cooperation

SIMA EHARAI WAS a forty-three-year-old widow with four children in Herat, Afghanistan, when she made the decision to migrate to Germany. Her eldest daughter, Sanaz, was already living in Frankfurt; her mother had managed to arrange a marriage for her to a German citizen of Afghan descent. According to her fifteen-year-old son, Redwan, she spontaneously made the decision to leave Afghanistan after watching a news report about Syrian families fleeing to Germany, which accepted them as refugees (Koelbl 2015). But although Afghans represent the second largest group (after Syrians) seeking asylum in Europe, the vast majority of claims are denied. In 2015 alone, 180,000 Afghans made asylum claims in Europe (Cunningham 2016), but the EU accepted just 25,915 applicants, less than 15 percent of the total (Eurostat 2016a). Many, like Sima, never even make it across a European border.

When Sima and her three younger children left Herat in 2015, they joined the approximately three thousand people illegally crossing the border into Iran every day (Koelbl 2015). Traveling by foot, they hoped to continue on to Turkey, where they could board boats to the Greek islands of Lesbos or Kos. From there, they could travel through the Balkans to Northern Europe. The family was only sixteen hours into their journey, exhausted and walking in the darkness, when Sima suddenly dropped to the ground. When Redwan reached her, he found her head soaked with blood, although he never heard the gunshot from the Iranian border patrol that killed her. He screamed for help, but instead found himself attacked by four border guards with assault rifles; they kicked him repeatedly in the stomach as they laughed and threw his mother's body into the back of their pickup truck. Redwan and his two younger brothers were held in a detention cell for a week before being deported back to Afghanistan with their mother's body. Back in Herat, the orphaned children found shelter with an uncle, with eight children of his own to support; the arrangement was only temporary (Koelbl 2015).

After almost fifteen years of war, the forces motivating Afghan migrants are complex. "We have nothing but war and violence here, and no work," explained an eighteen-year-old man who hoped to leave (Koelbl 2015). Politics ground to a standstill after the 2014 presidential elections, and the international presence that has fueled the economy for years is winding down. The influx of foreigners

caused wartime inflation and skyrocketing real estate prices, but this has col-
lapsed as foreign forces and organizations have withdrawn (Koelbl 2015). Although this was accompanied by a deteriorating security situation, including
persecution and violence, as the Taliban, al-Qaeda, and even Islamic State
gained ground, economic motivations are at least as powerful in stimulating
migration. While in practice these factors may be inextricably linked, there
remain important legal distinctions between economic migrants and asylum
seekers. For Sima, though, the distinction between the effects of the war and
her status a widow and mother with no income was irrelevant. "I can't continue
living like this," she told her daughter during her last phone conversation with
her. "Either I make it to you or I'll follow my husband into death" (Koelbl 2015).

Hamed Shurbaji, a twenty-four-year-old student studying French literature
at Damascus University, attempted to reach Europe by boat twice before finally
succeeding on his third, most treacherous journey. His route was circuitous.
He first left Syria for Egypt in 2012, traveling through Lebanon, but found the
situation there untenable. After forty days, he decided to head to Libya on foot,
where he hoped to catch a boat to Europe. He was quickly thwarted, however,
by the Libyan border patrol. After being detained for a few days, he was released
and traveled to Tripoli. He spent seven months there working and saving money
for his journey before engaging a smuggler who promised him passage to Europe. When the boat finally sailed, it was immediately intercepted by the Libyan
coast guard, and he was again detained for a few days before being released.
Discouraged but undeterred, Shurbaji paid a thousand dollars to another smuggler to secure passage on another boat. This time, the boat was so overcrowded
that it spent thirty hours at sea without getting anywhere; an Egyptian rescue
ship eventually took the passengers back to shore. His final trip was the most
overcrowded, with more than 730 people crammed on the boat, and it ended
in disaster for at least some of the passengers. Only hours into the journey, the
craft began to take on water and sink. Over the course of the next twenty-four
hours, the passengers bailed water and tried to keep it afloat. Finally, they spot-
ted a helicopter and a Danish ship, but the situation worsened after the ship hit
their much smaller boat. People began to jump into the water, and the ensuing
rescue took over five hours. Shurbaji was one of the lucky ones; thirty-nine
migrants drowned (al-Muqdad 2015).

Shurbaji ended up in a camp in Sicily, but he escaped and managed to continue on to Milan. From there, he and a friend tried to travel to France, which
they hoped would be their final destination. They were caught and turned back
by French police. Back in Milan, they hired a smuggler who drove them to
Germany. Once they arrived, Shurbaji immediately turned himself in to the
local police. Three months later, he received refugee status and became a legal
resident of Germany (al-Muqdad 2015).

Shurbaji's case highlights three important points. First, as in the case of Sima Eharai, individual migrants may be motivated by multiple factors. Certainly, Shurbaji fled Syria because of the ongoing war (and he had learned that he was on the government's radar after participating in student protests in 2011). But he was secure in Libya, where he worked for many months before continuing on to Europe; his motivation for migrating at that point was broader than security. Second, migrants' paths are not direct, and individuals may have contact with state authorities from several different countries along their journey; this young man traveled through (or attempted to travel to) six different countries before settling in Germany. He ended up there through a combination of state policies and his own preferences. Although his first-choice destination was France, he was effectively repelled by French police and chose Germany as a secondary option because of its opportunities and more open asylum policies.

Third, Shurbaji's experience may have been very different had he arrived in Germany a few years later. Until November 2015, almost all Syrians (and Iraqis and Eritreans) arriving in Germany were granted full refugee status, which provided residence rights in Germany for at least three years, generous welfare benefits, and the right to have family members join them. Then, in November 2015, the interior ministry announced that all successful applicants would be offered only "subsidiary protection"—temporary protection for a year with no right to family reunification. This announcement was followed by some confusion as the Social Democrats, junior partners in the ruling coalition government, denied the change (Traynor 2015). By January 2016, however, the government reached an agreement and implemented the new policy, which it hoped would bring the country more in line with other European states (Deutsche Welle 2016). The relatively generous policies meant that refugees were choosing Germany over neighboring states. Migrants like Hamed Shurbaji may be treated very dissimilarly by different governments at various points, even as states fulfill basic obligations under the refugee regime, which recognizes variations in temporary protection as legitimate (Orchard and Miller 2014; Ostrand 2015).

In 2015, more than half a million migrants had arrived in Germany by late September. Of these, about half had already applied for asylum, and 42 percent of these asylum seekers came not from Syria or Afghanistan but from Europe (Bennhold 2015). Albanians, Kosovars, Macedonians, and Serbians joined with the flood of migrants from far more dangerous places in hopes of both blending in and taking advantage of the new services established to help refugees. The new stream was also facilitated by Serbia's relaxation of travel restrictions on Kosovars in September 2015. In the late 1990s, tens of thousands of refugees flooded into the European Union from Serbia, escaping the war in Kosovo. In 2015, however, the "refugees" fled corruption and hopelessness, not war. With unemployment hovering around 35 percent (60 percent among young people) and 30 percent of the population living below the poverty line, Kosovars in particular felt that they were refugees, "forced" to flee, even if they failed to meet the legal requirements. The belief was fueled by stories of friends and family who had reached the EU successfully, and by rumors that Germany had an "open door" policy, provided four thousand euros upon arrival, and was looking for Kosovars to work. These rumors are often propagated by smugglers who transport migrants across the Serbian border to Hungary for as little as two hundred fifty euros. From there, migrants either file an asylum claim in Hungary, if they are arrested, or continue on to another country in the Schengen Area; most travel to Germany and file claims there (Chick 2015). Asylum applications from Kosovars in Germany increased by 572 percent between January 2014 and January 2015 (Ott 2015).

Ibrahim Haziro, a twenty-three-year-old unemployed man from Pristina, made this journey in early 2015. By mid-March, he had been living at a refugee center in Augsburg, Germany, for about a month, waiting for his claim to be processed. Confident that he would receive refugee status, he was surprised to learn that most Kosovars are rejected and repatriated (less than one-half of one percent of Kosovars are accepted). "Dreams stay dreams in Kosovo," explained Haziro. "There is no perspective and people have given up hope that things will change. Germany is the promised land. Here we can turn our dreams into reality" (Ott 2015). Germany, however, has established a quick and effective system for processing asylum claims from those least likely to meet the requirements, alongside systems to process true refugees. Most applicants get a response within weeks and will be on their way back to Kosovo shortly, with support from the Kosovar government, which is concerned that the migration wave is hurting its chances to negotiate visa-free travel within the EU (Chick 2015). Once again, from the perspective of migrants like Haziro, the line between refugee and economic migrant appears indistinguishable, even as the legal distinction shapes the policies of states and determines the outcomes of their migration attempts.

These three migrants are representative of the migration flow into the European Union that was labeled the "migrant crisis" in late 2015 (Erlanger and Smale 2015). Sadly, these stories are far from unique. The Rohingya and Bangladeshi flows in Southeast Asia in April of the same year were labeled the "Rohingya migrant crisis." In the United States, unaccompanied minors in the tens of thousands arrived at the southern US border beginning in May 2014, another "migrant crisis." And even as the European migrant crisis diminished, there was another "mini-migrant crisis" in Costa Rica, where Cubans seeking to enter the United States were blocked from moving north ("Cuban Migrants" 2016). There are undoubtedly other migrant crises that do not reach the front page of the *New York Times*.

What, then, do these migrant crises tell us about international migration and the role of international cooperation on migration issues? There are three main points. First, this international flow is decidedly different from other types of international flows. Other international economic flows can affect economies and people in many ways, destroying employment and displacing some residents even as they also enrich others. But trade in goods and services and international capital flows represent inanimate objects. Migrants, on the other hand, are individual human beings whose lives are at risk as they journey from one part of the world to another and who may experience discrimination upon arrival. Because humans are involved, it is all the more important to understand how these crises can be resolved.

The second point is that a refugee regime exists that permits states to sort individuals into refugees and voluntary, or economic, migrants, regardless of the motives or perceptions of the migrants themselves. As elaborated in the UN Convention Relating to the Status of Refugees, only specific types of individual persecution qualify individuals for refugee status, and states are also often unwilling to accept applicants if they have found an initial refuge. Thus, even though many would consider the migrants seeking entry into Europe and elsewhere to be refugees, or "forced" migrants, most actually fall into the legal category of "voluntary" migrants.

The third point is that migrant crises serve as exogenous shocks that modify the costs of the status quo for states in the international system, propelling them to the bargaining table in search of solutions. These periodic crises demonstrate that the current structure of national and international laws is insufficient to prevent the enormous human costs generated by the flow of individuals across international borders. This is the question that is central to our inquiry: Under what conditions will states discard unilateralism and cooperate on international migration? This is a book about the possibilities of collaboration among states on this issue. To date, international cooperation on voluntary migration has been limited, and this is striking given that states in the international system have cooperated over many other international economic flows, including of trade and capital.

THEORETICAL CLAIMS

Our first claim is that the patterns of international migration in the post–World War II period help us understand the shape of international cooperation on migration. The patterns have been predominantly unidirectional, from poorer, less stable countries to wealthier, more stable countries. Stability and wealth are relative. There are many countries in the Global South that are destinations for international migrants, in addition to wealthy Western democracies. Moreover, the patterns are unique to specific host countries—Canada attracts different flows than does the United States; migrants to the United Kingdom are distinctive from those to Germany; South Africa's migrants come from different countries of origin than those in Malaysia. The pattern of the flows is important because it suggests that the externalities associated with the flows affect only the specific pair of countries, the country of origin and the country of destination. Hence, bargaining over the externalities is likely to be bilateral rather than regional or multilateral. International cooperation on migration is more likely to resemble not the multilateral World Trade Organization but the bilateral investment treaties that characterize the international investment regime between the Global North and the Global South.

There is a caveat to our generalization connecting the pattern of flows to the structure of cooperation. Where flows have the potential to be reciprocal, where economic conditions are similar, as in the case of the European Union, there is the potential for regional agreements on migration that underpin freedom of movement (United Nations Development Programme [UNDP] 2009).

Our second claim is that the status quo ante and the distribution of power in the international system help explain the paucity of international cooperation on migration. The status quo is one that divides the world into "sending" and "receiving" countries and, in most instances, privileges receiving countries. According to international law, states have sovereignty over the admission of foreigners and, therefore, determine which applicants to admit and which to reject, subject to treaty commitments to not refoule (turn away) genuine refugees. It also permits receiving states to discriminate between citizen and noncitizen residents, subject to human rights treaty commitments. At the same time, international law requires that states permit their citizens to leave their country of origin and to readmit their citizens upon return. This status quo privileges receiving states by allowing them to determine the level and type of immigrants they receive as well as the set of rights to provide the immigrants upon arrival. Since receiving states prefer the status quo in most instances, they are unlikely to engage in negotiations that reduce their privileges. And sending states, because they are poorer and less stable, are unlikely to have sufficient resources to persuade receiving states to negotiate over admissions and treatment of immigrants.

Our third claim is that the cost of the status quo for receiving states is subject to exogenous pressure or shocks. When that raises the costs of the status quo, receiving states may seek to negotiate an agreement that provides for international cooperation. The terms are affected by the bargaining power of the parties within the context of the negotiations. One source of bargaining power is the range of available outside options or "best alternative to a negotiated agreement." The distribution of benefits from international cooperation is largely determined by the attractiveness of the outside options. Those states whose outside options are limited are more eager to reach agreement and make greater concessions than those whose outside options are better. Exogenous shocks, such as migrant crises, can alter the available outside options and thus explain why states might resort to international cooperation, but migrant crises are not the sole trigger. Domestic political actors or international nongovernmental organizations (NGOs) might also create costs that pressure a government into seeking international negotiations on migration.

Our fourth claim focuses on the institutional forums in which the negotiations take place. If sending states prefer an alternative to the status quo and if the chosen institution privileges sending states (countries of origin), then sending states may negotiate agreements that reflect their preferences. However, even where a treaty is negotiated, sending states usually lack the power to persuade receiving states to ratify it. So this avenue may not be very productive.

Finally, the term "international cooperation" tends to take on a normative hue that suggests greater openness to the international system. In migration, at least, cooperation can, and often does, lead to the reduction of migratory flows. States that agree to cooperate on international migration often do so to minimize the number of individuals crossing international boundaries. This contradicts, rather than supports, the ideals of a liberal world order.

As with all theories, our claims are probabilistic and we neither seek nor claim to explain every state activity involving voluntary international migration. Theories always abstract from the details of reality in order to sketch underlying patterns. Nonetheless, we provide a considerable amount of evidence that is consistent with our theoretical claims. Our theory attempts to explain *when* states will enter negotiations on international migration, the *shape* that cooperation takes, and the *outcomes* of the negotiations in terms of which states gain and lose from the negotiations.

THEORIES OF INTERNATIONAL COOPERATION AND MIGRATION

Although the scope of the theory is limited to voluntary international migration, there are potential lessons for researchers interested in broader issues of international cooperation. The theoretical literature on international cooperation is rich, but it is challenging to evaluate empirically. Much focuses on instances where cooperation has succeeded or (very occasionally) failed; it rarely examines instances in which cooperation was never pursued in the first place. This neglect of the "null cases" and selection on the dependent variable of cooperation increases the risk of mistaken conclusions about the causes of cooperation (Geddes 1991). We overcome this limitation by surveying all of the issue areas associated with international migration. Our empirical work on migration illuminates four lessons for those interested in international cooperation more broadly.

The first lesson is that patterns of interactions may be important for the degree of inclusiveness in international negotiations. We know that international agreements can be bilateral, regional, and multilateral; our research supplements what is known about the shape of international cooperation (Koremenos, Lipson, and Snidal 2001; Verdier 2008; Thompson and Verdier 2014). We are particularly interested in the way flows of migrants affect the regime costs and transaction costs of cooperation, which affect the relative attractiveness of bilateral, regional, and multilateral agreements. We argue, however, that the patterns of flows may be important for explaining cooperation in other arenas as well, from capital to arms flows.

The second is that, in the international system, it may be difficult to predict when cooperation will take place as it is driven in part by exogenous shocks that researchers are unable to predict. Being alert to these changes in the status quo when they do occur means that researchers may be better equipped to identify the moments when cooperation is most likely to succeed. Policymakers and activists pursuing cooperation can use this information to time their efforts to coincide with the ideal moment.

The third lesson is already well established but worth repeating: the normal trappings of power in the international system do not always predict the outcomes of international bargaining. However, the distribution of power in the international system continues to play an important role given the current status quo. As institutionalization of the international system progresses, there may be more opportunities for groups of states to use the rules of international institutions to propose and pass treaties addressing any number of issues beyond migration. Without support from traditionally powerful states, however, these new treaties will remain poorly ratified and unenforced.

Finally, as the record of cooperation on migration illustrates, international cooperation will not necessarily facilitate the neoliberal dream of fewer international barriers and more openness. States may, in fact, work together to restrict openness and preserve their own sovereignty. Those seeking to achieve other goals may find that their efforts are more effective when directed at domestic policy.

ORGANIZATION OF THE BOOK

To substantiate our claims, we begin in chapter 1 by delineating the domain of our theory and explaining how the term "voluntary migration," although ambiguous, fairly describes the vast majority of individuals who live outside their country of birth and that attention to international cooperation on voluntary migration is appropriate. We then describe the pattern of migratory flows in the post–World War II period and show how these patterns are expected to affect the shape of international cooperation. In chapter 2, we adopt a bargaining framework to explain both stasis and change in the degree of cooperation in the international system on migration issues. We explain our choice of states as the central unit of analysis and our division of states into two types—receiving and sending. We then employ a bargaining framework with attention to the status quo, state preferences, and the distribution of power. If powerful states prefer the status quo, we predict that international negotiations will not ensue. There are two conditions under which we predict the initiation of international negotiations—when exogenous pressure or shocks modify the costs of the status quo for states and hence bring countries that would otherwise be resistant to the bargaining table, and when the less powerful sending states can exploit their institutional power in forums that advantage their numbers. Finally, we show how external power and internal, bargaining power affect the negotiated outcomes. In the first instance, where flows are unidirectional, sending states are able to leverage their bargaining power to extract concessions from receiving states; where flows are reciprocal, states may choose freedom of movement. In the second instance, multilateral treaties may be negotiated but sending states lack the resources to persuade receiving states to ratify the resulting treaty and the treaty is ineffective.

In chapters 3 to 7, we take up issues central to international migration: restricting immigrant flows through internal immigration control; facilitating immigrant flows, which takes the forms of bilateral recruitment and freedom of movement; law enforcement to reduce criminality; and immigrant rights. In each chapter, we begin with the story of a migrant that illustrates the specific issue dimension. We then outline the preferences of the central actors—sending and receiving states—and the status quo ante. We describe the exogenous forces that lead states to retain the status quo or to enter into negotiations. We then describe external sources of power and sources of power internal to the bargaining situation. The distribution of power allows us to predict the outcomes of the negotiations. We follow with evidence that is consistent with our predictions. Finally, we explore alternative explanations of the same phenomenon and demonstrate that our explanation is at least as good as alternative theories and provides additional insights into the timing, shape, and contents of the agreement. Over the five issue dimensions, a common theory that can explain outcomes is simpler and more elegant than theories that explain cooperation on only one issue dimension.

The evidence we present varies based on the issue area. In some instances we employ quantitative analyses to connect our explanatory variables to the outcome variables. In other cases, we describe in more detail the historical record, to illustrate and illuminate the distribution of power and connect that to the distribution of benefits from the negotiations. We believe that the evidence over the five issue areas taken together provides support for the regularity of the patterns as well as illustrates the process or mechanisms by which the independent variables affect the dependent variables.

In chapter 8, we explain the strengths and weaknesses of our theory as applied to the two other dimensions of international migration—the refugee regime and the travel regime. We also outline lessons from our theory that would advance the study of international cooperation more broadly. Finally, we point to the policy implications of our theory. International migration affects individuals; this is a very human story. The fate of migrants can be improved only by a clearer understanding of the causal mechanisms that affect their mobility and the degree to which their rights are protected. International cooperation is one venue that affects these relationships, and it is therefore important to deepen our understanding of the prospects for international cooperation on voluntary migration.

MIGRANT CRISES AND MIGRANT PROTECTIONS

Our interest in international cooperation on migration stems in part from the intensely human story of international migration. We began our discussion with the stories of three migrants from the more than one million migrants who arrived in Europe in 2015 and 2016. These three migrants represent possible trajectories: death along the migrant trail; successful arrival in a destination that expands their life choices; and return to their country of origin, a failure in their aspirations. The European migrant crisis also represents the failure of existing national and international institutions to respond to large-scale violence and inequalities around the globe. We find theoretically and empirically that the prospects for international cooperation on migration are likely to be quite limited and that some cooperation efforts will reduce rather than expand flows.

Migrants, in many ways, are the canaries in the coal mines, warning that all is not well. Only when conditions are truly dire will people uproot themselves on a mass scale, leaving behind their homes, families, and friends, sometimes risking their lives, for an uncertain future in a new country. These conditions lead to periodic explosions that spew humans across international borders, generating migrant crises. What is more, these migrants are most likely the privileged ones, those with sufficient resources, both material and internal, to risk such a move. If we think of migrants in this way, then the significance of migrant protections becomes broader. Migrant rights are human rights, and humans are just migrants and potential migrants who remain behind. The story of human history is in part a story of migration; understanding how we respond to it, facilitate it, and manage it is crucially important.

Migrants have many advocates, including themselves, who petition to help ensure that individuals, resident outside their country of birth, are able to live with dignity and access to resources. The question that arises is where the advocates should focus their activities. But without a sound theoretical understanding of the structure of global governance on migration, activism can be wasted. Advocates need to employ their resources where they can best achieve their goals. We hope to persuade our readers that the locus of activity should vary depending on the issue addressed and that advocates should focus most of their attention on the local, national, and bilateral levels because these are the forums in which they will find the most success.

CHAPTER 1

Migration Patterns and the Prevalence of Bilateralism

The Empirical Puzzle

DOES INTERNATIONAL COOPERATION on migration exist? The fable of the blind men and the elephant is well known—each blind man examines one part of the elephant and projects this knowledge onto the whole, thereby drawing an inaccurate picture of the empirical reality. The scholars who study international cooperation in migration are similar to the blind men. There is a bewildering number of scholarly efforts to describe, explain, and promote collaboration in the international system among states on issues surrounding the flow of individuals across borders. Yet there is little agreement among scholars about whether there is no regime at all (Hollifield 2000; UNDP 2009), or whether efforts to manage international migration privilege wealthy and powerful countries in the international system (Lindley 2011), or whether there exists a "tapestry" of different kinds of cooperation depending on the type of collective action problem that arises (Betts 2011). Moreover, there is a new terminology that incorporates a broader set of actors in the international system, labeled "global governance." Migration cooperation, from this perspective, is not just the action of states but the action of both state and nonstate actors in the international system (Held and McGrew 2002; Woods 2002).[1] Yet these scholars are presumably all looking at the same empirical reality. How do we make sense of these different visions of cooperation?

We take this scholarly disagreement as a point of departure. It is useful to reexamine the parable of the elephant and the blind men in light of the literature that explores international cooperation on migration. Although one might draw a number of lessons from this parable, we emphasize that we cannot understand international cooperation on migration without understanding that the various components of cooperation are systematically connected into a larger whole. A single theoretical framework can account for the varying patterns of international cooperation on voluntary migration. We present this framework in two chapters. In this chapter, we argue that the dominant form of cooperation on voluntary migration is bilateral, because the dominant pattern of migration flows are unidirectional and unique to each state. In chapter 2, we provide a bargaining framework that employs the status quo and state preferences, along with exogenous shocks, to locate the timing and content of international agreements on migration.

We begin by addressing some definitional issues that help clarify the scope of our research: the definition of voluntary migration, the role of the state as the central actor in international cooperation, and the distinctiveness of migration as an international economic flow. We then outline a central theoretical lens, how the possibilities for cooperation are shaped by the unidirectional and unique patterns of voluntary migration. These patterns limit cooperation because the lack of reciprocity reduces an important element of cooperative behavior in the international system and because the pattern of flows generates externalities or market failures that are dyadic rather than regional or global in scope. In chapter 2, we introduce a bargaining framework that allows us to hypothesize about the conditions under which states may cooperate on migration issues.

VOLUNTARY MIGRATION

Our focus is on voluntary migration. As noted in our introduction, this focus presumes a clear distinction between "voluntary" and "forced" migration, yet we know that migrants often have multiple motives for moving and that the legal definition of "refugee," found in the UN Convention Relating to the Status of Refugees, is so narrow as to leave many migrants unprotected from violence and other threats to their existence.[2] Thus, there is an ethical definition of "forced" migration that differs significantly from the legal definition. However, this legal fiction is actually important in practice, and migrants are classified according to the legal criterion every day. A case in point is the 2015 European crisis, which has been labeled a migrant rather than refugee crisis, despite significant migrant flows from war-torn countries, as our three stories of migrants within that flow illustrate. Although the door clearly has been more open to Syrians, Iraqis, and Afghans whose countries are experiencing civil conflict, even these migrants usually gain temporary protected status rather than refugee status as defined in the UN convention (European Commission 2016). The remainder are treated as voluntary economic migrants whom the receiving state can accept or reject, depending on state preferences on immigration. Moreover, there is a specific constellation of treaties and organizations that deal with forced migration, as distinct from "voluntary" migration. So we employ the legal distinction to set apart a group of migrants not governed by the refugee regime with the purpose of examining whether there is a (voluntary) migration regime and how that regime works.

This question is important in part because the vast majority of individuals living outside their country of birth are defined as voluntary migrants. The UNDP reports that in 2008, of the approximately two hundred million migrants—those living for more than one year outside their country of origin—only around fifteen million were classified as refugees (UNDP 2009). Most of the individuals caught up in "migration crises" are classified as migrants rather than as refugees. If migrant rights activists and the international community more broadly hope to reduce the human tragedies involved in many migration flows, understanding the prospects for cooperation on voluntary migration is central.[3]

In order to make sense of the underlying structure of international cooperation, we focus our lens on the regime for voluntary migration. However, the entire picture of "global migration governance," according to Rey Koslowski (2011a), can be divided into three subregimes: the travel or mobility regime, the voluntary migration regime, and the forced migration or refugee regime. The travel or mobility regime deals with individuals who cross international borders and includes those who stay for short periods, such as tourists, family visitors, business travelers, and students, as well as voluntary and forced migrants. The refugee regime is defined by the UN Convention Relating to the Status of Refugees (1951) and subsequent protocol (1967) and is monitored by the UN High Commissioner for Refugees (UNHCR). In the conclusions, we point to characteristics of refugee and travel flows that are distinctive from voluntary migration and suggest modifications to our theoretical framework to account for different patterns of international cooperation in these migration subregimes, particularly the refugee regime.

MIGRATION AS A UNIQUE INTERNATIONAL FLOW

International cooperation forms a generic research agenda for scholars of international relations. There is a substantial amount of theoretical research that explores the conditions under which states in the international system find it beneficial to cooperate or coordinate their activities that we should be able to apply to a specific international economic flow. However, we agree with most scholars that migration is somehow distinctive from other international economic flows. The question, then, revolves around how migration might differ from flows of goods, services, or capital *in ways that affect the prospects for global governance.*

Migration and Identity Politics. Although migration and other international economic flows share a number of commonalities, migration has several distinct dimensions as well. One distinctive element may be related to the fact that migrants are individuals with their own cultures, customs, and languages, so the politics of migration often involve identity. In addition to societal concerns over economic issues, political organization arises in the form of anti-immigrant movements or political parties that adopt electoral platforms focusing on preserving a national identity and a cherished way of life.[4] Identity issues may generate greater opposition to migration than to other international economic flows, and the political backlash might be sufficient to discourage cooperation among states on migration issues.

It is difficult to disagree with the observation that vociferous political opposition has arisen in response to migration, and that anti-immigrant parties are common in many immigrant-receiving societies. It is also true that some migrants disrupt some members of the society in which they choose to live and work. Yet societal disruption is also a common feature of trade and capital flows. Trade can displace and decimate industries that were once a major source of employment and wealth—in wealthy as well as poor countries. Shifting patterns of comparative advantage can uproot a local population and set in motion vast internal migrations. Consumption patterns may change as well, sometimes for the worse, as the Nestlé infant formula scandal well illustrates.[5] Foreign direct investment may bring changes in social mores as well as increasing inequality, among other things (Alderson and Nielsen 1999; Choi 2006). So, although migration can be disruptive to the host society, it is certainly not the only international economic flow that is disruptive, and may not even be the most disruptive.[6] If the backlash to migration plays a crucial role in blocking international cooperation, one might expect the political backlash from international trade and foreign direct investment to prevent cooperation in those arenas. Yet we tend to see many instances of global cooperation for these international economic flows, such as encompassed in the World Trade Organization (WTO) and the Organisation for Economic Co-operation and Development (OECD) Guidelines for Multinational Enterprises (OECD 2011).[7]

Human Rights and Migration. One dimension that may well be distinctive, especially in the post–World War II era, and that has seen the acceptance of human rights as a central tenet of the international system is that migrants are human beings first and labor only second. Max Frisch, a Swiss playwright, famously noted that "we asked for workers. We got people instead." This insight might provide the key to understanding why the politics of international cooperation on migration are different than those of other economic flows in the most recent era. Prior to World War II, states unceremoniously expelled nonnationals when it suited their interests. This was true in democratic as well as autocratic regimes.[8] The advent of human rights regimes granted citizens as well as residents, documented and undocumented, some basic protections. Beginning with the 1948 Universal Declaration of Human Rights, the United Nations has created nine core human rights instruments that reduce the distinction between citizens and residents of any state.[9] This contrasts with flows of goods or capital, where no human rights are involved.

Ruhs and Chang (2004) bring this distinction to bear when they argue that migrants enter the host state with a bundle of rights.[10] While it is true that the size of the bundle may vary, Ruhs and Chang make a convincing argument that migration is distinctive from other international economic flows because these rights change the equation of costs and benefits of migration. Although we believe this observation is accurate, we do not believe that this distinction is crucial to the prospects for international cooperation. Like trade in goods and services, the costs and benefits of migration are borne differently by different groups in society. This helps establish the interested actors who enter the political arena—and thus affect domestic politics—but there is no systematic link between the costs associated with migrant rights and prospects for international cooperation.

Migration Externalities. Alexander Betts (2011) has pointed out that migration generates externalities in the international system, as have Sandra Lavenex and Emek Uçarer (2002). Externalities are defined as costs and/or benefits that accrue to individuals or groups who did not choose to incur them. Robert Keohane (1984), in *After Hegemony*, employs the concept of externalities to construct a neofunctionalist model of international cooperation. In essence, externalities generate problems of collective action for those subject to the externality, prompting cooperation among states to overcome the costs through bargaining with the generator of the externality. His is a provocative use of the economic literature on transaction costs to underpin the construction of international regimes or organizations that allow states to achieve better collective outcomes. However, he relies on the notion that externalities affect more than a single actor, creating problems of collective action. In the original work on externalities, Ronald Coase (1960) clearly distinguishes between an externality affecting a single actor and an externality affecting multiple actors. Unless the externality affects multiple actors, there is no need to organize to bargain over the costs of the externality. Otherwise, a situation of bilateral bargaining is generated by the externality—not multiple actors in need of multilateral cooperation. We argue that the patterns of migration in the postwar period have not, for the most part, generated collective externalities (also see Lockhart and Money 2011).

MIGRATION PATTERNS BETWEEN SENDING AND RECEIVING STATES

So, what are the barriers to international cooperation in international migration? We argue that migration patterns in the post–World War II era are characterized by both nonreciprocity and unique receiving country patterns (UNDP 2009; Hatton 2007). Both of these characteristics affect the degree and shape of cooperation.[11]

The first dimension is characterized by the labeling of states as either "sending" or source states, "receiving" or host states.[12] Some countries, such as Spain and Italy, have made a transition from sending to receiving state in the recent past, but even transition states normally do not experience reciprocal flows. Reciprocal flows are defined by the exchange of migrants between two countries. Those that experience both inflows and outflows during the transition from sending state to receiving state generally send their emigrants to one set of countries and receive their immigrants from another set. Italy, for example, sent its emigrants to wealthier Western democracies in Europe and the Americas while receiving immigrants from North and sub-Saharan Africa.

There are complex reasons why individuals choose to migrate (Castles, de Haas, and Miller 2014). However, barring state barriers to egress and entry, the general pattern in the contemporary era is from poorer and less stable states to wealthier and more stable states (UNDP 2009). Wealth and stability are relative so that some states in the Global South are receiving states and about half of all voluntary migrant flows are among countries of the Global South. This characteristic is unique to migration in the depth and breadth of international economic flows. It is characterized by predominantly one-way flows, hence the division of states into sending and receiving states (Hatton 2007; Sykes 2013).[13] The UNDP (2009) reports that 37 percent of migrant flows are from developing to developed countries, while only 3 percent move in the other direction.[14] Of all migrants, 75 percent enter a country with higher human development than their country of origin. These figures confirm that the flow of migrants among states is predominantly unidirectional.[15]

With the exception of movement within regional organizations such as the European Union by citizens of member states, this general pattern is reflected in individual countries. Table 1.1 illustrates the pattern of migration stock between two representative receiving countries, France and South Africa; the top six migrant nationalities are listed for each country.[16] In the absence of systematic data on flows to most developing countries, stocks of migrants offer the best picture we can present but one that is closely reflected in past flows. The imbalance is clear. The French migrant stock in Algeria is less than one-tenth of one percent of the Algerian migrant stock in France. As the numbers of immigrants in the recipient countries decline, the imbalance falls, but the highest proportion of recipient country stock in a sending country is 11.2 percent in the exchange between South Africa and Malawi.

In contrast to the imbalance in migration flows, trade and investment tend to be reciprocal. For example, foreign direct investment (FDI) patterns are

Table 1.1

Migrant Stocks in France/South Africa and French/South African Stocks in Sending Countries, 2013

	France			South Africa	
	Foreign stocks in France	French stocks in sending country		Foreign stock in South Africa	South African stocks in sending country
Algeria	1,406,845	1,116 (0.07%)	Mozambique	462,412	8,735 (1.8%)
Morocco	911,046	4,961 (0.5%)	Zimbabwe	358,109	11,571 (3.2%)
Tunisia	382,129	3,305 (0.8%)	Lesotho	310,925	1,060 (0.3%)
Turkey	259,514	23,658 (9.1%)	Namibia	129,488	7,203 (5.5%)
Madagascar	118,397	10,185 (8.6%)	Swaziland	92,854	10,216 (11.0%)
Senegal	115,909	10,652 (9.1%)	Malawi	70,038	7,849 (11.2%)

Source: United Nations, Department of Economics and Social Affairs, Population Division (2013).

Table 1.2

Reciprocal Foreign Direct Investment Flows (Percentage of Total)

	1990	2000	2013
Developed country inward stocks from other developed countries	75.2	75.6	63.0
Developed country outward stocks to other developed countries	93.2	88.6	78.9
Developed country inward flows from other developed countries		81.0	52.0
Developed country outward flows to other developed countries		93.0	61.0

Source: UNCTAD (2014).

beginning to change, but until very recently, these flows were primarily among wealthy Western democracies (UNCTAD 2014). As presented in Table 1.2, in 1990 developed countries generated 93.2 percent of outward FDI stocks and received 75.2 percent of inward FDI stocks; by 2013, both proportions had diminished but still accounted for the large majority of FDI stocks. As late as 2000, developed countries accounted for 81 percent of inflows and 93 percent of outflows. Developed countries invested in each other. Although developing countries are beginning to receive about half of the FDI inflows, even those are highly concentrated among a few states, which are now also generating the majority of developing country outflows. For example, in 2013, China, Russia, Hong Kong, and Singapore were among the top twenty destination countries for FDI; they were also among the top twenty source countries (UNCTAD 2014).[17]

Trade patterns are also dominated by reciprocity, that is, a country's largest export markets are also among its largest import markets. There is a large component of trade that consists of intraindustry trade, and even trade patterns between developed and developing countries tend to balance over time, although many developing countries export primary products and import manufactured goods (Dicken 2011). Patterns vary, of course, but most countries' top importers overlap heavily with top exporters. Three of Vietnam's top five export destinations are also three of Vietnam's top import sources; the same is true for Nigeria; four of five top trading partners in the Philippines as well as in Brazil are the same for exports and imports; six of Jamaica's top ten export markets are also top import sources; and, in the United States, the top seven export markets are also the same top seven import sources.[18]

If migration is nonreciprocal, why would this pattern of migration generate a barrier to international cooperation? Axelrod (1985) pointed out the importance of reciprocity to the evolution of cooperation; it is based on the ability to retaliate. If states receive reciprocal flows, then efforts to cooperate can evolve with a tit-for-tat strategy, producing higher payoffs for both parties. The tit-for-tat strategy adopts a position of cooperation on the first move and then copies the opponent's strategy thereafter. This means that when a state refuses to cooperate, it is punished in the next move. However, should it cooperate in the future, then forgiveness is demonstrated and allows cooperation to ensue. The WTO, for example, has created a decentralized enforcement mechanism that allows states whose economies have been hurt by unfair trade practices to retaliate against the trade of the opposing state. The absence of reciprocity represents a stumbling block to cooperation, as cooperation then requires linkage to some third issue.

In the limited number of cases where migration flows are reciprocal, states have been able to generate multilateral cooperation on migration—such as in the Nordic Union or the European Union. But this type of cooperation is the exception rather than the rule. Thus, we argue that the nonreciprocal nature of the flows is a crucial element in international migration that is absent in other international economic flows and one characteristic that distinguishes the possibilities for cooperation. However, as we shall see, linkage politics is central to bargaining over international migration. So lack of reciprocity reduces the likelihood that cooperation among states will emerge but, by itself, will not prevent cooperation if states can link migration to other issue dimensions in the international bargaining setting.

We argue that the central feature that shapes the type of international cooperation that arises is the fact that migration patterns are not only directional but country-specific as well. These patterns are well known to migration experts, and flows can be reasonably well modeled based on geography, historical ties, and wage differentials (Hatton and Williamson 2003a, 2003b). One example is provided in Table 1.3, which illustrates the top "third country" immigrant

Table 1.3
Top Non-EU Migrant Admissions, 2003 (Selected EU Countries)

France	Germany	United Kingdom	Sweden
Algeria	Turkey	Pakistan	Iraq
Morocco	Russia	India	Thailand
Tunisia	Ukraine	South Africa	Serbia
Turkey	United States	Nigeria	China
Congo	China	Afghanistan (data from 2006)	Somalia

Source: Migration Policy Institute (2012).

groups to the largest recipient states in the European Union in 2003. There is virtually no overlap in the migration source countries despite the fact that these are wealthy members of the European Union, which has adopted free movement among its members (there are eighteen unique observations among the twenty data points; Turkey and China are each listed twice). This pattern suggests that any market failures or externalities that are generated by migration are dyadic in nature. For example, if there is a large population of undocumented Algerians in France, this does not concern Germany, the United Kingdom, or Sweden.[19] The solution to this problem revolves around cooperation between France and Algeria. So, we argue, cooperation does exist but is structured by the nature of the flows, and hence the stocks of migrants, which privileges bilateral cooperation and disadvantages multilateral cooperation.

To demonstrate that these patterns are not unique to countries of the European Union and that the pattern remains important in the contemporary era, we provide data on non-EU migrant entries to the European Union in 2013, along with the United States' entries. For other regions of the world, data on flows are unavailable, so we present stocks of migrants by country of origin. As illustrated in Table 1.4, in 2013, the flows of third country nationals into the European Union are still distinctive, but now China and India, countries whose populations exceed one billion people and which, together, account for a third of the global population, are showing up more frequently as top origin countries. This is true of the United States as well, although the US pattern of entries is otherwise quite distinctive from those of Europe (of the thirty observations, twenty-two are unique; Turkey and the United States are reflected twice; China and India are listed four times each).

For Asia, there is a similar pattern of distinct unilateral flows. Geographically proximate countries receive very distinctive flows. As depicted in Table 1.5, the

Table 1.4
Top Non-EU Migrant Admissions, 2013 (Selected EU Countries and United States)

France	Germany	United Kingdom	Sweden	United States
Algeria	Russia	*China*	Syria	Mexico
Morocco	Serbia	*India*	Somalia	*China*
Tunisia	Turkey	United States	Afghanistan	*India*
China	*China*	Australia	Eritrea	Philippines
Turkey	United States	Pakistan	*India*	Dominican Republic
Senegal	*India*	Malaysia	Iraq	Cuba

Note: Italics are used for sending states that appear in the immigration profile of multiple receiving states.
Source: OECD (2015).

Table 1.5
Top Migrant Stock Countries in Asia

South Korea (2012)	Malaysia (2011)	Singapore (2013)	Thailand (2011)	Japan (2013)
Vietnam	*Indonesia*	Malaysia	Myanmar	South Korea
Thailand	Nepal	China	Cambodia	China
Indonesia	Myanmar	*Indonesia*	Laos	Brazil
Philippines	Bangladesh	*Philippines*		*Philippines*
Sri Lanka	India	Pakistan		Peru
Mongolia	Vietnam	Bangladesh		United States

Note: Italics are used for sending states that appear in the immigration profile of multiple receiving states.
Source: Imson (2013); for Japan and Singapore, United Nations, Department of Economics and Social Affairs, Population Division (2013).

largest origin countries are unique. There is more overlap if we look down the list, but two-thirds of the observations are unique. South Korea attracts migrants from Thailand, Sri Lanka, and Mongolia, while Malaysia attracts them from Nepal, Bangladesh, and India. Thailand, while also a sending state, receives migrants from Cambodia and Laos. And Japan's top immigrant stocks include Chinese, Korean, and US citizens.

The only region of the world that appears to have common stocks generated by common flows is the Persian Gulf. Although the order of the top countries of migrants is not identical, each of the five countries surveyed in Table 1.6 has the same top six source countries, with the single exception of Saudi Arabia, which

Table 1.6
Top Countries of Origin, Migrant Stock, Gulf States, 2013

Kuwait	Oman	Qatar	Saudi Arabia	United Arab Emirates
India	India	India	India	India
Bangladesh	Bangladesh	Bangladesh	Pakistan	Bangladesh
Egypt	Pakistan	Pakistan	Bangladesh	Pakistan
Pakistan	Egypt	Egypt	Egypt	Egypt
Philippines	Indonesia	Philippines	Philippines	Pakistan
Indonesia	Philippines	Indonesia	Yemen	Indonesia

Source: United Nations, Department of Economics and Social Affairs, Population Division (2013).

includes Yemen, rather than Indonesia. But, as these are autocratic governments, which appear unconstrained by human rights guarantees against mass expulsion, there appears to be little reason to cooperate with source countries.

The last point to make is that the profiles of states from different regions also differ dramatically. Important source countries in the Gulf region are different from source countries in Asia, Latin America, North America, Africa, and Europe. We have not traced empirically the patterns of emigration from source countries, but those profiles would be distinctive as well.

BILATERALISM

Having established empirically that patterns of migration flows are predominantly unilateral and unique, we provide the logic that connects these flows to bilateralism as an institutional design choice. The literature on institutional design is surprisingly thin on the conditions under which states choose bilateral versus multilateral institutions.[20] Alexander Thompson and Daniel Verdier (2014) speak directly to the choice between multilateral and bilateral treaties by juxtaposing the costs associated with each type of agreement. Bilateral treaties generate higher transactions costs as each state is required to bargain with every other state. Multilateralism, on the other hand, generates what Thompson and Verdier have labeled "membership surplus." In their formal model, the authors posit that a hegemon is soliciting an international agreement among states in the international system in order to enjoy a collective good (or avoid a collective bad). Because a principle of multilateralism is to treat each member in an identical fashion, the terms of the agreement correspond to the compliance costs of the member with the highest compliance costs. Members with lower compliance costs receive benefits that exceed their costs and, hence, experience a surplus.

Bilateralism provides tailored agreements that reduce the costs of the side payments but requires the hegemon to negotiate multiple agreements, increasing transaction costs. According to Thompson and Verdier, it is this trade-off that states must evaluate when deciding on a multilateral or bilateral agreement format.

We employ the concept of membership surplus to explain the shape of cooperation on migration, but we look at it from the perspective of the regime organizer. The concept of membership surplus has as a counterpart *regime support costs*. Receiving states prefer to minimize side payments when seeking international cooperation. Multilateral agreements increase side payments through two mechanisms. The first mechanism is the higher side payments to all members of the agreement, based on the compliance costs of the highest cost member. For example, in creating a multilateral agreement on migration, France would have to provide the same side payments to Algeria, Morocco, and Tunisia, when their compliance costs could be very different. The second mechanism that increases costs is the number of states to which France would have to supply side payments. France would want to tailor side payments to the compliance costs of each state that was presenting a migration issue and avoid side payments to all other states. There would be no reason for France to include Botswana or Argentina in a multilateral migration agreement. The organizers of the migration regime want to minimize the size of these payments. Given that the issues generated by migration involve a distinctive profile of states for each receiving state and involve a limited number of states, bilateral agreements, even though they involve transaction costs, are cheaper than multilateral agreements. The concept of "membership surplus" presented by Thompson and Verdier (2014) helps us consider how states prefer to minimize regime support payments and also how the regime support costs are generated. What we add is that the pattern of flows helps clarify how regime support costs are generated and shape the costs and benefits of institutional choice. Because the patterns are dominated by unidirectional and unique flows from sending states to receiving states, the externalities associated with the flows are bilateral. The costs of a multilateral agreement would be very large.

Nonetheless, Thompson and Verdier's model provides the basic components for understanding the shape or membership of any international agreement. Where global membership is required to achieve the agreement objectives, regime organizers would evaluate the regime support costs against the transaction costs of negotiating bilateral agreements among all regime member states. In our analysis of criminality in international migration, we find that regime effectiveness requires global membership and the regime organizer, the United States, preferred the lowered transaction costs of a multilateral regime, even though this increased the regime support costs. The specific hypothesis generated by our discussion of migration patterns reflects this trade-off.

H_{1a} Where migration flows are unidirectional and unique and regime support costs exceed negotiation transaction costs, international agreements on migration will be bilateral.

EXCEPTIONS TO THE RULE: RECIPROCAL MOVEMENT

In our model, we have divided the world into sending and receiving states. But the possibility exists for states to experience migration that is reciprocal. In these instances, there is the potential for cooperation that facilitates the movement of migrants across international boundaries. There are few examples of this historically, so we anticipate that the conditions under which migration flows will be reciprocal are rare: they include the Nordic Common Labor Market (including members of the Nordic Union, Sweden, Finland, Norway, Iceland, and Denmark), the Benelux Free Labor Movement Agreement (including Belgium, the Netherlands, and Luxembourg), and the best known example, the European Union. The Trans-Tasman Travel Arrangement (TTTA) between Australia and New Zealand represents yet another case. Two regional organizations in the Global South also meet these conditions: the Gulf Cooperation Council (GCC) and the Organization of Eastern Caribbean States (OECS). Despite the rarity of cooperation to facilitate reciprocal flows, our model needs to account for the possibility. These cases tend to be characterized by relative equality in wages and standard of living and experience low unemployment (UNDP 2009).[21] We employ the same bargaining framework for this type of cooperation: states prefer the status quo until exogenous shocks or pressures generate costs that bring the parties to the bargaining table, but power is not a central component of the bargain. Under these circumstances, we anticipate the presence of bilateral or regional agreements for free labor movement. In the absence of these two conditions, however, regional provisions for free movement may exist but will not be implemented (IOM 2011; UNDP 2009). Thus, our initial hypothesis emphasizing one-way flows and bilateralism is complemented by a hypothesis recognizing reciprocal flows and the potential for bilateral or regional freedom of movement.

H_{1b} Where migration flows are reciprocal, freedom of movement agreements may be negotiated.

CONCLUSIONS

In this first chapter, we have connected migration crises to the agenda on international cooperation. Migration crises reveal that the international institutional structure is riddled with holes that allow migrants to fall into perilous situations, resulting in discrimination, violence, and even death. The lack of international institutions in an era of human rights promotion and global governance is puzzling, especially since many other international flows are governed by international regimes. Although many researchers argue, and we agree, that migration is distinctive from many other international flows, we do not believe that these distinctions account for the lack of international cooperation.

We have described the structure of voluntary migration flows in the past sixty years and have argued that the structure of the flows shapes the costs of regime support. The flows are characterized by nonreciprocal movement from sending to receiving states; moreover, each receiving state's pattern of migration is distinctive. To minimize the costs of regime support, bilateralism is the most cost-effective structure. We hypothesize that, in most instances, where cooperation does occur, it will likely be bilateral in form. We do add three caveats. First, where patterns are reciprocal and states have similar migration profiles, other institutional arrangements may be more cost-effective. Second, where regime goals require global membership, the balance between regime support costs and transaction costs of negotiating bilateral agreements shifts in favor of a multilateral structure. Finally, as we develop in the next chapter, when a group of states seeks to change the status quo through institutional power, regional and multilateral agreements may be negotiated.

In the next chapter, we address international cooperation directly. We adopt a bargaining framework that focuses on the preferences of state actors, the status quo, and the distribution of power in the international system. If powerful states prefer the status quo, international cooperation is unlikely. However, migration crises and other pressures may change the cost of the status quo for powerful states, giving rise to international negotiations on migration. The outcome of the negotiations is a function of bargaining power within the negotiations, shaped by the outside options available to the negotiating parties. Alternatively, negotiations can be initiated by states that prefer a change to the status quo if they locate an institution that provides them with institutional leverage. Chapters 1 and 2 together provide the basis for a series of hypotheses that guide our empirical research.

CHAPTER 2

A Bargaining Framework for Understanding Cooperation

WE EMPLOY a bargaining framework to theorize the conditions under which states maintain the status quo or choose to initiate international bargaining on migration issues and the types of outcomes that result. We focus on the preferences of sending states and receiving states, the status quo ante, and their power resources, both external and internal to the negotiating arena. The status quo ante privileges unilateral control of migration, a position that tends to benefit the receiving states. Receiving states, by definition, have greater external power resources than sending states, which are poor in external power resources. When receiving states prefer the status quo ante, they will not initiate international negotiations. Hence, the status quo ante is a privileged solution.

We argue that there are two mechanisms that bring states to the negotiating table and structure the outcome of the negotiations. First, when exogenous events raise the cost of the status quo for receiving states, they will initiate bargaining with the sending states that are generating the costs. Once bargaining is initiated, sending states are able to extract concessions that reflect the costs to the receiving state of the status quo. Second, if sending states prefer an alternative to the status quo and locate an international forum that provides them with institutional power, they may initiate negotiations. That institutional power may be sufficient to negotiate a treaty but is insufficient to ensure that receiving states actually ratify the treaty; a regime exists in appearance, but the core participants required to put it into effect are absent.

To develop our argument, we briefly survey the types of international activities that exist in the realm of migration. We follow with a definition of international cooperation. We define and justify our unit of analysis as the state. We then present a bargaining framework that generates specific hypotheses about the conditions under which international bargaining will be initiated and the types of agreements that will result. Finally, we outline our research design to test our hypotheses. We describe, classify, and explain the types of international activity related to international migration that exist.

SURVEY OF INTERNATIONAL COOPERATION ON MIGRATION

To start, the International Labor Organization (ILO), a specialized agency of the League of Nations and subsequently the United Nations, has dealt with issues of international labor migration since its establishment in 1919. It currently has a migration section, and there are both ILO and UN conventions on the treatment of migrant workers. In the post–World War II period, the International Organization for Migration (IOM) was created to deal with refugees and "surplus" European populations. It has since evolved from a regional to a global organization and became an affiliate of the United Nations in 2016. The United Nations has promoted various dialogues on issues of migration, starting in 2006 with the High Level Dialogue on Migration that has since evolved into an annual Global Forum on Migration and Development. The IOM also organizes regional consultative processes (RCPs) that bring together regional actors on issues of migration. More recently, the Palermo Protocols of the UN Convention Against Transnational Organized Crime address issues of human trafficking and smuggling. And this list is not exhaustive. There are bilateral readmission agreements, bilateral treaties facilitating labor flows, regional agreements for free movement, and components of the WTO's General Agreement on Trade in Services (GATS Mode 4) that address the movement of people across international borders. Table 2.1 lists many of today's most important instruments that affect international migration.

WHAT CONSTITUTES INTERNATIONAL COOPERATION?

In addition to states' multiple and varied cooperative activities, there are also innumerable nonstate actors that deal with international migration, some of which participate in the dialogues listed above. Yet we need to delineate our area of scholarly inquiry. There is no standard definition of international cooperation employed in the scholarly literature, especially since the recognition that nonstate actors may play an active role in what has come to be known as global governance. However, as the research agenda has deepened over the past three decades, we find that many scholars now focus on international agreements as the marker of international cooperation (Koremenos, Lipson, and Snidal 2001). International agreements come in many forms (bilateral, regional, or multilateral) and can be formally binding or simply a nonbinding memorandum of understanding. They can create institutional structures or be self-implementing and enforcing. They define a set of behaviors to which state parties agree. International agreements bind states to action that is not unilaterally determined. We take up this position and for our purposes, define international cooperation as a formal or informal agreement among two or more states that binds them

Table 2.1
Overview of Interstate Interaction on Voluntary Migration

Type of agreement	
Bilateral agreements	• Bilateral labor agreements • Bilateral readmission agreements
Regional organizations, dialogues, and agreements	• Regional consultative processes (18 organized by the International Organization for Migration) • Regional organizations (e.g., European Union, ECOWAS, Mercosur, etc.)
Multilateral organizations, dialogues, and agreements	• General Agreement on Trade in Services Mode 4 • Palermo Protocols to the UN Convention Against Organized Crime for Human Trafficking and Smuggling • International Labor Organization Conventions No. 79 (1949) and No. 143 (1975) • UN International Convention on the Rights of All Migrant Workers and Members of Their Families • Global Forum on Migration and Development • Global Commission on International Migration • International Organization for Migration

to adopt a joint solution to an issue area that requires action on the part of the signatories.

Global governance is another term that has gained popularity in the international arena and in scholarly research. It covers a broader notion that incorporates the activities of nonstate actors, both domestic and international. Thus, multinational firms, for example, may develop practices that constitute informal rules governing the international behavior of firms, which may or may not be widely accepted. Corporate social responsibility programs are a case in point.[1] And other nonstate actors are clearly active in petitioning states, firms, and international organizations to adopt particular behaviors.

However, there are two reasons to focus specifically on agreements between states as the locus of our theoretical and empirical inquiry. The first is that our approach does not exclude the activities of nonstate actors; they are incorporated into the analysis by way of delineating the costs of the status quo, and changes to it, for states. Those activities are then reflected in the negotiating outcomes should states choose to initiate international negotiations. Second, the practices adopted by nonstate actors exist only when those actors have both the preferences and resources to implement those practices, with no scope for enforcement of any type. Although it is not impossible for nonstate actors, such as firms or international organizations, to adopt and implement such governance practices, such practices appear largely absent in the international migration arena. In our empirical analysis, we examine the conditions under which states cooperate and the presence or absence of other actors that actually implement global governance activities.

STATES AS CENTRAL ACTORS

We take the perspective that states are the primary actors in the international system, although we acknowledge that other nonstate actors can play an important role in shaping international collaboration.[2] This position is not controversial in the literature on international bargaining (Odell 2000; McKibben 2015). After all, we are interested in agreements that states sign, and this is one method of abstracting from the empirical reality to model the processes taking place.

Although states are the usual unit of analysis in international relations, scholars recognize that a state's national interest is an amorphous concept and that domestic politics play an important role in defining state interests in the international system. It is also true that migration is often a domestically charged political issue and that domestic actors have positions on the level and type of migration desired (both immigration and emigration). These actors' preferences, as filtered through the state's political institutions, are reflected in the preferences of the state regarding the level and type of migration desired by the state. Although we recognize that migration policies are defined primarily by the interplay of domestic actors and domestic political institutions, we do not explore the domestic origins of state preferences on migration policies per se. This is not to say that the topic is unimportant or uninteresting. To the contrary, a large and growing body of research is evolving to understand how states adopt and adapt policies governing entry to the territory (immigration control policy) and the treatment of migrants upon arrival (immigrant integration policy). There is currently no consensus on the factors that play into the domestic politics equation, although many domestic actors and interests have been enumerated and global actors included in the equation as well.[3] However, in order to fulfill our task of delineating the possibilities for cooperation in the international system, we take state interests (state preferences) as both given and visible to outside observers. That is, we "black box" the domestic politics of immigration policy (the level and types of migrants to admit and their treatment upon arrival) in order to focus on the potential for interaction among states in the international system on migration issues. This makes sense for migration, because, although domestic actors may have strong preferences over the level of immigration and treatment of immigrants, they often do not have specific preferences over whether those policy goals are met with unilateral, bilateral, regional, or multilateral action. And, we argue, because migration is central to the concept of state sovereignty, the state itself, through its representatives, has preferences for retaining control over its borders and population (Rudolph 2003).

There are some disadvantages to taking the state as the unit of analysis without incorporating domestic politics in some way. There is a large and growing intellectual tradition in international relations that privileges domestic political actors in shaping state preferences in international negotiations. A central source in the literature is Robert Putnam's (1988) discussion of two-level games. The state negotiator is required to negotiate an agreement with other states but is also required to obtain the consent of the domestic polity in order to ratify that agreement. In the subfield of international political economy, researchers look to the economic consequences of policy on domestic groups and their access to the corridors of political power as a determinant of state preferences (Lake 2009). More broadly, selectorate theory, or attention to audience costs, has brought domestic actors into the equation of international negotiations (Bueno de Mesquita et al. 2004; Bueno de Mesquita and Smith 2012).

Selectorate theory points to the size of the group that selects the state's leaders and to the preferences of the median person in that group as key to understanding state preferences. This literature focuses primarily on the differences in preferences based on the size of the selectorate—large selectorates are representative of democracies, and small selectorates are representative of autocracies. There is little work on variation in the preferences for migration between democracies and autocracies. In the absence of such work, we look to the economic consequences of migration on domestic political actors and argue that these appear to be indifferent to the shape of the state's political institutions. The largest benefits from migration accrue to employers in the host state and to the migrants themselves, as employers have access to a cheaper and more pliable labor force and the migrants receive higher wages than they could accrue in their home state (Castles, de Haas, and Miller 2014). The impact on labor in the home and host states depends in large part on the degree to which local labor is insulated from foreign labor (Piore 1979) and the incorporation of domestic political actors' policy preferences into the state's decision calculus based on the economic consequences of the policy on domestic groups. For example, the trade literature refers to import-competing versus export-oriented economic sectors as potentially important actors in determining the level of international cooperation on trade.

We do not dispute the underlying theoretical framework but argue that, for migration issues, democracies do not differ systematically from autocracies in preferences for international cooperation. Our basic distinction is between sending and receiving states regardless of regime type. We develop our reasoning below.

MARKET CONDITIONS AND STATE PREFERENCES

When examining the interests of states in the international system relative to migration, we divide states into two categories: sending and receiving states.[4] Just as John Odell (2000) refers to "market conditions" as central to understanding state preferences on trade and how those preferences change, we refer to market conditions that separate states into those that attract immigrants and those that generate emigrants.[5] We have noted above the blurred line between voluntary and forced migration and observe that forced migrants are concentrated in the poorer countries of the Global South (UNHCR 2015). But voluntary migrants seek destinations that provide them with expanded opportunities, and hence we are able to distinguish destination countries as more stable and wealthier than voluntary emigrants' home countries (UNDP 2009).[6]

This is a simplification of the migration profile of states in the international system. All states send as well as receive migrants. Some are also geographically positioned to act as "transit" states between those sending and receiving. Yet all states have a net migration flow that weighs the number of emigrants against the number of immigrants and, we argue, serves to help understand the types of interests they pursue relative to migration issues. Transit states may be receiving states, such as Spain, which serves as a conduit for migrants traveling to more northern states in Europe and also hosts a large migrant population of its own; transit states may be sending states, such as Morocco, which also serves as a conduit for migrants traveling to Europe, but remains a sending state with a net emigration balance. In Southern Africa, Mozambique is a transit as well as a sending state, as is Mexico in North America. As noted above, states may transition between sending and receiving status; when they do, we argue that their interests shift as well. This simple dichotomy of sending and receiving state is employed in each chapter to outline state preferences on the five migration issues central to issues of international cooperation. However, in our quantitative analyses, we refine the dichotomy by employing a continuum based on net migration figures.

The second attribute that we want to point out is the power characteristics of sending and receiving states. By definition, states that attract voluntary migrants are wealthier and more stable than countries of origin. Therefore, we attribute to receiving states greater levels of external power resources—military, diplomatic, and economic power. These attributes serve to reinforce the preferences of powerful states in the international system.

THE BARGAINING FRAMEWORK

The Status Quo Ante, State Preferences, and Power. Our bargaining framework begins with the status quo and the preferences of sending and receiving states. To illustrate, we can think of the status quo ante as the accepted behavior of states in customary international law related to admissions and departures of individuals at state borders. This can be depicted by a two-dimensional issue space, as shown in Figure 2.1. The most basic rule governing admissions is state sovereignty; the state has the right to turn away individuals seeking entry. This rule has been abridged in several ways in customary international law. For example, states are required to allow their own citizens to enter, should they leave the territory of the state. A second abridgement of the rule is associated with the 1951 refugee convention that requires signatories to not refoule (turn away) refugees. This requires states to evaluate asylum claims of individuals seeking entry to determine whether they meet the refugee definition. In the two-dimensional issue space, the status quo on this dimension would reflect a point close but not equivalent to total state sovereignty. Conversely, states are required by customary international law to permit their citizens to leave their country, save for concerns with public order. Thus, on the second issue dimension, the status quo would be reflected by low levels of state sovereignty.

This represents one specific two-dimensional issue space. Each migration

FIGURE 2.1
Customary International Law on Departure and Entry

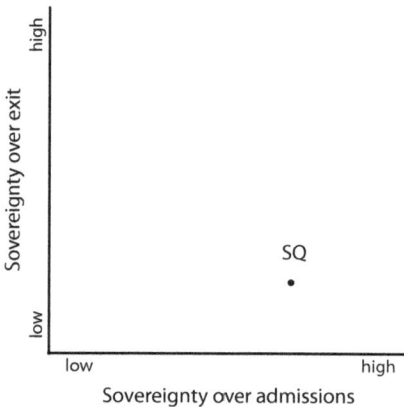

SQ = status quo (customary international law). The status quo point in the policy space represents high state sovereignty over admissions and low state sovereignty over exit.

FIGURE 2.2

Conditions That Promote Retention of the Status Quo

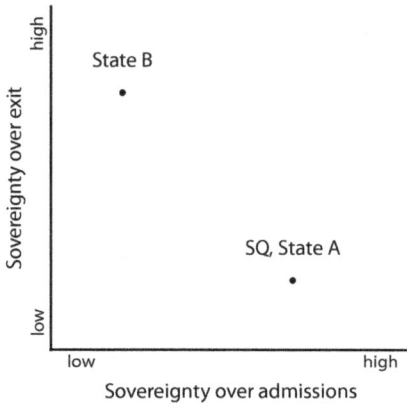

SQ = status quo (customary international law); *State A* = Receiving State A's ideal point; *State B* = Sending State B's ideal point. Receiving State A's ideal point is identical to the status quo, whereas Sending State B prefers a different point in the policy space. Generically, the win set of the status quo is empty because there is no point in the policy space that both State A and State B prefer to the status quo. Because Receiving State A is more powerful than Sending State B, it can resist efforts of the sending state to change the status quo. Hence, the status quo represents a privileged outcome; negotiations are unlikely to ensue.

issue area has a two-dimensional (or multidimensional) issue space and a specific status quo ante. For each of the issue areas, we describe a specific status quo and specific preferences of sending and receiving states. Generically, we point out that the win set of the status quo, the policies that both states would prefer to the status quo, is empty if one party prefers the status quo. As shown in Figure 2.2, State A prefers the status quo and State B prefers a position in the policy space that is different from the status quo. If State A is more powerful, State B has fewer resources to convince State A to change the status quo. If State B is more powerful, it can use its resources to provide side payments to State A to obtain State A's consent to change the status quo. Alternatively, if State B is more powerful, it may be able to change the status quo unilaterally.

Because we have defined receiving states as states with relatively more power and more stability, if State A is a receiving state and prefers the status quo, there is a strong likelihood that negotiations to change the status quo will not come to fruition, even though State B is dissatisfied with the status quo. This relationship holds, we argue, on both a bilateral basis and a multilateral basis. That is,

States A and B can represent two individual states in the international system or can represent a coalition of all receiving states and all sending states. Thus, we generate our second hypothesis.

H$_2$ When powerful states prefer the status quo ante, international cooperation is less likely to occur.

Weak states, however, are not totally without resources (Odell 2006). One of the resources they have garnered in the international system is the power of numbers achieved through institutional rules. An example is the United Nations where states of the Global South, individually less powerful than those of the Global North, can vote on provisions in the General Assembly and adopt by majority vote instruments that the Global North may not prefer. However, this resource is limited in the sense that states are unbound by treaties that they choose not to ratify. So when the less powerful states can agree on a policy and locate a forum that provides them with institutional power, negotiations may proceed and even result in an international agreement. However, the powerful states are not compelled to ratify the treaty.

On issues of international migration, we argue that if sending states prefer a policy different from the status quo and can organize a coalition that allows them to employ institutional rules to initiate negotiations, then sending states may be able to obtain an international agreement that modifies the status quo. However, sending states are unlikely to have the power resources to persuade receiving states to modify their opposition to the treaty proposals to change the status quo. An example of this type of event is the negotiation of the UN International Convention on the Protection of the Rights of All Migrant Workers and Members of Their Families between 1980 and 1990.[7] Our third hypothesis captures this form of weak state power.

H$_{3a}$ When less powerful states act as a coalition and find a forum that provides institutional power, bargaining is more likely to occur.

H$_{3b}$ When an agreement is negotiated without the support of powerful states, those states are unlikely to ratify any negotiated treaty.

Exogenous Pressures and the Changing Costs of the Status Quo Ante. Although powerful states may generally prefer the status quo, exogenous events may change the costs of the status quo and modify the preferences of powerful states. Exogenous events come in many forms. Domestic political actors may create political costs for the government. In the realm of international migration, there are a number of anti-immigrant actors—political parties and interest groups—that may be able to embarrass the government and create electoral costs that the government finds unacceptable. Migrant rights organizations and domestic media outlets may also bring attention to migration issues in a way that modifies the government's political calculus. International state and non-governmental actors may also be important in increasing the costs of the status quo to the government in power. Even market forces may create rising costs of the status quo. Peaks and valleys in the state's economic cycle may generate higher demand for migrants that is unattainable through the status quo system or increase calls to reduce the migrant population through methods that are unacceptable in the status quo system.

Migrants themselves are also actors. They can mobilize within a polity in a way that creates challenges to the government in power. Or, as we saw in the example of the European migrant crisis, they can increase the costs to the government of the status quo by moving across international borders. Regardless of the source of the exogenous pressures or shocks, as the costs of the current status quo rise, the preferences of the powerful state may change. In this case, the powerful state is likely to initiate negotiations. In terms of sending and receiving states, when the costs of the status quo for the receiving state rise, it is more likely to initiate international negotiations with the states that are generating the costs. An example of powerful receiving states entering the international arena in search of an agreement to reduce the costs of the status quo is the European Union, in light of the European migrant crisis. Negotiations with Turkey, the main transit country during that crisis, began in late summer 2015 and concluded only in March 2016. This leads to our fourth hypothesis.

H$_4$ When the costs of the status quo ante rise, receiving states are more likely to initiate international negotiations.

Bargaining Power and the Distribution of Benefits. Once a powerful state initiates international negotiations, the distribution of power may shift based on each state's best alternative to a negotiated agreement. The concept of "best alternative to a negotiated agreement" is central to the bargaining literature and reflects the idea that parties to the negotiation will examine their alternatives and choose the one with the highest payoff. If an alternative to a negotiated agreement provides a higher payoff, then the state will select it. If the negotiated agreement provides the highest payoff, then the agreement will be chosen.

When receiving states experience an exogenous shock, the rising costs of the current status quo make no agreement costly. Time is not on the receiving state's side; its leaders need a resolution that reduces their costs. They may try unilateral solutions to address the rising costs as alternatives to a negotiated agreement, but these solutions have been ineffective. They need an agreement. On the other side of the negotiating table, the sending or transit state may well be better satisfied with the status quo than is the receiving state. That is, although the sending or transit state prefers a policy position different from the status quo, that state's position is closer to the status quo than to the position desired by the receiving state.[8] The best alternative to a negotiated agreement that reflects the preferences of the receiving state may well be the status quo. In this case, the sending or transit state will not choose a negotiated agreement unless they are compensated for their compliance. The availability of alternatives to the negotiated agreement enhances the bargaining power of the sending state. As the receiving state's cost rise, the sending state can extract higher side payments and/or a change in the international rules governing migration. To continue the same example mentioned above, when the European Union was confronted with a large, and potentially unending, stream of migrants flowing through Turkey in 2015, it negotiated an agreement with Turkey to stop migrant departures—a change to the status quo. In the initial agreement in November 2015, Turkey was able to obtain three billion euros but ultimately realized that it could extract yet larger side payments. The second agreement, which took effect in March 2016, upped the ante to six billion euros—payments promised by the European Union to Turkey to help offset the costs of housing Syrians fleeing civil war within Turkey itself (European Commission 2016).

Figure 2.3 shows that A's preferences have changed; the state now desires a change in the status quo. State B is now closer to the status quo than A and can

FIGURE 2.3

Conditions That Promote Negotiations to Change the Status Quo

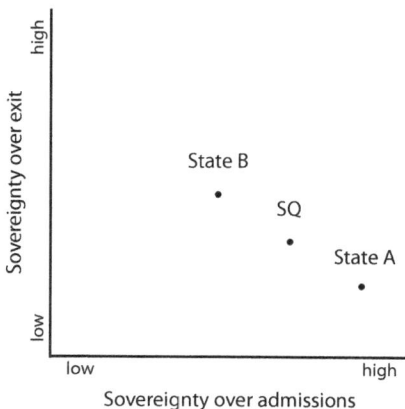

SQ = status quo (customary international law); *State A* = Receiving State A's ideal point; *State B* = Sending State B's ideal point. Receiving State A's ideal point is different than the status quo, whereas Sending State B prefers the status quo to Receiving State A's ideal point. Because Receiving State A has larger external power resources, it can use its superior resources to provide side payments to Sending State B to change the status quo to a point closer to its preferred position.

extract concessions from A to change the status quo closer to A's ideal point. This leads to our fifth hypothesis.

H$_5$ When the sending state has a better outside option than the receiving state, the sending state will be able to extract concessions from the receiving state.

THE STATUS QUO

In the abstract, it is easy to understand the concept of the status quo and posit the preferences of state actors at some point in the policy space. Empirically, locating these points is more problematic. Because each issue area represents a different status quo and a different set of state preferences, it is useful to address the issue of empirical referents generically. We adopt the position that customary international law is a good approximation of the behavior required of states in the international system. This is a useful and nonarbitrary method of understanding the status quo as customary international law is "the only vehicle for creating universal norms binding all States" and "is directly applicable by domestic courts in a substantial number of States" (Chetail 2014, 9). Although compliance with customary international law is never complete, there are characterics that permit us to define customary international law applicable to each of our issue areas.

We adopt the criteria presented by Vincent Chetail (2014) for locating the status quo ante. Chetail employs three criteria to determine whether a particular norm is considered part of customary international law. The first is whether the practice is particularly widespread and representative. The marker of representativeness is widespread state adherence to treaties that endorse the concept with few reservations. If the principle is enunciated in several treaties and those treaties are widely ratified, then it is likely that the principle is widely understood and accepted. The second is whether those states that fail to adhere to the treaties acknowledge the principle. Many states, even when they do not adhere to the principle, nonetheless still refer to the principle to explain their exception. For example, when turning away (refouling) individuals who might qualify for refugee status, states may argue that the act of returning individuals to their country of origin is not refoulement because there is no concern about persecution. Thus, even in the breech, the rule is accepted by the state. Finally, the third criterion for evaluating whether an international principle exists is whether the principle appears in a large number of international pronouncements and in domestic case law. Chetail (2014, 40) summarizes these three rules in the following statement: "In sum, the almost universal ratification of treaties, the general practice of states (including that of non-States Parties) and the numerous manifestation of *opinion juris* anchor the principle . . . within general international law." These criteria help to ensure that the status quo we describe is widely recognized by states in the international system, even though there are still controversies in international migration law over these issues. It is important to emphasize that this status quo represents not a normative position that is either positive or negative but the expected behavior of states in the international system. An analogy may help to understand why we choose to operationalize the status quo in this manner.

Take, for example, a thoroughfare in a town or city where the posted speed limit is forty-five miles per hour. Then add the construction of a new primary school that abuts this thoroughfare. Given the need to ensure the safety of the children who attend the new school, school leadership, or perhaps parents, may take unilateral action to build a wall between the thoroughfare and the school. Or perhaps the school or a parent association might hire a crossing guard to help the children cross the road. All of this can take place without changing the speed limit. Perhaps, despite the efforts of the school and the parents, children are hurt or killed crossing the thoroughfare. The parents and the school administrators may petition the local government to change the situation by reducing the speed to twenty-five miles per hour, or by putting in a stop sign or traffic light. Although this analogy is imperfect because this situation provides a specific decision process for changing traffic regulations, the issue of traffic regulations is analogous to international agreements on migration. We are interested in when states enter international agreements to change the regulations governing state behavior on migration issues. One can trace the pressures that build that make the existing status quo—forty-five miles per hour—costly for the school, the parents, and the children, and that lead them to negotiate with the government over the existing traffic regulations. Likewise, we trace the pressures that make the existing status quo costly to receiving and sending states. Employing the status quo in this fashion allows us to separate the pressures and costs from the existing legal framework. Because we adopt this definition of the status quo, we speak of state preferences as changing as a result of exogenous shocks rather than the status quo changing. States then negotiate to modify the guidelines that determine legitimate state behavior in the international system.

One may rightfully ask where the status quo we define originated. We suggest that, at least for migration issues, similar processes to the ones we trace here generated the status quo with which we initiate our analysis of each issue area. However, to avoid endless regress, we begin our analyses with the status quo—customary international law on migration—after the end of World War II in 1945. The one exception is on migrant rights when we begin with the period prior to World War I in order to trace the rise of the ILO, created in the Treaty of Versailles in 1919.

INTERNATIONAL MIGRATION ISSUES

To evaluate our hypotheses, we examine the *issues* generated by migration within the voluntary migration stream. We begin by delineating four generic issues generated by international migration: how to control and reduce migration; how to increase migration (recruitment and freedom of movement); how to deal with criminality; and migrant rights. In Table 2.2, we reorganize the international agreements by issue area and explain the origins of the agreements in terms of the preferences of sending and receiving states, the status quo ante, exogenous pressures or shocks, and the international institutional structure.

In each chapter, we begin by illustrating the issue with a description of the human dimension of migration. We proceed by describing the issue at hand and outlining the preferences of sending and receiving states and the status quo ante. We then explore exogenous pressures that raise the costs of the status quo for receiving states or institutional forums that permit sending states to

Table 2.2
Migration Issues and Types of International Cooperation on Migration

| Issue | Type of Agreement | | |
	Bilateral	Regional	Multilateral
Internal immigration control (chapter 3)	Bilateral readmission agreements	Regional consultative processes	None
Facilitating immigration: Labor recruitment (chapter 4)	Bilateral labor agreements	Regional organizations	GATS Mode 4; Global Forum on Migration and Development
Facilitating immigration: Freedom of movement (chapter 5)	Trans-Tasman Travel Arrangement	Regional organizations	None
Criminality (chapter 6)	Bilateral trafficking agreements	Regional consultative processes	Palermo Protocols to the UN Convention Against Organized Crime on Human Trafficking and Smuggling
Migrant rights (chapter 7)	Bilateral labor agreements	Regional organizations	International Labor Organization; ILO and UN migrant rights treaties; global forums

demand changes to the status quo. We trace the initiation of bargaining and the outcome of bargaining that are consistent with our theoretical claims, including bilateral, regional, and multilateral negotiations. Where possible, we generate a quantitative analysis that links the costs of the status quo with the generation of agreements. We complete each chapter by exploring alternative explanations for the phenomena we describe and demonstrate that our analysis fits the evidence better than, or is compatible with, alternative explanations. By providing analyses across multiple migration issues, our theory provides a more generic explanation of the conditions under which cooperation occurs on international migration.

We also point out that some of the existing international institutional framework is poorly ratified. Treaties can give the illusion of cooperation without the actual existence of cooperation, because few states are signatories to the agreement or because provisions in the treaties are never implemented. Thus our empirical evidence includes both genuine cooperation among states as well as institutions, treaties, and agreements that provide only the illusion of cooperation.

We emphasize that this is a broad view of international cooperation on voluntary migration—a bird's-eye view. And as some researchers will note in despair, we relegate external border controls to the travel (mobility) regime. This represents a large component of the cooperative behavior that we see in the international system on migration. However, this sorting is necessary if we are to understand the locus of state decision making on migration. We also do not claim that we explain each and every component of the voluntary migration regime—there are undoubtedly exceptions to the rule. However, we do claim that our broad outline is the best way to understand the types of cooperation that do exist as well as the shape of possible future cooperation.

SITUATING OUR CONTRIBUTION

As noted above, there have been multiple efforts to understand international cooperation on migration. Some come in the form of scholarly articles that focus on a single type of cooperation, for example, the RCPs that the IOM has promoted (Koehler 2011; Thouez and Channac 2006; Von Koppenfels 2001). Others take a normative position that cooperation is needed to resolve some specific problem generated by migratory flows (Ghosh 2000). Still others come in the form of edited volumes in which each author describes and explains different aspects of cooperation, including volumes to which we have contributed (Betts 2011; Gamlen and Marsh 2011; Ghosh 2000; Hansen, Koehler, and Money 2011; Koslowski 2011a; Kunz, Lavenex, and Panizzon 2011).[9] These efforts are useful to us as they illuminate arenas in which states have created dialogues and treaties, as well as highlight those areas in which states continue to act unilaterally. But we move beyond these compendia by providing a single theoretical framework to understand both the presence and absence of interstate cooperation on voluntary migration, and the form it is likely to take.

We exploit a body of theoretical insights from international relations to organize, analyze, and explain the shape, timing, and content of international agreements on voluntary migration, including when international cooperation should be absent. We provide a coherent picture of the types of behavior that we see in the international system on issues of international migration. We incorporate the role of ideas by focusing on exogenous pressures that emanate from domestic and international nonstate actors as well as domestic and international markets (Finnemore and Sikkink 1998). These forces become important when they change the costs of the status quo for receiving states and jolt them into the international arena in search of an agreement that modifies those costs.

Each of our issue areas represents one chapter in this volume. In each chapter, we take on the literature that deals specifically with that issue dimension to point out where our explanation is similar to or distinctive from the extant research. In each case, we provide new theory that either overturns or builds on the extant research to explain more fully the types of cooperation that exist. However, the primary contribution of the volume is synthetic: to bring a comprehensive theoretical and empirical picture of what type of interstate cooperation exists on issues of voluntary migration, and to distinguish which institutional structures have low ratification rates and which genuinely promote cooperation among states. We place all of these activities into a common framework that both explains and predicts the types of cooperation we anticipate.

CONCLUSIONS

Chapters 1 and 2 combined provide the scope of our research, the prospects for international cooperation on voluntary migration flows. In chapter 1, we argued that patterns of migration in the post–World War II period have been characterized primarily by state-specific, nonreciprocal flows. The theoretical work on the evolution of cooperation suggests that cooperation will be difficult in the absence of the possibility of reciprocity, and that where market failures or externalities are dyadic, the shape of cooperation is likely to be bilateral. These conclusions are reinforced by research that illuminates the shape of international agreements. When states initiate negotiations on migration flows, they weigh the costs of multilateral regime support against the transaction costs of negotiating a series of bilateral agreements. Where the costs of regime support outweigh the transaction costs of negotiating bilateral agreements, states will choose bilateral agreements. Given the observed empirical patterns, in most instances, cooperation will be bilateral. Rarely, the costs of regime support are lower than the transaction costs of negotiating bilateral agreements. We see this in the case of the Palermo Protocols on human trafficking and smuggling. We are able to explain both the dominance of bilateralism on issues of international migration and the conditions under which multilateralism will arise.

In this chapter, we have outlined a bargaining framework that generates several hypotheses about the stability of the status quo, the conditions under which international negotiations are likely to arise, and the shape that those agreements are likely to take. Although we take the state as the central unit of analysis, because states are the actors that sign international agreements, we incorporate nonstate actors into the explanation by acknowledging their capacity to change the costs of the status quo for receiving states. We argue that when powerful receiving states prefer the status quo, little international cooperation is likely to take place. We describe two circumstances under which negotiations over international migration are likely to take place. The first is when the costs of the status quo rise for receiving states; at that point, receiving states have incentives to undertake international negotiations to change the status quo and sending states are able to extract concessions. The second is when sending states that prefer an alternative to the status quo form a coalition and are able to locate an international forum that provides them with institutional power. Treaties may be negotiated under these circumstances, but receiving states, whose compliance is required to effectuate the terms of the treaty, fail to ratify the treaties.

Table 2.3
Recapitulation of Hypotheses

Hypothesis	
H_{1a}	Where migration flows are unidirectional and unique and where regime support costs exceed negotiation transaction costs, international agreements on migration will be bilateral.
H_{1b}	Where migration flows are reciprocal, freedom of movement agreements may be negotiated.
H_2	When powerful states prefer the status quo ante, international cooperation is less likely to occur.
H_{3a}	When less powerful states act as a coalition and find a forum that provides institutional power, bargaining is more likely to occur.
H_{3b}	When an agreement is negotiated without the support of powerful states, those states are unlikely to ratify any negotiated treaty.
H_4	When the costs of the status quo ante rise, receiving states are more likely to initiate international negotiations.
H_5	When the sending state has a better outside option than the receiving state, the sending state will be able to extract concessions from the receiving state.

Exceptionally, in regions where migration flows are reciprocal, agreements on free movement may be possible. We recapitulate our hypotheses in Table 2.3.

We now turn to the four issue areas central to international migration: internal immigration control, facilitating movement (recruitment and freedom of movement), criminality, and migrant rights.

CHAPTER 3

Controlling Immigration

Migrant Crises as a Key Driver of Cooperation

RAHIM WAS JUST sixteen years old when he fled Afghanistan in 2012 and ended up in Turkey, where he applied for refugee status with the UNHCR and was registered as an unaccompanied minor. After spending six months in dire conditions in a shelter in eastern Turkey, Rahim escaped to Istanbul and found work in a textile workshop. By late 2013, he had saved enough money to pay a smuggler to take him to Bulgaria, where he was promptly caught by police and returned to the Turkish side of the border. Turkish soldiers then transferred him to a removal center in Edirne. Rahim tried to escape to Europe two more times, attempting to reach the Greek island of Lesbos by boat. Both times, he was picked up by the Greek coastguard and sent back to Turkey:

> We were just 10m off the island when the Greek coastguard found us. . . . We were so close, we thought we can make it to the island. But the Greek coast-guard boat caught up with us. We punctured our boat and jumped into the sea so that the coastguard could not tow us back to Turkey. The coastguards picked us out of the sea on to their boat. . . . Then we sailed towards Turkey for half an hour or so. . . . They put an inflatable boat in the sea and pushed us onto it. They also threw two oars at us and pointed to the shore. And then they left. They just left us there.

Despite the risks, Rahim thinks that he will try to get to Europe again. "I would stay in Turkey," he says, "but I have no rights here. I can't legally work or go to school. I can't just continue working like this to survive. I feel stuck" (Amnesty International 2014, 8).

Rahim's case suggests that Europe expended substantial efforts to prevent both economic migrants and potential asylum seekers from reaching Europe. Although Rahim qualified for refugee status in Turkey, the "first safe country" of refuge, he was not considered a legitimate asylum seeker with onward movement. His pressing protection needs should have been met in the country of first refuge.[1] In his attempt to reach Europe, Rahim was viewed as an undocumented economic migrant.[2] And Rahim was joined on his quest for entry into Europe by myriad other migrants who would not meet the criteria for refugee status. In the most recent European migrant crisis, most Syrians and Eritreans received some type of protected status; on the other hand, Albanians and Kosovars were roundly rejected.[3] Despite the ongoing conflict in Afghanistan, almost half of the Afghans who applied for asylum in Europe were rejected.[4] If these individuals either fail to leave voluntarily or avoid detection, they add to the population of undocumented migrants in the host country.

In this chapter, we examine efforts by states to control and restrict migration. Rahim's story is not uncommon, particularly in Europe, where destination states have sought the cooperation of sending and transit states to accept the return of undocumented migrants, including both economic migrants and rejected asylum seekers. Most commonly, the cooperation has taken the form of readmission agreements, which continue to provoke controversy among advocates for migrant and refugee rights. Nevertheless, the European states and the European Union itself have only accelerated their pursuit of readmission agreements in response to the most recent "migration crisis" during which migrants from all parts of the world attempted to enter Europe.

If Rahim had been successful in his attempt to enter Europe, it is likely that his residence there would have been as an undocumented migrant or a rejected asylum seeker. He would not be unique. The UNDP's 2009 publication on human mobility reported that of the approximately 218 million individuals living outside their country of birth, "an estimated 40 million people today are living abroad with irregular status" (UNDP 2009, 2). This means that almost one in five immigrants does not have permission to stay in their country of residence.

Immigration control is usually addressed as a comprehensive package of policies that attempts to restrict immigration to the number and type of immigrants the state desires. A closer look, though, reveals that there are both internal and external dimensions of control: ensuring that only those individuals whom the state desires enter the territory of the state and detecting, apprehending, detaining, and deporting both those who evade the external controls and those who enter legally but overstay their entry provisions. The external dimension of control, or border management, falls squarely under the auspices of the travel regime, as proposed by Koslowski (2011a). Of course, the characteristics of the entrants can be quite varied: voluntary flows include short-term entrants such as tourists, family visitors, international students, and business visitors, as well as immigrants who intend to stay for at least twelve months; refugees and asylum seekers represent involuntary flows. And, as Koslowski suggests, multilateral, regional, and bilateral cooperation on international travel has been in existence for at least a century. However, because this is central to the travel regime, we do not deal with this component of migration cooperation here.

Here we focus on the internal dimension of immigration control. The problem of a resident undocumented population refers to individuals who have either successfully evaded border controls or entered legally and overstayed their visa provisions. This includes the so-called rejected asylum seekers or false asylum seekers who have petitioned the host state for refugee status and have been rejected but have failed to leave the host state. This population represents the issue we address in this chapter: under what circumstances do states cooperate on the internal dimensions of immigration control and, in particular, on the reduction of undocumented migrant populations?

In this chapter, we point to the rising costs associated with an undocumented resident population in the host state as the driver for the receiving state to initiate negotiations to enhance international cooperation on (internal) immigration control. Although the status quo initially favored receiving states, which could act unilaterally to both restrict entrance and deport unwanted immigrants, practices of migrants and sending states modified the status quo in favor of sending states, as receiving states' unilateral efforts became ineffective. Therefore, receiving states must persuade sending states to accept their citizens and transit migrants, a negotiation that generates costs. Receiving states continue to act unilaterally unless the domestic costs of the undocumented population are high. On the other side of the equation, international cooperation represents a cost to sending states; they will sign agreements only if the side payments from the negotiation are sufficient to offset these costs. Because of the unidirectional and unique flows of migrants, bilateralism is the dominant form of cooperation, as this reduces the costs of side payments receiving states must make to sending states. Even then, the win set of policies that both states would prefer to the status is usually empty, unless the ability of the receiving state to act unilaterally has also been curtailed in some way.

Our chapter begins with an overview of contemporary patterns of undocumented migration and the issues these flows raise in receiving states. We then present the status quo as reflected in customary international law and state preferences vis-à-vis the status quo. We proceed to develop theoretical propositions that explain the conditions under which international cooperation is likely to arise. We then present evidence to support our contentions at the bilateral, regional, and multilateral levels. At the bilateral level, we find the most extensive cooperation in Europe in the form of bilateral readmission agreements. Unilateral control has been eroded through the process of European integration. To compensate, European states facing higher costs from undocumented immigration have pursued readmission agreements with sending states. At the regional level, we find little cooperation. Although the European Union has pursued EU-wide agreement with sending states, very few have been concluded, even as member states continue to conclude ever greater numbers. Outside of Europe, we find that broader economic integration has *not* led to formal cooperation on internal immigration control (we look specifically at the Caribbean Community and Mercosur), supporting our claim that receiving states usually find it cost-effective to control immigration unilaterally unless their ability to do so has been eroded. We do find a broader range of informal cooperation, mainly in the form of RCPs, because this form of cooperation is less costly for both sending and receiving states. Finally, we point out that global multilateral cooperation on undocumented populations simply does not exist. Before we conclude, we evaluate our theory and evidence against alternative accounts and we also examine the European migrant crisis in light of our theoretical expectations.

INTERIOR IMMIGRATION CONTROL AND
UNDOCUMENTED MIGRATION

Undocumented migrants include both those who evade border controls and those who overstay the length of time permitted by their visas or the terms of their visa-free entry. Detecting, apprehending, detaining, and deporting undocumented immigrants have long been important elements of migration policy for states. *Undocumented* migration is not equivalent to *unwanted* migration, of course. There are often conflicting interest groups within states that support and oppose immigration. In response to these contradictory pressures, states might restrict legal immigration while tacitly supporting illegal immigration. The general public may oppose immigration for fear of labor competition, concern about the fiscal burden migrants pose for the welfare state, or xenophobia (Hainmueller and Hiscox 2007). At the same time, some domestic lobby groups may support maintaining or increasing immigration, particularly those that represent industries employing a large number of immigrants. For companies demanding immigrant labor, increasing the supply of immigrants lowers costs. Industries demanding high-skilled labor may look for an expansion of legal avenues for high-skilled immigrants; in the United States, for example, Facebook founder Mark Zuckerberg launched FWD.us, the US tech industry lobbying campaign that advocates for immigration reform. But for those industries demanding low-skilled labor, restrictions on legal migration coupled with lax enforcement can be even more beneficial. Undocumented migrants are less likely to demand higher wages or to report illegal working conditions due to their fear of deportation. To the extent, then, that these industries have political influence, the state policy may actually restrict legal immigration (appealing to populist demands) while tacitly supporting illegal immigration (appeasing politically influential and economically important industries).

On the other hand, documented migration is not always wanted. Christian Joppke (1998) points to two factors that allow migrants to enter and to stay legally, even though they are unwanted by a majority of the citizens of the receiving state. The first echoes our above description: states may respond to business interests for a less costly and more malleable labor supply and ignore citizen demands for greater restriction. The second points to the role of judiciaries, especially in wealthy Western democracies, that grant migrants human rights, such as the right to family reunification, which may expand the migrant population without any domestic political pressures at all (Hollifield 1992).

Although we acknowledge the differences between unwanted and undocumented migration, we posit that receiving states prefer to retain sovereignty over the ability to deport undocumented aliens. We assume that undocumented migration is unwanted at some level because it is illegal; it is a challenge to the legitimacy and capacity of the state to enforce its domestic laws. Moreover, the continued presence of large numbers of undocumented migrants does not indicate an actual preference for this specific level of undocumented migration, even if the state is doing little to reduce the number. There are two additional and important explanations for the continued presence of undocumented migrants. First, the state may not have the capability required to prevent undocumented migrants from entering the state or to remove them once they have arrived. Second, the state may have the capabilities, but it may not deem it worthwhile to expend resources preventing or removing undocumented migrants. At some point, the marginal cost of reducing the unwanted, undocumented population to zero is not worth it to the state; this means that states may support different levels of deportation. All of this is to say that the precise level of desired immigration and the cost of achieving it are unique to each receiving state at any given point in time, which helps explain why unilateralism has been widespread.

Historically, migrant-receiving states have largely pursued migration control unilaterally because receiving states' desired level of migration varies across countries and over time, and the costs of achieving this level vary as well. Settler countries, such as the United States, Canada, and Australia, have struggled with the issue for well over a hundred years and pursued different unilateral polices over time (Freeman 1994). At first, these countries embraced a laissez-faire approach to immigration, permitting it to proceed nearly unchecked, when land was plentiful, labor was in high demand, and immigrants were primarily European. As these countries became more established and conditions changed, immigration policies also changed. Over time, there was an increasing focus on restricting migration flows to keep out unwanted migrants. Control measures, however, have failed. At the peak in 2007, the United States was home to an estimated 12.2 million undocumented immigrants (Pew Research Center 2013a, 2013b). Estimates of undocumented immigrants in Canada range from 35,000 to 120,000. Even Australia, which has the advantage of sharing no land borders, has an estimated 50,000 to 100,000 undocumented immigrants, nearly all of whom overstayed visas.

Today, however, undocumented immigration is an issue not just for the historical settler countries but also for states in Europe, Asia, Africa, and South

America. According to estimates from 2008, the twenty-seven countries that were members of the European Union hosted between 1.9 and 3.8 million undocumented immigrants (Morehouse and Blomfield 2011). The Russian Federal Migration Service estimates that there are 3 million unauthorized migrants in Russia, mostly from former Soviet republics, but other estimates are much higher (Weir 2013). India hosts an unknown number of undocumented migrants, although India's minister of state for home estimated in 2011 that at least 1.4 million undocumented migrants had arrived from Bangladesh alone in the previous decade, in addition to the estimated 10 million who came during Bangladesh's war of independence (Ghosh 2012). South Africa hosts an estimated 10 million unauthorized migrants, including 3 million from Zimbabwe alone. In 2009, Brazil was home to between 200,000 and 600,000 undocumented migrants, many from neighboring Bolivia (BBC 2008). These statistics provide the sense that interior immigration control is a serious issue confronting many, if not all, receiving states.

THE STATUS QUO ANTE AND STATE PREFERENCES

The Status Quo Ante. Internal immigration control remains within the sovereign domain of the receiving state. Under customary international law, sending countries have long been expected to accept the return of their own citizens who are in another country illegally. This practice is a fundamental component of the basic concept of nationality, grounded in the individual's right of return to his or her own country (Hailbronner 1997; Panizzon 2012; Chetail 2014). States have been reluctant to codify this customary international law because doing so might imply that, absent a written treaty, states might not be obligated to respect the right of return (Coleman 2009). However, in the post–World War II era, human rights treaties have abridged this right in important ways. Chetail (2014) lists four constraints on states' ability to deport undocumented aliens. These include the prohibition against arbitrary detention, the prohibition of collective expulsion, the right of judicial review, and the right to human dignity. These four constraints increase the costs of deportation by requiring individual deportation decisions that can be appealed and by increasing the costs of transportation when individuals reject physical deportation.[5] Nonetheless, states retain the unilateral right to detect, apprehend, detain, and deport undocumented aliens. Thus, the initial status quo in the post–World War II period favored receiving states, although the status quo had become much more costly with the individualization of deportation decisions required by the adoption of human rights conventions.

This status quo has since been abridged informally by the migrants themselves and by the sending states. Whether by accident or by design, migrants became aware that, in the absence of identification documents, receiving states may be unable to identify the individual and his or her country of origin. In the absence of identification papers, states may simply be unable to deport an undocumented alien. Once the efficacy of this strategy became apparent, migrants in compromised situations began to destroy their identity documents, and smugglers and traffickers, as well as migrant networks, carried the message to newly arriving migrants. Sending states, too, soon discovered ways to delay or avoid receiving their citizens. Establishing the identity of the immigrant may be difficult for the receiving state, and the home state may balk at expeditious identification. It could, in many instances, claim that the individual was not a citizen. Moreover, states may also postpone or avoid repatriation of citizens by failing to provide the appropriate travel documents. Ellermann (2008) documents the case of the Vietnamese government simply failing to respond to diplomatic requests from the German government to repatriate sixty thousand Vietnamese citizens subsequent to the reunification of Germany in 1991. This new status quo privileged sending states as they had discovered methods to avoid their international responsibilities.

In the absence of identity documents, receiving states could turn to the entry point of the migrants to identify the last country of transit before reaching the destination country. However, the final element of the status quo ante is that states are not required to accept noncitizens, stateless individuals, or citizens of other states who have transited through their state on their way to the final destination (Chetail 2014). Thus, receiving states were also thwarted from returning undocumented aliens to the country they had transited.

Receiving State Preferences. On the side of receiving states with an undocumented population, deportation is a mechanism for maintaining "the integrity of the immigration system" and reducing the costs of unwanted immigration (Ellermann 2008, 172). In addition to the reasons enumerated by Ellermann, Adamson (2006, 176) adds the central issue of state security to the list. And Lloyd, Simmons, and Stewart (2012, 10) argue that an undocumented population represents a "challenge to the authority of the state itself." Thus, the status quo of unilateral deportation initially served receiving state interests, but this changed once migrants and sending states adopted techniques that reduced the capacity to deport. This change to the status quo propelled receiving states to the negotiating table.

Sending State Preferences. For sending states, readmitting a citizen deported by the receiving state generates a significant cost.[6] Castles (2004, 852) argues that "many less developed countries have identified labor export as important in reducing unemployment, improving the balance of payments, securing skills and investment capital, and stimulating development. In some cases, the export of discontent and reduction of political tension also become goals." These all become costs if the emigrant returns. In particular, the loss of remittances, pressure on labor markets, and social challenges associated with reintegrating the returning population are enumerated as costs to the sending state (Ellermann 2008; Wong 2012). Additionally, we add that transit states also face audience costs associated with agreeing to accept not only the state's own nationals, but also those of other sending states. Thus transit and sending states' interests conflict with those of receiving states; while sending and transit states opposed the initial status quo of unilateral deportation, they were powerless to compel receiving states to change their behavior. Once deportation became difficult, sending and transit states had no interest in negotiating unless offered significant side payments. As Antje Ellermann (2008, 171) puts it, "At the root of non-cooperation is a fundamental conflict of interest between the deporting state, on the one hand, and the deportee and his or her country of nationality, on the other."

PROSPECTS FOR INTERNATIONAL COOPERATION

As the status quo shifts from privileging receiving states to privileging sending states, receiving states face varying pressures to enter the negotiating arena. To enlist the help of sending states in restricting and controlling migration, receiving states must offer something in return. Under what conditions will this occur? We argue that there are three sets of conditions that are important for cooperation. First, undocumented immigration must be inflicting high costs on the receiving state. Second, the ability of states to control their borders must be diminished, thereby limiting the ability to control the number of undocumented residents. Third, sending states must find the agreement sufficiently attractive to overcome their costs. Unless these conditions are met, unilateralism will prevail. Furthermore, formalized cooperation is likely to be bilateral rather than multilateral, because migration flows are unique and nonreciprocal; multilateral agreements raise the costs for receiving states to reach agreement. Any multilateral cooperation will likely be informal, where it exists at all. We describe each of these conditions in more detail here.

Costs for the Receiving State: The Migrant's "Bundle of Rights." Unlike other international economic flows, migration brings costs for the state in addition to benefits. While other flows, like trade, may affect domestic distribution of wealth, they rarely impose costs on the state (Ruhs and Chang 2004). These costs stem from the bundle of rights immigrants receive when they enter the host state. Wealthy democracies provide migrants with the largest bundle of rights based on prior political processes that grant civil, political, and social rights to citizens, which, in many cases, are applicable to migrants as well. We argue that there are at least two types of costs associated with this bundle of rights: welfare costs and political costs.

Welfare Costs. The cost of providing social welfare benefits to immigrants may affect the incentives for receiving states to pursue cooperation. There is some evidence that generous benefits may actually attract immigrants to particular countries (De Giorgi and Pellizzari 2006). Immigrants generally do not use social welfare benefits more than citizens, controlling for other socioeconomic factors, but immigrants tend to be systematically younger, poorer, and less educated than host state citizens, which means that they are more likely to be eligible for welfare benefits (Brücker et al. 2001).

Two elements are important when calculating the welfare benefits costs of immigration. First, how great is the overall cost of the state's welfare expenditures? States that devote more resources to social welfare benefits will face an even greater burden from increased immigration. Second, how effectively can the state exclude undocumented immigrants from social welfare benefits? States that can avoid paying for the social welfare of undocumented immigrants will be much less concerned about restricting the flow of these immigrants.[7] Excluding undocumented immigrants from government benefits depends on both a legal ability to exclude migrants and the practical ability to identify undocumented migrants. In Germany, for example, there are strict laws that prevent undocumented migrants from accessing health care and education. There are also sophisticated, linked computer databases that streamline enforcement, and regular workplace checks. In France, on the other hand, undocumented immigrants have a legal right to health care, and the courts have been reluctant to enforce laws that make being caught without proper identification and documentation a deportation-worthy crime. Multiple agencies are responsible for investigating employers for illegally hiring undocumented workers, which makes enforcement cumbersome, and prosecution is rare (Doomernik and Jandl 2008). Thus, the social welfare costs due to undocumented immigrants incurred by France would likely be greater than those incurred by Germany. We argue that states with greater costs are more likely to pursue cooperative arrangements to reduce welfare expenditures.

Political Costs. There are also political costs associated with an undocumented migrant population. To citizens, states appear to be ineffective in protecting their borders, and public opinion polls suggest that citizens prefer fewer migrants.[8] Although the salience of the issue varies among states, a certain portion of the population may organize to protest the presence of unwanted migrants, to the detriment of the government in power. Thus, organized opposition to immigration that threatens the parties in power politically might push policymakers to cooperate with other states to control migration more effectively.

Mitigating Factors. Finally, there may be mitigating factors that reduce the costs of undocumented immigration. Immigrants may be useful to the state if they help promote economic growth and fill jobs that the native labor force shuns. The state of the economy is one indicator of the ability of immigrants to find employment and of the demand by employers for more labor. If the economy is growing rapidly and generating new jobs, there will be a larger demand for migrants than when the economy is growing slowly and unemployment is high. Previous research suggests that this relationship between the supply of immigrants and the demand for them holds for undocumented immigrants as well. Hanson and Spilimbergo (2001) find that states decrease border enforcement during positive shocks to sectors that employ a high number of undocumented workers. They argue that states respond to private lobbying by business interests to allow the inflow of at least some undocumented immigrants. At the same time, states must balance this against the demand by labor unions and anti-immigrant interest groups to crack down on undocumented immigration. These competing forces lead to an equilibrium level of undocumented immigration that changes in response to economic conditions within the receiving country (Bond and Chen 1987; Djajić 1987). We suggest that states will thus be less likely to pursue new enforcement and control mechanisms, including cooperative arrangements, when the state is experiencing a period of economic expansion and full employment.

In sum, the likelihood that receiving states will attempt to enter the negotiating arena to persuade sending states to accept their citizens and aliens who transited their territory depends on the level of costs associated with the undocumented population, costs that may be offset by the benefits that states may accrue from the undocumented immigrant population.

Diminished Unilateral Control. The second condition that propels states to the negotiating table is a loss of unilateral control. The post–World War II period has been characterized by both increased global mobility and the widespread adoption of international, regional, and bilateral agreements. These agreements address various human rights, labor mobility, and border control and represent a voluntary relinquishment of sovereignty that can affect a state's ability to sort and control migration flows through unilateral expulsion of anyone they do not want (Sassen 1996; also see Betts 2006 and UNDP 2009, 21). Most agreements, however, are weak enough that states can still enact enough unilateral control over immigration that the proliferation of international agreements does not motivate receiving states to cooperate formally with sending states. Instead, states may pursue informal cooperation with sending states, at most. The exception to this unilateralism, however, can be found where states adopt freedom of movement provisions and/or common travel zones. The most prominent example is Europe, where states have adopted freedom of movement via EU institutions and a passport-free zone via the Schengen Agreement. Because they have voluntarily relinquished significant levels of sovereignty over border control, they have been incentivized to construct much more formal and extensive cooperative arrangements with sending states than seen anywhere else in the world.[9] Other states lack these constraints over unilateral action and therefore find international cooperation to be an inefficient solution to immigration control. We explain below how freedom of movement and passport-free zones trigger the potential for undocumented migrants so the model can be generically applied outside of Europe.

Freedom of Movement Provisions. As we describe in chapter 4, the convergence of economic conditions within a group of geographically proximate states occasionally triggers an agreement to allow citizens of member states access to each other's labor markets, with the purpose of enhancing labor market efficiencies. Although these agreements relinquish states' ability to screen individual workers, and, in the case of the European Union, individual citizens of member states, the agreements generally do not provide for unlimited residence rights for all individuals. Thus, mobility agreements may generate a foreign population, with some proportion that does not fulfill the requirements of residence. Readmission agreements provide a mechanism whereby these individuals, once they are identified by a state, can be returned to their country of origin. Thus, we argue that states that adopt freedom of movement provisions relinquish some degree of immigration control and therefore turn to readmission agreements to shore up internal controls.

Historically, there are three notable agreements involving labor mobility in Europe prior to the advent of the European Economic Community (EEC): the Nordic Union, the Benelux Union, and the European Coal and Steel Community (ECSC). The EEC followed these agreements and expanded the ECSC provisions on labor mobility. The European Union incorporated the ECSC and EEC agreements and extended mobility rights to citizens of member states regardless of their employment status. Although, as we describe in chapter 4, there are additional regional organizations that have adopted freedom of movement, the European agreements are the broadest and have been in place the longest.[10]

Passport Unions and Common Travel Zones. A second mechanism whereby states relinquish immigration control is via passport unions or common travel zones. States that undertake this type of agreement with their neighbors allow citizens of member states to travel freely within the member states. They also create a common external border that represents the point of entry into the common travel zone and agree to a common set of criteria for permitting entry into the zone. Once a third country national enters that zone, he or she is free to travel across the borders of the member states without additional formalities that had been previously in place. The initial entry may be through ports of entry or through evading border controls. But, once inside the common travel zone, the individual is not required to present himself or herself to authorities to move across international borders. This is an important infringement of immigration control of the member states that relinquishes border controls to the least well protected border of the member states and is detrimental to the ability of the member states to control entry.

These agreements, too, are rare. The Nordic Union adopted a passport union in 1950s that permitted citizens of member states to travel freely among the member states; in 1957 they also signed a treaty allowing third country nationals to cross internal borders without border checks. The Benelux Union signed a similar agreement in 1958 (see chapter 5 for details). And, in the European Union, the Schengen Agreement, signed in 1985, radically changed the ability of member states to control their own borders.[11] Until this agreement, each state maintained and controlled its national borders, and all migrants still had to pass through border checks so that receiving countries could distinguish between citizens of EU member states and third country nationals. Schengen, however, abolished all internal border control mechanisms, which allowed for the free movement of everyone, not just Europeans. Each Schengen member agreed to common policies and procedures for visas, asylum requests, and border controls for its external borders (EU 2009). Once a foreigner entered a member country, she was free to move throughout the Schengen Area with no further documentation checks. So an Algerian could enter Spain, for example, and then travel to France with no additional paperwork or contact with French authorities. Thus, the Schengen Agreement relinquishes control over entry to the least well-policed borders, and to those countries with geographic proximity to poorer states. In addition, migrants can enter any country legally (even those with strong border controls), overstay the terms of their visas, and then move throughout the Schengen Area. There are only two other agreements of which we are aware that provide for a common travel zone—the Common Travel Area between Ireland and the United Kingdom and the Central American C-4 Border Control Agreement among El Salvador, Guatemala, Honduras, and Nicaragua, adopted in 2006. Again, these agreements facilitate economic integration but remain rare. Because this type of agreement reduces the ability of individual member states to control entry, it increases the possibility of undocumented entry and stay and may propel receiving states to the negotiating table.

Both freedom of movement and common travel zones make claims on states' ability to unilaterally determine which migrants may enter and reside. This phenomenon is not unique to these agreements or to this issue area; over the past several decades, world politics has become increasingly "legalized," with states voluntarily making binding commitments across a wide range of issues to reap a wide range of benefits.[12] But these benefits come at a price. The loss of sovereignty generates an effort to reclaim control through other means, and one way states can do this is through, ironically, further legalization. In the case of migration, bilateral readmission agreements are one legal tool through which states can reclaim sovereignty. In other words, receiving states' costs associated with the status quo rose, impelling them to the negotiating table.[13]

Costs to the Sending State. Wong (2012) and Ellermann (2008) have suggested that sending states are unlikely to sign or implement readmission agreements because of the domestic costs they face when repatriating deported citizens. The loss of remittances is first and foremost among those costs. Sending states may also incur audience costs in their political systems for being perceived as bending to the will of "Western" countries that were once colonial powers.[14] Most restrictions on migration are designed to serve the interests of the receiving states. The receiving state can still accept immigrants whom it wants, but it reserves the right to send back anyone who does not have the proper documentation. The sending state, however, has little desire to accept the return of its own citizens, and even less desire to accept the return of foreigners who simply transited through the state's territory. Receiving states must thus provide other incentives to the sending state in order to ensure cooperation in controlling migration (Wong 2012). These incentives can include larger quotas for legal migration, expedited and streamlined migration processes, and technical assistance (European Commission 2005). They may also receive benefits not directly related to migration, such as increased foreign aid payments (Betz and Ellis 2009).[15] Cooperative arrangements on migration control thus exemplify quid pro quo cooperation, where parties with divergent interests can nonetheless sustain a mutually beneficial cooperative arrangement through side payments.

Although we argue that receiving states create the demand for migration control and restriction, this is not to say that sending states are passive participants in the process. Sending states can use the negotiating process to achieve concessions like the ones described in the previous paragraph. Sending states may actually seek out agreements with receiving states as a relatively low-cost way to obtain these benefits. In addition, sending states can resist certain provisions or fail to implement parts of agreements, as Libya did in implementing a series of agreements with Italy, beginning in 2000 (Paoletti 2011). Clearly, sending states have their own interests and act to advance them as best as they can. We maintain, however, that receiving states drive the demand for migration control agreements, whether they be formal readmission agreements or other types of cooperation. Because receiving states are, by definition, wealthier, more powerful states, they also have the ability to coerce sending states into signing agreements; negotiations can include both carrots and sticks.

Finally, we point to the fact that migration flows tend to be bilateral, unique, and nonreciprocal. This is particularly important in shaping the nature of formal agreements (readmission agreements) on migration restriction and control. Readmission agreements are the result of quid pro quo bargaining, in which receiving states must offer something of value to sending cr transit states in order to gain their cooperation. However, each sending state comes to the bargaining table with different leverage, depending on their migration profile. Receiving states want to sign agreements only with those countries that generate flows, to minimize the cost of incentives. This is the primary reason that even region-wide agreements through the auspices of the European Union have been so limited. Why should Germany offer incentives to Algeria through an EU-wide agreement, when it receives few migrants from Algeria? We argue that host nations will want to sign agreements with only those countries that generate migrant flows. Having outlined the conditions under which we anticipate cooperation to arise, we now turn to the empirical evidence at the bilateral, regional, and multilateral levels.

BILATERAL READMISSION AGREEMENTS: FORMAL COOPERATION AMONG STATES

Readmission agreements both codify the expectation that countries will readmit their own citizens, setting out protocols for identifying citizens and providing associated travel documents, and expand it, usually requiring that signatory countries also admit stateless persons and citizens of third countries who entered the receiving country through the transit country. Readmission agreements generally apply to all unauthorized migrants, or "all persons who do not, or who no longer, fulfill the conditions in force for entry to, presence in, or residence on, the territory of the requesting state."[16] The agreements frequently include technical provisions on procedures, data collection, and human rights protection (European Commission 2005).

The first modern bilateral readmission agreements were signed between the late 1950s to the mid-1960s, mostly between Western European states. The earliest agreements followed the development of the ECSC (1952), the Nordic Passport Union (1954), the EEC (1957), and the Benelux Economic Union (1958). Having opened the door to labor market entry for citizens of member states, these same states wanted to be able to deport immigrants who were unable to find employment. The second wave of agreements began in the 1990s and was far larger. Whereas between 1950 and 1990 only 14 readmission agreements were concluded, from 1990 to 2000 the total jumped to 124. An additional 79 agreements were negotiated between 2000 and 2006.[17] Of these readmission agreements, the vast majority are bilateral treaties (IGC 2002, 2006). This wave of agreements was instigated by economically developed, net-recipient states in Western Europe and targeted less developed source countries in Eastern Europe, Africa, and beyond.

At first, these readmission agreements were concluded between European states and third countries and were completely outside the purview of the EU. In 1994, the EU adopted a model readmission agreement that would serve as guide for individual member states as they pursued agreements with states outside the union (EU 1996).[18] Figure 3.1 illustrates the number of readmission agreements signed by major receiving countries, while Figure 3.2 illustrates the number of sending countries that have signed readmission agreements. Table 3.1 presents a summary of readmission agreements signed by European states and other wealthy democracies. Although readmission agreements are not unique to Europe, according to the Intergovernmental Consultations on Migration, Asylum and Refugees (IGC), these treaties represent 89 percent of all readmission agreements, the vast majority of the agreements to date (IGC 2006). However,

FIGURE 3.1

Bilateral Readmission Agreements Signed by European Receiving States

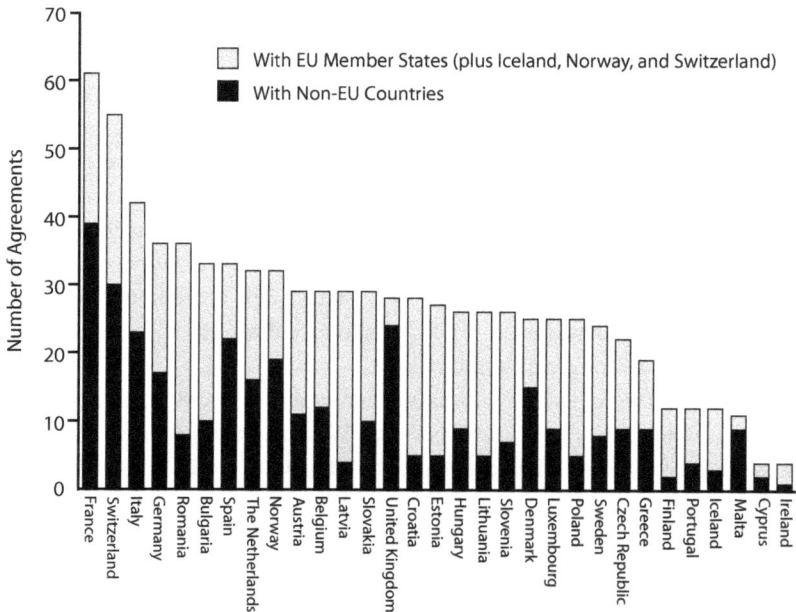

Source: Cassarino (2014).

FIGURE 3.2

Bilateral Readmission Agreements Concluded by Non-EU States with EU
Members (plus Iceland, Norway, and Switzerland)

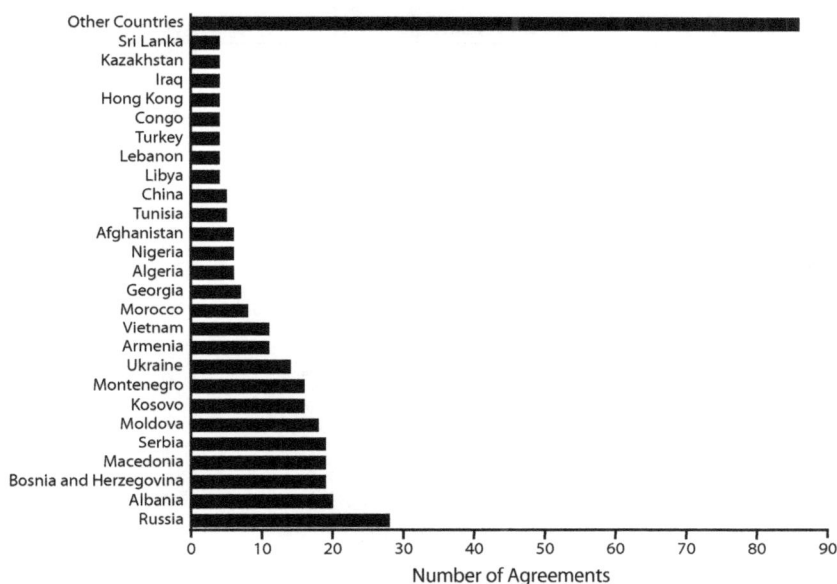

Source: Cassarino (2014).

the variation among countries in Europe is significant; by 2013, Ireland had
signed only four and the United Kingdom sixteen, whereas France had signed
sixty-eight and Italy fifty-one. Out of all the European agreements, multilateral
agreements negotiated by the European Union represent only 3 percent of the
total. A more detailed perusal of the agreements reveals that the signatories of
these agreements vary widely.

We note that bilateral readmission agreements are no longer the dominant
policy tool for European or other states dealing with undocumented migration
(Cassarino 2007). This is not because the problem of undocumented migration has dissipated; almost one in five migrants is undocumented. Although
the demand for cooperation by receiving states remains, sending states have
become more wary of signing readmission agreements as the benefits offered
by receiving states pale in comparison to the sovereignty costs generated by
signing. Rather, readmission procedures are now included, if at all, in informal
agreements or as part of broader partnership agreements so that the sovereignty
costs are less transparent and the side payments tied to a broader spectrum of
both carrots and sticks (Cassarino 2014).

This empirical overview illustrates the puzzles posed by the advent of bilateral

Table 3.1
Number of Readmission Agreements, 2002

State	Number of agreements
EU countries prior to 2004	
Ireland	4
Portugal	10
Finland	11
United Kingdom	16
Greece	19
Sweden	20
Denmark	21
Luxembourg	23
Netherlands	26
Belgium	26
Austria	28
Spain	31
Germany	35
Italy	51
France	68
Non-EU European countries	
Iceland	8
Norway	22
Switzerland	45
Mean for European countries	25.7
Other wealthy democracies	
New Zealand	0
United States	2
Australia	4
Canada	12
Mean for non-European countries	4.5

Source: MIREM (2009); IGC (2002).

readmission agreements, concentrated in Europe: the bilateral form of the agreements, the variation among states in number and signatories, and the timing of the agreements. This variation can be explained in part by the variation in costs experienced by the receiving states, offset by variation in the demand for immigrants. Although most states have signed international agreements that limit their ability to control the entry and residence of foreigners,[19] European states are the most constrained by treaties involving European integration and, hence, are the locus of most bilateral readmission agreements. Finally, because migration flows are unique, bilateral, and nonreciprocal, agreements governing those flows will be bilateral bargained agreements. Sending states' concurrence with the agreements is associated with the carrots and sticks offered by the receiving states.

We evaluate the factors central to the negotiation of a readmission agreement quantitatively. We anticipate that readmission agreements will be more frequent with higher state expenditures on welfare to immigrants and when anti-immigrant opinion is organized into competitive political parties. Readmission agreements should be less frequent as the host economy expands and unemployment declines. As host countries' control over borders declines via regional agreements, readmission agreements should become more frequent. Moreover, readmission agreements should be signed with those states that generate the largest undocumented flows.

The impetus for bilateral readmission agreements comes from the migrant-receiving states, as their costs of undocumented migration rise. Therefore, negotiations should be initiated with only those states whose migrants generate costs and should be undertaken only when the receiving state can offer incentives—or otherwise coerce—the sending state into signing an agreement. We are unable to operationalize either the sovereignty costs of sending states or the size of the side payments that receiving states offer to generate agreements by the sending states. We believe, however, that coercion may well play a role in eliciting cooperation from the sending state. Because receiving states seek to initiate bilateral readmission agreements, they would not be averse to using their leverage to threaten or coerce a sending state to ensure agreement. However, the usual coercive elements of military power are no longer viewed as either appropriate or effective in relations with sending countries. Alternatively, economic leverage may bring coercive power to bear. Therefore, we hypothesize that as the GDP per capita differential between sending and receiving states increases, host states have greater coercive capacity to bring sending states to the bargaining table and to conclude readmission agreements.

Data and Methods. In a perfect world, we would evaluate these hypotheses with a global dataset. However, we are extraordinarily limited in the availability of flow data, on both geographic and temporal dimensions. We therefore take advantage of the variation in European states' readmission agreements to evaluate our hypotheses. This variation exists not only on the dependent variable but on the independent variables as well. Our results, thus, provide substantial support for our hypotheses. We test the hypotheses summarized above with data from nine European states: Belgium, Denmark, Finland, Germany, Italy, the Netherlands, Norway, Spain, and Sweden. Our test is limited because historical data for bilateral migration flows are available only for these nine countries.[20] We analyze the data using the Cox proportional hazards model, which is a survival model. This method of analysis is appropriate because it allows us to find the probability that a state will conclude a readmission agreement with a particular country as time passes, accounting for changes in the independent variables. So, for example, we expect that as the number of immigrants from a particular country increases, the risk that the receiving country will sign an agreement will increase as time goes on. The Cox proportional hazards model allows us to test such claims (Box-Steffensmeier and Jones 2004).

The Risk Period. In survival analysis, one must identify the period of time in which there is a risk that the event of interest might occur; in this case, the event is the conclusion of a readmission agreement. Outside this risk period, we assume that there is no risk of the event occurring. We identify the risk period here as beginning with the European Convention on Human Rights and the establishment of the first European institutions, specifically the Nordic Passport Union, the Benelux Economic Union, the ECSC, and the EEC, in the early 1950s. Indeed, the very first readmission agreements were signed in 1952 between a small number of European states. The risk period continues through the present time.

The earliest date for which we were able to obtain data on source country-specific migrant flows for the widest number of countries is 1980. The data on migrant flows end between 2000 and 2004. This means that the data are both left- and right-censored. They are left-censored because countries were at risk of signing an agreement before 1980 and right-censored because countries may have signed agreements after 2004; in fact, they may continue to sign agreements into the future. Although this censoring is not ideal, the data still allow us to evaluate most of our hypotheses.

The Data. The unit of analysis in this study is the dyad-year. Each dyad includes a destination country (one of the nine European states mentioned above) and a source country. Only relevant dyads are included in the dataset; we define relevant dyads as ones in which at least one person from the source country has migrated to the destination country during at least one of the years in the dataset. This is a low bar to clear, but the record of readmission agreements shows that some destination countries do sign readmission agreements with states that send only a small number of migrants. Italy, for example, has signed a readmission agreement with Mexico, despite the fact that the greatest number of migrants that Mexico ever sent to Italy in a single year was 207, and in many years it sent none. Countries for which not a single migrant was recorded during the entire time period are excluded. We assume that countries that have no exchange of migrants are not at risk for signing a readmission agreement and, in fact, there are no readmission agreements between states in the absence of migration. The dyadic dataset allows us to test an important part of our theory, which is that readmission agreements with a particular sending country become more likely as the flow of migrants from the sending state increases. The drawback of this approach is that bilateral migration flow data are very limited, restricting both the number of receiving states we can include in the study as well as the time span. Table 3.2 provides the overall summary statistics for the data we analyze.

The Dependent Variable. Data on the signing of readmission agreements come from the MIREM project at the European University Institute. Once a receiving country has concluded an agreement with a sending country, this is marked as a "failure," which in a survival analysis means that the event of interest has occurred.

The Independent Variables. We test our hypothesis about the effect of international/regional agreements by including a dummy variable for signatories of

Table 3.2
Summary Statistics for Cox Model of Readmission Agreements

Variable	Observations	Mean	Standard deviation	Minimum	Maximum
Readmission agreements	33,063	N/A	N/A	0 (32,952 no events)	1 (111 events)
Migrant inflows	33,060	709	6,962.27	0	455,075
GDP growth rate (%)	33,063	2.08	2.35	−8.95	7.64
Unemployment rate (%)	33,064	8.47	4.47	1.3	20.4
Per capita welfare costs of migrant stock ($)	32,223	348.21	257.96	24.59	1,091.59
Support for right-wing parties (%)	32,881	3.72	5.99	0	26.3
Kilometers between capital cities	32,882	5,878	3,518	0	19,835

the Schengen Agreement, which was drafted during the time frame covered by our analysis. Ideally, we would like to test the effect of each agreement that we think was important in restricting state sovereignty over migration control: the ECSC, the EEC, the Benelux Economic Union, and the Nordic Union. Since our data begin only in 1980, these agreements are collinear during the period of the analysis, so we limit our focus to the effect of the Schengen Agreement. There is variation in the timing of European membership and adherence to Schengen; only three of the nine countries in our sample signed the agreement in 1985.

We measure the welfare cost of immigrants by multiplying the per capita cost of government social welfare programs by the total migrant stock within the receiving country, giving the sum of the per capita welfare costs of migrants. We then divide this number by the total population, which gives the welfare costs of migrants per capita (this accounts for the fact that larger countries likely host a larger number of migrants).[21] While these data accurately capture how much the states spend on social welfare, they do not necessarily capture differences in the level of access that immigrants have to government services. Our calculation assumes that migrants in different states have the same level of access to government welfare programs, when in fact some states may restrict access to these benefits to citizens only. However, there is likely to be a correlation between higher welfare expenditures and a greater absolute welfare expenditure on migrants, even if restrictions on access can prevent migrants from capturing some benefits.

We expect that the political costs of migration will grow when the political salience of migration is high, and this provides an incentive to receiving states to sign readmission agreements. We use the percentage of the vote won by right-wing parties as a measure of the political salience of migration. Growing support for right-wing parties indicates that the public thinks there are too many immigrants. Immigration restriction is a significant part of the platforms of right-wing parties across Europe, and anti-immigrant sentiment is a key determinant of support for the parties (Lubbers, Gijsberts, and Scheepers 2002).

We use the growth rate of real GDP per capita and unemployment rate as measures of factors that may mitigate demand for readmission agreements.[22] The ILO unemployment data come primarily from official employment office records, although the data from Finland and Italy come from the ILO's Labor Force Survey. Where possible, registered unemployment rates are used; total coverage figures are used for Finland and Italy. As the growth rate of real GDP per capita increases, we expect that demand for readmission agreements will decrease. When unemployment decreases, we expect that the demand for readmission agreements will decrease.

We argue that states will be more likely to conclude a readmission agreement the larger the inflow of undocumented migrants. However, there are no accurate data on annual inflows of undocumented migrants from particular source countries; any data that do exist are very broad and can provide only a rough estimate. We thus use the flow of documented migrants as a proxy for undocumented migrants. There are several reasons to expect that undocumented migrant flows would be highly correlated with documented migrant flows. First and foremost, migrant networks are mechanisms for continuing migration by providing information and resources for new migrants (Massey and Liang 1989). These migrants can be both documented and undocumented. Moreover, an original documented migrant can become an attractor to undocumented flows through unauthorized family reunification; these family migrants can usually enter the country legally for a visit, but become undocumented through overstaying. Second, the migrant's status depends on the host country's regulations. Documented migrants often end up as undocumented migrants, as their visas expire and they fail to leave the country. A good example of this pattern is the rise in undocumented Mexicans in the United States after the passage of the 1965 Immigration Act. Legal circular flows became permanent undocumented flows in light of the restrictions imposed on Western Hemispheric migration as a result of the act (Massey and Liang 1989; Money and Victor 2015). In the absence of data on undocumented flows, we assume that larger documented flows likely correspond with larger undocumented flows. The data come from the UN's "International Migration Flows to and from Selected Countries: The 2005 Revision" (United Nations, Department of Economics and Social Affairs, Population Division 2005).[23]

We expect that receiving states may attempt to coerce sending states into concluding readmission agreements. We measure a receiving state's coercive power as the GDP differential, subtracting the sending state's GDP per capita from the receiving state's GDP per capita, both adjusted for purchasing power parity (World Bank 2011).

Control Variables. The variation in the number of readmission agreements signed by European states may in part be due to bureaucratic inertia. Once one agreement has been signed, it becomes easier to sign another. The state then has a model for future agreements, and it also has negotiating experience, which reduces the cost of each future agreement. The process of concluding agreements may generate individual bureaucrats and even departments with an interest in pursuing more agreements as a way to expand their sphere of policy control. This effect may be especially strong when the incentives needed to induce the sending country to sign an agreement are low. France, for example, has signed an extraordinary number of readmission agreements, and it has even pursued agreements with far-flung countries (for example, in Latin America) that export a relatively small number of migrants to France. The effect of bureaucratic inertia is probably small, and it certainly would not override broader state interests (if there are any related to readmission in a particular case). However, it does seem reasonable that the more agreements that a state has signed, the more agreements it is likely to sign in the future. Bureaucratic inertia is measured simply by adding up the total number of readmission agreements signed by the receiving country up until a given year.

Last, we control for geographic distance between the sending and receiving countries (Cassarino 2010). We expect that states that are geographically farther apart are less likely to sign agreements with each other. The effect of distance may be overwhelmed by the effect of migrant flows, but distance may have a distinct effect, particularly since migration from geographically proximate states may be harder to control than migration from distant states. Persistent migrants from nearby states will likely have an easier time overcoming barriers that receiving states erect to control migration. Moreover, geographically proximate states can become transit states for migrants from more distant locations. Thus, receiving states may find that other tools, apart from readmission agreements, are sufficiently effective for controlling migration from distant states but insufficient for controlling migration from those nearby.

Quantitative Test: Results. The results of the analysis are displayed in Table 3.3. First, signing the Schengen Agreement has a strong and significant effect, as expected. Surrendering sovereignty over border control by creating a common border with Schengen member states is followed by an increase in readmission agreements. In an alternate model specification, Schengen implementation was measured rather than the signing of the agreement. In this specification, agreement implementation did not have a significant effect, and the model actually suggested that the effect is negative. This makes sense; the period of time between signing the Schengen Agreement and the date it went into effect is very long. The original signatories of Schengen in 1985 gave themselves an entire decade to prepare for the transition, which included standardizing admission requirements, streamlining procedures, and, it appears, preparing for negative externalities by pursuing bilateral readmission agreements with states outside the Schengen Area. By the time the agreement actually went into effect, the receiving countries had already signed the majority of the agreements that they intended to sign. States thus likely anticipated the changes that the Schengen Agreement was going to bring and planned accordingly.

The domestic welfare cost of migrants does not have the expected effect, but these are not significant results.[24] These results can be interpreted in two ways. First, it could be that economic costs in the form of welfare benefits for immigrants do not, in fact, move migration policy. If so, this is a surprising result; migration policy scholars and observers have argued that higher welfare

Table 3.3
Cox Model of Readmission Agreements

Readmission agreement	Log hazard ratios (standard errors)
Schengen signatory	1.343*
	(0.727)
Per capita welfare costs of migrant stock	−0.001
	(0.535)
Support for right-wing parties	0.036**
	(0.016)
GDP growth rate	−0.495
	(0.764)
Unemployment rate	0.114*
	(0.061)
Migrant inflows (logged)	0.176***
	(0.056)
Difference in GDP/pc between sending and receiving states	0.045***
	(0.009)
Total number of agreements signed	0.075*
	(0.042)
Distance between capital cities (in thousands of kilometers)	−5.272***
	(1.364)
GDP growth rate × time (logged)	0.226
	(0.570)
Distance × time (logged)	1.495***
	(0.460)
N	24,712
Log pseudolikelihood	−464.860

Note: Data are clustered by receiving country. Table uses Efron method of ties.

*$p < .10$; **$p < .05$; ***$p < .01$.

costs of immigration are a key determinant of negative public opinion toward migrants (Hanson, Scheve, and Slaughter 2007; Hainmueller and Hiscox 2007; Mayda 2006). If our result is accurate, then this casts doubt on existing theories of migration policy. But there is a second explanation: it could be that our measure does not accurately capture the welfare costs of immigrants. This may be because countries restrict access to social welfare benefits so that migrants cannot enjoy them. Thus, rising immigration rates alone may not increase social welfare costs. To determine which explanation is correct, further research on immigrant access to government welfare across countries and across time is needed. However, the fact that there are no readily available data on immigrant access to government welfare is, itself, a challenge to the theory that welfare costs drive restrictive migration policy. If we, as researchers, cannot assess the true welfare costs of immigrants, how can policymakers (or the public)? If costs are opaque, then they are unlikely to drive policy. It is possible that the *perception* of costs could drive policy; this might instead point toward political factors as far more important than government expenses. Only further research will allow us to untangle these competing explanations.

The political cost of unwanted migration, as measured by support for right-wing parties, is strongly significant and in the direction expected. As electoral support for right-wing parties grows, a country becomes more likely to pursue restrictive migration policy through readmission agreements. This result may perhaps support one of the proposed explanations for the insignificance of welfare expenditures: it is not welfare expenditures per se that influence readmission policy but the politically salient *perception* of high costs that mobilize anti-immigrant sentiment and fuel right-wing parties. Pursuing readmission agreements may be a way to politically signal that policymakers are "tough on immigration." Although we do not attempt to actually assess the effectiveness of readmission agreements in reducing unwanted migration and the accompanying fiscal costs, such effectiveness might not even be relevant if political costs are paramount. Readmission agreements might still serve as effective political signals even if they do not achieve their other goals.[25]

Unemployment has a positive and significant effect on the likelihood of signing an agreement, as expected. Countries experiencing low unemployment are more likely to demand more immigrants and thus are less likely to seek out readmission agreements to control immigration, and vice versa. Similarly, when economic growth and demand for immigrants increase, states are less likely to sign readmission agreements. This effect, however, appears to be relatively small and is not statistically significant.

The number of immigrants to the receiving country has a strong, significant effect on whether or not two countries conclude a readmission agreement. States do not pursue agreements with all others but focus on those with which they have a significant migrant flow. This explains both why receiving states pursue different numbers of agreements and why they pursue them with different sending states. In addition, this may explain why bilateral readmission agreements remain more popular than multilateral agreements. Since receiving states do not share the same migration profiles, they do not seek to conclude readmission agreements with the same sending states.

As expected, the greater the differential in GDP per capita between receiving and sending states, the more likely receiving states will be to conclude a readmission agreement, and this is a significant result. It is a broad measure of power inequality between the two parties to the agreement. We interpret the positive and statistically significant coefficient as a measure of coercive capacity of the receiving state. In this case, the greater the coercive power of the state, the more likely it is to obtain the agreement of the sending state.[26]

Bureaucratic inertia, as measured by the total number of agreements signed by a country, has the expected effect and is significant. The more agreements a country has signed, the more agreements it is expected to sign in the future. We suspect this is perhaps due to the entrepreneurial efforts of the individuals and agencies tasked with concluding and managing readmission agreements. In addition, familiarity and experience with readmission agreements may reduce the cost of drafting and concluding new ones, which would reduce the incentives needed to induce a receiving state to pursue a readmission agreement.

Last, geographic distance between sending and receiving states has a significant effect in the expected direction. States that are geographically farther away from each other are less likely to conclude agreements with each other. This relationship remains significant even though migrant flows are included in the model, which suggests that distance is not important simply because geographically proximate sending states send a larger number of migrants to receiving states than do more distant sending states. This could signify that receiving states are better able to control the flow of migrants from more far-flung states using tools other than readmission agreements. These other, more unilateral tools may be less effective on closer neighbors, creating an incentive to turn to readmission agreements. In addition, it may be cost-effective to offshore border control in geographically proximate states but not in more distant states.

Beyond basic conclusions about the direction and significance of effects, interpreting log hazard ratios in a Cox proportional hazards model is not always intuitive. In their simplest form, hazard ratios indicate that a unit increase in the independent variable signifies an increase in the probability that the event of interest (the signing of a readmission agreement) will occur in the next period (the next year) (Duerden 2009). In the results presented in Table 3.3, the logged hazard rates are presented, so that a coefficient above zero indicates a positive relationship, while one less than zero indicates a negative relationship.

The interpretation of the coefficients is complicated by that fact that diagnostic tests revealed nonproportional hazards in the original model. This means that the effect of the independent variables varies across time, while the model assumes that the effects do not vary with time.[27] To solve this problem, we interacted affected variables with a transformation of time (in this case, the natural log of time) and included the interactions in the model (Box-Steffensmeier and Jones 2004). We included interactions with the GDP growth variable and the distance variable, and this solved the nonproportional hazards problem. Unfortunately, this complicates the interpretation of the constituent coefficients. The constituent coefficients now must be interpreted as the effect only during the first year of the analysis (1980), and not the effect of the variables over the entire period.

Following methods suggested by Amanda Licht, we first calculated the point in time when the effect of the variables changes sign (Licht 2011). Distance between countries has time-varying effects. During the period of our analysis, states are more likely to sign agreements with geographically proximate states. However, after thirty-three years, the direction of this relationship changes. We suspect that this is because the number of geographically proximate states is quite limited. Over time, receiving states that continue to conclude readmission agreements are reaching farther and farther afield to find partners.[28]

Qualitatively, the pattern of European readmission agreements supports our theoretical framework. Figure 3.3 plots signed agreements over time for the nine receiving states that have concluded the greatest number of readmission agreements. Although the process of European integration began shortly after World War II, alongside the human rights agreements that constrained state sovereignty, readmission agreements were sparse in the initial period.

As noted earlier, the bilateral readmission agreements are concentrated in two periods, the early 1960s subsequent to the signing of the Treaty of Rome, which established free movement of labor among the original EEC member states, and the period after 1985 that saw the signing of the Schengen Agreement among the original participants (Germany, France, and the Benelux countries) and the Treaty of Maastricht (1992), which extended the right of movement to all citizens of member states. The plots show spikes in signing around the times when these regional agreements were concluded. Neither the United Kingdom nor Ireland joined the passport-free travel zone, retaining sovereign control over borders and obviating the need for bilateral readmission agreements—and hence these states are low on the list of signers. Italy, having been a net emigration country until the 1980s, delayed negotiating bilateral readmission agreements until it joined the Schengen Agreement in 1990; it then quickly became one of the most prolific signers of bilateral readmission agreements.

Switzerland is an interesting case because it is not a member of the European

FIGURE 3.3
Timing of Bilateral Readmission Agreements (Selected European States)

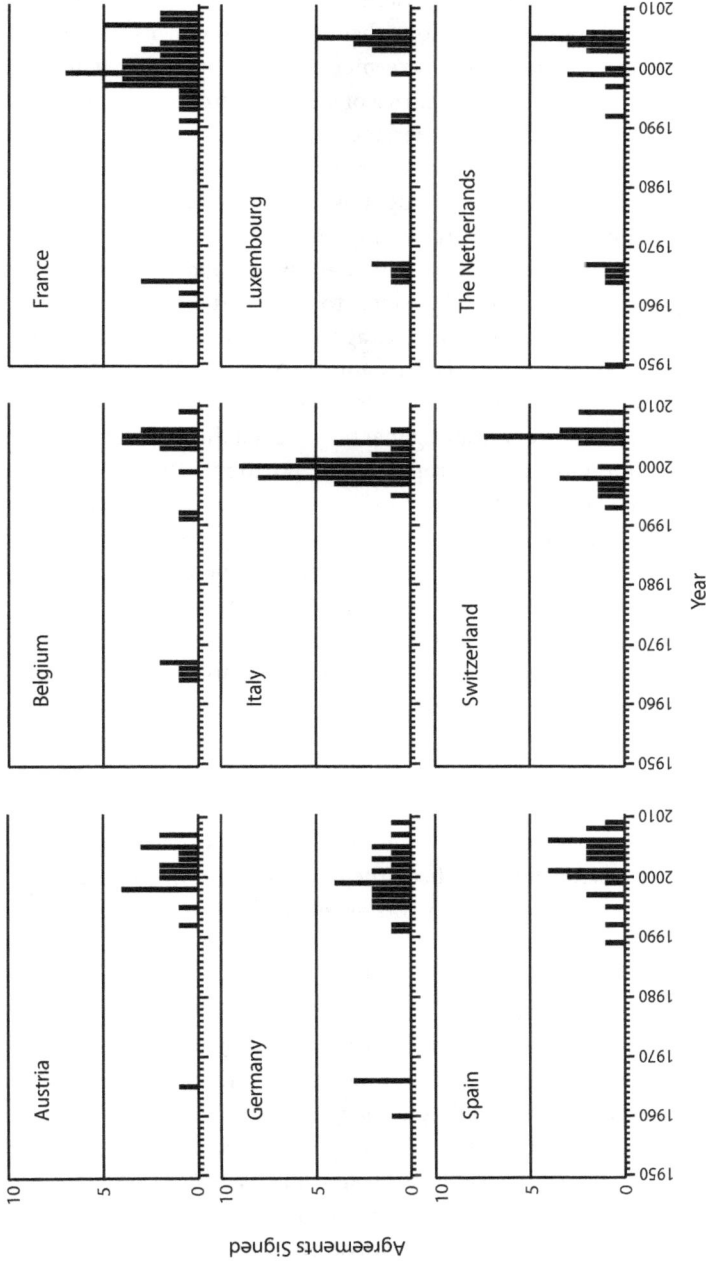

Figure includes the nine most active receiving country signers of readmission agreements.

Source: Cassarino (2014).

Union. However, beginning in 1994, Switzerland negotiated a series of bilateral agreements that ultimately brought it into the labor and mobility clauses of the European Union as well as accession to the Schengen Agreement in 2004. In anticipation of nonreciprocal flows that would follow, Switzerland negotiated a series of bilateral readmission agreements with EU member states—the earliest with the EU candidate countries of Central Europe—as well as with third countries (MIREM 2009). Switzerland follows the pattern of European states. Where national controls are constrained and flows are nonreciprocal, costs to the receiving state increase, leading those states to offer incentives to take back country nationals as well as transit migrants.

Finally, it is important to note that although bilateral readmission agreements are one tool of receiving states to control their undocumented population, sending states continue to drag their feet in implementing even those agreements that are reached (Ellermann 2008, 2009). Their behavior might be described as "passive-aggressive." Morocco, for example, continues to refuse third country deportees, arguing that they passed through Algeria, rather than Morocco, on their way to Europe (Cassarino 2007). This lack of cooperation has caused European states either to "informalize" bilateral readmission agreements, in the form of memoranda of understanding that are not legally binding, or to embed them in broader cooperation agreements (Cassarino 2007). Although this allows the agreements to be implemented flexibly and renegotiated as the costs to the sending state change, this brick in the wall of control is not well cemented. We turn now to the regional level to illustrate the nominal nature of cooperation at that level.

REGIONAL COOPERATION

Regional Cooperation on Deportation: The European Union's Readmission Agreements. European states have been the most active in the international system to employ readmission agreements as tools of interior immigration control. And most of these states are members of the European Union. It is important to ask whether the bilateral readmission agreements were supplemented at the regional level. As noted earlier, the European Union proposed a model readmission agreement for states to employ in 1994, which, in the language of Thompson and Verdier (2014), reduced the "transaction costs" of bilateral agreements by providing boilerplate language for future agreements. But it was not until 1999, after the Tampere European Council, that the EU gained the competency to conclude readmission agreements itself. Dispute continues over whether the EU should have (or does have) exclusive competence to negotiate readmission agreements, and the provision of the 2009 Treaty of Lisbon that was supposed to resolve the issue has failed to do so. Instead, the status quo of shared competency has prevailed and, so far individual states have continued to pursue their own agreements even while the European Union has pursued union-wide agreements (Panizzon 2012).

As our theory anticipates, region-wide agreements negotiated by the executive body of the EU, the European Commission, have been few. Member states have been reluctant to authorize the commission to negotiate agreements—thus far limited to eighteen—and the commission has had trouble in bringing those negotiations to a successful conclusion (European Commission 2005, 2011). This is in large part because the European Commission has few incentives to offer the sending states with which it seeks agreements. As Roig and Huddleston (2007) report, "Community readmission agreement negotiations are inconclusive for the simple reason that readmission agreements work solely in . . . the European Union's 'Eurocentric' interest." One carrot often mentioned is a visa waiver regime or a visa facilitation regime (Ellermann 2008; Wong 2012). States have proved willing to take back their undocumented citizens if their citizens are more able to move freely to the destination state. Although this is a prominent tool in bilateral readmission agreements, EU member states have been unwilling to offer visa waivers or visa facilitation to states from which they receive few immigrants and have not signed on to requests for cooperation from the commission. In the words of Roig and Huddleston (2007, 376), "The Commission has great difficulties in negotiating a visa facilitation regime, since this domain remains within the Member States' national competences."

While the European Commission continues to pursue readmission cooperation to facilitate deportations, bilateralism still dominates. The Council of the European Union—the body representing member states—requested that the commission include readmission clauses in all future cooperation agreements with third countries in 2002 (Roig and Huddleston 2007). The commission has taken up the task and, as of 2007, has negotiated 102 readmission clauses in third country agreements. The ability of the European Commission to insert such clauses in new cooperation agreements is a function of coercion: sending countries no longer have leverage to extract a specific quid pro quo because the agreements are embedded in broad aid and trade pacts. One specific example is the Cotonou Agreement with ninety-seven African, Caribbean, and Pacific countries, which entered into force in 2003. Article 13 contains a readmission clause that requires reciprocal readmission of nationals in other states party to the Cotonou Agreement. The issue of the readmission of third country nationals is minimized by requiring additional negotiations between the parties to the agreement. More important in terms of results, however, is the fact that readmission clauses are not self-executing and require additional bilateral negotiations to enter into force (Roig and Huddleston 2007). Per Roig and Huddleston (2007, 371), "The status of Article 13 [the readmission clause in the Cotonou

Agreement] remains unclear and disputed between both parties." So even in the region that produces the vast majority of readmission agreements, cooperation at the regional level is nominal.

An Absence of Formal Cooperation: CARICOM and Mercosur. European countries are the only ones that sign readmission agreements in large numbers, yet freedom of movement is addressed in other regional economic agreements. As it turns out, regional integration has not threatened unilateral state control of borders outside of Europe. Many regional economic agreements that address migration provide for the elimination of visas and the right to temporary stay in a member state. As noted in chapter 4, states maintain border controls, and policies toward third country nationals remain solely under state control (IOM 2007).

The two regional agreements that come closest to creating the type of free movement seen in Europe are the Caribbean Community (CARICOM) and the Common Market of the South (Mercosur). The CARICOM common market has fifteen member states and five associate members, and freedom of movement was listed as one of the community's goals in the Grand Anse Declaration, which established CARICOM in 1989. The various protocols of the common market were implemented over a period of several years between 1990 and 2002, with free movement slowly being implemented starting in 1995. First, university graduates were permitted to work and live in member states after providing proof of education at the border along with valid travel documents. This provision was then extended to athletes and artists. These classes of migrants, however, are quite small, and the facilitation of movement has yet to be extended to all workers. Furthermore, state leaders have made it clear that CARICOM seeks to facilitate movement only for workers, not for all citizens, in keeping with the economic goals of CARICOM. As Dominican prime minister Roosevelt Skerrit said at the 2010 meeting of the Conference of the Heads of Government, "Under the free movement regime, CARICOM has approved the free movement of labor, not the free movement of persons, and they are two distinct matters" (Jamaica Information Service 2010).

CARICOM goes further than almost all regional economic agreements in facilitating migration, but it does not go nearly as far as even the early agreements in Europe. Only small classes of migrants are affected by CARICOM policies, and states maintain control over their own borders. There is not complete free movement even for university graduates, athletes, and artists; they still must present documentation at state borders within the CARICOM zone, and thus states still have the ability to separate authorized migrants from the unauthorized.

The Mercosur common market agreement goes even further than CARICOM in establishing free movement, but the actual effect of the agreement on member states is far more limited. Mercosur was established in 1991 through the Treaty of Asunción with the intention to eventually create a broad market based on the "free movement of goods, services, and factors of production." This implies the free movement of labor, but labor was not explicitly addressed until 2002 when Mercosur members drafted the Free Movement and Residence Agreement (Jachimowicz 2006; Maguid 2007). The agreement, if implemented, would create open borders between the four member states (Argentina, Brazil, Uruguay, and Paraguay), Chile, and Bolivia (Jachimowicz 2006). This would establish a common external border and free movement within Mercosur, which would be very similar to the system in Europe's Schengen Area. The Free Movement and Residence Agreement has not yet been implemented, however, and it is unlikely that it will be implemented anytime in the foreseeable future.

Unlike the European Union, Mercosur is primarily intergovernmental, not institutional, and has no independent judicial body (Mecham 2003). Thus, Mercosur agreements are not enforceable, and individual state parliaments have been very slow to adopt domestic laws to fulfill Mercosur mandates (UNECA 2010). In addition, Mercosur's leadership has primarily focused on other aspects of the common market, like trade in goods, rather than migration and labor mobility. Mercosur's executive body, the Common Market Group, has ten working subgroups but only one is focused on migration and it has largely concentrated on border controls, not free movement (Maguid 2007).

As noted in chapter 4, very few regional economic agreements provide access to member states' labor markets, despite the fact that these agreements seek to establish some form of common market for the factors of production. The few agreements that explicitly seek some sort of free movement regime fall far short of what the European Union accomplished with the Schengen Agreement and what subsets of European states established as far back as 1953 (the year the Nordic Passport Union was created). Thus, no other state or group of states has faced the loss of unilateral control over immigration and borders that European states have faced. No other states outside of Europe have the same incentives to pursue readmission agreements in order to mitigate the costs of a free movement regime. We suggest that if Mercosur ever implements its Free Movement and Residence Agreement, or if CARICOM extends true free movement to a broader class of migrants, we would likely see member states in these organizations pursuing readmission agreements of their own. Furthermore, we would likely see readmission agreements anywhere free movement is incorporated into regional agreements. Until then, readmission agreements are likely to remain almost exclusively a European phenomenon.

Regional Consultative Processes and Informal Cooperation. RCPs have become the catchall international venues for states discussing migration-related issues. The first RCP, IGC, was created in 1985 in Bern, Switzerland. During the

1990s, fifteen new RCPs were sponsored by the IOM, following the model created by IGC. By 2018, there were twenty-seven active RCPs (twelve have been rebranded as Inter-regional Forums on Migration, or IRFs, a new term for the processes with memberships crossing regional boundaries). These are international forums that allow state officials, at both the political leadership level and the bureaucratic level, to meet with their counterparts in other states and discuss migration challenges. In some processes, NGOs are also invited to participate. The activities of the RCPs are in some cases confidential and designed to avoid public scrutiny. The goal of the RCPs is to provide opportunities for frank discussion and information sharing, not to create binding agreements between states. This means that the agendas and action plans of the RCPs reflect the interests of all participants; both sending and receiving states have equal voice within the processes. There is a disconnect between the contents of the agenda and of the action plans and what actually gets implemented, however. As we will see in the case of human trafficking, the agendas and action plans reflect the interests of all participants, while what is implemented (if anything) reflects the interests of powerful states with the resources to fund programs and perhaps act coercively. A review of the 5 + 5 Dialogue in the Western Mediterranean illustrates this point.

The 5 + 5 Dialogue in the Western Mediterranean.   The migration framework for the 5 + 5 Dialogue in the Western Mediterranean came from a ministerial summit in Lisbon in 2001 between the five Maghreb countries (Algeria, Libya, Mauritania, Morocco, and Tunisia) and five European countries (France, Italy, Malta, Portugal, and Spain). This summit was part of the broader Forum for the Dialogue in the Western Mediterranean, which began in 1990 but did not specifically address migration until 2002, when the first Ministerial Conference on Migration in the Western Mediterranean was held in Tunis (Economic Forum of the Western Mediterranean 2013). The foreign ministers laid out a plan for annual meetings to discuss migration issues, with the second held in Saint-Symphorien-le-Château, France, in October 2003. This was quickly followed by the first Summit of Heads of State in Tunis in December of that same year (the summit covered other issues in addition to migration). The resulting Tunis Declaration reiterated support for dialogue, trust building, and consultation among the ten countries, and it proposed three main areas for continued discussion: (1) Security and Stability, (2) Regional Integration and Economic Cooperation, and (3) Cooperation in Social and Human Affairs (Saadi 2005). The third Ministerial Conference was held in Rabat in 2004. They discussed proposals that arose from the Tunis Declaration, including organizing meetings and seminars with experts from both sets of countries, setting up "awareness campaigns" on the risks of illegal migration, and promoting new ways of managing migration through bilateral cooperation. The fourth Ministerial

Conference was held in Paris and began to hone in on the issue of clandestine immigration, with the aim of providing a "global response" to migration through control, integration, and codevelopment policies (Economic Forum of the Western Mediterranean 2013).

The annual meetings continued to cover similar ground in subsequent years. At the fifth Ministerial Conference, in Évora, Portugal, in 2008; participants reasserted the need for global cooperation among sending, transit, and receiving countries and proposed organizing two expert panels (Economic Forum of the Western Mediterranean 2013). At the seventh Ministerial Conference in Tripoli in 2010, the participants drafted a document with proposals for development projects intended to encourage potential migrants to stay in their home countries and reiterated the need to cooperate on preventing illegal immigration. A follow-up committee was assigned the task of designing an implementation strategy. However, the text of the conference report shows that, after seven years of dialogue, the participating states had agreed to very little substantively. Of the nine action points in the report, one "reaffirmed" the need for a global and shared approach to migration, two proposed "exploring" various migration issues, one "respected" human rights, one "developed" dialogue, and one "expressed appreciation." The remaining three points actually required action: one "ensured" the operation of the RCP's website (which, last time we checked, had not been updated in several years); another called for "cooperation" in implementing a media campaign in sending/transit countries that discouraged illegal immigration, funded by EU institutions; and the third reactivated the follow-up committee to make it happen.

The progress (or lack thereof) made by 5 + 5 Dialogue exemplifies both the benefits and the shortcomings of informal processes. A benefit is that they bring together states with disparate interests to discuss important policy issues in migration. But, despite the repeated calls for cooperation expressed by the representatives, the process itself does not change the fundamental nature of these interests; after seven years of dialogue, the participants did initiate cooperative projects for most of the issues under discussion. Those that were carried out were paid for by the receiving states and offered nothing objectionable or costly for the sending/transit states: media campaigns to combat illegal immigration.

In 2012, the Forum for Dialogue in the Western Mediterranean held its second Summit of Heads of State in Malta. The resulting Malta Declaration focused much more specifically on migration than the Tunis Declaration did, with most of the emphasis on migration control and combating irregular migration, although the section is titled "Migration and Development" (Statewatch 2012). The preamble to the section also recognized the importance of immigration and contributions that immigrants make, the benefits of mobility that simplifying immigration procedures "could" produce on a reciprocal basis, and the importance of development in resolving the root causes of irregular immigration. Of course, none of the participant states made any commitments to enact any sort of agreement in the document.

Although the probability of reaching any multilateral agreements between all participating states on anything of substance is very low, given the disparate interests and varying migration profiles, the costs are low too. They require no precommitment to anything beyond participation and discussion, and they can generate goodwill between states (both within the migration policy realm and in other policy areas; the 5 + 5 Forum covers everything from security to youth education). Unlike formal readmission agreements, which have been limited primarily to Europe where the loss of unilateral control has been the most extreme, RCPs are found around the globe. Four are in Europe and the former Soviet Union; three are in the Americas; one is in the Middle East; five are in Africa; two are in Asia and Oceania; and twelve are classified as IRFs. The threshold for participation in these informal processes, for sending, transit, and receiving states, is much lower. States facing even small costs are incentivized to participate, and loss of unilateral control over borders or the specifics of bilateral migration profiles do not significantly affect participation. This does not mean that all this talking will yield many substantive agreements. The price receiving states would have to pay to sending/transit states for their cooperation on the biggest issues of control is simply higher than most are willing to consider. It is not in the interest of receiving states to invest heavily in solving the "root causes" of illegal migration, including economic underdevelopment in sending states, that sending states desire. For the most part, then, RCPs will remain "talking shops," with low-cost but relatively insignificant projects paid for by receiving states.

MULTILATERAL COOPERATION

This section serves to reiterate that there is no multilateral cooperation on interior migration control to deport a state's undocumented population. As noted in chapter 6, states do coordinate their activities on human trafficking and smuggling. States also cooperate on external border controls, included in the international travel regime. No multilateral agreements exist on deportation, however.

ALTERNATIVE EXPLANATIONS

There is little research that addresses international cooperation on interior immigration control, primarily because it is seen as a prerogative of sovereign states. Recent research on deportations, much of which has focused on the normative and policy dimensions of the agreements, has highlighted the problematic aspects of interior control, including the implications for human rights

(Betts 2006; Bouteillet-Paquet 2003; Ellermann 2008; Wong 2015).[29] This literature has generally not examined the reasons why some states pursue readmission agreements and others do not, let alone why states rarely cooperate on migration control more broadly. Some researchers have directly addressed the determinants of readmission agreements, including Jean-Pierre Cassarino (2010), who argues that geographic proximity, migration salience, and incentives are the most important factors propelling formal readmission agreements.[30] According to his analysis, geographic proximity provides the source of the immigrants. Migration salience in the source country leads to a decline in readmission agreements, as the country of origin is less willing to sign a readmission agreement.[31] Finally, countries of destination provide incentives to transit and/or origin countries to persuade them to sign the agreements. The higher the level of incentives, the more likely the countries of transit and/or origin are to sign. His argument is conditional; given geographic proximity, readmission agreements will occur only if migration salience is low and incentives are high.

Cassarino, however, does not systematically evaluate these hypotheses. Moreover, the focus on incentives begs the question of the circumstances that would generate an offer of incentives. Thus we build on Cassarino's initial insights by focusing, in part, on the factors that would cause receiving states to offer incentives to sending states to sign readmission agreements. Implicit in Cassarino's argument is a bargaining framework that relies on the concept of best alternative to negotiated agreements.[32] As a state's best alternative changes, it reconsiders the benefits of international agreements. However, we provide the empirical referents to understand the state's calculus of the changing environment. We also draw on the migration literature to understand the pattern of flows as well as migration policy literature to elaborate why states are constrained in handling these flows.

The literature on policy diffusion, or how states come to adopt more uniform policy approaches to problems, represents another approach to answering why states might adopt bilateral, regional, or multilateral agreements. Simmons, Dobbin, and Garrett (2006) identify four mechanisms by which policy diffuses: coercion, competition, learning, and emulation. Coercion and competition reflect material concerns (Lloyd, Simmons, and Stewart 2012). Coercion occurs when powerful states manipulate less powerful states to adopt policies or sign onto cooperative agreements by offering incentives to those that comply and by threatening punishments to those who do not. Coercion is surely part of the answer to the rise of readmission agreements. However, if coercion was the primary explanation, then we should see the widespread rise of these agreements between all powerful receiving states and their prominent migrant-sending states. Coercion alone cannot explain which states initiate readmission negotiations and when. Moreover, coercion implies that powerful states consistently have leverage over weaker states; this explanation does not elucidate the conditions under which less powerful states simply walk away from the table. We discount the other mechanisms for policy diffusion in large part because of the very limited diffusion of bilateral readmission agreements. The diffusion theory is a prominent explanation of international cooperation, but it lacks the leverage to explain the cases we explore here.

Last, another possible explanation comes from the strand of literature on European integration that suggests a "spillover" effect of integration (Haas 1958). That is, one component of integration—in this case, agreements on labor mobility and border controls—will cause states to resolve the problems generated by the initial integration through further integration. This would suggest that the member states would direct the institutions of the EU itself to sign readmission agreements in order to deport more effectively the undocumented population. However, the history of readmission agreements at the level of the EU undermines this interpretation of spillover. The EU did draft model readmission agreements that were taken up by individual states, and it received authority to negotiate readmission agreements on behalf of all members for some eighteen states. Only thirteen of those negotiations have come to fruition—and constitute only 3 percent of all European readmission agreements. European states, including states that are not EU members (Switzerland and Norway, notably), are the main actors in negotiating readmission agreements.

THE EUROPEAN MIGRANT CRISIS AND BILATERAL READMISSION AGREEMENTS

We began our account of international cooperation on internal immigration control—deportations—with Rahim's story. After providing our theoretical argument and empirical evidence, we return to the European migrant crisis. In the second half of 2015 and the first quarter of 2016, more than one million irregular immigrants made their way to Europe, most through Turkey. Many migrants came from Syria, fleeing the growing violence, but migrants also came from other parts of the Middle East, Africa, and Asia as well as from poorer and less stable parts of Europe. There was even one report of a family of Haitians flying to Turkey to attempt to enter Europe through the Turkish channel ("Caribbean Migrants" 2016). This European migrant crisis represents a case study that illuminates our quantitative analysis. Did the most recent European migrant crisis follow the pattern suggested by our theoretical framework? The answer is a resounding yes; in tracing the construction of readmission agreements between the EU and Turkey, we can also assess the side payments that Turkey was able to extract from the EU. The cost of the migrant flows to EU member states was very high, and the corresponding price paid to stop the flows was also considerable.

The European migrant crisis has exacted a heavy toll on the EU and its member states. The costs of processing more than a million asylum claims are staggering, as are the costs of food, clothing, housing, and health care in the interim and, for those successful claimants, the continued cost of integration. The political price has also been high, with the rise of new, and the growing success of already established, anti-immigrant right-wing parties in Europe. The imminent withdrawal of the United Kingdom from the EU, cemented by a June 2016 referendum, was fueled in large part by anti-immigrant sentiment stirred by the European migrant crisis. These costs elicited action on the part of the EU to negotiate an agreement with Turkey. We describe the trajectory of the negotiations below.

As noted above, the EU was authorized to negotiate a small number of readmission agreements that would engage all member states. One authorized agreement was with Turkey. However, because not all states were implicated in flows from Turkey, an agreement was not forthcoming. The European Commission received its negotiating directive for Turkey based on an EU Council meeting of 28 November 2002. Negotiations commenced in May 2005 and continued for eighteen months but ground to a halt in December 2006. It was only in response to renewed flows from Turkey through the Western Balkan and Eastern Mediterranean routes beginning in 2008 that the negotiations restarted ("European Migrant Crisis" 2016). Unilateral action continued apace with Greece ultimately constructing a wall on the land border between Greece and Turkey that was not marked by the flow of the Meriç River. However, pressure to conclude a readmission agreement with Turkey continued. In 2009 a new draft text was prepared and forwarded to the Turkish negotiators. This new agreement was signed on 13 December 2013 and entered into force on 1 October 2014. The agreement provided for reciprocal readmission, including third country nationals and stateless persons. However, "the readmission obligation for third country nationals or stateless persons becomes applicable only three years after the entry into force of the whole agreement" (European Commission 2012, 3).[33] This meant that the readmission of third country nationals, central to the 2015 European migrant crisis, would commence only on 1 October 2017 (EU 2013).

In response to the crisis, which mounted in the second half of 2015, the EU negotiated the EU–Turkey Joint Action Plan, dated 29 November 2015. According to the European Commission (2015) the objective of the action plan was "to supplement Turkey's efforts in managing the situation of massive influx of persons in need of temporary protection." The three dimensions of the plan included addressing the root causes of the Syrian influx, supporting Syrians and their host communities in Turkey, and "strengthening cooperation to prevent irregular migration flows to the EU" (European Commission 2015). The action plan notes the mobilization of 4.2 billion euros to support Syrian refugees in Turkey, in light of the 7 billion euros already expended by Turkey. Turkey agreed to police its borders to prevent the flow of irregular migrants toward the EU. Nonetheless, the flows continued and a new agreement with new incentives was needed to stem the tide.

That agreement came in the form of the EU–Turkey Statement on 19 March 2016. This agreement brought the readmission of third country nationals into immediate effect more than eighteen months in advance of the official EU–Turkey readmission agreement date. The statement indicated that "all new irregular migrants crossing from Turkey to the Greek islands as of 20 March will be returned to Turkey." More importantly, Turkey again agreed and then acted to prevent the smuggling of third country nationals from its territory. The price paid by the EU was considerable and agreed to only in light of the high costs, financially and politically, of the more than a million irregular migrants that entered EU territory during 2015 and 2016. The EU agreed to speed up the disbursement of the 3 billion Euros promised in the Action Plan and to provide an additional 3 billion Euros to support the Syrian population in Turkey when the initial funding was used up.[34] More importantly, the EU agreed to accelerate the visa liberalization road map and to lift the visa requirements for Turkish citizens at the latest by the end of June 2016 (Kirişci 2014). The Turkish accession process would also be "re-energized" (European Commission 2016).

Visa-free travel for Turkish citizens is indeed a significant price to pay. Turkey is a country with more than seventy million citizens—larger than any EU country save Germany. The road map, however, does require Turkey "to implement in a full and effective manner the readmission agreement, to manage the borders and the visa policy in such a manner as to effectively prevent irregular migration, to have secure travel documents, to establish migrant and asylum systems in line with international standards, to have functioning structures for combating organized crime with focus on migrants' smuggling and trafficking in human beings, to have in place and implement adequate forms of police and judicial cooperation with the EU Member States and the international community, and to respect the fundamental rights of the citizens and foreigners with a specific attention to persons belonging to minorities and vulnerable categories" (European Commission 2014, 1).

In light of the July 2016 coup attempt in Turkey, the EU postponed the implementation of the road map. Turkey agreed to accept a delay in EU visa liberalization, which was supposed to take place by June 2016. The EU expressed concern that Turkey was using antiterror laws to attack critics of President Erdogan (Shalal 2016). Nonetheless, Turkey continues to threaten to walk away from its previous commitments unless the EU honors visa-free travel for Turkish citizens.

Thus, the European migrant crisis fits well with our theoretical expectations. The EU was authorized to negotiate a union-wide agreement with Turkey in

2002, but those negotiations went nowhere until flows from Turkey mounted and multiple EU member states were affected. Then a readmission agreement was negotiated, but the side payments were insufficient to actually achieve the readmission of third country nationals. The rise in irregular migration to Europe began in earnest in the second half of 2015, with more than one million migrants arriving on EU shores in the twelve months that followed. Europe stepped up its pressure on Turkey to arrest the flows, promising 3 to 4 billion euros to support Syrians in Turkey in the October 2015 Joint Action Plan. That payment was insufficient to elicit the needed cooperation, and the EU upped the ante to an additional 3 billion euros and a promise of visa-free travel in the EU–Turkey Statement.

CONCLUSIONS

Detecting, apprehending, detaining, and deporting undocumented migrants is one method states employ to control immigration; to be effective, receiving states require the cooperation of sending states to accept their own citizens as well as transit migrants. Yet unilateral action, as opposed to international cooperation, remains the preferred method of interior immigration control. Most states fall far short of eliminating irregular migration, despite the attention and resources devoted to immigration control. In part, this is due to the determination and ingenuity of migrants themselves; as states erect new barriers to restrict migration, determined migrants find ways to circumvent them. There are other reasons, however, why states fail to eliminate irregular migration through interior immigration control. First, states may prefer alternative methods to achieve their policy goals; second, states may be ambivalent about the level of irregular migration itself.

As noted in our introduction, efforts to combat irregular immigration can be divided into two types: those that focus on preventing unauthorized entry and those that focus on interior enforcement. States differ in the degree of emphasis they place on each type of policy; the traditional countries of immigration (the United States, Canada, Australia, and New Zealand) and island countries, like Ireland and the United Kingdom, have historically emphasized border control. Most continental European states have placed greater emphasis on interior enforcement (Martin 2004). The most obvious factor in explaining these differences is geographic location, followed by international constraints. Island states clearly have an advantage in controlling their borders, and European Schengen states are constrained by open borders among member states.

Logistical issues do not explain fully the differences between states in their unilateral approaches to migration control. The United States shares a border with Mexico that is nearly two thousand miles long, yet it has focused most of its attention on border control rather than interior enforcement. This suggests that states may be ambivalent about interior enforcement methods, which require a culture of monitoring that is more acceptable in some states than in others. Most Central European states, for example, require everyone to carry national identification cards, and police are permitted to randomly stop individuals and request the card. On the opposite end of the spectrum, the United States maintains no national identification system and places limits on the ability of police to stop individuals without cause. A discomfort with monitoring and concerns about discrimination, as well as constitutional restrictions, led to widespread protest against efforts in Arizona in 2010 to require individuals to present proof of legal immigration status upon police request. Although most of the state law was eventually allowed to stand, it was challenged in court by the federal government (Santos 2014). Unlike interior enforcement, border enforcement provokes less controversy, in part because citizens are not regularly confronted with it, and it does not infringe on the rights of citizens safely within the state.

Workplace checks, which can be an effective interior enforcement method of identifying undocumented immigrants, may also provoke dissatisfaction. Workplace audits fluctuate over time, but when they increase, they tend to generate political pushback from employers (Koslowski 2011b). For example, in the United States, the Obama administration switched from workplace raids to paperwork audits, which proved to be a much more efficient way to identify the companies employing undocumented workers. In the last year of the Bush administration, there were 503 audits; in 2009, the government conducted more than 8,000 (Sherman 2013). In 2008, federal authorities issued only 18 "final orders" against employers for hiring undocumented workers, collecting $675,209; in 2012, that number increased to 495, collecting $12.4 million (Doyle 2013). The successful effort, however, now faces strong political opposition. The agricultural industry, in particular, has been lobbying Congress aggressively to direct Homeland Security to lighten up on workplace enforcement. As California senator Dianne Feinstein wrote in September 2013, "The reality is that the majority of farmworkers in the US are foreign-born and unauthorized, which is well-known." She added that she was "afraid that this aggressive worksite enforcement strategy will deprive the agricultural sector of most of its workforce" (Doyle 2013).

Other countries face similar opposition to workplace enforcement, even when there is an established monitoring culture. During the 1990s, the German government stepped up workplace checks in the construction industry, which employed 550,000, including 200,000 foreigners, despite a 10 percent unemployment rate among German construction workers. The increased enforcement was undermined when employers began contesting the judgments, and subcontractors began going out of business (Martin 2004). Enforcement activities were then scaled back, without curtailing the influx of undocumented migrants; the political will to continue was not there. The opposition to interior enforcement by employers signals a second source of ambivalence: states may also be ambivalent about the number of undocumented migrants within their borders, as we noted in our discussion about unwanted versus undocumented migrants in our introduction to this chapter.

States have a number of unilateral policy tools at their disposal to control immigration. However, the political motivation to use these tools effectively is not always present. Thus, ineffective unilateral action alone does not indicate that the state is *unable* to act unilaterally, nor does it indicate that the state will pursue cooperation with other states. If there is ambivalence about the *goal* of restricting and controlling immigration, the state may be satisfied with the status quo of ineffective control. If the ambivalence is primarily about the *method of control*, states may seek to cooperate with other states as an alternative policy implementation. In this sense, cooperating with sending and transit states on issues of control is an extension of the border control method of enforcement, which focuses on preventing unauthorized entry. If interior enforcement provokes the most political opposition as citizens are confronted with the costs of immigration control, then outsourcing control to sending and transit states might provoke the least political opposition. The degree to which receiving states pursue cooperation with sending and transit states will thus be a reflection not only of the ability of the receiving state to act unilaterally, but of the underlying political will to actually control migration.

However, when receiving states do decide to act, sending, transit, and receiving states share few common interests in reducing the undocumented migrant population through deportation. Generally speaking, the number of migrants whom receiving states wish to deport exceeds the number of migrants whom sending and transit states wish to receive. In other words, the preferences of sending and receiving states diverge. In the contemporary era, it is sending states that prefer the status quo—in which migrants attempt to avoid deportation by eluding control agencies and by destroying identity documents when confronting control agencies. Transit states refuse the return of noncitizens and sending states adopt delaying tactics when confronting the return of their citizens. It is receiving states that prefer a change in the status quo. There are no collective action or coordination problems that these states can work together to solve. In the face of conflicting interests, the only possibility for cooperation lies in quid pro quo bargaining. In exchange for sending and transit states' cooperation in controlling migration, receiving states must offer side payments.

In cases where receiving states truly want to reduce their undocumented migrant population, two conditions will make cooperation more likely. The first relates to the cost of unwanted migration for the receiving states; the more costly unwanted migrants are, the more likely it is that cooperation will emerge. This cost is greater when the bundle of rights to which migrants have access in the host society is greater. When immigrants cannot be excluded from social welfare benefits such education, health care, and income support, receiving states will be more likely to cooperate with sending states. These costs are mitigated by a robust economy and exacerbated by a faltering one. The second condition relates to international restrictions on unilateral immigration control. When states are restricted in their ability to implement unilateral control policies, they are more likely to seek cooperative alternatives. The most extreme example of this type of loss of control is found in Europe, where states have voluntarily relinquished some sovereignty over border control by granting citizens of member states free movement and by joining the Schengen Agreement, which limits external border controls. Consequently, we see the most formalized cooperation on migration control emerging in Europe in the form of readmission agreements. Receiving states elsewhere, including those in the Global South, have not found it cost-effective to initiate international cooperation for interior migration control.

When formal cooperation occurs, it is likely to be bilateral, because bilateral migration profiles are unique and quid pro cooperation requires side payments. To minimize costs for the receiving states, they will prefer to negotiate with each state separately, offering the minimum incentive to elicit cooperation. In informal cooperation, the format will be much more flexible and there may be multilateral participation. Because informal processes are nonbinding and low-cost, there is no drawback to multilateralism, but the outcomes of informal processes will likely be much more modest for precisely the same reasons.

CHAPTER 4

Labor Recruitment

Market Forces and Market Failures

EARLY ON THE MORNING of 8 August 1956, disaster struck the Marcinelle section of the small Belgian city of Charleroi. Shortly after eight that morning, a coal car jumped the tracks and collided with a mine's ventilation shaft, breaking an electrical cable, which then ignited a fire that quickly spread throughout the mine (Nash 1976). Only 12 of the 274 miners working that morning survived the accident. Of those who perished, 136 were Italians who had been recruited from impoverished parts of southern Italy to fill labor shortages in postwar Belgium (Tino 2016). Labor shortages in Belgium were so severe that in June 1946, Italy and Belgium signed a bilateral protocol to facilitate the importation of Italian labor in exchange for Belgian coal. The agreement aimed to provide fifty thousand workers for Belgian mines, with the Italian government pledging to send some two thousand workers per week (Tino 2016). Migrants were given free train tickets and lodging and were promised jobs upon arrival. The attraction of these incentives was strong for the two to four million unemployed and underemployed in Italy (Randazzo 2014).

Sarina DiMartino's father was one of the thousands of Italians who ended up working in the Belgian mines, leaving his native Sicily with his wife and eleven children for opportunity abroad. "That was the reason my father brought us to Belgium," DiMartino recounted to Marianna Randazzo (2014). "Employment. Opportunity. Italians were told, 'Go to Belgium, it's good.' My father did not know better. . . . Italians were desperate for work, we were so many children."

DiMartino was just eight years old on the day of Marcinelle mine accident, but she clearly remembers the discrimination that she and other Italians faced in Belgium. "The Italians were mistreated," she recounted. "They did not want us here. They did not hide it. Do you know what they wrote above the signs in the bars and restaurants? NO DOGS, NO ITALIANS. Imagine seeing that? We were no better than the dogs? My father would tell us not to look at the signs. Yet, those were words we all understood" (Randazzo 2014).

The story of the DiMartino family has been told many millions of times over: lack of economic opportunity in their home countries and the chance of a better life, if not for the parents, then for the children. In this case, the Marcinelle disaster ended the formal cooperation on migration facilitation between Italy and Belgium, although no one was held criminally responsible for the unsafe conditions that precipitated the accident (Randazzo 2014). Stories of emigration have many different endings, but the origins are similar: men and women searching for better lives for their families than can be found in their country of origin, and countries that need their labor.

Although the DiMartino family did migrate under the auspices of a bilateral labor agreement (BLA) between Belgium and Italy, most migrants do not go through such channels. In the post–World War II period, most migrants have found employment in the absence of any cooperation between states. As Cornia (2011, 14, emphasis added) confirms, "The last 30 years have witnessed a surge in the number of migrants, exceeding 200 million by 2005. Much of this migration is *not the result of agreements between states* but reflects (often illegal) decisions of individuals, families, and firms in the countries of origin and destination." Markets, migrant networks, and private agencies have filled the gap between surplus labor countries and countries that desire additional labor.

The absence of international cooperation to *facilitate* international labor flows is distinctive from other dimensions of the postwar international economic system, which, by most accounts, relies on international cooperation to ensure other international economic flows. The Bretton Woods Conference in 1944 established the International Monetary Fund (IMF) and the International Bank of Reconstruction and Development (World Bank). International trading relations have been governed by the General Agreement on Tariffs and Trade (GATT) and, subsequently, by the WTO, established as a result of the Uruguay Round negotiations of the GATT. These international institutions, supplemented by a variety of bilateral and regional agreements, support an international economic system that facilitates the movement of goods, services, and capital around the globe. Yet, despite the existence of the UN ILO and the IOM, there is little systematic interstate cooperation to facilitate the movement of labor. States tend to act unilaterally to define who can enter legally and to sort immigrants at their respective borders. Moreover, bilateral and regional agreements that have proliferated on issues of trade and capital flows often exclude issues of migration. Why is there so little international cooperation to *facilitate* the flow of migrants in the international system?

This chapter is really a story about the dog that did not bark or, rather, one that barks infrequently. In the post–World War II period, market mechanisms and private actors are the primary forces facilitating migration, obviating the need for cooperation. Receiving states control migration unilaterally, sorting migrants in terms of numbers, characteristics, length of stay, and rights upon arrival while sending states are constrained by international law to allow their citizens to leave. Authoritarian regimes have sometimes sidestepped the latter international norm, but fewer and fewer states now control exit. The status quo is preferred by the powerful receiving states, and governments rarely negotiate to facilitate the movement of labor. Even sending states may benefit from and prefer the status quo when the demand for labor in international markets is strong.

Nonetheless, there are conditions under which states do seek to facilitate migration by negotiating and concluding international agreements. First, as developed in chapter 1, where agreements exist, they will be predominantly bilateral. Even when the unmet demand for labor in a specific country is large, it is not infinite. The costs of maintaining a multilateral regime, which provides uniform access to domestic labor markets, are substantially higher than the transaction costs of negotiating a few bilateral agreements. Second, as developed in chapter 2, powerful receiving states are usually satisfied with the status quo of unilateral action, since labor demands can usually be met through market mechanisms; only on rare occasions does a state fail to meet its labor market needs when it simply unilaterally removes restrictions to immigration.

Third, this status quo may be challenged by powerful receiving states only when exogenous shocks create very specific conditions: high labor market demand that cannot be met domestically and labor market failures that cannot be overcome by private sector actors. This increases the cost of the status quo for receiving states and triggers international negotiations. In this instance, sending states are likely to extract concessions from receiving states. Fourth, less powerful sending states may wish to negotiate for broader access to international labor markets, but they have neither found nor created an institutional forum within which to negotiate access.

We begin with an overview of the status quo ante that combines the right of departure with national sovereignty over admissions. We then present the preferences of sending and receiving states, which demonstrates an alignment of the state preferences, a preference for the status quo. We then discuss how market mechanisms and private networks work to equilibrate labor market supply and demand across international borders and the conditions under which markets fail. The demand for cooperation, the exogenous shock that triggers efforts to cooperate internationally, comes from receiving states when the demand for labor exceeds the supply, due to informational asymmetries between employers' demand for labor and the available international supply. Alternatively, sending states may desire broader access to receiving country labor markets to enhance social stability and increase remittances. Our empirical evidence is organized by level of cooperation: multilateral, regional, and bilateral. We argue that multilateral cooperation is never warranted in meeting limited labor market demands. GATS Mode 4 is the sole multilateral forum that implicates international migration, but it is narrowly tailored to avoid access to the domestic labor markets of receiving states. Sending states have been unable to leverage this institutional forum to address the issue because, even though sending states are a numerical majority, consensus decision rules prevent sending states from capturing the bargaining agenda.

Regional agreements represent a more promising venue for negotiating cooperation on migration but are limited to regions that have similar wages, working conditions, and standards of living. These conditions promote reciprocal flows that improve labor market efficiency while avoiding charges that may accrue to the state. We examine twenty-eight regional economic organizations (REOs) and provide evidence that only those regions with similar levels of wealth have negotiated freedom of movement.[1] Those cases are detailed in chapter 5. Otherwise, regional cooperation on migration is absent.

Finally, we turn to BLAs, the dominant form of interstate cooperation to facilitate migration in response to labor market demands. Because a universal repository does not exist, we provide evidence from an OECD survey (OECD 2004) and from a more recent global survey by the ILO that suggests that few agreements are negotiated and that more recently BLAs are turning into immigration control agreements in which labor market access in the receiving state becomes a reward for sending state control over managing undocumented flows (Wickramasekara 2015). Thus, although the name of the agreement remains unchanged, BLAs are shifting from facilitating to controlling migration. We provide case study evidence that is consistent with our hypotheses that the agreements are necessary only when market failures are not resolved through private actors.

Before concluding, we evaluate our analysis against other accounts of the phenomenon. In the conclusions, we draw from the theoretical propositions to point out that sending states, by empowering private actors to facilitate migration, are giving up potential leverage they may have when negotiating with receiving states to improve the lives of their citizens abroad.

In examining facilitation of international migration, we make a distinction between *freedom of movement* and *labor recruitment*. Freedom of movement agreements allow citizens of member states to seek employment in any of the member states at any time.[2] Labor recruitment, on the other hand, is associated with limited entry in response to specific labor market shortages that cannot be met through domestic labor markets. Quotas may govern the number of admissions or employers may be required to demonstrate the lack of qualified workers in the domestic labor force. Work and residence permits are also employed as mechanisms of control to ensure that migrants come when needed and go when demand subsides. It is not the open door policy associated with freedom of movement. Governments seek to retain control over the type and number of entries, as well as the length of stay. In this chapter, we address labor recruitment. In chapter 5 we deal with freedom of movement.

Research on labor recruitment often distinguishes between *high-skilled* and *low-skilled* labor. There are a number of reasons why this disaggregation of labor flows might be useful analytically. Although many states, including some states in the Global South, attempt to reduce low-skilled migration and enhance high-skilled migration, the demand for both high-skilled and low-skilled workers remains strong. Many of the jobs that nationals no longer want, the "dirty, dangerous, and difficult" jobs as well as the many "care" jobs that arise from aging populations and women's participation in the formal labor force, are filled by migrant labor and are classified as unskilled. At the same time, there appears to be a "competition for the best and the brightest," individuals with tertiary degrees, to spur innovation and economic growth. Because demand remains strong but states privilege high-skilled over low-skilled migration, analysts argue that the domestic politics of high- and low-skilled migration appear to mobilize different constituencies with different outcomes in terms of policies adopted (Cerna 2009). However, for our purposes, this distinction is less significant. When the explanatory variable of interest is *cooperation among states*, the skill level required by employers should not affect the trajectory of states. Once a policy choice is adopted, states can choose to act unilaterally to achieve that policy objective or to cooperate with other states, bilaterally, regionally, or multilaterally. Thus our discussion makes reference to high-skilled and low-skilled labor only insofar as they represent different state preferences for migrant labor and may thus be reflected in the content of the negotiated agreements.

STATUS QUO ANTE AND STATE PREFERENCES

The Status Quo Ante. As developed in chapter 2, for labor recruitment or facilitation of labor, principles of customary international law related both to departure and to admissions are important. Chetail summarizes these principles in Table 4.1.

The first principle to note is the right of citizens to leave and return to their country of origin. Without this principle, there could be no international migration. It is central to the notion of human rights and personal liberty—the ability to control one's own destiny. Jurists noted this as part of the development of the law of nations as early as the fifteenth century, when Europeans began to spread around the globe (Chetail 2014).

Of course, the opposing principle is national sovereignty over entry. "The competence of States to regulate the entry of non-citizens is traditionally considered as a well-established principle of positive international law" (Chetail 2014, 27). The legal rationale on which this principle is based is that of territorial sovereignty. It is echoed in much domestic jurisprudence, such as the oft-cited US Supreme Court case *Nishimura Ekiu v. United States*: "It is an accepted maxim of international law, that every sovereign nation has the power as inherent in sovereignty and essential to its self-preservation, to forbid the

Table 4.1

Customary Law in International Migration

Departure	Admission
Right to leave any country except when restrictions are provided by law, necessary to protect public order and consistent with other fundamental rights	Right to return to one's own country
	Non-refoulement (of those facing persecution as defined in the UN Refugee Convention [1951, 1967])
	Family reunion of children
	Prohibition of arbitrary detention
	Access to consular protection
	Prohibition of collective expulsion

Source: Chetail (2014, 71).

entrance of foreigners within its dominions, or to admit them only in such cases as it may see fit to prescribe."[3]

This fact is widely recognized in the contemporary era, although it was constructed slowly beginning in the seventeenth century. Chetail (2014) reminds us that state regulation of entry was not instantaneously adopted and implemented with the institutionalization of the interstate system in the Treaty of Westphalia (1648). Torpey (2000) provides a historical overview of the evolution in Europe from a feudal system that bound peasants to the land to a system of relatively free movement beginning with the French Revolution and expanding across the European continent in the nineteenth century, before passports and immigration control became the norm in the early twentieth century. Nonetheless, the system of passports and immigration control has been firmly in place since well before World War II (Torpey 2000; Salter 2003). Thus, the status quo in the post–World War II international system recognizes both the right to leave one's country of origin and the (constrained) national sovereignty of states to govern entry. This status quo allows receiving states to choose both the number and type of immigrants for entry regardless of the preferences of sending states. It is not an unlimited sovereignty, as it is constrained by states' commitments to international treaties to not refoule individuals defined in international treaties as persecuted as well as to protect the special rights of children in terms of family reunion. Nonetheless, state sovereignty over entry is well established in international law. When combined with individuals' right to exit, this status quo privileges receiving states.

Preferences of Receiving States. Outside of the imperative of ensuring state territorial security, the interests of states in the international system are often opaque. Here we posit that receiving states have two imperatives. The first originates in the imperative of ensuring territorial integrity. The second is an interest in efficiently functioning labor markets that promote economic growth and contribute to the state's legitimacy (Zolberg 2006).

The sovereign right of territorial integrity includes control over entry, which permits the state to define its citizen population. To quote *Nishimura Ekiu* again, this attribute is central to the state's "self-preservation." The inability to control entry, in the extreme, allows other states to invade and conquer. So control over entry is part and parcel of ensuring territorial integrity. And, in popular imagination, even peaceful entry of migrant populations in sufficiently large numbers can overwhelm the existing community (Wilders et al. 2015). Thus, receiving states have a preference for control over entry to the territory.

The state's interest in ensuring a functioning labor market, necessary for economic growth, moderates its preference for control over entry, since economic growth is an important component of a state's legitimacy (Zolberg 2006; Rudolph 2003). Given a specific set of productive factors and structure of the labor market, each state has a demand for different quantities and types of labor. Those demands may be met locally, from a broader national labor supply, or from international sources. At a basic level, economists suggest that capital-intensive countries would benefit from access to international labor and that labor-intensive countries would benefit from the export of their labor, suggesting a specific market demand process for international labor.

Michael Piore, in *Birds of Passage* (1979), provides a more theoretically sophisticated extension of this basic description. He describes the construction of dual labor markets in wealthy Western democracies. Workers in those countries develop sufficient economic and/or political power to generate protections from the vagaries of the market. Employers, in response, seek workers whom they can hire and fire easily as a mechanism to respond to changing market demand for their product. The dual labor market is then composed of a protected, stable primary sector, and a flexible secondary sector. The workers employed in the secondary sector of the labor market can include disadvantaged national groups, such as women, youth, or minorities. However, international migrants can also meet labor market demands. In both of these scenarios, the labor shortage state has an interest in expanding its labor supply. As Kindleberger (1967) explains in describing Europe's postwar economic growth, an expanding labor supply moderates wage increases and induces additional investment, creating a positive cycle of economic growth. If economic growth is one component of state legitimacy, then receiving states have an interest in moderating labor markets. One means of doing so is through international migration.

If receiving states are attentive to the efficient functioning of labor markets as well as territorial integrity, these states should prefer a system that allows them to pick and choose the number and characteristics of migrants. This allows them to enhance labor market efficiencies as well as to protect territorial integrity. We do not suggest that receiving states actually have the capacity to completely control the level and characteristics of international migrants that maximize labor market efficiency, only that these two criteria determine receiving state preferences. The central preference of receiving states is the retention of national sovereignty over entry—the ability to determine the permissible number of immigrants and to sort those immigrants on the desired characteristics and to determine the length of stay. This preference is consistent with the status quo ante.

Preferences of Sending States. In the contemporary era, most sending states view emigrants as a positive resource, as an outlet for domestic discontent and a source of foreign exchange earnings that migrants send home in the form of remittances (Ratha 2005).[4] This is not to say that all sending states prefer all types of emigration at all times.[5] We recognize that the preferences of sending states have changed over time, although the trajectory of these preferences varies from country to country. Scholarly research has debated the costs and benefits of emigration, with the downside emanating from the loss of skilled and energetic manpower, the "brain drain" and the "brawn drain" (de Haas 2008).[6] But the Global Forum on Migration and Development and much contemporary research promote the notion of the "triple win," where emigration benefits the migrants themselves, as well as countries of origin and destination (Hermele 2015).[7] The countries of origin benefit from exporting migrants in three ways (Stewart, Clark, and Clark 2007). First, exporting migrants leads to additional resources for the home country in terms of remittances. Second, the potential for high-skilled emigration can stimulate additional public and private investments in human capital in the country of origin, which promotes economic growth. Since not all skilled labor emigrates, the home country may benefit through an enhanced level of human capital (Beine, Docquier, and Rapoport 2008). Last, the home country may benefit from the diaspora effect, where international migration facilitates and increases international business contacts in the home country (Leblang 2010). In the contemporary era, most sending states prefer emigration and prefer for it to be legal. For the most part, this is consistent with the status quo; it is only when the desire for emigration exceeds the demand for immigrants that sending states depart from their support for the status quo.[8]

INTERNATIONAL COOPERATION TO FACILITATE MIGRATION

For much of the post–World War II period, the preferences of both sending and receiving states supported the status quo, that is, individuals are free to leave their home state in search of a better life and receiving states are free to accept as many migrants as they choose, of any characteristic and for any duration of stay, turning away those they do not want. However, exogenous shocks may modify the costs of the status quo and generate the demand for a negotiated agreement.

Labor Market Shortages. The primary exogenous shock or pressure that forces receiving states into the international arena in search of cooperation to *facilitate* migration is an unmet demand for labor. In the post–World War II era that is the focus of our inquiry, the primary mechanism for linking individuals to employment opportunities is the market.[9] If the underpinnings of the market mechanism are in place, there is little need for cooperation. Market mechanisms include employer recruitment efforts, the services of private recruitment firms (including smugglers), and migrant networks. In other words, the "invisible hand" of the market works to match the surplus labor with the appropriate employer, across international boundaries. There is no reason for states with labor market shortages to bind themselves to agreements with countries experiencing labor market surpluses; nor is there any reason for countries with labor market surpluses to bind themselves to agreements with countries experiencing labor market shortages. Signals from the labor market—wages and working conditions—will draw the appropriate responses from private actors. Thus, international cooperation is not required and we should expect few negotiated agreements to facilitate migration.

Market Failures and Labor Recruitment. There are two primary reasons that markets may fail to fulfill labor market needs. The first stems from informational asymmetries. Employers know the number and type of workers they want, but potential employees in foreign countries are unaware of these specific demands. In the absence of information, states with labor market shortages would need to publicize their job openings in labor surplus countries and may find that agreements with these states provide an inexpensive mechanism for advertising their labor market needs. We would expect demand for international agreements to increase if information is costly for individuals to obtain and to decrease if the opposite is true. There are at least two mechanisms that affect information costs. The first is communication technology. Over the nineteenth, twentieth, and twenty-first centuries, communication technology has changed dramatically. Even twenty years ago, an international telephone call was very expensive. Now, computers, the internet, and programs such as Skype have diminished the costs of communication to almost zero. Hence, we anticipate that as communication technology costs decrease, we will see fewer international agreements to facilitate labor migration. The second mechanism is networks that permit employers to match their job requirements to workers with the appropriate skills. An organizational infrastructure can be put into place that allows for the mechanical matching of workers in the foreign country to employers, but the informal network of workers themselves is also a critical mechanism. We know from the research on migrant networks that migrants themselves are often key to linking workers in the country of origin to employment in the host country (Massey 1987). Migrant networks may be difficult to initiate but, once in place, overtake formal placement mechanisms as cheaper and more reliable. Therefore, we anticipate that as migrant networks increase, international agreements to facilitate labor migration will decrease.

The second type of market failure stems from adjustment costs. Markets function well when adjustment costs are zero, but it is common knowledge that this is rarely the case in the real world. The higher the adjustment costs, the less likely that market forces will function properly. Even if workers in one country have knowledge of labor market opportunities in a second country, they need the resources to relocate to take advantage of those opportunities.[10] Migrant networks also serve a function here, tending to reduce adjustment costs of all types. Migrants who arrive first can help later arrivals meet practical needs, like securing housing and accessing services, as well as social needs, such as cultural adjustment and camaraderie. This is a second mechanism that connects migrant networks to the declining need for international agreements to facilitate migration. On the other hand, transportation expenses increase adjustment costs. That is why workers often migrate to the geographically closest countries with labor market shortages. More generically, as the cost of transportation decreases, market forces will more likely match workers with employers. Therefore, we anticipate that as transportation costs decrease, international agreements to facilitate labor migration will decrease. This also suggests that attracting migrant labor from more distant locations will also be a determinant of BLAs.

Where market mechanisms are deficient, receiving states respond to labor market pressures by negotiating agreements with migrant-sending states. Moreover, because labor market demands are ultimately limited, states negotiate bilaterally with a series of countries until the demand for labor is offset by a sufficient supply; at some point, private mechanisms, such as migrant networks and private recruitment agencies, may be able to keep up with demand. Thus, to facilitate labor migration, we anticipate bilateral agreements only under conditions of labor market pressures in the presence of information asymmetries and high adjustment costs. Given that powerful receiving states seek to modify the status quo, we expect sending states to extract concessions, such as greater migrant protections, in the ensuing agreements.

Access to International Labor Markets. Alternatively, migrant-sending states and their citizens may prefer greater access to international labor markets than is currently available. In recent periods, sending states and their citizens appear to have a preference for more robust access to labor markets in receiving states. This pressure is generated by continued high levels of inequality both within and between states in the international system and is reflected in the growing undocumented populations in receiving states (UNDP 2009). Given their dissatisfaction with the status quo, sending states have explored various international forums in an effort to extract greater labor market access. In this chapter, we examine efforts by sending states at the multilateral, regional, and bilateral levels to expand documented, legal access to receiving country labor markets. We argue that sending states have been unable to locate a forum to address these demands effectively. Powerful receiving states are unwilling to modify the status quo to open their labor markets more broadly to both skilled and unskilled labor in bilateral, regional, or multilateral forums in the absence of labor market failures addressed above.[11] We now turn to the empirical evidence and connect our theoretical expectation with the empirical reality.

MULTILATERAL AGREEMENTS: GATS MODE 4

GATS Mode 4 is the sole multilateral agreement that implicates migration. It is therefore a potential international forum for sending states to attempt to negotiate greater access for their emigrants. However, it has only recently been recognized as a potential forum for negotiating a change to the status quo and the unanimity rules for decision making prevent sending states from exploiting this forum. To support our contention, we present a brief history of the GATS and the current state of GATS negotiations, pointing out its narrowness in terms of state commitments as well as actual movement of individuals. We emphasize that when sending states sought to employ GATS negotiations to extract greater access to receiving state labor markets, they were unsuccessful.

A Short History of GATS Mode 4. The Uruguay Round of GATT resulted in the creation of the WTO and also incorporated other trade-related issues into the multilateral trading regime, including trade-related investment measures, trade-related intellectual property rights, and trade in services. Because in-person delivery of services is one method of trading services across international borders, GATS implicates migration and multilateral cooperation on migration.

The history of the international trading system is well known and will not be replicated here. We merely remind readers that the Uruguay Round began in 1986 with developing nations demanding greater access to developed country markets in agricultural and textile products. Developed countries countered with demands for greater market access and national treatment on FDI, trade in services, and protection for intellectual property generated in the developed world. The "Grand Bargain" allowed both groups of states to encode some of their preferences in the agreement, which was unanimously adopted by the 128 member states in 1994 (Ostry 2000; WTO 2013b).[12]

The Structure of GATS. The service sector is composed of economic activities whose products cannot be embodied in a physical form. There are 155 designated sectors within twelve economic categories and four modes of service delivery (GATS 2016): Mode 1 is the *cross-border* delivery of services, such as the current use of call centers in foreign countries. The workers in the provider country remain at home while servicing the needs of the consumer in the consuming country. Mode 2 is *consumption abroad*, as when the consumer travels to the producer country to consume the good. Tourism has been the most important good delivered under Mode 2, although there is now a growing trade in health services where consumers (in costly developed countries) travel to (cheaper) developing countries to consume medical services. Mode 3 (*commercial presence*) involves the establishment of a branch by a foreign company in the consumer country through FDI. Finally, Mode 4 is the temporary *movement of natural persons* from the producer country to provide a service in the consumer country. Mode 4 implicates migration and is, hence, the focus of our interest in multilateral cooperation on migration.

The negotiations on trade in services have generally been analyzed as between developed and developing states—the Global North versus the Global South—rather than between sending and receiving countries. It was the states of the Global North, in particular the United States, that placed trade in services on the GATT negotiating agenda (Drake and Nicolaïdis 1992). Developing nations are described as being opposed to opening their domestic markets to trade in services for which they do not have a comparative advantage, and they have granted limited access to developed country service providers. Throughout the Uruguay Round, migrant-sending countries did not perceive GATS Mode 4 as a method of providing a market opening for their unskilled workers in developed country markets. Based on the preferences of states in the Global North, the GATS specifically excludes permanent migration, access to domestic labor markets, and access to citizenship. It focuses on temporary movement for the provision of services and therefore also excludes even temporary access to labor markets in other sectors of the economy in which developing country migrants have found employment, such as agriculture and manufacturing.

GATS is nested within the WTO, which operates on the principle of unanimity; no agreement can be reached without the agreement of each member state. The bargains struck in each round of negotiations reflect this institutional rule. Moreover, by the 1980s, at least a few developing nations had the capacity to present their demands and were no longer willing to take a back seat in the GATS negotiations. Given the opposing interests of the developed and developing countries, GATS therefore reflects some of the interests of developing nations and differs in structure from the agreements on trade. GATS is structured as a "positive list" rather than a "negative list" document. This means that countries are unbound by GATS unless they choose to opt in by sector or by mode of service provision; this contrasts with trade of manufactured goods, where states sign up for the entire basket of trade concessions except for those sectors they choose to opt out of.

GATS Mode 4 Commitments. Under GATS, there are both horizontal commitments (the four modes of delivery) and sector-specific commitments. Initially, only 95 of the 128 member states submitted horizontal commitments and sectoral commitments of many states were quite limited. Mode 4 commitments are generally unbound, meaning that there is no commitment to allow entry for the provision of services, or commitments are limited to highly skilled individuals categorized as business visitors, intercorporate transferees, and professionals. Business visitors have both maximum stay restrictions (most commonly ninety days) and limits on the types of activities they can undertake. Intracorporate transferees must have professional qualifications, be previously employed by the foreign corporation, and demonstrate specialized corporate knowledge (GATS 2016). Professionals must demonstrate qualifications, and both intracorporate transferees and professionals are often subject to national legislation in order to obtain required work permits. There are no commitments that allow entry of unskilled service providers.

There is a general consensus that country commitments to GATS have not facilitated trade in services. According to Das (2006, ix), "Members at best bound the status quo for the most part and sometimes even backtracked on the status quo." The commitments, in general, reflect the competitive advantage of states in the delivery of services. And, although international trade in services has grown since the signing of GATS, the temporary movement of persons (Mode 4) has been insignificant in the delivery of these services. "A 2004 estimate suggests that the temporary movement of natural persons accounts for less than 2 percent of total world trade in services" (Dawson 2012, 1; see also Nielson and Taglioni n.d.).

The Status of Current Negotiations. Since the end of the Uruguay Round, some experts on development at organizations such as the World Bank have seized on GATS Mode 4 as a method to promote trade in services by developing nations and to facilitate economic growth and development in poor countries (Chanda 2002; Mattoo and Carzaniga 2003; Stephenson and Hufbauer 2011;

Sáez 2013). Additionally, some developing nations have begun to view GATS Mode 4 as an opportunity to expand trade in services in sectors in which they are beginning to have a comparative advantage. Both of these efforts reconfigure negotiating coalitions into sending versus receiving states rather than developed versus developing states, so it is important to examine the future prospects of GATS as a venue for increased migration.

Unlike the WTO, GATS had a built-in negotiating agenda that called for the commencement of a new round of negotiations on the liberalization of trade in services to begin no later than five years after its entry into force. So, in January 2000, GATS 2000, a new round of negotiations on services, commenced. Once the Doha Development Round of the WTO was launched in 2001, however, the negotiations for GATS 2000 were subsumed under the broader negotiations.

In the interim between the creation of GATS and the GATS 2000 negotiating round, the position of some developing countries shifted from opposition to trade in services to efforts to expand access. India, in particular, found a growing comparative advantage in services, especially in information technology, and has pressed for greater openness to markets in the industrialized world and for a "GATS visa" to facilitate the movement of natural persons on a temporary basis (Das 2006). Moreover, NGOs have made the case that GATS Mode 4 should include less skilled service suppliers, which would allow developing countries to take advantage of their comparative advantage in other types of services (Mashayekhi n.d.).

Thirteen years after the initiation of the GATS negotiations, in Bali, Indonesia, the Doha Development Round reached an interim Ministerial Declaration that produced a modest set of proposals that was able to garner consensus within the organization, now counting 159 members (Fabi 2013). However, the GATS portion of that agreement was limited to "operationalizing" the preferential treatment of service providers from the least developed countries, which was agreed to in 2009 (WTO 2013a). Efforts by India to employ the WTO institutions to expand labor market access for citizens of sending states have been completely unsuccessful. It has been difficult to build a sending state coalition in an organization that has had a primary dividing line between developing and developed nations.[13] And the rules requiring unanimity have caused negotiations to flounder across a wide array of issues including, but not limited to, migration of service providers through Mode 4.

Analysis. Although GATS Mode 4 represents the possibility of cooperation on international migration, it has not provided a venue for the management of even temporary migration. The agreement specifically excludes both permanent migration and access to the host country's domestic labor market. When the agreement was originally negotiated, developed countries wanted access to developing countries' service sectors, but most developing countries avoided commitments in most service sectors. However, developed countries protected their own low-skilled service sectors by admitting only a select group of temporary service providers, business visitors, intracorporate transferees, and professionals. Entry is not only limited in terms of length of stay but also subjected to national legislation that either bars access to the local labor market even on a temporary basis or requires labor market tests before granting a work permit. This scheme fit well with the growing emphasis on high-skilled migration in the developed world, the "global competition for the best and the brightest." Developing countries are only now attempting to push for greater market access to developed countries for their low-skilled migrants, with no success to date despite many years of negotiations. It is thus safe to conclude that, despite appearances, GATS Mode 4 is not a multilateral venue for international migration cooperation.

Our analysis finds support in some of the research on GATS. For example, Bhatnagar and Manning (2005, 176) remark that coordination or cooperation is unnecessary in light of market forces. "Critics of the WTO approach . . . sometimes argue that market forces are already operating to bring about a movement of workers from labour-abundant to labour-scarce countries, as, for example, the increased mobility of nurses into OECD countries. Why then, should countries carry out formal negotiations on Mode 4 in regional or multilateral settings?"

REGIONAL LABOR AGREEMENTS

At the present point in time, REOs remain in the wings rather than at the center of the international migration stage. We argue that regional agreements are more propitious than global agreements in facilitating migration but that the conditions that underpin cooperation on labor mobility are infrequently met. One example comes from the Association of South East Asian Nations (ASEAN): "The ASEAN experience shows that geographical proximity and a common historical and cultural tradition is not sufficient to free up entry of foreign workers" (Bhatnagar and Manning 2005, 195). Nonetheless, REOs present the future potential to incorporate cooperation on international migration. They can do so if they promote economic integration that reduces disparities in wealth and living conditions among the member states and generate full employment, thus setting the stage for reciprocal migratory flows. In this section, we outline the conditions under which freedom of movement is implemented in REOs; we provide evidence from twenty-eight prominent regional organizations that is consistent with our arguments.

Exploring regional agreements that facilitate labor migration represents a minefield. There are at least three problems that arise. The first is that the number of REOs is growing. The literature acknowledges two waves of regionalization; the first wave provided the initial model of economic integration in Europe during the 1950s and led to the emulation of that agreement around the world in the 1960s and 1970s, as Europe prospered. However, many of these agreements had become moribund by the 1980s. A second wave arose in the 1990s, with the widespread adoption of neoliberal economic policies in developing countries. The pressures of interdependence were compounded by the lack of progress on the WTO multilateral trade negotiations that began in Doha in 2001. Countries around the globe reinvigorated old regional agreements and drafted new ones. Thus, the number of regional agreements is constantly increasing, and each regional agreement is unique. The second problem is that the content of the regional agreements continues to shift. REOs are institutions that evolve as states negotiate new dimensions of integration. A free trade area can turn into a customs union and a customs union into a common market. Thus, it is difficult to keep track of the contents of the latest agreements, especially because the vocabulary takes on different meanings in different REOs: facilitation of movement, free circulation, freedom of movement, and rights of establishment can be narrowly or broadly defined to include or exclude rights of residence and access to the labor market. However, even if these problems are mastered, once agreements are negotiated, they are often not implemented. In some cases, states that have negotiated the agreements fail to ratify them, so they do not come into force. And those that have come into force may not be fully implemented in ways that are often opaque. Moreover, regional agreements are often supplemented by bilateral agreements that create the actual rules under which workers from one state in an REO migrate to another state in the same organization. Or, national legislation governs migratory movements, so that no international cooperation exists even as labor flows between countries.

To add to the confusion, the provisions for facilitating mobility can take several forms. The first is the adoption of visa-free entry and residence, usually for a period of ninety days. Many regional organizations have adopted measures such as these, but they preclude access to the local labor market so they do not represent access to labor mobility or migration, defined as residence in a host country for more than a year. The second model is a GATS Mode 4–type agreement that reiterates or extends the WTO concessions to regional partners; again, generally, these do not represent access to labor markets and, hence, cannot be counted as agreements to facilitate labor migration. Third, regional agreements can facilitate skilled migration either through extension of the "independent professional" category in the GATS Mode 4–type agreements or through the listing of specific professions for which entry is open. Finally, there are freedom of movement provisions, often modeled on the "four freedoms" incorporated in the EU: freedom of movement for goods, services, capital, and labor. In principle, freedom of movement allows access to the labor markets to nationals of the member states. This freedom is generally abridged in some way; for example, even the EU allows job searches for only six months and only with adequate resources and medical insurance to prevent access to host state social services. Nonetheless, freedom of movement generally provides national treatment to citizens of member states when applying for jobs.

Thus, it is hazardous to draw strong conclusions about the ability of regional organizations to cooperate in ways that facilitate labor migration. Nonetheless, we argue that, at present, disparities in wealth and working conditions are sufficiently large in most REOs so as to minimize the potential for actual implementation of labor mobility. Even where wealth and working conditions are similar, there must be an unfulfilled demand for labor to act as a trigger to initiate international negotiations to enhance international labor mobility. As Stephenson and Hufbauer (2011, 285, emphasis added) note, "The trading partners that have been the most willing to open their markets wider for foreign workers from developing PTA [preferential trade agreement] partners have been *countries that face considerable labor shortages.*" Their observation is consistent with our expectation that international cooperation to facilitate labor migration originates with a demand for labor that is unmet by domestic supply.

Chapter 5, on freedom of movement, covers those regional agreements that appear to promote the broadest access of member state citizens to labor markets. Here, we summarize evidence from twenty-eight prominent regional organizations, differentiating between agreements that have no mobility provisions, agreements that have not entered into force, agreements that are not fully implemented, and agreements that open labor markets to a select set of professions. Ours will not be the last word because, as noted above, these regional organizations are constantly evolving.

There are at least three systemic factors within which REOs are constructed. The first is the model of economic integration in Europe, which was initiated with the ECSC in 1952 and found full development in the EEC and EU. The creation of an area of "peace and prosperity" has provided a strong impetus for imitation elsewhere in the world. Moreover, the EU, believing in regional economic integration as a major source of its success in creating peace and prosperity, has proselytized regional organizations, contributing to their construction elsewhere. The second systemic factor is the propagation of a "theory" of economic integration that traces a path from free trade agreement to a customs union, a common market, an economic union, and a political union (Grimwade 2013). Factor mobility is a central component of a common market, and the free movement of goods, services, capital, and labor is viewed as a natural progression in economic integration. For states that organize regionally, labor mobility is a de facto component of the negotiation agenda. The third systemic dimension is growing economic interdependence and the desire of small states to increase their leverage in international negotiations through banding together in regional organizations that carry more economic and political weight. Each of these factors combines to put labor mobility on the agenda of many REOs.[14]

Our work on freedom of movement, presented in chapter 5, informs the criteria we employ to predict which REOs will actually implement labor facilitation agreements. Agreements may be negotiated in any region, depending on the preferences of the states within the region and the institutional rules governing introduction of legislation and decision making. However, we argue that the implementation of agreements that permit access to national labor markets will take place only where wealth disparities are small and reciprocal flows likely. We develop the argument in detail in chapter 5 but recapitulate our argument. States prefer efficient labor markets that allow employers to hire labor as demand expands and to lay off labor when demand contracts. But unemployed workers may draw on state social services and will be unable to contribute to state coffers when they do not earn an income. Therefore, economic efficiency also requires that unemployed workers be able to obtain employment elsewhere, either locally or abroad. States have a preference for the ability to export workers as well as import workers; they have a preference for reciprocal labor movements. However, reciprocity is viable only under very specific conditions. Foreign labor markets must attract unemployed workers with similar wages and benefits. Hence a requirement for freedom of movement is similarity in wages, benefits, and the general standard of living. Common language and common culture also facilitate ease of movement in both directions. Finally, national treatment of migrants ensures that employers will not undercut native employment, so that conditions close to full employment should prevail.

To support our claim that the implementation of labor facilitation requires small disparities in wealth and reciprocal flows, we present evidence from twenty-eight REOs. These REOs were selected by Yoram Haftel (2012) to ensure that the central focus of the organizations was some form of economic cooperation and integration. These are the most prominent REOs in the global community today and exhibit wide variation on the degree to which they incorporate some dimension of labor mobility. However, the list is not comprehensive.

Table 4.2 summarizes the pertinent information on the twenty-eight REOs. We provide a brief description of the degree of implementation for those agreements that incorporate labor mobility provisions. Rather than organize the table geographically, we present the REOs by variation in levels of wealth, which is a central predictor of the implementation of freedom of movement. In some cases, no free movement provisions are incorporated into regional agreements. In other cases, agreements that have been negotiated have never entered into force for lack of ratification. However, there are many instances where agreements

Table 4.2
REOs and Facilitation of Migration

Regional economic organization	Membership	Date	Mobility provisions	Implementation	Low-high ratio	Low-mean ratio
Southern African Development Community (SADC)	Angola, Botswana, Democratic Republic of the Congo (1997), Lesotho, Madagascar, Malawi, Mauritius, Mozambique, Namibia (1990), Seychelles, South Africa (1994), Swaziland, Tanzania, Zambia, Zimbabwe	1980	2005 Protocol on the Facilitation of Movement of Persons	Not ratified (by required two-thirds of member states)	55.5	16.0
Common Market for Eastern and Southern Africa (COMESA) (previously PTA)	Burundi, Comoros, Democratic Republic of the Congo, Djibouti, Egypt, Eritrea, Ethiopia, Kenya, Libya, Madagascar, Malawi, Mauritius, Rwanda, Seychelles, Sudan, Swaziland, Uganda, Zambia, Zimbabwe	1981 1994	1998 Free Movement Protocol	Not ratified (only four of nineteen member states have signed and only two ratified)	55.4	12.1
Economic Community of Central African States (ECCAS) (relaunched 1999)	Angola, Burundi, Cameroon, Central African Republic, Chad, Democratic Republic of the Congo, Equatorial Guinea, Gabon, Republic of the Congo, Rwanda, São Tomé and Príncipe	1983 1999	1983 Protocol on Freedom of Movement and Rights of Establishment of Nationals: "progressive facilitation"	Regulations facilitating movement not drafted	49.4	12.4
Communauté Economique et Monetaire de l'Afrique Centrale (CEMAC) (previously Union Douanière des Etats de l'Afrique Centrale [UDEAC])	Cameroon, Central African Republic, Chad, Equatorial Guinea, Gabon, Republic of the Congo	1964 1994	1964 initial goal of UDEAC was common market 2005 treaty on Economic Union with fifteen-year transition period	Gabon and Equatorial Guinea have not implemented	30.1	9.5

(continued)

Table 4.2
(*continued*)

Regional economic organization	Membership	Date	Mobility provisions	Implementation	Low-high ratio	Low-mean ratio
Association of South East Asian Nations (ASEAN)	Brunei Darassalem (1984), Cambodia (1999), Indonesia, Laos (1997), Malaysia, Myanmar (1997), Philippines, Singapore, Thailand, Vietnam (1997)	1967	2015 mutual recognition agreements for eight professions (2015)	Must still meet national migration regulations	25.8	7.5
Indian Ocean Commission (IOC)	Comoros, Madagascar, Mauritius, Réunion,* Seychelles	1982	No free movement provisions		18.5	8.3
Asia-Pacific Trade Agreement (APTA) (originally Bangkok Agreement)	Bangladesh, China (2005), India, Laos PDR, Mongolia (2013), Republic of Korea, Sri Lanka	1975 2005	No free movement provisions		11.6	3.1
Economic Cooperation Organization (ECO) (previously Regional Cooperation for Development)	Iran, Pakistan, Turkey; 1992 accessions: Afghanistan, Azerbaijan, Kazakhstan, Kyrgyzstan, Tajikistan, Turkmenistan, Uzbekistan	1964–79 1985	No free movement provisions		10.2	5.0
Economic Community of West African States (ECOWAS)	Benin, Burkina Faso, Cape Verde, Côte d'Ivoire, Gambia, Ghana, Guinea, Guinea Bissau, Liberia, Mali, Niger, Nigeria, Senegal, Sierra Leone, Togo	1975	1980 visa-free entry 1986 right to reside and take up employment Right of establishment not yet implemented	Requirement for work permit after ninety days; limits on the categories of workers	8.5	3.0
Eurasian Economic Union (EEU) (previously Eurasian Economic Community)	Armenia (2015), Belarus, Kazakhstan, Kyrgyzstan, Russia (Uzbekistan suspended membership in 2008)	2000 2014	2012 common economic space with four freedoms: goods, capital, services, and people (in force 2015)	Movement governed by bilateral agreements and domestic legislation	7.5	4.6
Arab Maghreb Union (AMU)	Algeria, Libya, Mauritania, Morocco, Tunisia	1989	No free movement provisions		7.2	3.6

Organization	Members	Dates	Free movement provisions		
Southern African Customs Union (SACU) (updated 1969)	Botswana, Lesotho, Namibia (1990), South Africa, Swaziland	1910 1969	No free movement provisions	5.3	3.2
South Asian Association for Regional Cooperation (SAARC)	Afghanistan, Bangladesh, Bhutan, India, Maldives, Nepal, Pakistan, Sri Lanka	1985	No free movement provisions	5.3	2.8
Caribbean Community/CSME (CARICOM) (previously Caribbean Free Trade Area)	Antigua and Barbuda, Bahamas (1983), Barbados, Belize, Dominica, Grenada, Guyana, Haiti (2002), Jamaica, Montserrat, Saint Kitts and Nevis, Saint Lucia, Saint Vincent and the Grenadines, Suriname (1995), Trinidad and Tobago (CSME members exclude Bahamas, Montserrat, and Haiti)	1965 1973 Community	2005–6 single-market economy (twelve states) which allows for free movement of skilled workers (eight categories); also GATS Mode 4–type provisions	4.0 CSME	1.8 CSME
Mano River Union (MRU) (reactivated 2008)	Côte d'Ivoire (2008), Guinea (1980), Liberia, Sierra Leone	1973 2008	No free movement provisions	3.7	3.2
Latin American Integration Association (LAIA) (previously Latin American Free Trade Association)	Argentina, Bolivia, Brazil, Chile, Colombia, Cuba, Ecuador, Mexico, Panama, Paraguay, Peru, Uruguay, Venezuela	1960 1980	No free movement provisions	3.5	2.3
North American Free Trade Agreement (NAFTA)	Canada, Mexico, United States	1994	1994 GATS Mode 4 provisions, extended to some classes of skilled workers	3.3	2.3
West African Economic and Monetary Union (WAEMU)	Benin, Burkina Faso, Côte d'Ivoire, Guinea Bissau (1997), Mali, Niger, Senegal, Togo	1994	1994 "progressive implementation" of free movement of workers and self-employed	3.2	1.8
Communauté Economique des Pays des Grands Lacs (CEPGL) (relaunched in 2008)	Burundi; Democratic Republic of the Congo, Rwanda	1976 2008	1976 progressive implementation of visa-free entry and right of establishment Intrastate and regional conflicts prevent implementation	3.1	1.9

(continued)

Table 4.2
(*continued*)

Regional economic organization	Membership	Date	Mobility provisions	Implementation	Low-high ratio	Low-mean ratio
East African Community (EAC)	Burundi (2009), Kenya, Rwanda (2009), South Sudan* (2016), Tanzania, Uganda	1967–77 2000	2010 common market with free movement provisions	Work permits still required, although Rwanda and Kenya dropped requirement	2.9	2.0
Central European Free Trade Agreement (CEFTA)	Albania, Bosnia and Herzegovina, Kosovo,* Macedonia,* Moldova, Montenegro, Serbia (prior members: Bulgaria, Croatia, Czech Republic, Hungary, Poland, Romania, Slovakia, Slovenia)	1992	No free movement provisions		2.6	1.8
Mercosur (Common Market of the South)	Argentina, Bolivia (2015), Brazil, Paraguay, Uruguay, Venezuela (2012); associate members: Chile (1991), Colombia (1994), Ecuador (1994), Peru (1991), Suriname (1994)	1991	2002 Mercosur Residency Agreement, in force 2009; includes full and associate members	Domestic legislation not adopted; must go through a review desk and other procedures with immigration agency	2.3 2.2 (M-4)	1.9 1.5 (M-4)
Organization of Eastern Caribbean States) (OECS) (previously West Indies Associated States)	*Antigua & Barbuda, Dominica, Grenada, Montserrat, Saint Kitts, Saint Lucia, Saint Vincent and the Grenadines*	*1981*	*2001 Agreement on Economic Union* *2006 OECS Economic Treaty (in force 2010) includes free movement of labor*	*Full implementation is under way*	2.2	1.4
Andean Community of Nations (previously Andean Pact)	Bolivia, Colombia, Ecuador, Peru	1964 1996	2003 Decision 545: Andean labor migration instrument	Employment contract necessary; contract, seasonal, and border worker facilitated movement	2.1	1.7

	Members	Year	Movement provisions	Low-high ratio	Low-mean ratio
Gulf Cooperation Council (GCC)	Bahrain, Kuwait, Oman, Qatar, Saudi Arabia, United Arab Emirates	1981	2001 Unified Economic Agreement authorizes free movement of labor	2.1	1.2
Central American Integration System (CAIS) (previously Central American Common Market)	Belize (2000), Costa Rica, Dominican Republic (2013), El Salvador, Guatemala, Honduras, Nicaragua, Panama	1960–73, 1993	Access to labor market governed by national immigration legislation; 2006 C-4 (El Salvador, Guatemala, Honduras and Nicaragua) common internal borders and passport	1.7 (C-4), 4.0 (CAIS)	1.4 (C-4), 2.2 (CAIS)
European Union	Twenty-eight member states (twenty-seven when the UK negotiates departure; see chapter 5)	1957	Freedom of movement with six-month maximum for employment search and adequate resources	1.3 (1957)	
European Free Trade Association (EFTA)	Remaining members 2016: Iceland, Liechtenstein,* Norway, Switzerland	1959, 1994	European Economic Area Agreement signed in 1994 providing for freedom of movement within EU/EFTA area; Switzerland is not in EEA but has bilateral freedom of movement agreement with the EU	1.2 (1994)	1.1

Note: The low-high ratio represents the ratio of GDP/pc/PPP of the wealthiest country relative to the poorest county in the REO at the time of the agreement. The low-mean ratio represents the ratio of GDP/pc/PPP of the mean wealth of the REO relative to the poorest country. REOs set in italics have implemented broad but not unlimited freedom of movement.

*Indicates no information on GDP/pc/PPP and therefore exclusion from calculations.

Sources: IOM (2007) and additional sources as noted: For SADC, Rubia (2011); Tralac (2016); Kitimbo (2014). For ECCAS, ECCAS Treaty (1983); Meyer (2015). For CEMAC, Gatsi Tazo (2009); Sommo Pende (2010); "Cémac" (2013). For ASEAN, Jurje and Lavenex (2015); Stephenson and Hufbauer (2011). For ECOWAS, Kitimbo (2014); Adepoju, van Noorloos, and Zoomers (2010); Cronjé (2013, 2014). For EEU, Schenk (2015). For CARICOM, CARICOM (2016); "14,000 CARICOM" (2014); "Study" (2011); Biswaro (2011); Watson, Leander-Watson, and Allbrook (2007). For NAFTA, Stephenson and Hufbauer (2011); Jurje and Lavenex (2015). For WAEMU, Stephenson and Hufbauer (2011); Ibriga and Sourwema (2014). For CEPGL, CEPGL (1976); Kabamba (2003–4); "Amendement" (1980); "CEPGL" (2014). For EAC, Kitimbo (2014); Rubia (2011); EAC (2015); Stephenson and Hufbauer (2011); Ogalo (2012). For Mercosur, Horizon Brazil (n.d.); Margheritis (2013); Acosta (2016); Acosta and Geddes (2014); Acosta and Freier (2015); Cernadas (2013). For OECS, OECS (2010); "Free Movement of Persons" (2014); Webbie (2015). For the Andean Community of Nations, Gabriel Pérez et al. (2013); Baquero-Herrera (2005). The GCC, EU, and EFTA are covered extensively in chapter 5.

foresee some type of labor facilitation but remain ineffective due to lack of implementation by the member states. To ensure that our assessments are accurate, we researched each REO and provide citations that support our empirical findings.

By our count, almost one-third of the twenty-eight regional organizations, nine, provide no access to national labor markets. Of those that do, the EU (and associated organizations, the European Free Trade Association [EFTA] and the European Economic Area [EEA]), the GCC, and the OECS have the only fully implemented freedom of movement, addressed in chapter 5.[15] As anticipated, these REOs implemented freedom of movement only when differences in wages, working conditions, and standards of living were low. And as will be demonstrated in chapter 5, because there is little economic incentive to move, migratory flows were small and reciprocal.

Asian regional organizations, whose countries encompass large disparities in wealth, have made few provisions for labor facilitation. Although Russia's efforts to create a single market in the Eurasian Economic Community look good on paper, labor mobility remains dominated by national regulations.

African regional organizations have often modeled their economic unions on the EU's promise of four freedoms; sooner or later, protocols are negotiated with free movement provisions across the continent. More recently, the Abuja Treaty (1991), which established the African Economic Community, called on "the Regional Economic Communities (RECs) and their Member States to consider the adoption and implementation of appropriate protocols in order to progressively achieve the free movement of persons, and to ensure the enjoyment of the right of residence, the right of establishment and access to legal employment in host countries" (African Union 2006). This has been supplemented by the Joint Labor Migration Program for Africa (ILO 2015; Manuh 2016). However, despite their aspirations, many of the agreements remain on paper only. Even ECOWAS, with a longer history of attempting regional mobility and freedom of movement, has a poor record of implementing labor mobility provisions. In fact, the United Nations Commission on Africa (UNECA 2016) does not even rank African countries on freedom of movement; they are ranked only on mobility provisions that permit visa-free entry for citizens of member states.[16] And even on this narrower definition of mobility, the average level of implementation in African REOs, on a scale of 0 to 1, is less than .5. These are all REOs where the disparities in wealth are at least four to one, that is, the wealthiest state has four times the per capita gross national income in purchasing power parity terms (GNI/pc/PPP) as the poorest state in the regional organization. And, in a large number of cases, the wealth disparities are even more substantial, up to fifty to one. In these cases, documented flows reflect migration from the poorer, less stable states to the wealthier, more stable states (Castles, de Haas, and Miller

2014). Because receiving states prefer national control over the type and number of international migrants at any specific time, they remain unwilling to implement mobility agreements even when they are negotiated and ratified. This portrait of the lack of mobility on the African continent is confirmed by a recent *Economist* article ("A Dream" 2017): "It is still remarkably hard for Africans to get around their own continent."

There is more promise in the Americas, largely because wealth disparities are substantially smaller, approaching the ratio of wealth disparities among European states when they negotiated freedom of movement in the 1940s and 1950s. Here the ratio of wealthiest to poorest state is in the range of 1.3 to 2.2. This represents a potential wage premium of 30 to 100 percent—significant but not significant enough to propel large, one-way movement, given the material and nonmaterial costs of moving away from home and family. This is reflected in the documented flows in Latin America, which remain lower than the global average of 2.9 percent and far lower than the level of migration in wealthy OECD countries (Castles, de Haas, and Miller 2014). Nonetheless, even in these states, movement is mostly limited to high-skilled professionals or has not been fully implemented. CARICOM has implemented freedom of movement for specified categories of professionals, and the smaller grouping of island states, the OECS, has recently (2010) negotiated and is in the process of implementing region-wide access to its labor markets for citizens of member states. Mercosur adopted a Residency Protocol in 2002 (in force in 2009), which promises freedom of movement but faces delays in implementation due to lack of translation of the protocol into domestic legislation (Margheritis 2013; Acosta 2016; also see below). The North American Free Trade Agreement (NAFTA) provides expanded GATS Mode 4 access to a broader array of professionals, that is, it facilitates specific categories of high-skilled migration. This is a relatively new phenomenon in the region. A little more than a decade ago, Temprano Arroyo (2002, 4.6) argued that "the sub-regions under analysis have made little progress in liberalising the intra-regional flow of labour, in contrast with the EU." However, the landscape is changing quickly.

GCC is another anomaly regarding freedom of movement in the Global South. It also appears to have both adopted and implemented freedom of movement for citizens of member states; it, too, represents one of the lowest ratios between the wealthiest and poorest states, a ratio of 2.1 from the poorest to the wealthiest state and a ratio of only 1.2 from the poorest state to the regional average.

Analysis. Although states prefer efficient labor markets that allow employers to hire workers when demand expands and lay off workers when demand contracts, states continue to seek national control over labor markets, vetting the number, characteristics, and length of stay of immigrants. Only when market mechanisms are unable to meet demands do states contemplate negotiations to facilitate larger migratory flows. REOs do not, in themselves, overcome the differences in preferences we have described between sending and receiving states. Many regional organizations include neither short-term mobility provisions nor labor market access. In those regions that do adopt, either as a future goal or as a right of citizens, facilitated labor market access, that access is usually implemented only for high-skilled labor for which there remains a demand even when low-skilled labor is experiencing unemployment, or when relative equality of wealth and living conditions promise reciprocal rather than one-way flows.

We have explored twenty-eight prominent REOs and have found only four that appear to have fully implemented freedom of movement, those where the standard of living is similar so that the distinction between sending and receiving states becomes moot. Two are European, the EU and the EEA, which incorporates freedom of movement for the members of EFTA. The other two also reflect economic conditions that promise reciprocal movement and low mobility and indicate that the Global North is not the only area where conditions exist for freedom of movement: GCC and OECS. Our conclusions are shared by Bhatnagar and Manning, who argue that "achievements in regional trade negotiations do not differ greatly from those made by the rest of the world when it comes to regulating the entry of foreign service providers under Mode 4, even in a relatively dynamic trading region like ASEAN" (2005, 173).

BILATERAL AGREEMENTS

Our theory suggests that BLAs should be the exception rather than the rule. It is difficult to marshal evidence to support this position as there is no required repository for these agreements and no agreed baseline against which to compare the number of agreements. Moreover, there are many different types of agreements, including those that privilege cooperation on short-term mobility rather than on voluntary migration—defined as movement across international borders for at least one year. And the contents of the agreements change over time.[17] Nonetheless, we survey the quantitative evidence available and demonstrate that few countries actually negotiate bilateral agreements. We also provide a most similar case analysis, juxtaposing the United Kingdom and France, which traces the variation in market failure that generates the impetus to negotiate BLAs on the part of France and the absence in the United Kingdom. Finally, we trace the trajectory of BLAs and conclude that most agreements in the most recent wave actually represent immigration control rather than facilitation of migration.

Survey of Quantitative Evidence. No one knows for sure how many BLAs have been negotiated, how many remain in force, the contents of the agreements, or the signatories.[18] Nonetheless, a recent ILO report estimates both formal and informal BLAs on low-skilled migration at 358 (Wickramasekara 2015). An earlier survey by the OECD performed in 2003, which included both short- and long-term employment agreements, counted 277 unique agreements in OECD member states (OECD 2004). This represents only about one-tenth of existing bilateral investment treaties, another bilateral mechanism for states to cooperate internationally on FDI (Elkins, Guzman, and Simmons 2006).

The 2003 OECD survey identifies multiple types of agreements including seasonal employment, project-based workers, guest workers, trainee and apprenticeship programs, cross-border employment, working holidaymakers, and others (Bobeva and Garson 2004). Only 19 percent of the total were the typical "guest worker" agreements that allow migrants access to host labor markets for at least one year. To add to the confusion, the agreements can take at least two forms, formal and informal. A memorandum of agreement (MOA) is a binding document, whereas a memorandum of understanding (MOU) is nonbinding. To this list of BLAs, recent research has added agreements that expand GATS Mode 4–type agreements negotiated at the bilateral level. And some migration arrangements are now embedded in trade agreements or "framework agreements" that address a broad array of economic ties between countries (Kunz, Lavenex, and Panizzon 2011).

Of the 277 unique agreements, many are with the same countries, dealing with different categories of labor. In Germany, for example, of the 57 agreements, only 23 countries are affected. Germany has signed at least seven agreements with Poland and five agreements each with several Central European neighbors. Canada favors seasonal worker agreements, while France and Switzerland emphasize trainee programs. Australia and New Zealand promote working holiday exchanges, and only Germany appears to favor the traditional guest worker programs.

Many of the bilateral agreements collected by the OECD cover short-term employment rather than long-term labor market access and therefore do not meet the criteria of voluntary labor migration. Seasonal employment agreements generally cover migrant workers who work abroad for less than one year. Training agreements also fall predominantly under the category of short-term employment rather than voluntary labor migration. Many of these agreements are reciprocal, and most quotas are in the range of fifty to two hundred. Working holiday agreements originated in Australia and New Zealand as reciprocal agreements to allow young adults to travel and support themselves while traveling. The agreements are now virtually all between wealthy Western democracies and are reciprocal. Many of the programs have overall quotas or country-specific quotas.

There are many ways of thinking about the import of these agreements, but regardless of the measure employed, BLAs are the exception rather than the rule. For OECD countries, there are 595 possible bilateral agreements that could be reached among the 35 member states. The 153 unique agreements between OECD member states are reduced to 120 country dyads (because of the multiple agreements between two countries); this amounts to 20.1 percent of the total possible dyad agreements. If we think of the agreements in terms of agreement years (between 1947 and 2003), the possible number of agreements then becomes 33,915. The dates of enforcement are not available, but if each were in force for one year, this would represent 0.4 percent of the total possible agreement years. If each were in force for ten years, that would represent 4.5 percent of the possible agreement years. If we took only guest worker agreements, as these are the only agreements that represent access to labor markets for at least one year, this would represent 6.2 percent if the agreements were in force over the entire time frame. The vast majority of the agreements became moot because of freedom of movement within the EU. Because the data are so poor, the only real conclusion that can be drawn from this overview of OECD BLAs is that they are the exception rather than the rule, even in countries that value institutionalized agreements.

The Determinants of BLAs. It is widely held that the recovery of Europe in the postwar period was dependent on the availability of cheap immigrant labor (Kindleberger 1967). The question addressed here is whether the availability of cheap immigrant labor required international cooperation—negotiations between states to achieve the desired goal of obtaining larger flows of immigrant labor. France and the United Kingdom provide a nice comparison in that both experienced strong labor market demands in the early postwar period: France signed twelve BLAs with nine countries in the two decades after World War II, the United Kingdom only one (OECD 2004). France provides an example of a country with a strong demand for labor but insufficient networks to link that demand to the supply of foreign workers in neighboring countries as well as farther afield. The United Kingdom provides a contrasting case of already established migrant networks that linked the demand for labor through informal migrant network channels, bringing colonial and Commonwealth citizens to the United Kingdom to fill labor market vacancies in the absence of BLAs. These two cases illustrate our argument about the need for international cooperation only when market mechanisms fail to equilibrate domestic labor markets. The French case also demonstrates how the negotiated agreements became moot once market mechanisms developed to respond to surges in the demand for labor.

Bilateral Labor Agreements in France. In France directly after World War II, pressure came from many quarters to relax the immigration restrictions implemented during the Great Depression.[19] "Populationists" promoted the idea of French demographic growth through immigration to overcome both war losses and low rates of population growth. Alfred Sauvy, head of the newly created National Institute of Demographic Studies, proposed a figure of 5.3 million permanent immigrants. The French national planning commission (Conseil General du Plan), in light of the demands of postwar recovery and in response to employers' interests, drew up the first national economic plan for the 1946 to 1951 period, projecting a need for 1.3 million foreign workers, or more than 200,000 net entrants per year. This consensus for greater immigration was translated into the creation of the National Office of Immigration (Office national d'immigration, or ONI) via the ordinance of 2 November 1945. The ONI was granted a monopoly over recruitment of immigrant workers. The populationist side of the equation was reflected in the 1946 Law 46-550 that allowed migrants with the appropriate residence and work permits and with adequate housing to be joined by their families.

The labor shortages alluded to above were addressed in the first instance by the ONI. In theory, when confronting a labor shortage, employers were to request foreign workers from the ONI, either by name or by job classification. The ONI would recruit workers in the country of origin, evaluate their health and skill levels, and send approved workers to employers endowed with the appropriate work and residence permits. This structure reduced not only information asymmetries between French labor markets and workers abroad but also adjustment costs for the recruited workers by providing them with free visas, transportation, medical and skills exams, and often housing upon arrival in France. To facilitate international labor market recruitment, France negotiated agreements with Italy in 1946 and 1951, West Germany in 1950, Greece in 1954, and Spain in 1961. Because an adequate supply of foreign workers was still lacking, the government reached farther afield to Portugal and Morocco (1963), Tunisia (1964), and Turkey and Yugoslavia (1965) (Money 1999).[20]

In their scramble to obtain an adequate labor supply, however, employers found the ONI recruitment system cumbersome and time-consuming. They therefore revived their prewar practice of recruiting workers directly from source countries or hired resident foreigners who lacked the appropriate permits. Thus a laissez-faire system of immigration was inaugurated. This practice was actively accommodated by the state through the establishment of a process whereby immigrants with employment contracts but without the proper work and residence permits were "regularized." By 1968, more than 80 percent of all immigrants legally installed in France during that year had been regularized bypassing the ONI and therefore the negotiated BLA (Tapinos 1975). Thus, in France, BLAs initiated the flow of immigrants under conditions of severe labor market shortages. Once the flows began, however, market mechanisms and networks kicked in to facilitate additional immigration. Employers actively recruited in foreign countries, reducing information asymmetries. More importantly, migrant networks acted as recruitment agents, providing information to family and friends at home about job opportunities, wages, and working conditions in France. It is little wonder that the last BLA was signed in 1965. The BLAs inaugurated the flows but were quickly overtaken by private actors. The initial informational asymmetries that generated the need for formal cooperation between states were erased by employer recruitment practices and informal migrant networks.

In initiating these agreements, the sending countries were able to extract concessions, as our theory suggests. The type of concession was informed by the ILO's "Model Bilateral Labor Agreement" (Recommendation 86, 1949) that provided a template for bilateral negotiations. Other researchers confirm the details of the French case on a broader scale. According to Miller and Martin (1982, 42), "Western European bilateral labor agreements with emigrant labor-sending nations generally conformed to the international norms established by the ILO's convention 97 and recommendation 86." Consequently, most treaties contain similar requirements for translated contracts, signature of contracts prior to departure, and specification of the host society's role in recruitment, transportation costs, medical examinations, family entry, adequate housing, and equality of treatment.[21]

However, we have reason to be skeptical of the benefits to migrants from sending countries for two reasons. First, most immigrants did not enter under the auspices of these bilateral agreements but came through informal channels, so they did not benefit from travel and other benefits contained in the bilateral agreement. Second, the focus of these bilateral labor accords was on recruitment procedures. Most did not include quotas but relied on employer requests to fill specific labor market shortages. Although these BLAs contained some basic protections for migrant workers, which were not always implemented, these agreements were basically recruitment tools to link employers with a migrant labor supply. Miller and Martin (1982, 43) quote the conclusions of Maurice Flory, one of the leading European experts on bilateral manpower treaties: "The treaties were primarily written to ensure the provision of sufficient quantities of foreigners who were young, healthy, and capable of doing often difficult work. The interests of the foreign workers and their native societies were poorly protected because most treaties did not contain concrete, detailed provisions for foreign-worker vocational training, adequate living conditions, socioeconomic rights, and so on."

Moreover, the equality of treatment provision "did not commit host governments to specific actions in favor of migrant workers" (Miller and Martin 1982, 42). Because of the short term of the agreements, they could be abrogated at any time. As Miller and Martin (43) note, "The unilateral nature of the decisions to halt labor recruitment testified to the essentially unequal nature of Western European bilateral labor agreements signed in the 1960s." And, in the case of France, these agreements did not actually cover the vast majority of the migrant labor force.

The Absence of Bilateral Labor Agreements in the United Kingdom. The United Kingdom did not follow the path of France and other continental countries in adopting BLAs. The single agreement included in Table 4.2, signed with Belgium, appears to have facilitated no Belgian immigration—Belgium itself was a receiving state at that time.[22] Rather, the United Kingdom employed unilateral government programs and employer-based recruitment to deal with labor market shortages, supplemented with migrant networks of Irish, Commonwealth, and colonial workers.

Kathleen Paul (1997, chap. 1) vividly describes British labor market shortages subsequent to World War II; the government not only recruited foreign workers but actively recruited women to join the labor force and called for school holidays to allow children to help with agricultural harvests. Yet the British government did not feel the need to negotiate BLAs to facilitate the flow of labor. We argue that this is due to the already established migrant networks and active labor market recruitment by private employers as well as government employers.

The immigration status quo in the United Kingdom after World War II involved three sets of foreign-born populations: the Irish, Commonwealth and colonial citizens, and aliens.[23] Aliens' entry was restricted by legislation enacted in 1905 and 1914, which authorized immigration officers to refuse entry and to deport aliens who were unable to support themselves and their dependents. Immigrants were required to register with the police and to apply for a work permit in order to enter the labor force; their freedom of movement in the United Kingdom was also restricted. However, the Irish and Commonwealth citizens and colonial subjects were governed by the custom of free entry.

In the immediate aftermath of World War II, the British government responded to the demand for additional labor through several unilateral schemes to recruit aliens. The government established the Foreign Labor Committee to oversee recruitment. It organized the Polish Resettlement Corps, the European Volunteer Workers program (Westward Ho!), the Official Italian Recruitment Scheme, the Private Domestic Worker Scheme, other employment schemes to attract single women (Blue Danube, North Sea, and Official Italian Scheme), and the Prisoners of War program (Paul 1997). Through the "aliens" channel, an estimated 345,000 Europeans entered Britain under these schemes over a ten-year period (Paul 1997).

The United Kingdom, however, had two other classes of migrants who were not controlled at entry and who did not need work permits to join the labor force: the Irish and colonial and Commonwealth citizens.[24] Ireland has a long and troubled history with Great Britain, beginning with colonization in the seventeenth century. It won independence in 1921 and subsequently withdrew from the British Commonwealth in 1949. Nonetheless, the 1948 British Nationality Act stipulated that the Irish in Britain were to be regarded as "neither British subjects nor aliens but Irish citizens with all the rights of British subjecthood" (Paul 1997, 98). The Irish were free to come and go, with unlimited access to the British labor market. This proved to be an important channel that supplemented the domestic labor force in numbers that far exceeded the "aliens" channel. Paul (1997, 90) reports that "on average in the period 1946 through 1962, between 50,000 and 60,000 Irish men and women entered the UK labor market for the first time each year," a number almost twice that of alien entries.

The second channel proved equally important. After the war, in light of the gradual disintegration of the empire, the 1948 British Nationality Act created a distinction between citizens of the United Kingdom and colonial and Commonwealth citizens. But Commonwealth citizens as well as British subjects maintained the right to enter British territory freely and retained access to all rights and privileges of citizenship, including voting. Registration for British citizenship required only twelve months' residence (Money 1999).

During World War II, the British government and private employers called on imperial subjects and Commonwealth citizens to support the war effort in Britain. There was a large influx of both groups into the United Kingdom during the war. Labor market shortages in the United Kingdom, along with immigration restrictions on European migrants, led employers (including government employers such as the National Health Service) to tap immigrants from the Commonwealth whose entrance remained uncontrolled. Although colonial subjects recruited to work in Britain during the war were initially sent home, when economic conditions in their home countries provided limited opportunities, they quickly returned to the United Kingdom (Money 1999). These were the migrants who initiated the migrant networks from the Caribbean and the Indian subcontinent; these migrants, followed by their family and friends, rapidly took up employment in the United Kingdom, obviating the need for BLAs. Although statistics are not readily available for total immigration into the United Kingdom in this period, new Commonwealth immigration exceeded Irish immigration by 1955 and was more than triple the level of Irish immigration by 1961 (Money 1999).

Analysis. The juxtaposition of France and the United Kingdom suggests that the respective governments handled labor market shortages, common to both countries, in different ways. In the United Kingdom, employer recruitment and migrant networks alleviated the need to recruit immigrant labor via BLAs. In France, the government intervened to start the immigrant labor flow through BLAs, but once the pump was primed, France had little need for additional agreements. In both cases, the import of migrant labor was halted at or before the 1973–74 oil crisis. The decline in the use of bilateral agreements after the oil shocks demonstrates the one-sided nature of this first wave of BLAs.

Although we do not marshal systematic cross-national evidence, we can see patterns similar to France in the Federal Republic of Germany in light of the rapid economic growth after World War II. West Germany, however, had access to a skilled and German-speaking population from the German Democratic Republic and from the expellees from farther east. It was only the construction of the Berlin Wall in 1961 that brought an end to this labor flow, and German labor demand was subsequently met through the construction of a guest worker program. Five of Germany's eight BLAs were negotiated after 1961. Elsewhere in Europe, "the strong economic growth and the resulting labor shortages in the second half of the 1950s and the 1960s induced a number of Western European countries to open up for immigration" (Zimmerman 2005, 431).

Secular Trends in BLAs. Although no characterization incorporates all agreements, we describe "three waves" of BLAs. The first wave of agreements is explained by informational asymmetries in international labor markets due to the costly communication, costly transportation, and lack of migrant networks. The second wave is primarily a function of changes in the international political and economic systems that generated a need for agreements between first-wave receiving states and new sending states and between new receiving states and new sending states. Most recently, there may be a third wave of agreements that employ BLAs as a method of restricting migration and controlling undocumented migration, either on their own or as a complement to bilateral readmission agreements (discussed in chapter 3; see also Sáez 2013).

Table 4.3 provides a summary of the initial wave of BLAs in Europe. The rise of immigrant labor in Europe after World War II is widely known, but much less research has focused on whether the movements were spontaneous or generated by cooperation between migrant-sending and migrant-receiving states. The number of actual agreements between sending and receiving states is small even in this initial period when labor market demands were acute and there appeared to be little knowledge of the long-term consequences of guest worker programs. As is visible in Table 4.3, many European receiving countries initially signed agreements with a small number of neighboring sending states. In the 1960s, agreements extended to Mediterranean countries. The last agreement in this first wave was signed in 1968.[25]

Table 4.3
First-Wave Bilateral Labor Agreements in Europe, 1946–68

Receiving country	Sending country	Year of agreement
Belgium	Italy	1946, 1954
France	Italy	1946, 1947, 1951
Netherlands	Italy	1948, 1960
Germany*	Italy	1955
Luxembourg	Italy	1957
France**	West Germany	1950
United Kingdom	Belgium	1947
France	Spain	1956, 1961
Germany*	Spain	1960
Germany*	Greece	1960
France**	Greece	1954
Germany*	Morocco	1963
France	Morocco	1963
Netherlands	Morocco	1964
Germany*	Portugal	1964
France**	Portugal	1963
France	Tunisia	1964
Germany*	Tunisia	1965
Germany	Turkey	1961
Austria	Turkey	1964
Belgium	Turkey	1964
France	Turkey	1964
Netherlands	Turkey	1964
Sweden	Turkey	1967
Germany*	Yugoslavia	1968
France**	Yugoslavia	1965
Total agreements	26	

Sources: *"Anwebeabkommen" (n.d.); **Money (1999); other countries, OECD (2004).

The ILO notes a surge in BLAs in the 1990s, continuing into the 2000s. Table 4.4 provides an overview of these agreements beginning in the 1990s. We argue that this second wave was responding predominantly to new labor market shortages, both in Europe and around the globe, generating new flows of migrant labor. If the demand for labor in Europe in the "trente glorieuses"—the thirty glorious years of economic growth in Europe between 1945 and 1975—generated a demand for BLAs, that came to an abrupt halt by the first oil crisis in 1973–74. But the flip side of economic stagnation in Europe and other OECD countries was the rapid accretion of wealth in the Gulf oil states and their efforts to diversify their economies. This generated a rapidly expanding demand for labor—both skilled and unskilled—in the Gulf oil states. The growing oil wealth generated in the Persian Gulf region allowed those states to undertake an unprecedented number of development projects. The GCC member states emerged "as one of the largest regions relying on temporary labor migrants since the early 1970s" (Rahman 2012, 218). The initial reliance on neighboring Arab workers generated political and security concerns by the autocratic leaders in the region. These concerns, along with the growing demand for foreign labor, exerted a shift to other countries, especially from the Indian subcontinent and from Southeast Asia (Kapiszewski 2004; Rahman 2012). It is difficult to trace whether the GCC countries signed BLAs in the period to generate flows from Asian countries that were, until that time, relatively unconnected. It is possible that private recruiters were able to meet the labor market demands of the GCC countries without the help of state intervention.

In Southeast Asia, by the 1980s, following decolonization and the rise of independent nation-states, several states in the region achieved sustained levels of high economic growth based on export-led development strategies (Haggard 1990). The expansion of job opportunities for their citizens in the Gulf States and East Asia further exacerbated the situation and labor shortages became critical, first in Singapore and then in Malaysia, followed by Thailand. According to Kaur (2010, 6), "Labor migration entered a new phase in Southeast Asia after the 1970s and has resumed its considerable role in the region's geopolitics, coinciding with the independent Southeast Asian states' greater integration into the global economy, the redistribution and relocation of manufacturing production to the region and regional labour shortages." Since the data begin in 1990, we miss any agreements negotiated by the Gulf oil states and the Asian tigers in the 1970s and 1980s.

In Europe, the agreements signed in the 1990s were with the countries of Central Europe after the fall of the Berlin Wall in 1989. As is well known, these countries had authoritarian regimes that prevented the exit of their citizens. Once those regimes were overthrown in the "velvet revolutions," European countries experiencing labor market shortages again resorted to BLAs. Finland signed agreements with Russia in 1992 and Estonia in 1991. Germany signed agreements with Bulgaria, Croatia, the Czech Republic, Hungary, Poland, Romania, the Slovak Republic, Slovenia, Latvia, Albania, and Estonia, from 1989 to 2002. Greece signed agreements with Albania and Bulgaria in 1995. Italy signed an agreement with Albania in 1997. Spain signed agreements with Romania and Poland in 2002 (OECD 2004). Not all countries with a history of BLAs signed new agreements. Some that had previously been on the sending side of the agreements, such as Spain and Italy, became countries of immigration and began signing bilateral agreements. These agreements were predominantly for seasonal employment but included some guest worker programs as well. More recently, European countries such as Norway and the United Kingdom have signed agreements that are specific to shortages in particular labor market sectors, such as health care, engineering, and other high-skilled areas. Of the BLAs signed between 1990 and 2004, 75 percent were signed by European countries as the Central European countries prepared for accession to the EU in 2004 and 2007. Accession did not promise instantaneous access to freedom of movement—there was a seven-year transition period.[26]

All of these examples demonstrate that some economic sectors in some states experience labor market shortages at some points in time. Migration is one, although not the only, solution. International migrants in labor surplus countries can be matched with job opportunities in labor scarce countries. If market forces work well, government intervention in international migration is superfluous, so we anticipate few instances of states actively pursuing agreements in the international system. However, if market mechanisms are not in place, international agreements may become necessary to facilitate international labor flows.

In the most recent period, there are probably at least two types of third-wave agreements (see Table 4.5 on the regional and temporal distribution of BLAs). The first is generated by the demand for high-skilled workers in wealthy Western

Table 4.4
Second-Wave Bilateral Labor Agreements, 1990–2004

Period	Africa	Asia	Europe and the Americas	Total	Percentage of total
1990–94	0	0	11	11	21.6
1995–99	2	4	4	10	19.6
2000–2004	1	6	23	30	58.8
Total	3	10	38	51	
Percentage of total	5.9	19.6	74.5		100.0

Source: Wickramasekara (2015).

Table 4.5
Third-Wave Bilateral Labor Agreements, 2005–14

Period	Africa	Asia	Europe and the Americas	Total	Percentage of total
2005–9	17	32	10	59	69.4
2010–14	2	18	6	26	30.6
Total	19	50	16	85	
Percentage of total	22.4	58.8	18.8		100.0

Source: Wickramasekara (2015).

democracies. The second perverts the agreements into immigration control for which access to the receiving country's labor market is the reward for controlling undocumented migrant flows.

In the contemporary global economy, the watchword is shortages of high-skilled labor, for which wealthy countries are exploiting labor resources from the developing world. According to the McKinsey Global Institute, "The world could have 40 million too few college-educated graduates by 2020. In the United States and other developed economies in North America and Europe, companies will require 16 to 18 million more college educated workers than will be available in 2020" (Wright 2012). Zimmerman (2005, 427) argues that "all developed economies face a strong and increasing excess demand for skilled labour, fostered by technological change, population ageing, and a subsequent decline in the future native European workforce." This is echoed in the prognosis for specific countries and for specific economic sectors. For example, Wright (2012) claims that "a major finding of the study is that the German labor market cannot provide enough nursing care professionals for the elderly care sector by 2030. Secondly, most of the other European Union member states are facing similar challenges, at least in the long run." Constant and Tien (2011, 6) reinforce this impression for Germany more broadly: "In contrast to other developed economies, the German economy managed to recover rather swiftly and vigorously from the global economic downturn of 2008. . . . Currently, Germany's problems are related to labor supply shortages." However, BLAs to recruit skilled labor are important only in their absence: less than 20 percent of the BLAs in the contemporary period are generated in the Global North. These are primarily associated with the Philippines, covering the export of Filipino nurses (OECD 2004).

The second type of third-wave agreements rewards sending countries' immigration control efforts with limited access to the receiving countries' labor markets. These agreements provide temporary migration quotas of ten to three hundred places annually for efforts to quell undocumented migration or as a reward for signing a bilateral readmission agreement. We draw this conclusion based on a detailed analysis of several recent BLAs—the full set of the Philippines agreements, detailed in chapter 7, the MOU between the Laos and Thailand, and the summary analysis of 144 recent bilateral agreements provided by the ILO. The modest protections provided for migrant labor in the European BLAs of the 1950s and 1960s are almost completely missing from the third wave of BLAs. In general, these new agreements are short, spell out recruitment structures, and, at best, require written contracts for the migrant workers. Another distinguishing feature of the new wave of BLAs, at least in Asia, is the systematic incorporation of private recruitment agencies to take over what, in Europe, had been governmental recruitment activities. This delegation may represent gains in efficiency, but without adequate oversight, it also represents yet another crack in the wall of migrant rights.

The ILO compared 144 BLAs to the twenty-nine articles in the 1949 ILO Recommendation 86 Model Bilateral Labor Agreement. These protections include access to adequate and correct information, provisions for facilitated entry, equal treatment to that of domestic workers, and supervision of workplace rights and safety. We evaluated the Lao/Thai MOU against the twenty-nine articles and found provisions for only four, and even for those, only nominal protections are provided rather than adopting the verbiage of the Model Agreement. The MOU is really about recruitment and control of undocumented migration in the guise of reducing human trafficking. The goals are for effective recruitment and the return of the migrants at the end of their contracts. One of the most egregious components of the agreement, in contrast with the Model Agreement that calls for return transportation provided by someone other than the migrant, is the agreement to tax the migrant 15 percent of monthly wages to pay for the return.

The survey by the ILO provides only a slightly rosier picture in the larger survey of 144 BLAs. The protections that are provided in the fewest agreements are equality of treatment and supervision on living conditions, exactly those elements of the Model Agreement that provide the most protection for migrant workers. The most frequently provided protections, Articles 1, 5, and 6, are concerned only with solving market failures—providing information to facilitate the matching of workers to employers.

Analysis. The ILO has touted "a 'revival' of bilateral and multilateral agreements between countries of origin and destination . . . [which] have drawn inspiration from the ILO Model Agreement on Temporary and Permanent Employment" (ILO n.d.-a). We argue that the rosy assessment of the ILO is overdrawn. European agreements generally do contain migrant worker protections and guarantees of equality to local workers, but many agreements between receiving states elsewhere and other countries of the Global South are short on protection and long on recruitment. In chapter 7, on migrant rights, we demonstrate a connection between the strength of domestic labor movements and the national protection of human rights to the rights of migrants. This suggests that countries with weak labor movements and that have authoritarian regimes that fail to protect the human rights of their citizens are likely to be states where migrant rights are abused as well.

Moreover, although states continue to negotiate BLAs, they remain the exception to the rule that most migrant flows are governed by national regulations, obviating the need for cooperation between states. Where agreements are negotiated, they now tend to take the form of nonbinding MOUs and, because of the imbalance in power between sending and receiving states, serve primarily to facilitate recruitment rather than to protect migrant workers. The most recent spate of BLAs tends to emphasize immigration control rather than recruitment.

Contemporary observers of BLAs often echo the comments of observers of first-wave BLAs. Martin (2011, 1), for example, notes, "So far BLAs have concerned only a very small share of total bilateral migration flows between the countries involved, their implementation has caused quite a lot of frustration in countries of origin and they have problems of sustainability and continuity over time." This observation confirms our hypothesis that BLAs are the exception rather than the rule.

ALTERNATIVE EXPLANATIONS

There is little by way of research and theory that specifically address the sources of cooperation to *facilitate migration*. This is likely because of the perception that, in the contemporary period, receiving states desire fewer migrants than sending states would like to export (Joppke 1998). However, generically, economists point to the global welfare gains of relaxing immigration restrictions and to the externalities that incentivize cooperation. These gains are not trivial. Hamilton and Whalley (1984) posit that global gross domestic product would double if states opened their doors to migration. Dani Rodrik (2002) argues that facilitating migration should be central to the global negotiating agenda as the gains from migration are expected to be twenty-five times higher than continued reduction of barriers to trade. The potential for global welfare gains motivates the research on cooperation on migration policies.

Timothy Hatton (2007) provides an important overview of the possibilities for international cooperation on migration. He explores the parallels between trade and migration and points out that the key difference between the two is not public attitudes toward trade and migration—on both issues the public is skeptical of greater openness—but the fact that trade is based on comparative advantage and generates reciprocal flows (globally) whereas migration is based on absolute advantage (based on total factor productivity), which generates one-way flows and a lack of reciprocity. The absence of reciprocity reduces the likelihood of international cooperation on migration (Axelrod 1985). Hatton reviews four possible solutions—issue linkage, regional agreements, temporary migration, and multilateral agreements, although his multilateral scheme precludes entry rights of any type. However, he is pessimistic that any of these will provide the desired international cooperation.

Although we agree with Hatton's observation that flows are one-way, we draw different conclusions. First, we believe the one-way flows are central to the pattern of externalities that arise and that privilege bilateral rather than multilateral cooperation. Second, we agree that reciprocity facilitates cooperation, but the absence of reciprocity does not prevent cooperation—rather we describe two conditions under which cooperation is likely to arise: when the costs of the status quo become costly for receiving states (resulting in either bilateral recruitment agreements or freedom of movement agreements) and when sending states find an institutional forum where they can catapult their preferences to the international stage. Our model can explain when and where the appearance and the actuality of cooperation on migration arise, whereas Hatton's model remains skeptical of the possibility of cooperation.

Alan Sykes (2013) also focuses on the "one-way problem." He begins his presentation with a series of externalities generated by migration: a "terms of trade" externality, the costs of unilateral enforcement of national migration laws, and spillover effects in other receiving countries by shifting immigration flows to them.[27] These externalities are welfare reducing; therefore cooperation represents the potential for welfare enhancement. Sykes argues that the greatest obstacle to cooperation is the "one-way problem," the fact that migratory flows move from poor states to wealthy states. It then becomes difficult to negotiate a cooperative solution that leaves both sides of the bargain better off. Nonetheless, migration externalities reduce global welfare because "governments tend to consider the benefits of policy to their own citizens and constituents but tend to ignore or discount the effects of their policy choices on foreigners." This is the typical problem described by Ronald Coase, and the solution that Coase proposed was that bargaining can lead to Pareto efficient outcomes if transactions costs are sufficiently low (Coase 1960). Like Hatton, Sykes cites the potential for issue linkage, regional agreements for countries with similar levels of development, and circular migration. And, like Hatton, Sykes suggests that sending countries may be unwilling to come to the bargaining table because it is the migrants themselves who are the primary beneficiaries of migration, rather than the home country government.

There are a number of differences between the economists' approaches to international cooperation on migration and ours. First is attention to the status quo and to state preferences for deviation from the status quo. Economists' arguments are constructed based on a notion of Pareto efficient outcomes at the global level. However, global welfare is not central to national politicians' political function. Although we "black box" the construction of state preferences for migration, we acknowledge that states may prefer high or low levels of migration, skilled or unskilled labor flows. The national preference functions recognize that even Pareto efficient outcomes at the national level are likely to divide the gains from bargaining unequally domestically. So these national migration preferences are not likely to generate global Pareto efficient outcomes.

Second, the promise of a welfare-enhancing bargain does not necessarily lead states to the bargaining table. There are two reasons for this. First, the status quo privileges powerful receiving states, and less powerful sending states do not have the resources to bring receiving states to the bargaining table. Second, politicians do not want to disrupt the distribution of gains (costs) of migration that internal negotiations threaten. It is only when the costs of unilateral action rise that receiving states prefer to negotiate to change the status quo.

One component of our explanation is very close to that proposed in a working paper by Margaret Peters (2013). She segregates a specific type of BLA from the many other types and labels it recruitment agreement. She argues that employers face two costs: vacancy costs and screening costs. Vacancy costs are those employers incur when they have insufficient workers to meet production goals. For example, with sufficient demand, a plant might be able to add a second or third shift to increase production but lack the workers to increase production. Likewise, when agricultural crops are ready for harvesting and there are insufficient workers for the harvest, the produce may rot in the fields. This is consistent with our observation that unmet labor market demands are the source of receiving state preferences to change the status quo. Screening costs, on the other hand, are closer to the informational asymmetries we refer to in our framework. That is, employers need workers with specific qualities, be they personal or skill-based. Workers know whether they have the required skills but have no incentive to share that information with employers, as then they might not receive the job offer. Peters argues that vacancy and screening costs generate the need for BLAs. Our argument is similar but focuses on the lack of information available to prospective immigrants rather than screening costs of employers. However, we emphasize the paucity of such agreements in the absence of market failures, even though we have similar ideas about the determinants recruitment agreements. Moreover, we point to the most recent wave of bilateral agreements as being more control-oriented rather than facilitating labor flows.

CONCLUSIONS

In this chapter, we have argued that when states are interested in facilitating international migratory flows, there is usually little need for international cooperation. Unilateral action on the part of states results in Pareto optimal outcomes. The evidence we have presented is centered around the absence of cooperation—the dog that does not bark. It is a difficult task to persuade readers that cooperation does not exist, except as the exception. Nonetheless, we marshal evidence at the multilateral, regional, and bilateral levels.

The central multilateral agreement that deals with the "movement of natural persons"—GATS Mode 4—is strongly anchored in the interests of wealthy Western states to sell services abroad and limits movement to high-skilled professionals for short periods. Fourteen years of GATS negotiations within the WTO have proved insufficient for sending states to change that status quo to one more generous toward their service providers, whether low- or high-skilled.

REOs have some experience with freedom of movement but, as we have demonstrated in our survey of twenty-eight of them, freedom of movement is the exception rather than the rule. It exists only among nations of relatively equal wealth, which allows labor markets to work efficiently across national borders without generating large, unidirectional flows that generate costs for the state.

Bilateral agreements to facilitate flows are employed when states decide that international migration is a preferred solution to sectoral labor market shortages. They overcome incomplete markets due to informational asymmetries and adjustment costs by creating recruitment structures that match international migrants to job openings in receiving states and providing support for migrants to travel to these states and establish themselves. Because of power imbalances, the contents of the agreements usually favor the receiving states' interests in recruitment, although migrant protections are more often included when the receiving states in question have strong labor movements and themselves protect human rights (see chapter 7). The recent proliferation of BLAs is, in large part, a result of the changing global division of labor, which has generated economic growth in the Global South and, hence, labor market shortages elsewhere in the world. However, many recent agreements cannot be truly characterized as facilitating labor movement; rather, these agreements either condition labor market access on controlling undocumented migration or are a reward for signing readmission agreements that facilitate deportation from receiving countries to source or transit countries.

This portrait of facilitating flows reflects the bargaining framework presented in chapter 2. The status quo provides receiving states the ability to determine the level and characteristics of international migrant inflows, so they prefer the status quo. Sending states, too, tend to benefit from the status quo by allowing their citizens to emigrate in response to labor market demands in the international system. Where both sending and receiving states prefer the status quo, there is little need for international cooperation: a harmony of interests ensues. Thus, cooperation to facilitate migration flows is the exception rather than the rule.

There are two conditions under which we would anticipate international cooperation. When receiving states experience unmet labor market demands, where informational asymmetries create market failures, receiving states may negotiate with sending states to facilitate labor migration. We distinguished between negotiations among states of comparable levels of wealth, which anticipate reciprocal flows, and negotiations among states of disparate levels of wealth, which anticipate unilateral flows. In the first instance, we anticipate agreements that incorporate freedom of movement—unrestricted access to citizens of member states—as a method of enhancing labor market efficiencies. In the second instance, we anticipate BLAs that trade access to labor for a broader package of rights for those migrants. Agreements are negotiated as a method of overcoming market failures and information asymmetries, in light of continuing labor market shortages. These agreements represent one method for sending states to extract concessions from receiving states and to enhance migrant rights protections but, given the asymmetries in power between sending and receiving states, these concessions are not a foregone conclusion. However, the asymmetry in power between sending and receiving states often leaves international migrants with few protections in the negotiated agreements.

Sending states now prefer broader access to receiving state labor markets than is available through unilateral action or bilateral and regional agreements. This is reflected in the growing levels of undocumented populations in receiving states. Sending states have a two-pronged strategy to gain greater access to the more vibrant labor markets of receiving states. The first is to open negotiations in multilateral arenas such as GATS negotiations—in which they have achieved no success—and in multilateral rights arenas such as the UN General Assembly—where, again, they have failed to bring receiving states to ratify migrant rights agreements that would equalize labor market access and treatment of undocumented migrants in receiving country labor markets.

There is at least one policy-relevant observation that emerges from this theoretical and empirical presentation. If, and when, sending states delegate to private actors, such as recruitment agencies, or authorize direct employer recruitment, they are facilitating the entry of private actors to improve the efficiency of international labor markets, ultimately reducing the unmet demand for migrants on the part of receiving states. When they do this, one consequence is that receiving states have no incentive to enter into BLAs to enhance access to migrant labor. Therefore, sending states are relinquishing one mechanism by which they can extract concessions—whether these are greater access to receiving country labor markets or greater rights for their migrants. Sending states are not completely without resources. Recent reporting notes that some states, such as Nepal and the Philippines, have barred domestic workers from working in some GCC countries unless minimum conditions are met. Sending states can choose to boycott labor markets that provide insufficient worker protections, much as Algeria did in the early 1970s when France failed to protect its workers (Money 1999). However, there are two reasons for pessimism. Migrants from these countries may choose to circumvent their country's controls, through gray or black markets, because they are willing to accept poor conditions in the host state—because the conditions are better than those found in their home state. Second, there is likely to be competition for access to labor markets by citizens of other states. Citizens of other states may fill the labor market demand and acquiesce to the poorer wages and working conditions. Thus, receiving states are better placed to have their preferences reflected in international migration flows.

CHAPTER 5

Freedom of Movement

Reciprocal Flows and Facilitating Immigration

TOMASZ DYL WAS THIRTEEN years old when Poland joined the EU in 2004, along with seven other Eastern European states (Sherwood 2014). Shortly after that, Dyl emigrated with his parents from his native Krakow to Southampton when the United Kingdom became one of just three EU states to immediately allow citizens of new member states to live and work freely within their borders. The UK census bureau estimated that only about 13,000 Poles would take advantage of the new opportunity to immigrate, but this assessment was wildly low. There were 58,000 Polish-born UK residents in 2001, 520,000 by 2008 (Trevena 2009).

The United Kingdom's motivation for so quickly embracing freedom of movement was economic. In 2004, economic growth was brisk and unemployment was low, at 5 percent. This resulted in labor shortages that immigration could alleviate (Trevena 2009). And although the size of the flow from Poland did provoke an anti-immigrant backlash,[1] Tomasz Dyl's trajectory supports the economic case for encouraging immigration. While his parents supported the family by picking fruit and packing flowers in their new country, Tomasz went to school and learned English. At seventeen, he went to college and simultaneously started a marketing business. By age twenty-three his business employed six people, he was about to close the purchase of his first home, and his adopted hometown had proclaimed him its young entrepreneur of the year. "There is a better standard of life here, and the UK gives you more chances," he said. "It's fantastic seeing the number of Poles starting their own businesses" (Sherwood 2014).

In this chapter, we focus on freedom of movement, a migration policy that is both distinctive and exceptional. Tomasz Dyl's story is only one of the millions of stories of individuals who have been able to take up residence in another country without a visa, work permit, or residence permit.[2] However frequently this story has been told in Europe, it is the exception elsewhere in the world. Europe is the central focus of our inquiry in this chapter, as there have been three distinct groups of states that have adopted freedom of movement in the twentieth century: the Nordic Common Labor Market (1945/1954), the Benelux Community (1926/1958), and the precursors to the EU (1952/1957). We disaggregate the historical evolution of the EU by examining the development of both the ECSC (1952) and the EEC (1957), as these represent distinct institutional arrangements regarding freedom of movement. The EU has since incorporated the EFTA's remaining members into its free movement regulations through the EEA and has, through bilateral negotiations with Switzerland, applied free movement rules there as well. The Nordic Common Labor Market and the Benelux Community are now amalgamated into the EU, but their individual institutional origins allow us to evaluate our theoretical claims.[3] We include an examination of the TTTA between Australia and New Zealand as a fifth example of free movement, which confirms the conditions under which it is likely to arise. Finally, our sixth case focuses on the GCC's freedom of movement provisions, as one of the two regional organizations in the Global South that appear to have fully implemented regional access to their labor markets.[4]

We argue that negotiations that generate free movement are triggered by a variety of exogenous forces including, but not limited to, labor market shortages, similar to those discussed in chapter 4 on bilateral recruitment. However, specific conditions among the states encourage reciprocal migration flows and allow states to improve efficiency in labor markets as well as minimize the potential costs of migration through freedom of movement. Similar levels of wealth, wages, and social benefits ensure that flows will tend toward reciprocity. Full employment mitigates social welfare costs for the state. Linguistic, cultural, and historical similarities are also present in all our cases. Our argument is complicated by attention to the institutional structures within which these bargains take place. Institutions can constrain states' future actions, requiring them to accept free movement even when conditions are not met; this, we argue, was the road to Brexit.[5] Alternatively, institutions can be flexible and allow states to renege on free movement when conditions change, as was the case with the TTTA (Krasner 1976).[6]

Although the term "freedom of movement" implies that citizens of member states party to such an agreement can move and live at will, freedom of movement in the international sphere is generally constrained in some way. A comparison to internal movement makes this distinction clear. In most cases, to move internally within a state, individuals are free to pick up stakes and move when and where they please.[7] They can move for a job, for training, to join a family member, or simply for personal choice. International freedom of movement is virtually always circumscribed in some way. The initial agreements in Europe applied to workers only, ensuring that free movement applied only to active labor market participants (and their families). Inability to find employment required the worker to return home (although subsequent unemployment generally did not).[8] When freedom of movement was expanded in the Treaty of Maastricht to citizens of EU member states, including those not in the workforce, those individuals were subject to specific conditions. They must be self-supporting and provide their own health insurance, to ensure that the state of residence is not burdened with social welfare expenses. Only after five years' legal residence can individuals make any claims on the welfare state.[9] So international freedom of movement is not the same as internal freedom of movement. Nonetheless, international freedom of movement is extraordinary in the sense that, with or without border checks, citizens of member states have permission to reside and to take up employment without regard to quotas or labor market conditions of the national labor force. The states party to such agreements relinquish sovereignty over immigration for a select group of countries, as Britain discovered much to its dismay when immigration from the ten new EU member states in 2004 exceeded expectations by a factor of ten to one (Sherwood 2014). This policy is exceptional in that only European states and Australia and New Zealand, along with the GCC and the OECS, have adopted *and implemented* freedom of movement.[10]

To explain freedom of movement, we first outline the status quo ante and state preferences. The status quo is disrupted by unmet labor market demands, or other exogenous shocks, which become sufficiently powerful to send states to the negotiating table. However, unlike the agreements between powerful receiving states and weak sending states described in chapter 4, prior flows among the bargaining states reflected some degree of reciprocity. States desired the efficient functioning of labor markets—where unmet labor market needs could be fulfilled by immigrants and unemployed workers could find work abroad. Full employment reduced the demands on the state for social welfare and enhanced state revenue through taxes. Unilateral flows were to be avoided as these represented potential claims on the state. The translation of this set of preferences into policy is conditional on similar standards of living and on "full" employment. Our theoretical claims are illustrated in the six cases of free movement. In the last section, we juxtapose our argument against other accounts of this phenomenon.

THE STATUS QUO AND STATE PREFERENCES

Status Quo Ante. As developed in chapter 4, the status quo ante directly after World War II is reflected in the notion of state sovereignty over entry in combination with international norms guaranteeing exit proclaimed in the UN Universal Declaration of Human Rights adopted in 1948. This status quo permits emigration but allows countries of immigration to select those migrants it wishes to admit. The status quo in this set of cases also includes a long history of migratory movements among the member states. Freedom of movement tends to ratify prior flows rather than initiate new flows. The basic difference in this chapter, as distinct from the examination of labor market recruitment in chapter 4, is that countries are not easily divided into sending and receiving states vis-à-vis each other. One of the earliest agreements on freedom of movement between Sweden and Denmark is based on a long history of reciprocal movement between the two states, leaving Sweden with a net migration inflow in some years and in other years reversing (Meade, Liesner, and Wells 1962).

State Preferences. The central preference of states is to be able to respond to the business cycle and the changing division of labor in the global economy while minimizing costs to the state for the welfare of its residents and maximizing revenue from tax contributions of workers and employers. Economic efficiency requires that firms be able to hire the necessary workers as the demand arises, generating a potential demand for immigrants.[11] However, economic efficiency also requires that firms be able to lay off workers when necessary. Unemployed workers may draw on state social services and do not contribute to state coffers when they do not earn an income. Therefore, economic efficiency also requires that unemployed workers be able to obtain employment elsewhere, either locally or abroad. States therefore have a preference for the ability to export as well as import workers; they have a preference for reciprocal labor movements. However, reciprocity is viable only under very specific conditions. The foreign labor markets must attract the unemployed workers with similar wages and benefits. Hence a requirement for freedom of movement is similarity in wages, benefits, and the general standard of living. Common language and common culture also facilitate ease of movement in both directions. Finally, national treatment of migrants ensures that employers will not undercut native employment so that conditions close to full employment should prevail.

As we describe below, in each case an exogenous shock modified the preferences of states that sent them to the bargaining table. The shock varied across our cases; in some instances, it was similar to the shocks described in chapter 4, labor market shortages. In other instances, it was required by the construction of a larger economic unit, the instance of regional economic integration. In the case of the TTTA, bargaining between Australia and New Zealand was triggered by changes in migration policy of a third country, the United Kingdom. These agreements have always been negotiated with geographic neighbors. Knowledge of the geographic neighbors informed the type of agreement that was preferred—one that relinquished sovereignty to promote reciprocity in the name of economic efficiency or one that sorted immigrants according to specific labor market needs. Rather than bilateral agreements between labor surplus and labor shortage countries that foresaw one-way movement, the conditions that generated potential reciprocity acknowledged that workers could and would move both ways; states could experience both net inflows and net outflows but, over time, net flows would converge toward zero. States negotiated

freedom of movement only when they were assured that the flows would address labor market efficiency rather than result in population shifts or changes
in the welfare burden.

As in chapter 4, in the absence of an external shock, no agreements are anticipated. However, where an exogenous event or shock modifies the status quo,
freedom of movement agreements will be negotiated and implemented only
between countries with similar standards of living, national treatment of the
migrants, and the presence of full employment.[12] In the following case studies, we describe the status quo ante and the exogenous shocks that disturbed
the status quo. Although we do not have detailed accounts of the actual negotiations, we can describe the status of the states in terms of the similarity in
wages, benefits, and living standards. The TTTA is a useful comparison to the
European cases as it was informal and was therefore easy to modify when the
underlying conditions changed. The GCC's freedom of movement provisions
are little known but help confirm our theoretical expectations. We conclude the
chapter by juxtaposing our explanation against alternative theories.

THE NORDIC COMMON LABOR MARKET

Migration for employment among Scandanavian countries reflects longstand-
ing patterns of cross-border movement. As Salvesen observed in 1956, "It is
anything but a new situation to see Finnish lumberjacks in the Swedish forest,
Swedish construction workers helping to build Norwegian electricity plants,
Norwegian industrial workers in Swedish factories, Danish agricultural workers taking jobs with Norwegian farmers, Norwegian girls working in Danish
homes, and Icelandic boys signing on for Norwegian ships. Nonetheless, the
1954 creation of the Nordic Common Labor Market, buttressed by the Nordic
Passport Union in 1953 and the Social Security Convention in 1955,[13] represents
one of the earliest formal agreements on freedom of movement. These three
treaties combined to create the ability of workers within any of the five Nordic
countries to move freely among the member states, take up employment on
terms equal to nationals, and receive the same benefits that nationals received.
Prior requirements for work and residence permits were dropped. These three
agreements arose from both informal institutional cooperation through the
Nordic Inter-Parliamentary Union and the more formal Nordic Council. This
case is also interesting because, unlike the EU and its predecessor organizations, this regional organization was never able to create a free trade area or
customs union, the example of which may confound our understanding of the
relationship between freedom of movement and regional economic integration
more broadly. And, because its institutional trajectory is little known, it helps
us establish the viability of our hypotheses.

The Nordic states of Norway, Sweden, Denmark, Finland, and Iceland have a long history of cooperation that culminated in the creation of the Nordic Council in 1952.[14] The most immediate predecessor to the Nordic Council was the Nordic Inter-Parliamentary Union, an informal meeting of members of the Nordic parliaments to discuss issues of common concern, beginning in 1907. Denmark promoted more formal institutional cooperation and proposed a Nordic Council in 1938 and again in 1951. The latter proposal sprang to life with its legislative adoption by the member states in 1952, and the first meeting of the Nordic Council was held in early 1953. Although the Nordic Council is only an advisory organization, once it began having annual meetings, the council proposed additional areas of cooperation and drafted agreements that were subsequently adopted by the member states. One of the first items on its agenda was the free movement of labor.

The status quo ante is reflected in the fact that the Nordic countries have a long history of workers moving easily among the nations of Scandinavia. This region also reflects a common history, religious preferences, and strong linguistic similarities (Wendt 1981). The movement of workers had been regulated by work and residence permits, allowing states to control entry into their territory and labor markets.[15] The exogenous shock that disturbed the status quo was the demand for labor in Sweden. As a neutral country during World War II, Sweden's territory and economy remained intact; unlike those of Finland, Norway, and Denmark, the Swedish economy had not been destroyed by either occupation or combat. It was and remains the largest country by population in the Nordic Council but does not have the heft of a regional hegemon.[16] Nonetheless, its labor market needs were both larger and more dynamic than those of the other regional members during the war, continuing into the early postwar period. In response, Sweden unilaterally abolished its work permit requirement in 1943. This move allowed it to incorporate refugee populations from Denmark and Finland rapidly into its labor force. Strong labor market demand persisted even in light of the "surplus populations" knocking around Europe in the aftermath of World War II.

Sadly, there is very little literature in English that allows us to trace the negotiations on the creation of the Nordic Common Labor Market. However, we do know that only months after the war was concluded in Europe, the ministers for social affairs of the five governments met in Copenhagen in September 1945 and drafted a convention creating a common labor market, eliminating the need for a work permit or a residence permit for the citizens of member states (Wendt 1981). This is distinctive from the bilateral agreements examined in chapter 4, which are recruitment agreements signed between sending and receiving countries where migrants flow from one country to the other. This convention, however, met with approval only by Denmark and Sweden, both of which ratified the convention in late 1946. Despite having participated in the negotiations, Finland and Norway failed to join over concerns for their own labor market shortages generated by their reconstruction efforts (Wendt 1981, 220).

Mobility within the Nordic area remained an issue of high priority. First came efforts to facilitate travel across international borders. The Parliamentary Committee for Freer Communications was established in 1952 to deal with various policy issues including the requirement for passports for travel within the Nordic region, reestablished in 1939 at the outset of World War II. The Parliamentary Committee proposed and member governments adopted a convention that abolished the need for passports at internal borders and allowed stays of up to three months. This cooperation was deepened in 1957 upon the recommendations of the Nordic Council to create a common passport zone.[17] Subsequent movement across internal borders was ungoverned.

The establishment of the Nordic Council in 1952 provided a new forum for discussion of labor mobility, and the council generated a new draft convention in 1954, which again abolished the use of work and residence permits for citizens of member states. The preface of the agreement set the larger context for freedom of movement in the Nordic countries, already well known for their social democratic traditions. It stated that "free movement of labour within the Nordic area would be of benefit to the economic and social development of all the countries" and that "full employment was a necessary condition for the free labour market" (Wendt 1981, 221). Although Finland did not join the Nordic Union until 1955, it participated in the drafting of the convention and was one of the four member states to sign the convention. Iceland, with a total population of 142,000 in 1951, failed to sign on, fearing the impact of the agreement on its small labor market. Reciprocity, in this case, would overwhelm the local labor market.[18] The agreement was broad but excluded self-employed workers and did not constrain the ability of states to apply national legislation for professional licensing.[19]

The short-term consequences of the Nordic Common Labor Market appear to have been small. For example, Salvesen (1956, 340) reports that "in 1955 there were 4,242 Swedes, 5,869 Danes, and 449 Finns registered as employed in Norway; in the same year the Norwegians in Sweden numbered 11,637." This is consistent with our claim that freedom of movement is negotiated where reciprocal flows are likely. Norwegian emigrants in 1955 amounted to 110 percent of Nordic immigrants to Norway, and the immigrants accounted for only 0.3 percent of the Norwegian population. The longer-term consequences appear to be more significant. Wendt (1981, 220) reports that between 1951 and 1976 "about one million Nordic citizens changed their land of residence within Scandinavia (a third returning home and a quarter gaining citizenship of their new country of residence)." This amounts to almost 5 percent of the total Nordic Council population in 1976. However, as anticipated by our theory, net migration was much smaller.[20] The only state that produced a significant net outflow was Finland, to

Sweden. There were about 200,000 Finns in Sweden in 1976, or about 2.5 percent of the Swedish population.[21]

Analysis. This agreement reflects our theoretical claims that freedom of movement is possible only among countries that experience unmet labor market demands and have similar standards of living and wages, as well as our claim that flows tend to be reciprocal. The wages and standard of living in these five countries were (and remain) similar. The ratio of GDP per capita from the lowest (Iceland) to the highest (Denmark) was .73 in 1950 (Heston, Summers, and Aten 2009).[22] Although there is little primary research in English on the political determinants of these agreements, clearly reciprocal flows were a central component. Over time, around 5 percent of the Nordic population worked in other Nordic countries, about a third of whom returned home. Iceland, with its tiny labor market reflecting a population ratio of 85 to 1 (Denmark, Finland, Norway, and Sweden to Iceland), could not handle reciprocal flows and retained a work permit requirement.[23]

Table 5.1 presents the contemporary migrant stock in the Nordic Common Labor Market. Between 1 and 3 percent of the population lives in another Nordic country. The pattern is consistent with what we know about international migration flows: countries with small populations generate higher levels of out-migration, while countries with larger populations, which create greater labor market opportunities, generate smaller outflows proportionate to the population. The largest imbalance is between Finland and Sweden, but it remains small and has declined from 2.5 percent of the Swedish population to less than 2 percent.

Table 5.2 provides an overview of the unemployment rates at the points in

Table 5.1
Stocks of Member State Migrants: Nordic Common Labor Market, 2013

Country	Nordic Council emigration	Percentage of country population	Nordic Council immigration	Percentage of "other" Nordic Council population	Net migration
Denmark	63,861	1.13	44,522	0.21	(19,339)
Finland	200,096	3.66	29,822	0.14	(170,274)
Iceland	13,727	4.22	5,214	0.02	(8,513)
Norway	63,335	1.24	63,666	0.29	331
Sweden	81,365	0.84	279,160	1.60	197,795
Total			422,384	2.26	

Sources: United Nations, Department of Economics and Social Affairs, Population Division (2013); "Population Pyramids of the World from 1950 to 2100," http://populationpyramid.net.

Table 5.2
Unemployment Rates: Nordic Common Labor Market

Country	1945 (%)	1954 (%)
Denmark	13.4	8.0
Finland (1958)	n/a	3.1
Norway (1947)	3.1	2.2
Sweden	4.5	2.6

Source: Mitchell (2003).

time when freedom of movement was considered. The conditions that generated the reciprocal agreement between Denmark and Sweden in 1945 look more like a BLA, in the sense that unemployment was high in Denmark and very low in Sweden. However, by the 1954 agreement, all four countries had achieved full employment.[24]

It is not clear whether the institutional environment played a role in the creation of the Nordic Common Labor Market. The initial agreement in 1945 was drafted without the presence of the Nordic Council. However, the council proposed the 1954 agreement that was adopted by the member state governments. Even though the Nordic Council has only an advisory status, proposals can be initiated by states (via ministers) or members (of parliaments), so it provided an institutional forum for discussion and negotiations. After the 1945 proposal of the ministers of social affairs failed to garner the support of Finland and Norway, the Nordic Council represented a second body that could raise the issue again and address the concerns of all the member states. By 1954, the tightness of the Finnish and Norwegian labor market had slackened and diminished concerns about labor market shortages. The second time around, the agreement won the approval of the council and of the respective governments. It is interesting to note, though, that the Nordic Common Labor Market is not nested inside an economic union; it appears that broader regional economic integration is not a necessary component of a regional agreement on freedom of movement.

THE BENELUX ECONOMIC UNION

The Belgium-Netherlands-Luxembourg (Benelux) Treaty of Economic Union was signed in 1958 and came into force on 1 November 1960 based on a fifteen-year negotiation process that generated several conventions, protocols, and ad hoc ministerial agreements. Similar to the Nordic Common Labor Market, the agreement incorporated freedom of movement based on previously negotiated bilateral agreements. Although not all of the early bilateral agreements were nested inside an economic union, the multilateral agreement was clearly nested within an economic union based on the principle of a common market in goods, services, capital, and labor.

Efforts were initiated during World War II to create an economic union between the Netherlands and the Belgium-Luxembourg Economic Union (BLEU).[25] The governments in exile in London concluded two agreements, the first a monetary convention signed on 21 October 1943, the second a customs union signed on 5 September 1944, with the idea that both would go into effect upon liberation. These initial conventions were to prepare for a "total economic union" (Gay and Wagret 1970, 118). Because of differences in timing of liberation and in the state of the economies, the conventions were not enacted until January 1948. A new agreement was negotiated in July 1949 that set a four-stage path to economic union (the Pre-Union Agreement): provision for a common external tariff, reduction of internal tariffs, reduction of quantitative barriers to trade, and relaxation of currency exchange. In 1951, a new protocol called for the convergence of tax policies and economic policies. The Treaty of Economic Union (1958) brought these various treaties and protocols together in a single document, with full effect in 1960 (Meade, Liesner, and Wells 1962).

The labor market component of the Economic Union found precursors in earlier bilateral agreements. A labor mobility treaty was signed between Belgium and Luxembourg in 1926; Netherlands negotiated similar treaties with both Belgium and Luxembourg in 1933 (Eyck 1954; Robertson 1956). The agreements allowed citizens of member states unlimited access to temporary work permits that could then be transformed into permanent work permits at the end of six months of employment, as opposed to ten years for citizens of other countries. Thus, the bilateral treaties granted privileged access to each other's labor markets that did not depend on labor market conditions, but mobility was governed by work permits (Meade, Liesner, and Wells 1962). The free movement of workers was reconfirmed in a 1956 treaty specifically dealing with labor mobility and folded into the 1958 treaty. Specifically, the treaty granted the right of nationals to establish themselves in the other contracting states and to free movement within the Benelux area. Interestingly, the three countries also negotiated a common external border and lifted internal border controls in 1960, a precursor to the larger Schengen Agreement ultimately incorporated into the EU.

Analysis. The evidence is consistent with our theoretical claims that freedom of movement requires similar levels of wealth and labor market demands. In the early postwar period, the Netherlands was perceived as having a surplus population, and Belgium had the more dynamic economy. But wealth disparities

Table 5.3
Stocks of Member State Migrants: BLEU and Benelux Economic Union, 2013

Country	Benelux emigration	Percentage of country population	Benelux immigration	Percentage of Benelux population	Net migration
Belgium	60,783	0.54	107,624	0.37	46,841
Netherlands	100,459	0.59	46,830	0.16	(53,629)
Luxembourg	11,287	2.07	18,074	0.06	6,787
Total			172,528	0.59	

Sources: United Nations, Department of Economics and Social Affairs, Population Division (2013); "Population Pyramids of the World from 1950 to 2100," http://populationpyramid.net.

were small; the Dutch GDP per capita in real terms was 92 percent of its Belgian counterpart in 1955 (Heston, Summers, and Aten 2009). And the Netherlands' economy quickly took off and relieved population pressures. Dutch is one of the nationally recognized languages in Belgium and is employed by more than half of the population. The goal of economic union also propelled the Benelux states to the negotiating table. As it turns out, even with freedom of movement inside the Benelux Economic Union, there was reciprocity but at very low levels of migration, in large part because wealth disparities were so small (Meade, Liesner, and Wells 1962, 11).

Table 5.3 provides a snapshot of Benelux migrant stocks as of 2013. Labor mobility appears to be lower in the Benelux Union than in the Nordic Common Labor Market, with only about one-half of one percent of the population living in another member state. However, imbalances are even smaller in the Benelux Union — amounting to around a fifty thousand positive net balance in Belgium, a minuscule proportion of the total population.

Table 5.4 presents the unemployment rate for Belgium for the period of economic union with Luxembourg and for the subsequent periods during which bilateral and multilateral agreements on freedom of movement were negotiated (unemployment rates for Luxembourg are unavailable). It is easy to see that the bilateral agreement between Belgium and Luxembourg in 1926 was adopted during a period of full employment. The bilateral agreements that the Netherlands negotiated with Belgium and with Luxembourg in 1933 are more puzzling as unemployment rates were very high in both Belgium and the Netherlands. However, this appears to be an outlier. Despite descriptions of Belgium as the more dynamic economy in the early postwar period, in the early 1950s Belgium had relatively high unemployment rates. However, those rates dropped rapidly in the mid-1950s, so by the time the multilateral agreement on freedom of movement of labor was negotiated in 1956, both Belgium and the Netherlands

Table 5.4
Unemployment Rates: BLEU and Benelux Economic Union

Country	1923–29 (%)	1931–39 (%)	1948–49 (%)	1950–55 (%)	1956 (%)
Belgium	1.3–2.4	13.8–23.5	4.0–8.6	5.8–9.2	4.5
Netherlands		14.8–32.7	1.0–1.5	1.9–3.5	0.9

Source: Mitchell (2003).

experienced full employment. The case of the Benelux Union is also important from an institutional perspective. There is a long history of bilateral agreements that facilitated labor mobility along with the recognition, from experience, that flows would be small and reciprocal.

THE EUROPEAN UNION

European regional integration is the world's most developed and advanced form of regional governance, and migration has long been central to European integration. Free movement for nationals of member states is part of the core EU objective of economic integration.[26] Moreover, the geographic scope of freedom of movement expanded as the union itself broadened its membership from the original six member states of France, Germany, Italy, Belgium, the Netherlands, and Luxembourg to the now twenty-eight.[27] Each geographic expansion widened the scope of movement, although transition periods were almost invariably employed to ensure that labor market flows would enhance the economic efficiency of labor markets rather than generate one-way flows.[28]

We begin with the ECSC, negotiated in 1950–51 and implemented in 1952. The ECSC forbade discrimination based on nationality for a subset of workers, skilled workers, in the coal and steel sectors of member states. However, this treaty article neither promised nor created freedom of movement in these sectors. Earlier analyses suggest that these provisions were the basis for freedom of movement incorporated into the EEC in 1957 (Maas 2006; Money and Geddes 2011). However, we show that the freedom of movement for workers incorporated in the 1957 treaty is quite distinct from the ECSC provisions and is closely associated with the Benelux experience. The EEC's freedom of movement was expanded in the Treaty of Maastricht in 1992 to include citizens of the member states, rather than just workers, and allowed for conditional settlement of those citizens in any member state. Freedom of movement, therefore, was constructed over several decades. We also emphasize the institutional constraints created by the evolution of the EU that forced member states to permit freedom of movement to new member states in 2004 and subsequent accessions, even though the underlying conditions we assert are necessary were, in fact, absent.

The European Coal and Steel Community. The story of the creation of the ECSC is well known. The French foreign minister, Robert Schuman, on 9 May 1950 invited European states to create a customs union for coal and steel. The announcement, coming on the tenth anniversary of the German invasion of France, was seen as an effort to integrate the German economy so tightly with other European economies that it would preclude German ability to develop an independent war-making capacity. The invitation for the negotiations focused on a *customs union* rather than a *common market*. A customs union would involve the free flow of goods across national borders, but the fourth freedom of labor, now recognized in the EU, had not yet seen light of day.

Although Jean Monnet, the French bureaucrat behind the Schuman Declaration, envisioned a "citizens' Europe," the declaration did not include any verbiage that suggested either freedom of movement or a common labor market. The invitation stated, "The French government proposes to place Franco-German production of coal and steel under one common High Authority in an organization open to the participation of other countries of Europe. . . . The movement of coal and steel between member states will immediately be freed of all customs duties and it will not be permitted for it to be constrained by differential transport rates" (Schuman 1950). The declaration included a section devoted to "the equalization of improvement in the living conditions of workers in these industries." So workers' interests were included, but freedom of movement was excluded from the negotiating agenda.

There are no published *travaux préparatoires* for the ECSC negotiations, so we know of the negotiations only through position papers of various member states, press coverage, and memoirs of the negotiators themselves (Diebold 1959). There is no indication that any of the six negotiating states sought to include freedom of movement for labor. Even the Italian government made no mention of migration in its instruction brief to negotiators ("Letter" 1950). Rather, the negotiating brief focused on the customs union as a means to ensure cheaper intermediate products (coal and steel) for its industrial production. Negotiators talked of a "coal and steel pool." When the Benelux countries met to harmonize their negotiation positions, the list included the words "free movement," but it was reserved for "coal, coke, iron ore, scrap, and steel products of all kinds." For workers, the Benelux countries were interested in "guaranteeing a constant improvement in the living and working conditions of the labor force in the industries under consideration" ("Meeting" 1950). Free movement of labor was absent from the negotiating positions.

Nonetheless, the Treaty of Paris that established the ECSC does have provisions that prevent member states from discriminating based on nationality when hiring *skilled* workers who originate in other member states in the coal and steel industries. Maas (2003, 2006) reports that this clause was inserted at the insistence of the Italian negotiator as the price for Italian participation in the agreement. If this is true, the Italian delegation was hoodwinked, as Article 69 (1) clearly states, "The member States bind themselves to renounce any restriction based on nationality against the employment in the coal and steel industries of workers *of proven qualifications* for such industries who possess the nationality of one of the member States" (Treaty Constituting the European Coal and Steel Community 1951, emphasis added). There were virtually no skilled coal miners in Italy, in the absence of coal deposits, and their steel industry was very small. Virtually all Italians who moved north to work in France, Belgium, and Germany were unskilled laborers from the Italian Mezzogiorno and did not fall under the provisions of the ECSC.

The flows from Italy to Northern Europe were already well established when the call from Schuman brought negotiators to the table. Italy had been a country of emigration for over a century, with most flows prior to World War II moving to the Americas (Moch 1995). After World War II, Italians headed to Northern Europe to work in many unskilled occupations, including in coal and steel, as this was central to the reconstruction efforts at the end of the war and because Italy experienced a surplus of labor especially from the South (Moch 1995). Such was the need for foreign labor that bilateral agreements regulating the flow of Italian workers were signed with Belgium in 1946, France in 1947, and the Netherlands in 1948. Germany subsequently signed a BLA with Italy in 1956 (OECD 2004).[29] However, unlike the bilateral agreements between Nordic Union member states and the Benelux states that preceded the construction of freedom of movement, those with Italy were recruitment agreements establishing one-way flows from Italy to Northern Europe.

ECSC Analysis. In 1950, as the ECSC negotiations commenced, the preconditions that we argue are necessary to freedom of movement were lacking among the six states that sought to integrate their coal and steel industries. Although there were clearly labor market shortages in some coal- and steel-producing regions, the living conditions were not sufficiently similar to generate reciprocal flows and full employment was absent. In 1950, the ratio of the lowest to highest standard of living among the six states negotiating the ECSC treaty was .55 (Italy/Netherlands), and we know that the conditions in Italy's Mezzogiorno were much poorer. Moreover, high levels of unemployment in Italy, ranging from 8.3 to 9.5 percent during this period, suggested that the one-way flow would become permanent. In any event, there was virtually no movement under the

ECSC provisions from Italy or elsewhere. The treaty, signed and implemented in 1952, specified that member states would establish common definitions of skilled trades and qualifications. The implementation of this provision was slow, and ultimately the negotiated agreement defined professional qualifications very narrowly (Haas 1958). Free movement was assured for only 20 to 25 percent of ECSC labor; Italians who worked in Belgian coal mines, for example, were unskilled agricultural workers and were therefore excluded completely (Haas 1958).[30] Moreover, the negotiation process took so long that the labor mobility agreement was ratified only in June 1957 and took effect in September 1957, the same year that the European Economic Community Treaty was signed that *did* include freedom of movement (Maas 2006; Bok 1955).[31] Our analysis suggests that there was no intent on the part of the original ECSC six to promote a common labor market or freedom of movement, even in the sector-specific coal and steel community, because the conditions that would guarantee reciprocity were lacking in terms of both standard of living and unemployment. Italian migration north continued but was governed by BLAs.

The European Economic Community. The broadening of economic cooperation in Europe proceeded with the establishment of a committee, headed by Belgian foreign minister Paul-Henri Spaak, to prepare a report on the feasibility of a common market and an atomic energy agency. Many of the institutional structures negotiated in the ECSC were adapted in the Treaty of Rome that created the EEC and the European Atomic Energy Community. But the "four freedoms" for which the EEC is famous were based in part on Spaak's experience with the negotiation of the Benelux Economic Union, in which he participated starting with the original agreements of the governments in exile in London in 1943 and 1944 (Spaak 1956). His efforts were seconded by the Dutch foreign minister Beyen, who was also familiar with the Benelux negotiations, as an advisor to the Dutch government in exile in London during World War II (Harryvan 2009). Both these statesmen had not participated in the ECSC negotiations but served in important government roles prior to and subsequent to the ECSC agreement.[32] The report that the Spaak committee produced, "Report of the Heads of Delegation to the Minsters of Foreign Affairs," is known informally as the "Spaak Report." His experience is reflected in its chapter 3, "The Free Movement of Workers," and draws on the Benelux Union's experience that suggested a freedom of movement clause would not produce large flows.[33] In Spaak's words, "In considering the free movement of workers we should not overestimate the size of the movements of the work force that would be produced in a completely free common market. We know the reticence to changes of profession or residence, even within the same country. . . . For all these reasons, the most recent tendency is on efforts for development and the creation of employment on location [where workers are unemployed]" ("Report" 1956, 88, authors' translation).

The report also echoes our list of conditions necessary for free movement to be adopted. The authors cite ensuring full employment ("the reconversion of economic activities and the creation of new activities"); the granting of residence only when employment is obtained ("the right to apply in all the countries of the community for jobs that are offered and to stay in the country [only] if employment is obtained"); and the nondisplacement of local workers (identical wages, working conditions, and benefits "so that employers have no incentive to call for a migrant labor force except to fill open positions") ("Report" 1956, 88–89). Additional evidence that the Benelux Union was the model for the EEC's freedom of movement for labor comes from the wording of the treaty articles. The EEC and the Benelux Economic Union use freedom of movement (*la libre circulation*) terminology rather than copying the ECSC's terminology preventing discrimination based on nationality. To be sure, the Benelux Economic Union was signed in 1958 and entered into force in 1960, subsequent to the Treaty of Rome (signed 1957, in force 1958). However, the separate treaty dealing with freedom of movement of labor was negotiated and signed in 1956 among the Benelux member states, as the Spaak committee was meeting to discuss economic union in the wider geographic region. The Benelux countries had long experience, dating from 1926 and 1933, which permitted the free flow of workers, exclusive of economic union.

The inclusion of freedom of movement in the Treaty of Rome, which created the EEC, was undoubtedly also facilitated by the fact that all six original member states were democracies where workers were organized economically and politically. Spaak was a member of the Belgian Socialist Party and brought the workers' perspective to the table. Unions were eager to ensure that economic cooperation included a social dimension (Haas 1958; Maas 2006). Freedom of movement was one mechanism (of several) for achieving harmonization of working conditions and wages.

Article 48 of the Treaty of Rome, signed in 1957, established free movement rights for all workers with the exception of those employed in the public service. The provisions were subject to a transition period scheduled to end by 1 January 1970, thirteen years from the date of treaty ratification. This transition phase would allow the conditions in Italy to improve so that flows could become reciprocal.

EEC Analysis. Table 5.5 shows the unemployment rates among the six states that negotiated the ECSC and the EEC.[34] Initially, not only was there a large discrepancy in the standard of living between the Northern European countries and Italy, full employment had not been achieved. Reciprocity was not in the

Table 5.5

Unemployment Rates: European Coal and Steel Community and European Economic Community

Country	1949–52 (%)	1957 (%)	1958–74 average (%)
Belgium	7.6–9.0	3.9	3.7
France	Low	Low	Low
Federal Republic of Germany	8.3–10.0	3.4	1.5
Italy	8.3–9.5	8.2	4.5
Netherlands	1.0–3.5	1.2	1.8

Note: The French authorities did not report the unemployment rate until 1977 but instead reported the number of unemployed. This number ranged from 78,000 in 1948 to 196,000 in 1967. During this entire time, the unemployed represented a small portion of the labor force.

Source: Mitchell (2003).

cards. That situation had begun to change by the mid-1950s, and the thirteen-year transition period ensured that both the standard of living in Italy and the unemployment rate would converge on the Northern European countries before full freedom of movement was implemented.

There were three steps for full implementation of Article 48. The 1961 directive opened national labor markets to the citizens of member states and abolished entry and exit visas for all intracommunity movement. It abolished quotas on EEC workers. It provided equal access to employment but required that workers obtain work permits and protected national labor markets by allowing states to hold vacancies for nationals for three weeks. It also provided that workers could be reunited with their spouse and children under the age of twenty-one, dependent on adequate housing. The 1964 directive included seasonal and frontier workers in the free movement and labor market access provisions, and it limited the circumstances under which states could protect national labor markets for nationals. Workers could now be joined by all dependent relatives and any other relative living in the workers' home. The final step, taken in 1968, ended any discrimination against nationals of other member countries and abolished work permits as of 31 December 1969 (although states could maintain a requirement for residence permits) (EU 1968; Keesing's Report 1975). In 1970, these rights were further extended to allow member state workers to remain in the member state after having been employed there (Keesing's Report 1975).

Although these provisions were wide-ranging in providing labor mobility, they essentially confirmed rather than initiated new flows of workers. The presence of labor market shortages in the 1950s and 1960s in Northern Europe is widely documented (Kindleberger 1967). And there was a long transition period to ensure that wages and working conditions would not generate a large and permanent flow in any one direction. In 1950, when the ECSC treaty was being negotiated, the ratio of real GDP per capita between the lowest and highest states was .55 (Italy/Netherlands). That increased to .64 in 1955 and to 0.75 by 1970 (Italy/Netherlands).[35] This most recent ratio is almost identical to the ratio in the Nordic region when the Nordic Common Labor Market was negotiated in 1954 (.73, Iceland/Denmark). Although a 25 to 35 percent wage premium is not insignificant, it is insufficient to attract large permanent waves of migration. By comparison, the Mexico–US wealth gap was .28 in 1955 and .33 in 1970 (Heston, Summers, and Aten 2009).

Extensions of Freedom of Movement. Freedom of movement and establishment in the ECSC and EEC applied only to economic actors, that is, workers seeking employment. The Single European Act, signed in 1986, was an effort to provide new momentum for regional integration. In terms of labor mobility, the act implicated measures requiring mutual recognition of professional training within the EEC and rights of establishment. Subsequently, in June 1990, the Council of Ministers of the EU adopted three directives on the right of residence for students, retirees, and any other citizens who could show that they had sufficient means to live in another EU host country (van Oudenaren 2005). The next step to full freedom of movement was therefore relatively small. The Treaty on European Union (Maastricht Treaty), signed in 1992, established EU citizenship. It did not grant any further privileges in terms of freedom of movement. Rather, EU citizenship shifted the free movement of persons from an economic right, guaranteed as a function of the single market, to a human and political right guaranteed to people as a function of their citizenship (van Oudenaren 2005).

This brief summary of the various EU provisions on freedom of movement and establishment demonstrates that the current system was adopted over a long period, starting with the Treaty of Rome in 1957 (rather than the Treaty of Paris) and incorporated active labor market participants and their families; freedom of movement extended subsequently to professionals and finally to noneconomic actors. There remains a series of safeguards in place for health and public safety, as well as requirements for self-sufficiency. Nonetheless, these rights are the broadest of any among contemporary states in the international system (with the exceptions that we describe below).

Expansion of Membership. As these rights expanded, the number of individuals to which the rights applied broadened as well, as the initial membership in the ECSC and the EEC grew from the original six to the current twenty-eight. Ireland, the United Kingdom, and Denmark joined in 1973; Greece in 1981; Spain and Portugal in 1986; and Sweden, Austria, and Finland in 1995. Central European states were incorporated in 2004 and 2007, and Croatia in 2013. Additional membership applications are pending. The most controversial in terms of labor market access prior to 2004 were the Southern European accessions. Greece, Spain, and Portugal all had significant migrant communities in the EEC and economies that were relatively underdeveloped. Spain, in particular, was a medium-sized state with relatively high unemployment at the time of accession.[36] Member states feared a flood of migrants when free movement provisions took effect in countries whose unemployment rates had risen dramatically in the decade after 1975. Therefore, transition provisions for access to EEC labor markets were built into the accession treaties (Maas 2006; Geddes and Boswell 2011). The idea was to give Spain and the other Mediterranean countries time to bring their economy, employment, wages, and working conditions in line with those of the other member states, thus decreasing flows from the south. For comparison purposes, the ratio of Spain's standard of living to that of the Netherlands was .68 in 1986 (the highest within the EU at that time) and .72 in 1993, at the end of the transition period to free movement. Put differently, in 1993, the ratio of Spain's standard of living to the unweighted EU average was .90. Clearly, wage premiums had significantly diminished by the time Spain's citizens could freely access other European labor markets. The accession of Northern European countries (Austria, Finland, and Sweden) in 1995 was uncontroversial from a free movement perspective; the standards of living of Austria and Sweden were above the EU average and Finland's only slightly below. Subsequent accessions of Central European countries again elicited fears of labor market swamping.

Table 5.6 shows that the full employment criterion was present in the 1973 accessions but absent thereafter.[37] This explains the hesitance of the member states over free movement, especially with the Spanish and Portuguese accessions in 1986. However, the institutional foundations were already enshrined in the *acquis communautaire* so that the four freedoms, including free movement of labor, were offered to all new member states. The long transition period adopted for the Spanish and Portuguese accession actually brought the standards of living into alignment, and weak labor market demand in the established EEC countries was insufficient to generate large unilateral flows. The transition period, initiated in the original Treaty of Rome, also became part of the *acquis communautaire*, allowing the new member states to converge on the standard of living of the old member states and thus reduce potentially dislocating migration flows.

After the fall of the Berlin Wall and the implosion of the Soviet Union, Cen-

Table 5.6
Unemployment Rates: Membership Expansion of the European Union

Country	1973; United Kingdom, Ireland, and Denmark (%)	1981; Greece (%)	1986; Spain and Portugal (%)	1995; Austria, Sweden, and Finland (%)
Belgium	3.6	10.9	12.3	9.3
France	Low	7.4	10.4	11.6
Federal Republic of Germany	1.2	5.5	9.0	10.1
Italy	6.4	10.1	11.1	11.3
Netherlands	2.8	9.1	14.7	7.0
Denmark	2.4	9.2	8.1	7.0
Ireland	7.2	10.1	18.1	12.2
United Kingdom	2.6	8.0	10.9	8.6
Greece		2.7	7.4	10.0
Spain			20.0	22.9
Austria				11.5
Finland				11.6
Sweden				7.7

Source: Mitchell (2003).

tral European states were eager to renew their ties with the West and to gain some of the material wealth that had accompanied economic integration. Applications for membership in the EU came fast and furious. Ultimately they were embraced, with accession dates set for 2004 and later. The standard of living differences were more on the order of those between Mexico and the United States than earlier accessions. For comparison purposes, we take the ratio of Poland, the largest accession state, to the Netherlands, the EU country with the highest GDP per capita in purchasing power parity terms (although the EU average is substantially lower). In 1990, the ratio of Poland's standard of living to that of the Netherlands was .28. The ratio was .35 by accession in 2004, .43 at the end of the labor market transition period.

The German government led calls for a seven-year transition period before introduction of full rights to free movement for nationals of the Central European states. The final agreement was a 2 + 3 + 2 formula from 2004 until 2011, which stated that the situation would be reviewed after two years and then again after three years. Sweden, Ireland, and the United Kingdom were the only states that allowed free movement from the date of accession. Thus, free movement of the new member states that were substantially poorer than the old member states was subject to a long transition period. However, given that freedom of movement was well entrenched in the treaties governing the EU, member states were in a sense trapped by this institutional constraint. Admission to the EU meant admission to freedom of movement. The transition period was identical to the earlier accessions of Spain and Portugal—seven years—but the original EU member states could not bar freedom of movement altogether, even though the conditions that were present at the establishment of free movement and at earlier expansions via long transition periods were absent in the case of Central European accessions.

Mobility in the Contemporary European Union. In April 2004, the EU brought together in one directive (2004/38/EC) the previous arrangements contained in one regulation and nine directives, all governing free movement and mobility rights (EU 2010a, 2010b). This single directive covers the rights of EU citizens and their family members to move and reside freely within the territory of the member states. The directive specifies the conditions under which EU citizens can move freely and imposes only minor constraints on movement, linked, for example, to public order or public health concerns, and specifies a right of permanent residence for EU citizens exercising mobility rights.

In practical terms, this means that all EU citizens able to present a valid identity card or passport have the right to enter another EU member state. Family members have the same rights as the EU citizens they have accompanied. If residence is to be for longer than six months, certain conditions can be imposed. These are interesting because they reveal the concern of EU member states to minimize the costs of free movement. To acquire a right of residence for more than six months, EU citizens must (1) be engaged in economic activity or be self-employed and (2) have sufficient resources, including health insurance, so that they do not become a burden on the member state that they move to; or (3) be following vocational training and have sufficient resources to support themselves; or (4) be a family member of an EU citizen who falls into one of these categories. EU citizens acquire a right to permanent residence following a five-year period of uninterrupted, legal residence. This right is not subject to any conditions. This same rule also applies to family members.[38]

This overview is an important clarification of the mobility provisions within the EU. It is the most advanced (except for the TTTA) agreement that provides for free movement among member states. However, it is not unlimited mobility. Workers must be employed, and although they have access to unemployment insurance and other social welfare benefits, they cannot live indefinitely in another member state if they have no source of income, unless they have an established residence and record of income for a minimum of five years. Other individuals must prove that they have adequate resources and will not require recourse to the welfare provisions of their host state.

And in fact, mobility among the EU member states remains limited because citizens of member states choose not to move; only about 2 percent of all EU citizens reside in another member state. In terms of overall migration *flows* in Europe, though, internal migration represents a substantial portion of EU migration in the contemporary era (Herm 2008). Around 40 percent of the migrants arriving in the EU 27 in 2006 were citizens of member states. The flows are generally reciprocal, although still unbalanced with regard to the 2004/2007 accession states (Herm 2008).

Analysis. Although the EU now represents the pinnacle of free movement and residence rights in the world, this brief description of the evolution of these rights poses the question of how they were achieved. Our account of the mobility provisions in the EU focuses on the components that we argue are central to this type of migration cooperation: reciprocity as demonstrated by minimal differences in the standard of living of the parties to the agreement, labor market shortages in one or more parties to the agreement, and full employment. Empirically, with the exception of the latest accessions of Central European states, wage and living standard differentials existed but were relatively small. Moreover, accessions were negotiated to ensure that those differences diminished before free movement was allowed. That said, mobility provisions in the EU are clearly path-dependent. For an EU of fifteen in 1995 with a forty-year history of mobility, it was impossible to negotiate membership with the Central European states and exclude labor market access, even though wealth and wages were substantially lower in the Central European states even at the end of the seven-year transition period.

In Table 5.7, we provide the data on migrant stocks for the fifteen old EU member states similar to those provided for the Nordic Common Labor Market and the Benelux Economic Union (this table does not include the 2004/2007 accessions). The first thing to note is that intra-EU migration among the EU 15 is small: 1.7 percent of the total population. In 2013, the stocks are reasonably well balanced. We see that Finland is still an outlier, although this is due to Finns migrating to Sweden rather than elsewhere in the EU. The net outflows from Greece and Ireland are likely the direct reflection of the effects of the 2008 global financial crisis and the ensuing bailouts imposed by the European Central Bank. However, these flows are small relative to the overall population of the EU. The two other countries that have produced substantial negative net outflows to other EU member states are Italy and Portugal, whose populations are concentrated primarily in France and Germany. These more permanent

Table 5.7
Stocks of Member State Migrants: EU 15 Only, 2013

Country	EU emigration	Percentage of country population	EU immigration	Percentage of EU population	Net migration
Austria	212,402	2.50	202,699	0.05	(9,703)
Belgium	328,558	2.90	590,821	0.14	262,263
Denmark	120,853	2.14	83,356	0.02	(37,497)
Finland	272,404	4.99	39,978	0.01	(232,426)
France	788,379	1.23	1,967,844	0.49	1,179,465
Germany	1,242,810	1.54	2,196,132	0.55	953,322
Greece	365,251	3.30	146,441	0.03	(218,810)
Ireland	659,240	14.11	281,435	0.07	(377,805)
Italy	1,372,713	2.29	175,583	0.04	(1,197,130)
Luxembourg	38,047	6.99	114,607	0.03	76,560
Netherlands	326,516	1.94	307,792	0.07	(18,255)
Portugal	1,033,905	9.88	157,488	0.05	(876,417)
Spain	700,161	1.50	560,218	0.14	(139,942)
Sweden	146,901	1.52	332,463	0.08	185,562
United Kingdom	823,719	1.28	1,278,684	0.32	454,965
Total			6,845,422	1.7	

Source: United Nations, Department of Economics and Social Affairs, Population Division (2013); "Population Pyramids of the World from 1950 to 2100," http://populationpyramid.net.

outflows reflect the unilateral flows governed by bilateral agreements in the 1950s and 1960s rather than the freedom of movement available through membership in the EU. Italy was an original member of the EEC, but the flow of its emigrants north was not covered by EU mobility provisions until the end of the transition period in 1970. Portugal joined the EEC only in 1986 and was subject to a long transition period that did not end until 1993. Population censuses from France and Germany show that the imbalances between these two states are long-standing.

We have presented earlier evidence on the standard of living disparities among the member states and have argued that the disparities were too large initially among the six states negotiating the ECSC. The standard of living in Italy was half that in the Netherlands. However, that rapidly shifted and when the treaty creating the EEC was negotiated in 1956 and 1957, and borrowing from the Benelux Economic Union experience, freedom of movement was incorporated with a long transition period. The ratio of lowest to highest standard of living as reflected in the GDP per capita in purchasing power parity terms was .75, almost identical to the variation among the countries of the Nordic Union in 1954 when the Nordic Common Labor Market was adopted. Full employment was also a characteristic of European labor markets up through the late 1970s. Subsequent geographic expansion depended on long transition periods to ensure that the basic conditions to generate reciprocal flows were met. But ultimately, the institutional stickiness of the EU constrained the flexibility of the EU 15 when negotiating with the Central European countries after the fall of the Berlin Wall and the reunification of Europe. Brexit, or the British exit from the EU, decided by referendum in June 2016, can be attributed to many factors but, clearly, one important factor is the institutional inflexibility that forced existing member states to open their labor markets to the 2004 accession states before economic conditions had converged. This did lead to one-way flows, with Tomasz Dyl, the Polish migrant introduced at the beginning of the chapter, as a prime example. Intra-European migration was a central issue in the Brexit campaign.[39]

This institutional stickiness is absent in our next case, the TTTA. As a result, the parties to the agreement, Australia and New Zealand, remained free to unilaterally change or renegotiate the terms of free movement when the underlying conditions supporting reciprocity declined. It is to that agreement that we now turn.

THE TRANS-TASMAN TRAVEL ARRANGEMENT

As far-flung outposts of the British Empire on the edge of Asia, Australia and New Zealand have a common history as immigrant societies heavily influenced by decades of migration from Europe, primarily from Great Britain and Ireland. From the time of the initial British settlement, as members of the British Empire, New Zealanders and Australians have enjoyed free movement between each other's countries.[40] In 1973, this freedom of movement was officially confirmed in the TTTA, which allowed Australians and New Zealanders to live and work as permanent residents in the other country without going through any visa application process, as well as to receive all state-supplied social benefits on the same terms as the host population.[41]

As "developed" nations and neighbors, both Australia and New Zealand have long recognized the importance of economic cooperation. Trade agreements were signed between the two nations in 1922 and 1933. In 1966, as part of the New Zealand–Australian Free Trade Agreement, tariffs were lowered by 80 percent. In the Closer Economic Relations agreement in 1983, the two countries found common ground in trade, tariffs, customs, and investment. This agreement represents one of the most comprehensive regional economic accords between sovereign states in existence today (Sampson 2003). The TTTA, like freedom of movement in the EU, is nested in a dense network of economic agreements, but unlike in the EU, the agreement has never been incorporated into the broader economic integration arrangements. Rather than a treaty, the TTTA is a set of immigration regulations that each state may change unilaterally. Therefore, although the agreement facilitates migration, each state is not legally bound and can change the terms at any time, as we describe below.[42] The remainder of this section describes how the immigration policies of New Zealand and Australia diverged because of their distinct historical legacies and labor market needs.[43] These divergent policies led to a change in migration flows, resulting in a reassessment of the TTTA.

The Origins of the Trans-Tasman Travel Arrangement. The development of the TTTA was largely a response to changes regarding travel within the British Commonwealth. Until the early 1970s, most immigrants to Australia and New Zealand came from Great Britain and Ireland, with some from other parts of Europe. At the same time, as citizens of the British Empire and subsequently British Commonwealth countries, Australians and New Zealanders enjoyed the right to travel and settle in the United Kingdom. Although Britain initiated some controls over Commonwealth migration with the 1962 Commonwealth Immigrants Act, it was not until 1971 that most of the privileges for Commonwealth citizens were abolished. This change in British policy prompted reciprocal action from Australia and New Zealand. Rather than labor market shortages, the exogenous shock that changed the status quo in this case was the British legislation that placed both Australians and New Zealanders on a different footing.

With these changes in the privileged status of Commonwealth citizens in Britain, it became necessary for the two nations to renegotiate their relationship. As neighboring members of the Commonwealth, both with a settler heritage, New Zealand and Australia had first recognized the importance of free movement across the Tasman Sea in 1846, and this was formalized in the 1920s. The TTTA of 1973 simply asserted that citizens of the two countries could continue to live, work, and receive benefits in either country, despite the changes in immigration policies toward the United Kingdom. Later amendments in 1981 required passports, but no other documentation was necessary. These residents were entitled to the same health, welfare, and pension benefits to which citizens were entitled regardless of employment status (unlike the EU).

The 2001 Change to the Trans-Tasman Travel Arrangement. Throughout their histories, Australia and New Zealand have repeatedly asserted their "special relationship," and open movement between the countries has been a bedrock policy for both (MacKellar and Gill 1976). Their economic integration in the

1980s and 1990s seemed only to further cement this relationship. However, in the past two decades, a rift has developed over immigration policy that has threatened the stability of this relationship. In 2001, the TTTA was amended to restrict the ability of New Zealanders to become permanent residents, requiring all new arrivals to go through the same process as other immigrants. This means that they have to apply and meet the qualifications set for all immigrants to gain permanent resident status, which allows them to access social security benefits (after a two-year waiting period), to obtain citizenship, or to sponsor other immigrants (Birrell and Rapson 2001; Betts 2003). If New Zealanders fail to meet the requirements, they may continue to live and work in Australia indefinitely as "temporary" residents, but they are not able to access any of the benefits available to permanent residents. Australians, on the other hand, continue to enjoy full benefits in New Zealand.[44]

This one-sided change to the TTTA reflects the diverging patterns of immigration in Australia and New Zealand that began in the 1980s and accelerated in the 1990s. Although in the 1960s immigration tended to favor New Zealand, beginning in the 1970s, Trans-Tasman immigration has tended to be directed toward Australia. This increased dramatically in the 1990s, when the number of New Zealanders coming to Australia to live permanently nearly quadrupled. By 1999, annual flows had reached 31,615 permanent settlers from New Zealand, representing 34 percent of all settlers that year. This represented a 28 percent increase from the previous year (Khoo 2002).

There has not been an equivalent increase in the number of Australians moving to New Zealand. In 2000, there was a total of about 435,000 New Zealanders living in Australia and only about 54,000 Australians living in New Zealand (Birrell and Rapson 2001; Hoadley 2003). These numbers clearly depict a dramatic shift in the pattern of migration flows between Australia and New Zealand and provide support for one of the primary components of our theory. Table 5.8 provides a detailed analysis of the changing flows from New Zealand to Australia. An unbalanced migration flow is not conducive to free movement provisions. The changes in the 1990s meant that, for the first time, migration between New Zealand and Australia was severely unbalanced.

The dramatic increase in movement from New Zealand to Australia is largely due to the better economic climate in Australia, as well as a larger and more vibrant labor market (Ward and Young 2000).[45] In response to the hemorrhage of New Zealanders to Australia, New Zealand relaxed its own immigration laws to attract foreign skilled labor. In so doing, it changed the composition of its immigrant flows from predominantly European to predominantly Asian (Birrell and Rapson 2001). New Zealand's 1991 change to the points system had an immediate effect on the number of immigrants arriving from Asia (New Zealand Ministry for Culture and Heritage 2005; Birrell and Rapson 2001). In

Table 5.8
Patterns of New Zealander Settlement in Australia

Year	Total number of New Zealand citizen settlers	Total number of New Zealand nonnative citizen settlers	Percentage of New Zealand settlers born in third country	Percentage New Zealand settlement of total settlement
1995	16,238	3,832	23.6	16
1996	17,508	4,237	24.2	20
1997	19,508	4,539	23.4	25
1998	24,686	5,900	23.9	29
1999	31,615	9,486	30.0	34

Sources: Australian Department of Immigration and Multicultural Affairs, as cited by Birrell and Rapson (2001); "Settler Arrivals 1993–1994 to 2003–2004," https://www.dss.gov.au/our-responsibilities/settlement-and-multicultural-affairs/publications/settler-arrivals-1993-94-to-2003-04.

1986, only 18 percent of immigrants arriving in New Zealand were Asian; by 1995, nearly 60 percent were Asian (New Zealand Immigration Service n.d.).[46] However, unlike the Australian points system, New Zealand did not require that immigrants' academic and professional credentials be recognized by the relevant regulatory bodies in New Zealand. In addition, there were no caps on the number of people admitted in a particular category or profession. This meant that large numbers of immigrants arrived to find themselves unable to work in their chosen profession (Bedford 2003). This problem was exacerbated by a sluggish economy and the disproportionate effect of unemployment on ethnic minorities. Although the 1996 overall unemployment rate was 7.7 percent, it stood at over 16 percent for Asians and 14 percent for Pacific Islanders (Statistics New Zealand n.d.). New Zealand residents also earned less than their counterparts across the Tasman in Australia. In 1999, New Zealander incomes were only 73 percent of Australian incomes, which was the result of a long slide from 92 percent in 1984 (Collins 2006). These factors, combined with rapid economic growth in Australia, worked to draw New Zealanders across the Tasman Sea, and this included immigrants to New Zealand who had subsequently become New Zealand citizens.[47]

According to the Australians, the increase in the number of New Zealanders in Australia was taking a toll on the social welfare system. This illustrates the costs of unbalanced flows to the state. The Australian government projected that annual welfare costs attributed to New Zealand immigrants would grow from A$930 million in 2000 to over A$1 billion in future years (Hoadley 2003). The TTTA prevented Australia from denying New Zealanders access to state benefits, and this made the agreement increasingly costly for the Australian state. These rising costs, compensation for which Australia started agitating in

1999, further increased concern about the Trans-Tasman relationship. In particular, parties on both sides feared that the immigration dispute might cause problems in other areas of cooperation between New Zealand and Australia, particularly in the economic sphere (Hoadley 2003).

The anti-immigrant political climate in the mid- to late 1990s, the rapid increase in the total numbers of New Zealanders settling permanently in Australia, the greater percentage of New Zealanders in Australia of third country origin, particularly of Asian origin, and steadily growing welfare costs culminated in the change to the TTTA in 2001. It is impossible to be certain which, if any, of these factors played the crucial role in the change, but the patterns since 2001 suggest that growing welfare costs were the driving force. Although both the total number of New Zealanders and the percentage of arrivals born in a third country peaked in 2000–2001, both figures have since stabilized at the relatively high levels seen in the mid-1990s. Furthermore, the decrease in the level of migration from New Zealand after the all-time high in 2000–2001 may have had as much to do with New Zealand's improving economy as with the changes to the TTTA (Australia Department of Immigration and Citizenship 2005). The result of the 2001 TTTA reforms, then, has not been to reduce the level of either overall migration from New Zealand or the percentage of Asians arriving from New Zealand. Instead, the main effect has been to shift the burden of providing social welfare benefits to these migrants away from the Australian state.

For New Zealand, though, the 2001 amendment was not the solution to its own Trans-Tasman problem and, in fact, it has made it only more severe. Despite New Zealand's successful attempts to attract immigrants, it continues to hemorrhage them into Australia, which undermines its efforts to retain skilled labor (Birrell and Rapson 2001). Australia can now pick and choose which New Zealanders it wants, offering the benefits of permanent residency only to the select few who meet its requirements. Although those who fail to meet the requirements will still be allowed to remain in the country, Australia will not have to pay for their upkeep. This is a perfect solution to Australia's problem, offering the best of both worlds in that it still gets the highly skilled, desirable emigrants from New Zealand, but avoids footing the bill for the accompanying nondesirables. For New Zealand, on the other hand, it is the worst of both worlds.

The changes to the TTTA demonstrate the costs of unbalanced flows that underpin our theorization that freedom of movement agreements can exist only when the likelihood of reciprocal flows is large. They also illustrate the inequitable distribution of the benefits of migration agreements. The country on the receiving end of the migration flow can largely dictate the terms of the agreement, while the sending country can either agree to the terms or forgo the agreement, knowing that it will suffer worse consequences than the wealthier receiving country will experience. In the market of human capital, the supply is plentiful, and receiving countries can set the price. Sending countries know that if they refuse an agreement, there will be plenty of other countries willing to take their place. Although the 2001 changes to the TTTA did not benefit the New Zealanders, they were well aware that an amended agreement was far more desirable than no agreement at all.

Analysis. The case of the TTTA provides useful insight into the significance of maintaining reciprocal flows in agreements that facilitate freedom of movement. The TTTA was even more generous than the freedom of movement in Europe, as the social welfare systems provided immediate benefits to immigrants, rather than restricting movement only to workers looking for jobs or those outside the labor force with sufficient resources to support themselves. Once the unilateral nature of the flows became obvious, the receiving country unilaterally changed the terms of the agreement to limit the state's financial responsibility to those covered by the agreement. The change from reciprocal to unilateral flows follows from the increasing disparities in the standards of living of the two countries: the ratio of New Zealand to Australia stood at .91 in 1960 and rose slightly to .92 in 1984; after that, the disparities grew larger, declining to .73 in 2000 (just prior to the changes in the TTTA initiated by Australia) and to .69 by 2010. It seems remarkable that the states that are able to maintain freedom of movement appear empirically to need a ratio of at least .75 to maintain an adequate amount of reciprocity to sustain the agreement. The TTTA suggests just how rare the conditions are for labor mobility agreements to be agreed and maintained.

As with our other freedom of movement states, in Table 5.9, we provide an overview of the stocks of migrants in 2013 to illustrate the imbalance in flows from New Zealand to Australia. This imbalance led the Australian government to modify the terms of free movement. It did not reject free movement altogether but modified the agreement to select those immigrants from New Zealand whom it was willing to incorporate in its economy and social welfare system.

Table 5.9
Stocks of Member State Migrants: TTTA, 2013

Country	Emigration	Percentage of national population	Immigration	Percentage of TTTA population	Net migration
Australia	56,173	0.2	355,875	1.52	299,702
New Zealand	355,875	7.9	56,173	1.25	(299,702)

Sources: United Nations, Department of Economics and Social Affairs, Population Division (2013); "Population Pyramids of the World from 1950 to 2100," http://populationpyramid.net.

THE GULF COOPERATION COUNCIL

There appear to be only two REOs in the Global South that have made substantial progress on implementing freedom of movement that permits access by citizens of member states to national labor markets without work permits across all categories of labor: the GCC and the OECS. Both have been widely overlooked in the research on freedom of movement. Here we discuss the progress of the GCC, consisting of six member states, all located in the Arabian Peninsula and all with substantial oil deposits that have created the wealth and subsequent demand for labor, providing the impetus for freedom of movement. The GCC states are better known for the recruitment of workers, both high- and low-skilled, from other Arab states and, more recently, from Asia, as well as concerns over the treatment of those workers, particularly low-skilled workers. The freedom of movement of citizens of member states has received little attention.

The cooperation among the six GCC member states (Bahrain, Kuwait, Oman, Qatar, Saudi Arabia, and the United Arab Emirates) on labor mobility fits well with the model proposed for European states and applied to the TTTA. Similarities in wealth, language, and culture, combined with low unemployment and a strong demand for labor, led to the negotiation of a freedom of movement clause in the economic agreement that accompanied the creation of the GCC in 1981. The GCC member states have periodically adapted their regulations to account for the changing structure of national labor markets and accompanying regulations. Similar to the EU (prior to the accession of Central and Eastern European states in 2004), freedom of movement has not generated high levels of labor mobility. Wage differentials are insufficient to attract large flows in any direction.

The Arabian Peninsula was peopled by Semitic tribes over the centuries, but the rise of Islam as a religious and political movement united the peninsula in the seventh century. The intervening centuries brought innumerable conflicts among the various tribes and religious branches of Islam as well as between the Arab population and the Ottoman overlords. The establishment of independent states during the twentieth century set the stage for regional cooperation. Talks among the smaller Gulf oil states began in the early 1970s, but it was not until 1981 that the Charter of the Gulf Cooperation Council was signed by the states of Bahrain, Kuwait, Oman, Qatar, Saudi Arabia, and the United Arab Emirates. The charter begins with an acknowledgment of their common heritage; the states proclaim themselves "fully aware of the ties of special relations, common characteristics, and similar systems founded on the creed of Islam which bind them" (Charter of the Gulf Cooperation Council 1981). There has even been an effort to promote a regional identity, *Khaleeji* (Babar 2011). Yet this common heritage did not prevent the exclusion from the GCC of the seventh

Arabian Peninsula country, Yemen. Central to our argument, the wealth disparities and potential for unilateral flows from Yemen prevented the inclusion of this country in the GCC and in the free movement provisions. Moreover, freedom of movement has not been extended to citizens of other Arab states, which, according to many sources, reflect "centuries of common history, religion, and language [that] have resulted in a high degree of cultural, political and social integration in the Arab region" (Nassar 2010, 11; see also Babar 2011).

The shock that disrupted the status quo ante was the growing oil wealth of the Gulf countries, especially after the oil price shocks of the 1970s, which catapulted these countries from low to high human development status in just two decades. The oil shocks of 1973 and 1979 transferred enormous amounts of wealth to these states, which then undertook vast development projects that required significant amounts of labor to implement. However, the populations of these states were small with low labor participation rates. In 1970, the entire region comprised only 7.8 million people, and labor market participation rates were between 30 and 40 percent. Moreover, formal employment was concentrated in the public sector. Thus there was an enormous need for labor to complete the development projects that would diversify these oil economies (Winckler 1997). Responding to this demand for labor, the national strategies were twofold: to increase natality and education—that is, to grow their own labor force—and to import labor, at least in the interim. These strategies attest to the low unemployment despite the lack of systematic records of unemployment rates during this period, a fact confirmed by Winckler (1997, 2010). The import of labor included Arabs, especially Palestinians. But the GCC states ultimately turned to Asians to fill low-skilled labor positions. The Asian population working in the GCC states rose from 342,589 in 1975 to 3,258,500 ten years later (Winckler 1997).

In the midst of this economic explosion, the six Gulf oil states negotiated the charter that created the GCC. At the same time, the six countries also adopted an economic agreement providing an impetus for economic integration. The Free Trade Agreement took effect in 1983. Article 8 provides for "freedom of movement, work, and residence" as well as "the freedom of engagement in economic activity."

It is difficult to confirm with certainty that freedom of movement is fully implemented. Nonetheless, several sources appear to agree that freedom of movement is partially or fully implemented (Babar 2011; Haftel 2012).[48] The implementation of the policy was slow. The list of agreements and pronouncements by the Supreme Council of the GCC, provided in Table 5.10, provides evidence that implementation was not immediate. A protocol was signed in 1993 that ensured equal treatment of GCC nationals, initially in the private sector where nationals were generally employed in very low numbers, followed by

Table 5.10

GCC Council Regulations regarding the National Labor Movement among GCC States

Year	Treaties and protocols on freedom of movement
1981	Economic agreement: Guarantees of free movement and equal treatment in terms of work, residence, and inheritance
1993	Protocol: Equal treatment of GCC citizens in the private sector
1995	Protocol: Statute to facilitate employment and free movement
2000	Protocol: Extension of measures for equal treatment of GCC citizens in the public sector
2001	Unified economic agreement: • Reemphasized and extended the national treatment of GCC nationals in movement, residence, and employment • Removal of national labor mobility barriers • GCC nationals are considered part of the nationalization targets • No discrimination in pursuing professions among GCC nationals • Coordination among GCC states to achieve human resource development and employment
2002	Protocol: Equal GCC employment treatment stressed and deadline for implementation set for 2005 at the latest
2003	Protocol: Emphasized timetable and the fields of equal treatment in both private and government sector employment and full economic nationalization
2004	Announcement: Measures to facilitate employment and movement of nationals such as ease of travel and border formalities
2004	Protocol: Extension of umbrella of insurance protection to GCC nationals working in other GCC states in both private and public sectors; unified system optional from January 2005 and obligatory from January 2006

Source: Adapted from Ibrahim (2010).

a protocol to facilitate employment and free movement. The guarantees of equal access were extended to the public sector in 2000. In 2001, the six states negotiated the Unified Economic Agreement to deepen economic integration. As the population increased and was educated, reflecting earlier policy choices of the state governments, young GCC nationals began to enter the job market; states created labor market "nationalization" policies to ensure that they found employment. The 2001 Unified Economic Agreement ensured that GCC nationals were treated equally in terms of "nationalization targets," goals for employment of nationals. This was followed in 2004 by the extension of social insurance to GCC nationals. Thus, the GCC Supreme Council appears to have taken very seriously efforts to ensure freedom of movement. Nonetheless, as is characteristic of other regions with freedom of movement, where living standards and wages are similar, the impetus to move is slight. As of 2010, only twenty-one thousand nationals of GCC countries were living in a member state different from their country of origin (Ibrahim 2010).[49]

Analysis. Our story of the construction of the GCC economic agreement that incorporates freedom of movement points to labor market shortages that potentially could be filled by citizens of member states. The similarities in wealth when regional cooperation was first established are substantial, this despite the small population base that distorts differences in income. In 1985–88, the ratio of the standard of living of the poorest GCC country to the wealthiest GCC country was .47; taking the regional wealth average, which discounts the outlier of the United Arab Emirates, the ratio rises to .83—comparable to those found in regional freedom of movement countries in Europe. What is interesting to note, in addition, is the place of the seventh Arabian Peninsula country that is not blessed with oil wealth. Yemen, the odd country out, has a ratio of .21 to the wealthiest country. Moreover, even with their numbers swollen by the enormous influx of international migrants, Yemen's population was more than half of the GCC's combined population in 1981. Admitting Yemen, even with the common history, language, and culture, would have generated substantial one-way migratory flows over which individuals states desired unilateral control. Thus, Yemen was excluded. In later periods, wealth disparities among GCC countries broadened, as oil revenues are subject to economic shocks and because populations are small. Yet a second measure of similarities of living conditions, the Human Development Index, suggests highly similar standards of living (UNDP 2009). Yemen remains the outlier on the Arabian Peninsula and an outcast of the GCC and its freedom of movement provisions. The status of Arabian Peninsula countries is provided in Table 5.11.

It is interesting to stumble across the little-known policy of freedom of movement in the Global South and to see that it, too, fits well with the theoretical frame generated by the analysis of those dimensions of regionalization in the Global North that privilege freedom of movement.

ALTERNATIVE EXPLANATIONS

As it turns out, very little research exists that focuses specifically on the evolution of freedom of movement or, in the vocabulary of this volume, cooperation on international migration (but see Pécoud and de Guchteneire 2007).[50] The focus has been almost entirely on the EU, understandably so since this is the best-known agreement on freedom of movement. But the literature does not deal with freedom of movement per se—it focuses on regional integration more broadly construed. This theoretical focus is problematic as we have seen that,

Table 5.11
Gulf Cooperation Council Countries

Country	GDP/pc/PPP 1985–88 ($)	Population 1981	GNI/pc/PPP 2013 ($)	HDI 2013
Bahrain	9,490	373,000	32,072	0.813
Kuwait	9,310	1,448,000	85,826	0.813
Oman	9,290	247,000	42,191	0.781
Qatar	11,800	1,217,000	119,029	0.850
Saudi Arabia	9,350	10,521,000	52,109	0.839
United Arab Emirates	19,440	1,092,000	56,068	0.825
Total GCC population		14,898,000		
Average across GCC	11,447		64,549	
Yemen (non-GCC)	2,410 (1992)	8,344,000	3,945	0.499

Source: UNDP, Human Development Data, http://hdr.undp.org/en/data; UNDP (1990).

in only three of the six cases, the EEC, the Benelux Economic Union, and the GCC, freedom of movement was nested inside a regional agreement. The Nordic Common Labor Market stands alone; the Nordic Council countries tried several times to create a customs union but failed. In the case of the TTTA, Australia and New Zealand do have a regional agreement that is similar to the EU, but freedom of movement remains outside of that regional framework, subject to unilateral change. (The sixth case, the ECSC, did not provide broad freedom of movement provisions.) Nonetheless, we begin by describing the literature that seeks to explain regional integration. We turn, then, to our five successful cases and employ our explanatory variables to demonstrate the connections among the cases theoretically and empirically. Finally, we turn to very recent research that examines Mercosur's Residency Agreement that appears expansive in theory but problematic in implementation. We attempt to disentangle the origins and practice of freedom of movement and place our contribution in context.

An entire cottage industry of researchers has sprung up to describe and explain the evolution of European integration. Three main theoretical frameworks are often invoked to explain regional integration in Europe.[51] The first is labeled neoinstitutionalism and focuses on state interests (derived from domestic sources) and state power as explanatory variables.[52] From this perspective, cooperation proceeds because one or more powerful states have an interest in cooperation and bargain with other states over the shape of that cooperation, bringing along less powerful states through side payments (Moravcsik 1998). In contrast, the neofunctionalist explanation, as the label implies, focuses on the functional need for a specific policy, especially in light of rising interstate transactions (Sandholtz and Stone Sweet 1998). In this mode., subnational actors bypass the state and petition supranational actors for policies that reduce transaction costs of cross-border transactions. Supranationa. institutions that act as engines of integration, such as the European Commission, play a key role in neofunctional theories. A third model, constructivism, explores the social effects of European integration over time. It analyzes how preferences and identities of state actors may shift as a consequence of sustained interaction. To put it another way, the focus is on how policymaking elites .n member states begin to adopt a European perspective on various issues, including migration and asylum. The theory incorporates the role of ideas and the political leaders who act as "moral entrepreneurs," disseminating the new ideas to the political elite and cementing the idea in the broader population through social learning and socialization (Checkel 2001).

The neoinstitutionalist framework comes closest to our argument. According to the major proponent of the neoinstitutionalist perspective on the construction of the EU, Moravcsik (1998) argues that when state interests converge, powerful states negotiate agreements to fulfil those interests, providing side payments to promote the cooperation of smaller states, though he does not provide an explanation of the origins of state interests, arguing only that they arise from domestic politics. Here we define the locus of state interests on migration—an interest in labor market efficiency that promises to maximize state resources. We do argue, though, that an agreement will be struck when interests converge. This convergence is unique to states that, due to underlying similarities in standards of living, anticipate reciprocal flows. However, we also need to supplement our argument with an examination of institutional stickiness, to determine the longevity of the agreement.[53]

Constructivism might also provide a theoretical frame for understanding the conditions under which freedom of movement arise: these agreements take place among neighbors with a shared history, often a common language and a common culture. Perhaps it is the "shared identity" of these states that permits them to relinquish sovereignty. We have identified two individuals—Spaak and Beyen—who, as foreign ministers for Belgium and the Netherlands, respectively, incorporated the ideas from the Benelux Union to the EEC. But although there is surely an informational advantage to concluding agreements with neighboring states, a constructivist framework has difficulty in identifying the timing of these agreements. A constructivist explanation could not distinguish between the 1945 failed efforts to create the Nordic Common Labor Market and the 1954 successful efforts to negotiate the same. Similarly, the constructivist frame would be unable to determine the difference in outcomes between the ECSC in 1952 and the EEC in 1957. It also fails to explain why the TTTA, which confirms a centuries-old labor flow, would be modified unilaterally to constrict labor mobility in 2001. Common history, rather, works to inform the potential participants that the flows will be reciprocal rather than unilateral.

The theory that fits least well with the evidence is the neofunctionalist argument that privileges substate and supranational actors in constructing integration. The neofunctionalist argument does not do a good job of explaining the rise of supranational actors in the first place. Once a treaty has been signed that creates supranational institutions, such as the High Authority in the case of the ECSC and the commission in the case of the EEC, these institutions and actors exist to facilitate the construction of additional elements of integration. There is no single set of established supranational actors as these freedom of movement agreements are negotiated. The prominent players in the Benelux Economic Union and EEC treaty negotiations, Spaak and Beyen, are foreign ministers representing their own countries, rather than supranational actors. Moreover, the reliance on the EU as the central case from which theory is generated proves deceptive because it is heavily institutionalized. None of the other five cases of freedom of movement have much of a supranational apparatus that would promote labor market integration. We have identified subnational actors such as unions and employers as playing a prominent role in the European negotiations, but they did so primarily through petitioning their own national governments (Haas 1958; Moravcsik 1998; Maas 2006). However, there is little evidence that subnational actors were prominent in the other four cases.

It is always difficult to evaluate theory with a single case; even if we look at the EU as several episodes of integration, it is difficult to discern the idiosyncratic from the general. That is why it is useful to present other cases of cooperation that facilitate mobility. Because we are able to break down the origins of freedom of movement in the EU in its institutional trajectory, we actually have four European cases. Our central variables are present in three cases, the Nordic Common Labor Market, the Benelux Economic Union, and the EEC, and absent in the fourth case, the ECSC. We confirm our understanding by presenting evidence from two additional cases that are usually overlooked in the research on migration cooperation: the TTTA and GCC.[54] Although six cases do not constitute a large-N study, they do provide multiple observations and allow us to see common patterns that underpin freedom of movement. These six cases allow us to evaluate our theoretical claims alongside the claims of theorists of regional integration and demonstrate that they fall short on this element of regional integration, while our variables can explain all six cases, five of success and one of failure. Chapter 4 presents complementary evidence from twenty-eight regional organizations that confirms that wealth inequalities are consistently associated with the absence of freedom of movement.

Incorporating a case of freedom of movement in the Global South confirms the value of our emphasis on reciprocal flows and the conditions that generate reciprocal flows. The freedom of movement provisions in the economic agreement negotiated among the GCC member states in tandem with the charter creating the GCC also fit our emphasis on similarities in wealth, low unemployment, and a demand for labor. Moreover, the patterns of flows produced by freedom of movement find parallels in Europe, at least until the accession of the ten member states in 2004 that did not meet the criteria for freedom of movement and have produced one-way flows. In the GCC, few citizens of member states move, in large part because the conditions are so similar. The noneconomic costs of migration mostly outweigh the economic gains, leading to small intraregional flows.

There has been a burst of activity as well as scholarly interest in the recent agreements in Latin America that appear to move in the direction of freedom of movement (Margheritis 2013; Acosta 2016; Acosta Arcarazo and Geddes 2014). The limited scholarly work on this phenomenon in South America attempts to extract the theoretical debate from the European regional integration debate and provide a more generic framework. Acosta Arcarazo and Geddes (2014, 30–31) provide one of the most theoretically developed attempts to understand regional migration cooperation as a singular phenomenon. The elements of their analytical framework are consistent with our own, which reinforces our emphasis on patterns of migration, the status quo ante, the interests of sending and receiving states, and international institutions. Acosta Arcarazo and Geddes argue that material and ideational factors are important, while regional diffusion (between Europe and South America) is minimal. They cite patterns of migration in South America as the most important material factor: "a dramatic increase in the turn of the century in the number of South American emigrants, mainly to the US and Spain" as well as the fact that "immigration in South American countries shifted from being extra-continental until the 1960s to mainly intra-regional flows from the 1970s onward." They also note that "by and large, all countries can be considered as senders and recipients," echoing our emphasis on reciprocity of flows. Thus, they cite patterns that we have posited as being central to freedom of movement agreements. The ideational factor they highlight is associated with "the large number of South American migrants in an irregular situation, both outside and inside the region, and the rejection of the criminalization of their situation" (Acosta Arcarazo and Geddes 2014, 30). This second ideational component fits with our emphasis on the difference in interests of sending and receiving states. Enhancing regional freedom of movement in South America might be interpreted as killing two birds with one stone. In the first instance, it reflects the changing patterns of migration away from unilateral flows to reciprocal flows (reinforced by decreased levels of cross-national inequality) (Cornia 2011). Second, it allows Mercosur member states, as sending states that desire to enhance legal flows to other regions, to employ an institution in which they have institutional power to create an alternative set of rules to govern international migration. Of course, what we have found is that the proposed alternative to the status quo will not be adopted by the receiving states if they prefer the status quo. The fact that Mercosur decriminalizes undocumented migration will not cause other regions or states to do the same. Nonetheless, as noted in chapter 4, Mercosur's Residence Agreement has not been implemented; it reflects "implementation gaps and a weaker regional governance setting" (Acosta Arcarazo and Geddes 2014, 20). In fact, Acosta Arcarazo and Geddes argue that "due to the lack of supranational oversight of its implementation, migrants still largely depend on national laws and procedures" (Acosta Arcarazo and Geddes 2014, 32). This is the reason that we do not include Mercosur in our case studies of freedom of movement while including it in our overview of regional agreements that have not yet implemented freedom of movement.

Our argument distinguishes between facilitated mobility—visa-free entry—and labor market access for citizens of member states—freedom of movement. In distinguishing between the "mobility regime" and the "migration regime," we limit our theoretical claims to those agreements that generate access to national labor markets. We also privilege the distinction between a negotiated agreement and an implemented agreement. Thus, our framework is nuanced in what we claim. Thus far, our theoretical frame has performed well, but it is a starting place for understanding the possibilities for international cooperation rather than an ending point.

CONCLUSIONS

Freedom of movement is a distinctive type of international cooperation on migration that is exceptional. It does not require economic integration, and the institutional frame that organizes freedom of movement varies from nominal to substantial. Because there are so few instances of freedom of movement, it is difficult to construct theory that does not rely inductively on the specific instances that we are trying to explain. Nonetheless, within our broader question of international cooperation on migration, we have noted the significance of unilateral flows versus reciprocal flows and employ reciprocity as a mechanism for generating a theory about the conditions under which reciprocity can take place. Reciprocity in migration is a solution to the dilemma of inefficient labor markets: states agree to the free inflow of immigrants but demand that emigrants have free access to each other's labor markets. Reciprocity, in turn, depends on specific conditions: similar standards of living and assurance that native workers will not be displaced by immigrant workers. This means that immigrants must receive the same benefits in terms of wages and welfare as the native population so that employers will not replace domestic labor with foreign labor. Moreover, full employment ensures that the state is not burdened with welfare benefits for either the domestic workforce or the foreign labor force.

We have employed both primary and secondary resources to provide evidence to underpin our empirical analysis. We take advantage of the independent institutional origins of four separate instances of freedom of movement (three successful and one unsuccessful) in Europe to evaluate our hypotheses about the determinants of international cooperation. We employ a fifth instance, the TTTA, to validate our hypotheses and bring in a sixth example, the GCC, of which we were unaware when developing our theory. The fact that this last case fits our framework well suggests that the basic causal relationships that we posit are more generalizable.

Our argument is complicated by the institutional environment in which these agreements may be embedded. If the institutional structure is nominal, as in the case of the TTTA, the agreement can be modified when the conditions underlying the agreement change. However, if freedom of movement is embedded in a wider agreement, then institutional stickiness prevents the agreement from being modified even when the conditions that we argue are required are absent.

CHAPTER 6

Criminality in Migration
Successful Multilateral Cooperation

"GRACE" QUIT SCHOOL IN the tenth grade to help support her family in Nigeria. After working at various jobs in her home country for three years, her father introduced her to a woman whose sister lived in Germany. The woman arranged for Grace to travel to Germany, where she was told she would have to work for the sister to pay off the expense of her trip, after which she could find other work and send money home to her family. Once she arrived in Germany, she was told that her debt was €50,000 (approximately $56,000), and that she would have to work off her debt as a prostitute in a legal brothel. She had arrived in the country under a false passport, and she was told that if she did not comply, she would be deported. "I cried every time a man slept with me, because I was brought up Christian," she shared with Equality Now's Survivor Stories Project. "Back in Nigeria, the father of my son had raped me, and this reminded me of that over and over."

Seven months later, when police carried out a check of the brothel, Grace confirmed that she was there voluntarily. They arrested her after realizing that her paperwork was not authentic, and she was taken to an immigration detention facility, where she became very ill. Once hospitalized, she was diagnosed with AIDS. After her release, the trafficker for whom she had been working tracked her down and told her that she still owed more than €25,000. By then, Grace had come into contact with SOLWODI, an international NGO that supports victims of trafficking and abuse, which eventually helped Grace settle legally in Germany and report her traffickers to the police (Equality Now 2014).

Ima Matul's story has many similarities to Grace's experience, although the countries are different and she was not forced into prostitution. Seventeen-year-old Ima was working as a housekeeper in her native Indonesia in 1997 when her employer introduced her to a cousin in Los Angeles who was looking for a nanny. She was offered the job and was excited about the prospect of working in the United States. But, upon arrival, her "employer" confiscated her passport and threatened to report her to the police if she ever ran away. She worked seven days a week, with no pay, facing constant verbal and physical abuse. Finally, after two years, she learned enough English and worked up enough courage to pass a note to a nanny working in a neighbor's home, asking for help. The nanny shared the note with her own employers, who arranged to rescue Ima and take her to a shelter run by the Coalition to Abolish Slavery and Trafficking. As in so many cases of trafficking, her captors were never prosecuted (Hargreaves 2013).

Every year, approximately 800,000 people are trafficked across international borders, generating an estimated $32 billion in annual profits for traffickers, approximately $40,000 per trafficked individual (US Department of State 2007; ILO 2005). Estimates suggest that approximately 66 percent of trafficked individuals end up in commercial sexual exploitation, although the figures for women are even higher (US Department of Justice 2004a). Women and girls make up 80 percent of the trafficked population, and 70 percent are sexually exploited (US Department of State 2007; US Department of Justice 2004a, 2004b). Human trafficking represents a significant violation of human and migrant rights, particularly for women. It also represents a huge source of revenue for international criminal syndicates, which may also be involved in drug trafficking, the illicit arms trade, piracy, and other illegal activity.

The figures for smuggled individuals are much more elusive, and the numbers reported vary widely, particularly because there is no consensus on the methodology used to count smuggled migrants. Three elements distinguish smuggled individuals from trafficked individuals: the source of profit, transnationalism, and presence of victimization (Bouteillet-Paquet 2011). Traffickers earn their profits from the labor of trafficked individuals, while smugglers earn profits from fees collected from the smuggled individuals. While trafficking can occur within or between countries, smuggling is transnational by definition. Last, trafficked individuals are victimized by traffickers, while smuggling does not necessarily involve victimization (although it can); individuals may freely engage smugglers to transport them across borders for an agreed on fee, free of coercion.

In practice, it can be difficult to distinguish smuggled individuals from other types of undocumented migrants (who are also difficult to count). The EU has attempted to develop common measurement tools to track migrant smuggling. Yet even in Europe, there is no consensus on the percentage of irregular migrants who are smuggled. Dutch authorities, for example, estimated in 2000 that 60 to 70 percent of irregular migrants were smuggled (Bouteillet-Paquet 2011; Aronowitz 2001). In Switzerland, one NGO estimated that 100 percent of irregular immigrants were smuggled (Bouteillet-Paquet 2011; Doomernik and Kyle 2004). However, Richard Staring (2004) estimates that only 15 to 30 percent of irregular migrants in Western Europe are smuggled (Bouteillet-Paquet 2011). In the United States, an estimated 80 percent of undocumented migrants use smugglers (Zhang 2007). Given that there are 1.8 to 3.3 million undocumented migrants residing in Europe, and an estimated 11.1 million in the United States, the number of smuggled migrants is likely very large, even if the lower end of the estimates is accurate (Yen 2012; Bouteillet-Paquet 2011).

Human trafficking and the related but distinct phenomenon of smuggling fit under the broader category of migration problems facing states that we defined as "illegality" in the introduction. Problems of illegality also include undocumented migration, but trafficking and smuggling present challenges that both overlap with those of undocumented migration and are unique. First, trafficked and smuggled individuals are often undocumented migrants. By default, if not by design, policies that seek to address undocumented migration may apply to trafficked and smuggled migrants as well. But stricter enforcement of migration policies meant to curb undocumented migration may unintentionally fuel trafficking and smuggling as determined migrants grow more desperate in their attempts to enter desirable destination countries. Where previously they may have been able to find their own way in, they become increasingly reliant on smuggling networks to which they pay large sums of money, or vulnerable to traffickers who make false promises about what awaits them on the other side of the border. Criminal entrepreneurs emerge to meet the demand of migrants seeking ways into destination countries and the demand for trafficked or smuggled labor (sexual and nonsexual) from segments of the host society. These entrepreneurs present a unique challenge to state authority, distinct from that of the individual undocumented migrant; their criminal activity undermines law and order, contributes to the black market economy, and may fuel violence and other illicit activities.[1]

The unique features of trafficking and smuggling lead us to predict that the international community will respond to the problem differently than it does to other migration-related problems, even other problems of illegality. In this chapter, we identify the trafficking- and smuggling-related policy space in which states, both sending and receiving, have similar preferences that have facilitated international cooperation. These shared interests have facilitated relatively easy bargaining between states, resulting in two protocols to an international treaty, the UN Convention Against Transnational Organized Crime: the Protocol to Prevent, Suppress and Punish Trafficking in Persons, Especially Women and Children, and the Protocol Against the Smuggling of Migrants by Land, Sea, and Air.[2] These protocols, in turn, have facilitated formal and informal international cooperation between states (bilaterally and regionally) on trafficking- and smuggling-related law enforcement. They complement a preexisting informal regional framework to address smuggling and trafficking through RCPs. But, we note that enforceable international obligations to protect the rights of trafficking and smuggling victims are noticeably weaker or even nonexistent, indicating that states have been unwilling to bargain their way to agreements on these issues due to divergent interests and sovereignty costs.[3] Instead, unilateral action has been the preferred path. In particular, we examine the case of the United States, which has willingly extended far more extensive protections to trafficking victims (and, to a much lesser extent, smuggling victims) than it has been willing to commit to internationally. In addition, the country has unilaterally pursued a program to coerce other states into combatting trafficking and smuggling domestically while simultaneously supporting the international agreements.

To understand the timing and shape of international cooperation on criminality, we first present the status quo ante, which reflects a long history of multilateral cooperation, followed by a description of sending and receiving state preferences. We point to a changed trafficking environment that required states to return to the bargaining table. We explain why multilateralism arises in contrast to what we have argued is the predominant form of international cooperation on migration, bilateralism. We then turn to the multilateral, regional, bilateral, and unilateral evidence that supports our contentions. Finally, we juxtapose our explanation with alternative efforts to understand interstate cooperation on illegality.

THE STATUS QUO AND STATE PREFERENCES

The Status Quo Ante. Human trafficking and smuggling have been on the international agenda since at least 1904, when European states negotiated and subsequently ratified the International Agreement for the Suppression of White Slave Traffic (Bruch 2004; Morcom and Schloenhardt 2011). This is merely the starting point of a long history of international cooperation on human trafficking underpinned by numerous multilateral treaties. Because trafficking is a multidimensional issue, it involves treaties on trafficking for sexual exploitation, slavery, forced labor, and child labor. Most of the treaties were negotiated in the first half of the twentieth century, predating the rise of the human rights agenda after World War II. A number of the most prominent international instruments are listed in Table 6.1 to provide an indication that, unlike migrant rights, which we address in chapter 7, multilateralism is common when dealing with illegality in migration. Moreover, the UN "Toolkit to Combat Trafficking in Persons" (UNODC 2008, 18–24) lists a wide array of other international instruments that address human trafficking either directly or indirectly. These include six human rights treaties, eight humanitarian treaties, nine treaties concerning migration, four additional labor instruments, one gender-specific treaty, four additional child-specific instruments, five additional treaties on slavery, and

Table 6.1

Multilateral Agreements on Trafficking

	Date of convention	Number of ratifications
Trafficking instruments		
International Agreement for the Suppression of the White Slave Trade (amended 1947 and 1949)	1904	78
Protocol Amending the International Agreement for the Suppression of White Slave Traffic (amended 1947 and 1949)	1910	54
International Convention for the Suppression of the Traffic in Women and Children (amended 1947)	1921	73
International Convention on the Suppression of the Traffic in Women of Full Age (amended 1947)	1933	45
Convention for the Suppression of the Traffic in Persons and of the Exploitation of the Prostitution of Others	1949	82
Labor instruments		
Convention Concerning Forced or Compulsory Labour (ILO Convention No. 29)	1930	178
Convention Concerning the Abolition of Forced Labour (ILO Convention No. 105)	1957	175 (2 denounced)
Convention Concerning Minimum Age for Admission for Employment (ILO Convention No. 138)	1973	169
Convention Concerning the Prohibition and Immediate Action for the Elimination of the Worst Forms of Child Labour (ILO Convention No. 182)	1999	180
Slavery instruments		
Slavery Convention (as amended by 1953 Protocol)	1926	118
Protocol Amending the Slavery Convention	1953	61
Supplementary Convention on the Abolition of Slavery, the Slave Trade, and Institutions and Practices Similar to Slavery	1956	123
New instruments		
Protocol to Prevent, Suppress, and Punish Trafficking in Persons, Especially Women and Children, Supplementing the United Nations Convention Against Transnational Organized Crime	2000	169
Protocol Against the Smuggling of Migrants by Land, Sea, and Air, Supplementing the United Nations Convention Against Transnational Organized Crime	2000	142

Sources: UNODC (2006); ratifications from WhatConvention.org and ILO (n.d.-b).

three treaties on development. One may rightly ask why new treaties on trafficking and smuggling were required as well as why these issues were addressed as protocols to the UN Convention Against Transnational Organized Crime.

The multilateral status quo involving trafficking and its associated dimensions was in place by 1957, with only two treaties on child labor added in 1973 and 1999. The major instruments we describe here were negotiated in 1999 and 2000, subsequent to UN General Assembly Resolution 53/111 of 9 December 1998 that called into existence an Ad Hoc Committee on the Elaboration of a Convention Against Transnational Organized Crime. The new instruments were required because existing international agreements and definitions were not adequate to deal with the trafficking and migrant smuggling that emerged in the late 1980s and early 1990s. First, already existing transnational criminal networks realized that a new opportunity for profits was available by diversifying their criminal activities to include trafficking in persons. Combatting transnational criminal networks required new types of coordination. Second, existing definitions did not encompass the many types of trafficking that arose. And third, transnational trafficking and smuggling flows increased starting in the 1980s.

Examining the various multilateral instruments dealing with human trafficking reveals both the changing human rights discourse as well as the novel forms of enslavement. The original trafficking agreement emblazons in its title a concern for "white" slavery, rather than a racially neutral terminology. Subsequent conventions focus on women and children and limit the activity to prostitution. The initial slavery convention addresses "chattel" slavery, where one person "owns" another person. It does not address the various forms of indentured servitude that reflect the types of trafficking and smuggling patterns in the contemporary era. Thus, new definitions were required.

There was also an increase in the level of transnational trafficking. In Europe, this increase was facilitated by the economic collapse of the Soviet Union and Eastern Europe, which generated a huge pool of new potential migrants seeking entrance into Western Europe and developed countries more broadly (Outshoorn 2004). Then, the political collapse of the authoritarian regimes in Eastern Europe and the Soviet Union removed the strict exit controls that had been in place for decades. The fledgling states of the former communist bloc did not have the capacity to manage the flow of their own citizens leaving for Western Europe, nor were they able to manage the inflow of individuals from other countries, particularly in Asia, looking for backdoor access to Western Europe (Laczko 2003). As a result, Western European receiving states faced challenges to regulating their borders and controlling migration that simply had not existed before.

In North America, traffickers and smugglers increasingly exploited the relative weakness of Mexican authorities to use Mexico as a transit route to the United States. Illegal migrants from China, Southeast Asia, and Central and South America smuggled and trafficked to the United States largely came through Mexico, and sometimes through Canada (Finckenauer and Schrock n.d.). The number of these migrants increased in the 1980s and 1990s as the number of people wanting to come to the United States exceeded the available spots.

The large pool of economically desperate people in less developed parts of the world, along with the chaos of the postcommunist period, combined with a decreased desire for immigrants in Europe coinciding with the first oil crisis beginning in 1973, created an opportunity for human trafficking and smuggling. This, combined with an increasingly globalized economy in which transnational communication, travel, and economic exchange are easy and common, led to the rise of criminal operations involved in trafficking and smuggling across multiple borders. These criminal enterprises grew and flourished where corruption and lawlessness were rampant, in places like post-Soviet Eastern Europe and Mexico (Stoeker 2000). By the 1990s, it was clear that the major global smuggling and trafficking pipelines ran across Asia into Europe and through Central America into the United States (Winer 1997).

The increase in the size and sophistication of trafficking operations drew the attention of both states and human rights activists. The women's movement, particularly in developed states, made combating trafficking a priority beginning in the 1980s (Bruch 2004). Their efforts gained traction as the problem grew in the 1990s. In the United States, a number of high-profile cases involving smuggled or trafficked migrants grabbed the attention of local politicians, law enforcement, immigrant rights activists, and the general public. One investigation in New York, for example, found dozens of deaf Mexican migrants living in cramped quarters, selling trinkets on the street. All of the profits went to the criminal gang that had brought the migrants to the United States, who threatened, beat, tortured, and sexually abused those who didn't meet daily quotas (DeStefano 2007). Cases like these highlighted the dangers and problems posed by illicit migration. From the perspective of states, trafficking and smuggling presented a threat to law and order that existing laws and strategies were unable to address. For human rights and migrant rights activists, trafficking and smuggling created a class of victims that was inadequately protected from both the traffickers/smugglers who sought to exploit them and the states that sought to expel them.

State Preferences. All types of states (sending, receiving, and transit) have an interest in reducing trafficking and smuggling, because it represents a "challenge to the authority of the state itself" (Lloyd, Simmons, and Stewart 2012, 10). The accompanying criminality can provide an avenue for the corruption of state officials, a challenge to state sovereignty over who may enter the state's territory, and a new funding stream for organized crime outfits. Specifically, because both victims and perpetrators of transnational trafficking cross borders, successful efforts to combat trafficking required cross-border collaboration on a wide array of law enforcement issues. Mattar (2013, 1) argues that combatting trafficking requires transnational cooperation on "the three EXs": exchange of information, extraterritoriality, and extradition. The exchange of information allows law enforcement officials to better detect, deter, and prosecute criminal activities through "information sharing, collection of evidence, investigation of criminals who commit cross-border crimes, facilitating judicial cooperation, witness protection in criminal proceedings, substantive and procedural protective measures designed to assist trafficking victims, repatriation of victims, and reducing re-victimization" (Mattar 2013, 9). Extraterritoriality expands the ability to prosecute crimes even if they do not take place on the territory of the state. Extradition allows states to move criminals from one jurisdiction to another to facilitate prosecution. This is to say that if both sending and receiving states prefer reduced trafficking and smuggling, only multilateral efforts will provide the outcomes desired. In terms of the international relations literature on cooperation, this can be classified as a coordination problem in which there is little incentive to defect once the focal point on which states can coordinate is found.

In addition, trafficking and smuggling produce real harm for victimized segments of society. That said, trafficking and smuggling manifest differently in traditional sending and receiving states, so that state preferences on protection of victims—migrant rights—diverge. In particular, trafficking is not just a transnational problem; 34 percent of trafficking is domestic, and another 37 percent cross-border but within the same subregion (UNODC 2014). Only 26 percent of trafficking flows are transregional, and these flows tend to be directed toward North America, Europe, and wealthy areas of the Middle East (UNODC 2014). Transregional trafficking tends to be much more complex, involving logistical hurdles like intercontinental travel, passports and visas, lodging, and supervision before exploitation begins. Within-country or subregion trafficking is less sophisticated, so the level of organization of the traffickers is simpler. In addition, in countries of origin, 95 percent of traffickers are citizens, while in destination countries, 58 percent of traffickers are foreign (UNODC 2014).

The challenges of combatting trafficking and smuggling are different in sending and receiving states. Receiving states are dealing with an international problem, and many of the key perpetrators may be able to seek refuge in their home countries, making cooperation with sending states crucial to effective law enforcement. Sending states face what is largely a domestic problem, except for the victims. Their interest in international cooperation, then, may lean toward protecting their citizens who are victimized abroad.

Both of the mechanisms that we identified in chapter 2 drove states to the negotiating table: both receiving states and sending states were motivated to pursue cooperation. On one side, exogenous events (the collapse of the communist bloc and increased flows through Mexico) created bigger and more sophisticated trafficking and smuggling operations that receiving states found difficult to combat unilaterally. Sending states, too, were concerned with criminality. Thus, the status quo of unilateral action on human trafficking and smuggling was not favorable to either sending or receiving states, since it fueled lawlessness and criminality on both sides. Although receiving states needed the cooperation of sending states in order to prosecute traffickers and smugglers, more than the other way around, the best alternative to negotiated agreement was not the status quo for either side. Reaching an agreement therefore required fewer side payments, leading to a low member surplus,[4] at least on the facet of the issue where shared interests were greatest: law enforcement. The costs of negotiating a series of bilateral agreements among the 169 states that have ratified the Trafficking Protocol are large; more than 14,000 bilateral agreements would be necessary to bind all states, rather than the one agreement. It is not surprising, then, that the international community was able to create formal, international treaties (the Palermo Protocols) to address the criminality aspect of human trafficking and smuggling.

Other facets of the trafficking and smuggling problem have not been quite so amenable to negotiation. Sending states are also interested in ensuring the protection of their citizens, the "victims" of trafficking and smuggling, abroad. At the same time, they are not eager to facilitate the return of these trafficked and smuggled migrants, many of whom wanted to migrate and did so to escape poverty and other desperate conditions at home. Thus, sending states may support policies that allow victims of trafficking and smuggling to remain in the receiving state while simultaneously condemning the illegal operations that facilitate their migration.

Sending states are not the only ones concerned about the rights of trafficked and, to a lesser extent, smuggled victims. Both international and domestic human and migrant rights activists, feminists, and others began to increasingly pressure state governments, particularly in receiving states, to protect victims in the 1980s and 1990s. In the United States in particular, the issue brought together an unusual coalition of feminists, human rights activists, and evangelical Christians that effectively lobbied the United States to protect victims (again, with a much greater emphasis on trafficked rather than smuggled individuals). As we highlighted in chapter 2, domestic political pressure is one of the exogenous pressures that can change the cost of the status quo ante for states, and in this case, it certainly contributed to receiving states' determination to pursue international cooperation. In the end, though, receiving states have made few international commitments to protecting victims, even as they succumbed to pressure to do so domestically. Sending states found that they had limited power to move receiving states on this issue in international forums, succeeding only to get the issues of victim rights on the agenda in a nonbinding fashion or informal environments. Receiving states found that they could effectively manage political pressure from activists through domestic law rather than international commitments, avoiding any sovereignty costs.

In the following sections, we examine the development of formal, multilateral cooperation in form of the Palermo Protocols; the bilateral cooperation that has ensued subsequent to the protocols; the informal, regional cooperation occurring prior to (and concurrently with) the formal, multilateral cooperation; and the unilateral action taken by the United States.

MULTILATERAL COOPERATION: THE PALERMO PROTOCOLS

In this section, we describe the process that led to the Trafficking and Smuggling Protocols to the UN Convention Against Transnational Organized Crime. These two protocols represent the most global and most binding form of cooperation that has emerged to address the problems of trafficking and smuggling. We argue that the lens of criminality emerged as the most successful one to coordinate formal international action because it served the dominant interests of powerful receiving states while also appealing to sending states, which minimized the side payments needed to reach agreement. The criminality frame appealed to the broadest swath of states, both sending and receiving.

The Trafficking and Smuggling Protocols to the UN Convention Against Transnational Organized Crime were initially discussed at an April 1997 session of the UN Commission on Crime Prevention and Criminal Justice (CCPCJ 1997). Argentina proposed a new convention against the trafficking of children as part of a program to address transnational organized crime, in part because it was dissatisfied with efforts to incorporate this into the UN Convention on the Rights of the Child (Gallagher 2001). At a subsequent meeting in September, Austria proposed that a similar protocol focusing on smuggling be drafted.[5] These suggestions were embraced by the United States and a number of Western European states, which had begun to develop antitrafficking and antismuggling efforts of their own. Both the United States and Argentina submitted draft proposals for a trafficking protocol in preparation for the first meeting in January 1999 of the Ad Hoc Committee on the Elaboration of a Convention Against Transnational Organized Crime, which was charged with drafting the protocol.

By the second meeting of the committee, however, it was the clear that the US proposal would serve as the basis for the protocol; the more expansive Argentinean proposal did not garner the necessary support (Schloenhardt 2009).

The Trafficking and Smuggling Protocols had the support of a broad base of states, including powerful ones like the United States. But the debate over the language of the protocols quickly turned contentious as the Ad Hoc Committee met in a series of eleven sessions, which came to be known as the Vienna Process. The Ad Hoc Committee comprised state delegates involved in the UN crime control program, which usually receives little attention from the human rights and migration policy communities. However, the UNHCR and the UN High Commissioner for Human Rights mobilized human rights and migration IGOs and NGOs in an effort to shape the protocol in a way that would prioritize the rights of trafficked and smuggled migrants (Fitzpatrick 2003).

The debates during the Vienna Process centered on two issues. The first issue was whether the trafficking and smuggling problem should be approached as a crime and border control issue or as a matter of state obligation to safeguard the human rights of trafficked and smuggled people. The second issue was whether or not the definition of trafficking should include migrants involved in "voluntary" prostitution (Chuang 2006). Sending states and their allies in the human rights and immigrant rights policy communities worked together to advocate for the human rights lens in the protocol, but their efforts had a very limited effect. Receiving states had embraced the idea of a trafficking protocol to the Convention Against Transnational Organized Crime precisely because it allowed them to maintain a focus on law enforcement solutions rather than the obligations of receiving states to protect trafficked and smuggled migrants. The receiving states had no intention of signing anything that imposed new obligations, or expanded existing obligations, under international law. So while debate and discussion about the human rights aspects of trafficking and smuggling were plentiful during the Vienna Process, there was little hope that they would become part of the final agreement in any meaningful way.

The final versions of the Trafficking and Smuggling Protocols said little of substance about human rights, beyond recognizing that states already have obligations to trafficked and smuggled migrants under existing human rights treaties and general legal principles that are not nullified by the Palermo Protocols (Fitzpatrick 2003). One concession that the sending states and human rights activists did achieve is the inclusion of the protection of human rights as one of the three "purposes" of the Trafficking Protocol. States, however, are not obligated to do much to actually protect the rights of trafficking victims; they must only "endeavor" to provide for their safety, "ensure" that their domestic legal systems provide privacy for victims and the possibility for victims to seek compensation, "consider" cooperation with NGOs to provide services for trafficking victims, and "consider" measures to allow trafficking victims to remain in the country. At the same time, receiving states are also free to arrest, prosecute, and deport trafficked or smuggled individuals. Sending states, however, do face obligations under the Palermo Protocols to accept the return of any trafficked or smuggled citizen or permanent resident; these obligations are stated in much more forceful language (Fitzpatrick 2003). Every section of Article 8 of the Trafficking Protocol, for example, asserts definitively that sending states "shall" carry out specific obligations, including accepting the return of trafficked individuals, showing due regard for their safety, providing travel documents to the requesting receiving state without delay, and so on.

The second issue that generated divisions during the Vienna Process was the issue of "voluntary" prostitution. On this issue, the human rights community was divided, and it led to rancorous debate among the various representatives of human rights organizations, women's organizations, and immigrant rights organizations participating in the process. One NGO bloc, operating under the name of the Human Rights Caucus and led by the International Human Rights Law Group and the Global Alliance Against Trafficking in Women, brought together human rights activists, antitrafficking activists, and sex worker rights activists. The caucus advocated for a distinction between trafficking and prostitution on the grounds that a migrant could, of her own free will, choose to engage in prostitution. The opposing bloc, led by the American-based Coalition Against Trafficking in Persons, argued that all prostitution was inherently coerced and thus all sex work should be considered trafficking in the protocol. This disagreement over the definition of trafficking in relation to prostitution so occupied the representatives of the various NGOs and IGOs at the Vienna Process that they were limited in their ability to find enough common ground to move onto other issues addressed in the protocol (Ditmore and Wijers 2003).

The two blocs of NGOs found allies in the state delegations. Initially, Argentina (the original proponent of the Trafficking Protocol) and the Philippines sided with the antiprostitution bloc. On the other side, the United States took the lead in advocating for a more restrictive definition of trafficking that included only "forced" prostitution (Gallagher 2001). It eventually backed away from the position, at least publicly, most likely because of increasing domestic pressures (Bennett and Colson 2000). In the end, though, the Trafficking Protocol excluded consensual prostitution and cleverly avoided defining prostitution altogether, instead referring to "exploitation of prostitution of others" and "other forms of sexual exploitation," leaving these terms up for interpretation by domestic legal systems (Chuang 2006).

It is unsurprising that the bid to define all prostitution as forced failed during the Vienna Process. The antiprostitution argument was premised on the idea that no one would voluntarily engage in sex work unless her circumstances were so dire that she had no other choice. Following this logic, the same claim could be made about all migrants who make great sacrifices to escape dire conditions, working at dangerous or menial jobs because they have no better option. By defining all prostitution as trafficking, the line between "smuggling" and "trafficking" would have become irreversibly blurred. As it stands, "trafficked" migrants are victims while "smuggled" migrants have agency. While the Smuggling Protocol intentionally stops short of criminalizing smuggled migrants, it does not identify them as victims in need of special protection (International Council on Human Rights Policy 2010). Receiving states have no interest in redefining all smuggled migrants as victims of trafficking, which would generate new state obligations toward migrants who choose to get themselves smuggled across borders. So, for receiving states, there was a significant incentive to maintain the distinction between voluntary and forced prostitution that had nothing to do with their views on prostitution as a legitimate occupation. This interest was strong enough for the US administration to resist significant pressure from domestic groups advocating a more expansive definition of trafficking. And in the end, the distinction between trafficking and smuggling was maintained in the Palermo Protocols, serving the interests of the powerful receiving states while carefully maintaining language that all signatories could support.

The Trafficking Protocol received much more attention than the Smuggling Protocol because of the heated debate about prostitution and the more extensive obligations that states should have toward victims of trafficking. Despite this public controversy, there was a broad consensus that trafficking produces victims to whom the state has some obligation and that traffickers are criminals who should be prosecuted. The consensus on the issue of smuggling was not quite so complete. First, while some smugglers are hardened criminals who present a danger to society, many are part of smaller operations that may even be driven by a somewhat altruistic motivation to help migrants cross borders, even if they also get paid (International Council on Human Rights Policy 2010). Sending states may thus be less enthusiastic about cracking down on migrant smugglers than receiving states; some types of smuggling may be no more detrimental to the sending state than other types of undocumented migration (it could even be beneficial). Second, there is less consensus on the degree to which smuggled migrants are victims than there is on the victimization of trafficked individuals. In practice, the line between smuggling and trafficking is often unclear. Migrants sometimes start off as smuggled, but once they are in the destination country, they may be forced to work to pay off their smuggling debts. In both trafficking and smuggling, there can be elements of free choice and coercion, despite the fact that coercion is supposed to be one of the legally defining differences between the two (Bouteillet-Paquet 2011). Furthermore, migrant rights advocates would argue that smuggled migrants are "coerced" to emigrate by poverty, oppression, insecurity, and a host of other problems. If the level of victimization determines the degree of obligation that a state has to migrants, then recipient states will want to narrow the definition of a victim while sending states will want to expand it.

In the end, the Smuggling Protocol represented a compromise on these two issues rather than a consensus. It called for the criminalization of the smuggler, but it made clear that the migrants themselves are not criminals. It also recognized that states should seek to address the dire circumstances that lead migrants to seek out the services of smugglers, but it did not enforce any specific obligations toward smuggled migrants. By contrast, the Trafficking Protocol received a great deal of attention and provoked greater debate, but the basis for consensus (on both the criminalization of traffickers and the victimization of the trafficked) was stronger.

An examination of the states that have signed, ratified, and/or acceded to the Palermo Protocols demonstrates the slightly greater consensus that the Trafficking Protocol generated versus the Smuggling Protocol. Overall, both received widespread support; 80 states promptly signed the Trafficking Protocol, and 77 states signed the Smuggling Protocol in December 2000. As of 2016, the Trafficking Protocol has 117 signatories and 169 states are party to it; the Smuggling Protocol has 112 signatories and 142 parties (parties to the treaty may have accepted the treaty as legally binding while not signing or ratifying it). In most cases, countries treated the Trafficking Protocol and the Smuggling Protocol similarly. However, there were significant differences in forty-five cases. In only five of these did it take longer for the state to sign, ratify, or accede to the Trafficking Protocol.[6] In every other case, it took states anywhere from a few months to nearly five years longer to become a party to the Smuggling Protocol, if they ever did. Fifteen states that at least signed or acceded to the Trafficking Protocol refused to sign, ratify, or accede to the Smuggling Protocol; most of these are countries of origin, suggesting their reservations come from a difference in interests between sending and receiving states on the smuggling issue.[7] A complete list of differences in signatories, ratifications, and accessions to the two protocols can be found in Table 6.2.

The reservations recorded in the Palermo Protocols provide small insights into some of the concerns that states had. Most of the reservations for both protocols concern the requirement that interstate disputes about the treaty be brought to the International Court of Justice. Knowing that this would be a contentious requirement, the protocols specifically allow signatories to opt out of this provision, and a number of states chose to do so. This allowed signatories to preserve a greater degree of sovereignty. The only other reservations of interest come from Qatar, Saudi Arabia, and Syria, which expressed reservations to parts of the Trafficking Protocol, and Ecuador, which declared reservations

Table 6.2

Differences in Signatures, Ratifications, and Accessions between the Palermo Protocols

Country	Trafficking protocol	Smuggling protocol
Afghanistan		No accession
Australia	+1 year to sign and ratify	
Austria		+2 years to ratify
Belize		+3 years to accede
Benin		+1.5 years to sign
Bolivia		No ratification
Cambodia	+1.5 years to ratify	
Chad		No accession
China		No accession
Colombia		No signature, ratification, or accession
Czech Republic	+1 year to ratify	
Denmark		+3 years to ratify
Dominican Republic	+3 months to ratify	
Egypt		No signature, acceded +1 year after Trafficking Protocol ratification
Equatorial Guinea		No ratification
Gabon		No accession
Guinea		+6 months to accede
Guinea-Bissau		No ratification
Guyana		+3.5 years to accede
Honduras		+6 months to accede
Iceland		No ratification
Ireland		No ratification
Jordan		No accession
Lesotho		+1 year to ratify
Luxembourg		+3.5 years to sign and ratify
Malaysia		No accession
Micronesia		No accession
Nicaragua		+1.5 years to accede
Niger		No signature, +4.5 years to accede after Trafficking Protocol ratification
Paraguay		No signature, +4 years to accede after Trafficking Protocol ratification
Qatar		No accession

(continued)

Table 6.2
(*continued*)

Country	Trafficking protocol	Smuggling protocol
Rwanda		+3 years to ratify
São Tomé and Príncipe	+4 years to accede	
Singapore		No accession
Sri Lanka		No ratification
St. Lucia		No accession
Sudan		No accession
Sweden		+2 years to ratify
Thailand		No ratification
Togo		+1 year to ratify
United Arab Emirates		No accession
Uzbekistan		No ratification
Venezuela		+3 years to ratify
Vietnam		No accession
Zimbabwe		No accession

Source: United Nations Treaty Collection, https://treaties.un.org/.

about parts of the Smuggling Protocol. The three Middle Eastern countries, all of which are authoritarian, asserted some reservations about providing opportunities for victims of trafficking, particularly employment and housing. Both Syria and Saudi Arabia have signed and ratified the treaty; Qatar acceded to the treaty in 2009 but never signed it. All three of these states are both transit and destination countries for human trafficking; the 2013 US Trafficking in Persons Report lists both Saudi Arabia and Syria as Tier 3 countries, meaning their governments are doing very little to comply with the Trafficking Protocol, neither providing support to victims nor pursuing traffickers. Qatar is ranked as a Tier 2 country, which is only slightly better. These reservations suggest that destination and transit states with a weak commitment to human rights might not prioritize fighting trafficking as a crime and might resist assuming additional responsibilities to victims. However, even these states have either ratified or acceded to the treaty, demonstrating the broad international consensus against trafficking.

The Smuggling Protocol provoked one very different reservation from Ecuador. Ecuador, a source and transit country for smuggled migrants, asserts in its reservation that smuggled migrants are victims of smugglers and that the Palermo Protocol can be understood only in conjunction with the International Convention on the Protection of the Rights of All Migrant Workers and Members of Their Families and other human rights instruments. Ecuador's reservation may give voice to the concerns of many source and transit countries that resisted signing, ratifying, or acceding to the Smuggling Protocol. For them, the protocol did not go far enough in recognizing the victimization of smuggled migrants and the obligations that receiving states should have toward them.

The Palermo Protocols represent formal coordination on the issues of trafficking and smuggling. As expected from our bargaining theory, the only elements included in the agreements are ones on which every state party could agree or where side payments (from powerful receiving states to sending states) were quite cheap. Thus, the Palermo Protocols represent a far from comprehensive approach to the problem, and it is important to note that the protocols do not include enforcement mechanisms,[8] the absence of which dramatically reduces states' potential costs of signing. The agreements do, however, both raise awareness of the problems of trafficking and smuggling and facilitate greater efficiency in national approaches to combating the problems.[9] The Palermo Protocols also provide the foundation for, and work in conjunction with, other types of cooperation at the regional and bilateral levels, as well as unilateral action by states. It is to those efforts we now turn.

REGIONAL COOPERATION: REGIONAL CONSULTATIVE PROCESSES

The Palermo Protocols represent one of the very few instances of formal cooperation on a migration-related issue. But since the early 1990s, informal international discussions on migration issues have flourished in the form of RCPs. In this section, we argue that the informal character of the RCPs allows state members (and partner organizations) to raise virtually any migration-related issue. And, because the RCPs are premised on the idea that each member is equal within the context of the process, issues important to less powerful members are frequently given greater prominence than in formal cooperation. However, the driving force behind the RCPs has always been powerful states, and the most concrete outcomes of the RCPs reflect the interests of these states. These include combating trafficking and smuggling. The existence, form, and outcomes of RCPs thus support both of the mechanisms that bring states to the negotiating table as we outlined in chapter 2. On one side, exogenous events raise the costs of the status quo for receiving states and incentivize them to pursue international cooperation. On the other side, sending states that are dissatisfied with the status quo can use the structure of RCPs, which institutionally treat every state as equal, to put issues important to them on the agenda. As we expect, though, the concrete outcomes of RCPs tend to favor the interests of powerful receiving states.

The first RCP was the IGC, established in 1985 within the UNHCR, with support from Sweden, to examine asylum policy within Europe (IGC 2009; ICMPD 2012). The IGC became autonomous in 1991, and in 1993 the secretariat transferred all administrative duties to the IOM (IGC 2009). The IGC evolved to become a confidential forum for states to discuss a broad range of migration-related topics and to share information. There are now working groups focusing on Admission, Control, and Enforcement; Asylum/Refugees; Country of Origin Information; Immigration; Integration; and Technology.

During the 1990s, sixteen RCPs emerged that followed the model of the IGC (see Table 6.3). In most cases, the impetus for the processes came from states

Table 6.3
Regional Consultative Processes

Name	Year established	Number of member states
Inter-Governmental Consultations for Asylum, Refugee and Migration Policies (IGC)	1985	17
Budapest Group	1991	49
CIS Conference (not active)	1996	12
Manila Process (not active)	1996	16
Puebla Process	1996	11
South American Conference on Migration (Lima Process)	1999	12
Migration Dialogue for Southern Africa	2000	15
Migration Dialogue for West Africa	2001	13
Söderköping Process	2001	10
Inter-Governmental Asia-Pacific Consultations on Refugees, Displaced Persons, and Migrants	2002	34
Bali Ministerial Conference on People Smuggling, Trafficking in Persons, and Related Transnational Crime (Bali Process)	2002	40
5+5 Dialogue on Migration in the Western Mediterranean	2002	11
Ministerial Consultations on Overseas Employment and Contractual Labor (Colombo Process)	2003	11
Dialogue on Mediterranean Transit Migration	2003	37
Inter-Governmental Authority on Development Regional Consultative Process on Migration	2008	6
Ministerial Consultations on Overseas Employment and Contractual Labor for Countries of Origin and Destination in Asia (Abu Dhabi Dialogue)	2008	20
Prague Process	2009	50

Source: IOM, https://www.iom.int/rcps-region.

with an interest in addressing particular problems. The second RCP, for example, was the Budapest Process, which was created in response to the collapse of the Soviet Union and the Eastern Bloc, to address the uncontrolled flood of migrants seeking entrance into Western Europe. The RCP sought to facilitate a harmonized approach toward irregular migration. In some cases, however, the IOM or other international organizations took the lead in creating the RCPs. In all cases, the primary membership belongs to states, with international organizations involved either as members or as nonmember partners. International organizations also provide administrative and technical support for the RCPs. In most cases, the IOM fills this role, but other organizations do as well; for example, the Budapest Process is managed by the International Center for Migration Policy Development. The creation of RCPs has thus been a result of both state interests and the entrepreneurial efforts of international organizations to expand on the successful RCP model.

For states, the informal structure of the RCPs offers a number of advantages. First, informality avoids unnecessary sacrifices of national sovereignty. Binding agreements limit the policy choices that states may make in the future; while states can break binding agreements, the diplomatic costs or punishments inflicted by built-in enforcement mechanisms are likely to be higher than in nonbinding arrangements (Cassarino 2007). States may also have a desire to avoid formal or visible pledges to other states, which could have reputational or precedent-setting effects (Lipson 1991). The United States, for example, might want to work with Mexico on migration issues, but it would be hesitant to create a highly visible agreement that other states in Central and South America could use as a model to pressure it into similar agreements. Informal processes lower these stakes and give each country an exit option at any point.

Second, informal interaction makes fewer informational demands and is well suited to situations where there is a high level of uncertainty (Lipson 1991; Cassarino 2007). This is especially important in the area of migration because states are uncertain about future levels of migration inflows and outflows in particular countries, workforce demands, and public opinion regarding migration. States are reluctant to make long-term commitments to particular countries, whether they are to facilitate legal migration or to coordinate border control, if the flow of migrants is going to shift to another country, increase dramatically, or decrease dramatically. Informality allows states the flexibility to deal with changing circumstances and makes them more willing to engage now with less concern about future ramifications. Informal arrangements can be renegotiated more quickly than binding agreements.

Third, informality allows states to avoid protracted, and perhaps unwinnable, domestic battles (Lipson 1991). Binding international treaties require ratification by the states party to the agreement, and this can be difficult to achieve. While any formal international agreement might provoke opposition from those who oppose conceding any national sovereignty to international institutions, public opinion on migration issues in particular is very divided, making it politically difficult to ratify international agreements (Cassarino 2007). Receiving countries face competing political pressure from anti-immigrant groups and business interests in need of a labor source (Sölner 1999). The controversy over how to address immigration issues in receiving countries has been an obstacle even to unilateral, national legislation; the US Senate's rejection of comprehensive immigration reform in 2007 highlights the political challenge of managing immigration (Weisman 2007). Source countries may also face public pressure to protect emigrant rights and facilitate migration. While source states may want to take advantage of the economic, technical, and training incentives that host countries may offer in return for their cooperation in controlling migration, it may be difficult for source countries to convince their own publics that cooperation is beneficial.

Informality allows states to largely circumvent both the legislative process and public scrutiny. Because informal processes are nonbinding, the national bureaucracies can begin working directly with their counterparts in other states without going through a ratification process. Informal processes simply allow bureaucracies to implement national policies in a more effective, efficient way. Because informal arrangements do not have to be debated in the legislature, they are less visible to the public and provoke less public controversy. At the same time, informality keeps policymaking in the hands of the executive and the bureaucracy, away from legislative influence. In the domestic struggle for political power, informal processes are thus favored by the executive and the agencies in charge of implementing policy (Benvenisti 2006).

Informality also provides further benefits for the executive branch, since national bureaucrats may be reluctant to cede any of their policy authority to international bureaucracies (Benvenisti 2006). Formal, binding cooperation is more likely to create standing organizations with their own bureaucratic employees who may come to develop independent expertise and independent influence over policy (Barnett and Finnemore 1999; Nielson and Tierney 2003; Pollack 1997). In contrast, informality allows states' bureaucracies to maintain their dominance over information and expertise in their policy arena. In the RCPs, the bureaucratic apparatus remains very limited; interactions and logistics are managed by the IOM or other existing international organizations, and the overhead cost is low.

RCPs themselves do not represent "cooperation," informal or otherwise. Instead, they are a venue for facilitating cooperation. RCPs create structured opportunities for state representatives to meet on a regular basis and discuss issues of concern. Sometimes, these are high-level meetings that focus on developing policy goals, but the RCPs can also facilitate communication between lower-level officials in charge of implementing policy. The informality of the RCPs, along with their confidentiality, allows states to raise nearly any issue related to migration. Whether or not this communication will result in cooperation is dependent on state interests. In most cases, states do not share interests. Even when there are no shared interests, states may gather information through the RCPs that could allow them to make offers of side payments that are attractive enough to induce cooperation (chapter 3 addresses this type of cooperation in depth).

More typically, however, the concrete cooperative outcomes of the RCPs are quite small given the number of meetings, working groups, committees, and reports generated by the processes on a wide range of migration topics. RCP documents often lack concrete plans of action and frequently address the same issues, year after year. The following excerpt from the Chair's Summary of the Joint Conference of UNODC and the Budapest Process with the Organization of the Black Sea Economic Cooperation on "Trafficking in Human Beings in the Black Sea Region" in 2007 demonstrates this lack of action: "Regional cooperation in the field of data collection shall be strengthened. To facilitate this process, cooperation and coordination of the information flow between different actors along the trafficking chain is needed. It must ensure that all relevant information and data is available, accessible to the actors involved and exchanged regularly with due regard to the right to privacy and data protection" (Ministry of Foreign Affairs of Turkey 2007). While trafficking represents an area of shared interest, the manner in which it was addressed at this meeting was shaped by the informality of the RCP. The grammatical structure of the passage itself is striking; nowhere can one find an actor who will actually undertake any of these tasks. "Data collection shall be strengthened," but who shall strengthen it? "Cooperation and coordination" may be "needed," but who will cooperate and coordinate? The RCPs are designed to be safe, open forums for state delegates to freely discuss any migration-related issue, and the range of topics covered in RCP reports reflects this intention. By design, the RCPs' primary accomplishments are creating opportunities for state representatives to meet (at conferences and seminars) and producing reports on the topics covered. These types of outcomes are very low-cost and low-risk for participating states.

There are, however, a few instances of RCPs producing more tangible outcomes. What explains whether an issue within an RCP gets relegated to an endless cycle of meetings and reports or provokes concrete action? First, in all cases that produce tangible outcomes, states must share a particular interest, although the interest may be of varying importance for different states. In other words, states must prefer a change to the status quo, and the "win set," the policy space preferred by all states to the status quo, cannot be empty. At minimum, none of the states can have an actively *opposing* interest in the given issue. The informal character of RCPs means that there is no mechanism to coerce or mandate compliance with any agreement made within the context of the RCP, so a shared interest (or absence of a conflict of interest) is essential. Second, some state (or group of states) must assume the financial and logistical costs of concrete action. It follows, then, that the issues important to wealthy, receiving states will be addressed in tangible ways, since the wealthy states are more willing to fund such projects. In the following section, we examine the action plans of the Regional Conference on Migration to support this argument.

REGIONAL CONFERENCE ON MIGRATION (RCM OR PUEBLA PROCESS)

The RCM was the product of a summit of Central American presidents and the Mexican president, called Tuxtla II, held in February 1996. The summit produced a declaration calling for a process to address migration-related issues as part of the ongoing integration of the region. The preamble discussed the countries' shared democracy and the economic integration occurring under the WTO, which contributed to a shared interest in economic development for all countries in the region. The declaration reaffirmed each country's sovereignty and the needs to eliminate the use of force in international relations, to cooperate for development, and to fight for justice and equality. The twenty-eight clauses of the declaration addressed numerous areas of shared concern, from narcotrafficking to trade relations. The third clause addressed migration in particular, calling for an examination of the causes and consequences of migration in the region, focusing on structural components of migration and the adoption of programs to create economic opportunities in migrant-producing regions while respecting the human rights of migrants in transit and destination countries. The declaration was signed by the presidents of Costa Rica, El Salvador, Guatemala, Honduras, Nicaragua, Panama, Belize, and Mexico (Declaración Conjunta Tuxtla II 1996).

The first meeting of the RCM was held one month later, in March 1996, and it included the United States and Canada, neither of which had been part of the meeting that produced the Tuxtla II Declaration. The meeting was organized and hosted by the Mexican government, with technical and administrative support coming from the IOM. At the meeting, the participating countries created a basic framework for ongoing interaction, establishing an annual high-level meeting of vice-ministers (with both open and closed sessions) and creating the Regional Consultation Group on Migration, which includes state representatives from the technical and operational levels of government and observer organizations and meets annually, before the ministerial meetings. In subsequent years, the RCM established other structures, including a technical secretariat, the Liaison Officers Network to Combat Migrant Smuggling and Trafficking in Persons, and the Liaison Officers Network for Consular Protection.

By 2002, the RCM had succeeded in drafting a plan of action to guide its activities. The plan indicated a shift in the priorities first presented in the Tuxtla II Declaration, in part because of the inclusion of the United States and Canada in the process. The RCM shifted focus from the interests of sending states (the development of economic opportunities at home and the protection of migrant rights) to those of receiving states (migration control). The action plan presented three issue areas for the RCM, with objectives in each category: Migration Policies and Management (twelve objectives), Human Rights (five), and the Link between Development and Migration (seven) (RCM 2009a, 2009b).

Most of the RCM's objectives are being addressed through seminars, conferences, reports, and research undertaken by member countries, affiliated NGOs, or the IOM at the RCM's request. Of the twelve objectives under Migration Policies and Management, eight were addressed with actions beyond meetings and reports. Of the combined twelve objectives under Human Rights and the Link between Development and Migration, only two have been addressed with such actions (one under each category). While human rights and development may have been a primary motivation for the sending countries that signed the Tuxtla II Declaration in creating the RCM, the agenda has since turned toward issues of migration control and criminality. Half of the objectives in the RCM's action plan focus on human rights and development, but these issues are much less likely to be addressed with concrete action. The informal structure of the RCM allows the issues to remain on the agenda, but the powerful receiving states of Canada and the United States use their money to make sure that their issues remain at the forefront.

The objectives under Migration Policies and Management that produced concrete actions, beyond seminars and reports, dealt with repatriation of returned migrants, technological development, and human trafficking. In addressing repatriation, the United States paid for pilot projects in Honduras and El Salvador, which sought to facilitate reintegration for returned migrants (the IOM and a partner NGO launched a similar project). Mexico, El Salvador, Guatemala, Honduras, and Nicaragua signed an MOU to facilitate voluntary returns. In technological development, donor countries provided computer equipment and the IOM began working with member countries to create an integrated migration information system. The three objectives addressing human trafficking led to a number of concrete projects. The RCM established a liaison network for trafficking, coordinated by Canada, to work specifically on trafficking issues. They created a comparative legislation matrix to assess the compatibility of domestic laws, and Canada funded an IOM study to assess the state of trafficking and smuggling in Central America. Canada and the United States delivered trainings to consular officers and immigration officials on document security to prevent trafficking (and irregular migration more broadly). Last, the United States, Canada, and Mexico launched a pilot program for the interdiction of irregular migrants in Central America.

The objectives focused on human trafficking represent the shared interests of all RCM states. But the actions that the RCM has undertaken have favored the priorities of the powerful receiving states since they are funding the actions. The actions have focused on interdiction instead of victims' rights, which also serves the receiving state interest of reducing all irregular migration. This pattern also extends to the objectives in the Human Rights category. Human Rights Objective 3 calls for "strengthening respect for the human rights of all migrants regardless of their migrant status, with special attention to protection of rights of vulnerable groups such as women and children." However, not only are the actions for implementation weak,[10] the proposed activities differed dramatically from what was done in the end. First, the action plan proposed a regional project to establish a shelter for victims of trafficking, but this never happened. Instead, the United States financed a training program to combat trafficking. Second, El Salvador and the IOM designed a project to care for people who suffered severe disabilities due to the migration process, but the project was never executed. Third, Mexico proposed developing a human rights training program for migration officers. The UN Special Rapporteur on the Human Rights of Migrants created a proposal for the training program, but it was never executed.

The structure of the RCM and other RCPs provides each member state a nominally equal voice, and all decisions are made by consensus. Nevertheless, the influence of powerful states is somewhat evident in the objectives of the RCM and clearly evident in the implementation of RCM projects. While half the objectives reflect interests more important to sending states (human rights and development), only one objective in each of these categories has actually been implemented with something other than a meeting or a report. In the case of the activities addressing the human rights objective, the projects changed from ones clearly furthering human rights to ones more suitable to the Migration Policies and Management objectives. RCP projects depend on voluntary contributions from member states, and wealthy receiving states contribute the greatest amount. Thus, projects that serve wealthy state priorities get funded while others languish. Poorer, sending states still participate in the process since none of the objectives contradict their interests, but the RCPs fail to deliver on priorities most important to sending states. In the case of human trafficking, the result of the informal process is similar to that of the formal process exemplified by the Palermo Protocols. The criminality lens ends up dominating the actual projects that the RCM and the other RCPs deliver, while the human rights and migration lenses receive only limited attention, coupled with extremely low-cost actions such as further meetings and research reports.

BILATERAL COOPERATION

Although we know that bilateral cooperation exists, it is virtually impossible to collate all bilateral agreements on trafficking and smuggling as there is no single repository of bilateral agreements and states are not required to submit these agreements to a repository. We do know that states have pursued, and continue to pursue, both formal and informal bilateral agreements.

Asian states have been particularly active in pursuing bilateral arrangements, which makes sense since experts estimate that the majority of trafficking victims are living or originate in Asian countries (Shelley 2010; Yamada 2012). But bilateral arrangements cover every region of the world. They are encouraged and supported by the Palermo Protocols, as well as by international organizations, including the United Nations Children's Fund (UNICEF) and the Office of the High Commissioner for Human Rights (OHCHR), which champion bilateral agreements as a method to reduce human trafficking (UNODC 2014; OHCHR 2014; UNICEF 2014). For example, the OHCHR has published "Principles and Guidelines on Human Rights and Human Trafficking," which proposes "adopting bilateral agreements aimed at preventing trafficking, protecting the rights and dignity of trafficked persons and promoting their welfare" (OHCHR 2002, Guideline 11.1).

The UNODC published two toolkits for implementing the Palermo Protocols: "Toolkit to Combat Trafficking in Persons" (2008) and "Toolkit to Combat Smuggling of Migrants" (2010). In addition to providing guidance in implementing domestic programs to fulfill the obligations of the Palermo Protocols, the toolkits provide suggestions for interstate cooperation and examples of promising "best practices." A cursory comparison of the two toolkits suggests that states have been more active in pursuing cooperation around trafficking than smuggling. The trafficking toolkit highlights a broad range of formal, informal, bilateral, and regional cooperation that is both directly and tangentially related to trafficking and smuggling. These include the Police Cooperation Convention for South-East Europe (a formal, regional agreement signed after the Palermo Protocols covering security more generally) and the Bali Process (an informal, regional process predating the Palermo Protocols). Included in the list are seven bilateral agreements related specifically to trafficking, primarily focusing on protecting and repatriating victims along with joint efforts to investigate, arrest, and prosecute traffickers.[11] While we have not been able to generate a definitive list of bilateral arrangements addressing trafficking, we know that states continue to pursue them. India and Bahrain, for example, signed an MOU about trafficking in 2016.

Bilateral agreements tend to be memoranda of understanding rather than memoranda of agreement, meaning that they are not legally binding. Thus there are no enforcement mechanisms that require states to adhere to the "understanding," and states may modify the terms of the memorandum unilaterally. This format underscores the informality of so many of these agreements. The bilateral agreements appear to be almost exclusively devoted to trafficking rather than smuggling. We were unable to locate a single bilateral agreement on human smuggling and found only three references to human smuggling in broader bilateral agreements on international crime.[12] The agreements usually incorporate three aspects of bilateral cooperation: repatriation of victims, extradition of criminals, and information sharing (Yamada 2012). However, in her analysis of Thailand's set of bilateral agreements with its neighbors, Yamada argues that "repatriation is the raison d'être for such memoranda" (11).

The focus on repatriation has been tied to patterns of trafficking flows that are similar to the generic "voluntary" migration flows described in chapter 1. As Yamada (2012, 1) notes, "In many cases of cross-border human trafficking, there are patterns and trends of human trafficking routes from one specific origin country to a specific destination country." Because of this, the interests of origin and destination countries differ, which provides support for our argument that states reach agreement only through bargaining, and that receiving states can reduce member surplus costs by doing this bargaining and offering side payments bilaterally. Thompson and Verdier (2014) anticipate that states will choose to pursue a combination of multilateralism and bilateralism when transaction costs and member surplus are high. Human trafficking and smuggling might provide an example of such a scenario, explaining the dual approach that states have taken. The Palermo Protocols allowed states to hash out, through contentious negotiations, the definitions of trafficking and smuggling, as well the basic legal obligations of states in dealing with these problems. Doing this multilaterally was feasible and reduced transaction costs in that the basic framework did not need to be renegotiated with each state. But as with all migration flows, patterns of trafficking and smuggling are unique to each dyad of states and usually nonreciprocal, as are the criminal networks that facilitate these flows. Actually implementing strategies and targeting resources toward the problem makes more sense at the bilateral (or sometimes regional) level.

Our brief empirical survey of bilateral trafficking agreements is consistent with our theoretical expectations. The agreements tend to be between a destination country and geographically proximate origin countries. Consistent with our arguments about the role of power in bilateral agreements, the wealthier destination countries are able to insert their central interest in repatriation into the agreements.

UNILATERAL ACTION: THE TRAFFICKING VICTIMS PROTECTION ACT

The United States played a key role in the drafting of the Palermo Protocols. The Clinton administration advocated strongly for a transnational approach to address the trafficking and smuggling problem throughout the 1990s. Just weeks before the UN General Assembly adopted the Palermo Protocols in 2000, the US Congress passed its own unilateral antitrafficking legislation, the Trafficking Victims Protection Act (TVPA), which was signed into law by President Clinton (Chuang 2006). This legislation was more far-reaching than any legislation yet passed by any country, and it received broad, bipartisan support in Congress. The juxtaposition with the Palermo Protocols was striking. While the Clinton administration expressed a commitment to international cooperation on the global stage, the domestic legislation made a strong unilateral statement. In addition to strengthening the ability of the government to prosecute traffickers and smugglers domestically, the TVPA created new standards and a monitoring body by which the United States would judge other states' antitrafficking efforts. It authorized the president to apply unilateral sanctions against any state that did not meet these standards, although it did not require him to do so (Chuang 2006). While the Clinton administration argued that the TVPA and the Palermo Protocols were complementary, critics asserted that TVPA undermined the emerging international regime and questioned the authority of the United States to stand in judgment of other states' actions.

An examination of the similarities and the differences between the Palermo Protocols and the TVPA illuminates the distinct interests that dominate policymaking at the international versus the domestic level. Free from concerns about relinquishing sovereignty, making long-term commitments in a volatile international environment, or reaching consensus with other states, the United States was able to enact much stronger policies in the TVPA than were possible in the Palermo Protocols. Not only was the United States able to enshrine, in domestic law, policies that other countries would have opposed, it was also able to pursue policies that it would have opposed if included in an international agreement! Nevertheless, the Palermo Protocols and the TVPA share many common features, given the strong influence the United States had on the shape of the international agreements. Most significantly, the Palermo Protocols and the TVPA approach trafficking and smuggling through a criminal justice lens.

In this section, we describe how the TVPA developed simultaneously alongside international efforts, as both a complementary and competing strategy to address trafficking and smuggling. We show how domestic interest groups were able to appeal to both Republicans and Democrats to get the TVPA passed, along with reauthorizations in 2004 and 2007. These groups, coming from both the left and the right, challenged the government's position in the international negotiations that prostitution could be a choice and was not always a sign of coercion. At the international level, this only led the US government to quietly withdraw from the debate; at the domestic level, it led to a greater (but limited) focus on maintaining an abolitionist stance on prostitution. In essence, the final versions of both the Palermo Protocols and the TVPA illustrate the tight rope the United States is walking in responding to the state interest of combating trafficking and smuggling, the state interest of maintaining the ability to deport unwanted migrants, and the public interest in opposing prostitution. In sum, the policy outcomes at both the international and domestic levels reflect the partisan differences between the Democrats and the Republicans, the interests of domestic activist groups, and the overriding state interest in maintaining legitimate authority to expel unwanted migrants.

By 1995, trafficking and smuggling had become a major concern for policy-makers in many countries, and this pushed the issue onto the agenda of the United Nations Fourth World Forum Conference on Women held in Beijing that year. At the conference, First Lady Hillary Clinton included remarks about the effect of trafficking on women and children in her address, and subsequently spoke about the issue in various speeches at other conferences and events (Stolz 2007). In 1998, President Clinton issued a presidential directive to federal agencies to enforce laws applicable to trafficking and to assist victims. The directive also gave the President's Interagency Council on Women (PICW) the task of leading further efforts to address trafficking (Gulati 2012; Miko 2004; Masci 2004). The directive presented an integrated policy framework for both domestic and international efforts, referred to as the "three Ps": prevention, protection and assistance for victims, and prosecution of traffickers (Chuang 2006).

While the Clinton administration worked to advance antitrafficking efforts at the global level, the Republican-led Congress took the lead in crafting domestic legislation (Chuang 2006). Congressional committees led by Republicans with strong ties to evangelical Christian groups active in the antitrafficking movement held hearings on trafficking (Gulati 2012). These groups found common cause with women's groups, human rights groups, and labor groups, all traditionally associated with the Democratic Party. While the groups did not necessarily share the same motivations, they did share similar end goals, namely, the elimination of trafficking. Each group conducted independent lobbying efforts, but collectively they were able to reach nearly every lawmaker by tapping into their unique networks of legislative relationships. Thus, Republicans and Democrats worked across the aisle to cosponsor antitrafficking legislation. The final bill, titled the Trafficking Victims Protection Act, received nearly unanimous support in both chambers; the Senate voted 95 to 0, the House 371 to 1. President Clinton signed the bill into law on 28 October 2000 (McReynolds 2008; Gulati 2012).

Two features of the TVPA stand out. First, the strong bipartisan support of the TVPA belies the fact that it reflected clear Republican priorities; the end result would likely have looked much different if Democrats had been in the majority. Second, the bill went much further and offered more protections to trafficking victims than any international effort, demonstrating a willingness by both parties to implement policies at the national level to which the state would be unwilling to commit at the international level.

The TVPA reflected Republican priorities through three key elements: its unilateralism, its specific focus on sex trafficking, and its minimization of labor issues. First, the bill created a new, unilateral sanctions regime to punish states that did not comply with minimum US standards to combat trafficking. Under the regime, the US government could deny non-humanitarian, non-trade-related foreign assistance to any country that did not make significant efforts to comply with these standards.[13] The bill tasked the Department of State with conducting annual assessments of any country with more a hundred trafficked individuals and issuing its findings in an annual Trafficking in Persons Report (Chuang 2006). The Clinton administration strongly opposed the unilateral sanctions provision of the TVPA, believing that it would be both ineffective and "profoundly counterproductive" (Chuang 2006). First, it undermined the administration's simultaneous efforts to reach an international agreement through the Vienna Process. The fact that Congress quickly passed the more comprehensive TVPA in 2000 while not ratifying the Palermo Protocols until 2005 indicates the reluctance of the Republican-led Congress to make multilateral commitments, not a reluctance to address the problem of trafficking. Second, it would incentivize states to hide the seriousness of their trafficking problems in order to avoid sanctions. Third, it would cause governments to view the antitrafficking efforts of both international and local NGOs as a threat, since their attempts to raise awareness about the problem of trafficking might expose the state to sanctions. Fourth, the entire introduction of a new sanctions regime contradicted the administration's new policy of limiting the use of sanctions, in light of the fact that sanctions had been used with increasing frequency and decreasing success in recent years (Chuang 2006). If the Democrats had been in charge, a unilateral sanctions regime would likely not have been part of the final bill.

The TVPA also reflected Republican concerns in the way it addressed the definition of "trafficking." The same controversy around "forced" versus "voluntary" prostitution that dominated the debate during the Vienna Process also arose during the congressional debate. This time, however, the antiprostitution side succeeded in defining sex trafficking as "the recruitment, harboring, transportation, provision, or obtaining of a person for the purpose of a commercial sex act." Unlike the definition in the Palermo Protocol, the TVPA thus included consensual prostitution as a form of trafficking, reflecting the influence of the evangelical Christian activist groups who lobbied Republicans that prostitution could never be consensual. While the TVPA was more inclusive in defining victims of sex trafficking, it was less inclusive in including victims trafficked for other types of labor. First, the TVPA does not cover smuggled migrants, although other laws do (including the Immigration and Nationality Act). While the Department of State acknowledges that the line between smuggling and trafficking can be hard to define, such as when migrants believe they are being smuggled and then end up trafficked, the TVPA provides services and programs only for trafficked victims, not smuggled individuals (US Department of State 2006). Second, nonsexual labor trafficking is defined as "labor or services obtained through the use of force, fraud, or coercion AND resulting in involuntary servitude, peonage, debt bondage or slavery" (US Department of State 2006). Questionable practices like "deferred payment" (essentially indentured servitude, where migrants agree to work off the cost of their transport) are not covered under the trafficking definition (US Department of State 2006). The more inclusive definition of sex trafficking and more restrictive definition of nonsexual labor trafficking reflected the interests of the Republican majority in Congress.

The final version of the TVPA reflected the influence of both assorted public interest groups as well as broader state interests. Antitrafficking legislation was first introduced in the House of Representatives by Chris Smith, a Republican from New Jersey, along with Marcy Kaptur, a Democrat from Ohio, in 1999 (HR 1356: "The Freedom from Sexual Trafficking Act of 1999"). Representative Sam Gejdenson, a Connecticut Democrat, introduced competing legislation that same year (HR 3154: "The Comprehensive Anti-Trafficking in Persons Act of 1999"). The two bills differed in ways that reflected both the ideological positions of their sponsors and the influence of the interest groups with the most access to the lawmakers. Smith's bill focused solely on sex trafficking, while Gejdenson's was much more inclusive, reflecting the greater influence of labor groups. He met primarily with interest groups on the left and staff from the PICW (Stolz 2005).

In the Senate, Sam Brownback, a Republican from Kansas, and Paul Wellstone, a Democrat from Minnesota, each introduced antitrafficking legislation that was very similar. Both bills addressed both sex trafficking and involuntary servitude through coercion, fraud, force, or deception. They differed, however, in their enforcement mechanism; Brownback's bill called for unilateral sanctions, while Wellstone's did not. Wellstone's bill thus reflected the Clinton administration's preference to limit the use of unilateral sanctions. Brownback's interest in trafficking stemmed from his earlier work on slavery in Sudan, and he was influenced by a coalition of evangelical Christian and human rights groups that had worked closely with him on drafting earlier legislation related to religious freedom (Stolz 2005). This may explain why his bill, unlike that of his Republican counterpart in the House, paid greater attention to other types of labor trafficking.

The issue of forced versus consensual prostitution arose in the TVPA debates just as it did during the Vienna Process. In comparison to the international negotiations, however, there were few American groups that advocated for a distinction between types of prostitution. Instead, Christian organizations, human rights groups, and mainstream feminist groups and individuals, including the National Organization of Women and Gloria Steinem, argued that all forms of prostitution should be considered coerced (Stolz 2005). Only a small minority of groups, most notably the International Human Rights Law Group, which also advocates for the legalization of prostitution, supported the distinction between prostitution and forced prostitution (Stolz 2005).

Despite the even greater consensus in the United States than in the international community, across a broad range of ideologically diverse interest groups, that prostitution should not be distinguished from forced prostitution, the final version of the TVPA adopted the distinction, at least in terms of the actual enforcement of the law's provisions.[14] Legislators from both parties, along with the White House and the PICW, all made it clear that they opposed the legalization of prostitution (Shenon 2000). However, they also all resisted defining prostitution as always forced, despite pressure from interest groups and an active debate in the media. Interviews with those involved in process suggest that there was an overriding concern that any migrant who declared herself to be a prostitute would be entitled to benefits under the new law (Stolz 2005). Thus, the TVPA remained a law focused on criminal justice, human rights, and (to a lesser extent) labor rights, but lawmakers were careful to not stray too far into the realm of immigration policy, a much more contentious and divisive policy arena.

Although US lawmakers refused to define trafficking too broadly, the TVPA did address immigration policy more directly than the Palermo Protocols, and the United States unilaterally committed to more than it would at the multilateral level. The TVPA allowed for the possibility of either temporary or even permanent residency for victims of trafficking, provided that the victims assist in the prosecution of their traffickers. It authorized up to five thousand special "T-Visas" per year to be allocated to trafficking victims (US Department of Health and Human Services 2003). The law also made public assistance available to victims and some family members, and it provided them with the ability to sue their victimizers. Within the first few years after the TVPA was signed into law, eighteen to twenty thousand trafficking victims were being assisted in some way (US Department of Health and Human Services 2003). Additionally, the TVPA established programs to strengthen capacity in sending countries, to provide economic alternatives to potential targets of traffickers in their home countries, and to raise public awareness in sending countries about the dangers of trafficking (Chuang 2006). Although these types of concrete provisions and commitments were feasible at the domestic, unilateral level, the United States would never have committed to them in the Palermo Protocols.

ALTERNATIVE EXPLANATIONS

Another useful approach to understanding the development of international co-operation on trafficking and smuggling, and particularly why some efforts took hold and succeeded while others did not, comes from the literature on policy diffusion. Policy diffusion describes a broader phenomenon than cooperation or coordination, but it encompasses these processes as well. Common policy can emerge through simultaneous (or sequential) independent policy adoption by individual states. It can also emerge through coordination or cooperation by state actors. Thus, insights on policy diffusion are directly applicable to international cooperation and coordination. Simmons, Dobbin, and Garrett (2006) identify four mechanisms by which policy diffuses: coercion, competition, learning, and emulation. Coercion and competition reflect material concerns (Lloyd, Simmons, and Stewart 2012). Coercion occurs when powerful states manipulate less powerful states to adopt policies or sign onto cooperative agreements by offering incentives to those that comply and by threatening punishments to those who do not. "Soft" coercion is more difficult to identify, but it can also play a key role in policy diffusion. Powerful states often have the ability to be policy leaders and "go it alone." By acting unilaterally, they create a focal point for coordinating policy, and other states follow their lead (Simmons, Dobbin, and Garrett 2006). Soft coercion can also occur through ideological hegemony. Because powerful states play a central role in policy networks and international organizations, they have a significant influence in framing debates (Simmons, Dobbin, and Garrett 2006; Lloyd and Simmons 2012). Powerful states can influence which problems rise to the top of the international agenda, what types of outcomes are most desirable, and which means will best lead to these outcomes.

Competition is another material explanation of policy diffusion. More decentralized than coercion, it explains policy diffusion as a market-based phenomenon. States adopt particular policies that they would otherwise not because if they do not, they will lose out on benefits that will instead go to states that do. Competition is most often used to explain economic policies, particularly the trend toward greater liberalization, which is rewarded by international markets. The competition explanation differs from coercion in that states are not intentionally rewarded or punished by powerful states; instead, natural competition leads to policy diffusion without direction from particular actors.

Diffusion through learning bridges the gap between material explanations and explanations based on less tangible social structures and peer effects. In their simplest manifestation, learning explanations suggest that policy diffuses as states observe the behavior of other states, seeing the good results of best practices and the failure of poor policies. Through information sharing in policy networks, states gravitate toward common policies that are objectively more productive and efficient; no coercion or outside incentive is needed. In a more complex manifestation, learning is not a completely rational process in which states come to commonly identify an objectively "best policy." Instead, learning is rational only in a bounded sense, since available information is always limited. Power dynamics may influence which policies are even considered, as powerful states have significant influence over what policymakers learn and what information is available to them.

On the far end of the spectrum, the "emulation" explanation sees policy diffusion stemming not from material structures and effects at all but rather from less tangible social structures and peer effects (Lloyd, Simmons, and Stewart 2012). Unlike the simple learning explanation, the emulation explanation does not rely on the idea of a "best policy" diffusing at all. Instead, it explains the consensus that emerges around "best practices," and their subsequent diffusion, as a socially constructed process that occurs through emulation over time. Policy dispersion can spread from developed states to developing states, not because of coercion by developed states, or even because these policies are objectively the "best," but because developing states aspire to become developed states. Similarly, policy can also diffuse through peer states, as states look for solutions to policy problems within states that they perceive to be similar.

The mechanism of policy diffusion is not easy to discern for a particular issue area. There could be multiple mechanisms at work, and some of these mechanisms may appear observationally equivalent. In particular, it can be difficult to determine whether states are adopting common policies because they freely seek to emulate other states or because powerful states have coerced them into adopting similar policies. In the fuzziest cases, where dominant states have used their softest powers to cajole weaker states into adopting particular policies, the individuals involved may not even be sure which mechanism is truly at work.

In two separate articles, Lloyd and her coauthors argue that the cooperative agreements and common policies that have emerged to address human trafficking in the past fifteen years are due to a combination of diffusion mechanisms that include both material and ideational factors (Lloyd, Simmons, and Stewart 2012; Lloyd and Simmons 2012). These diffusion mechanisms affect both states' adoption of domestic antitrafficking laws and participation in international agreements. They provide evidence that these policies are a response to both material interests and a global discourse linking trafficking to broader criminal activity. Controlling for material interests, increased media coverage linking trafficking as a criminal activity with a particular country makes it more likely that the country will adopt antitrafficking policies (Lloyd, Simmons, and Stewart 2012).

These findings within the policy diffusion literature are not contradictory to our own argument, but there are some key distinctions. First, we highlight differences in states' preference structures much more directly. States have different resources, different problems, and different priorities. In the case of trafficking and smuggling, the most obvious difference between states is that some produce trafficked and smuggled migrants and some receive them. Thus, we do not assume that there is some objective "best practice" policy that states will learn of or emulate. What is good for one state may not be good for another. Following from this, we place a much stronger emphasis on material interests and structure, particularly power dynamics and the coercive abilities of strong states, not simply "natural" competition between states to adopt efficient policy. Last, distinct interests and international power dynamics play an even stronger role in explaining international cooperation and coordination than they do in explaining policy diffusion more broadly, which includes the independent adoption of common policies at the domestic level. Committing to a binding international agreement, in particular, is something states are generally reluctant do, since it necessarily weakens their sovereignty and independence. Thus, the material benefits must be high and/or the risks low for a state to reach the threshold at which it will make such a commitment. We expect that ideational factors would play a larger role in the domestic policymaking environment than in international agreements, although material interests should remain dominant. This is indeed what we found in comparing the US position during the negotiations over the Palermo Protocols to the domestic negotiations over the TVPA.

The diffusion literature also fails to address the timing, shape, and specific content of the international cooperation that ensued. As noted in our description of the status quo, there were already many multilateral agreements on trafficking, slavery, and forced labor in place. The Palermo Protocols were not the first effort to address the issue. Our focus on the status quo ante and state preferences, as well as exogenous shocks to the status quo, allows us to trace the initiation of efforts to renegotiate existing multilateral trafficking agreements. We also explain why the multilateral agreement was supplemented by bilateral agreements, reflecting the specific trafficking patterns that receiving states experience. This reflects both the shared preferences for the reduction in criminality and the specific bilateral patterns of flows. Finally, many domestic actors and international actors privileged victim protection in the trafficking debate but were unsuccessful in obtaining international cooperation on this issue—the Palermo Protocols are addendums to the Convention Against Transnational Organized Crime, not to the International Convention on the Protection of the Rights of All Migrant Workers and Members of Their Families. The diffusion literature does not contradict and may well supplement our analysis, but it does not provide a complete picture of the timing, shape, and content of international cooperation on criminality in migration.

CONCLUSIONS

Criminality in migration, manifested through trafficking and smuggling, is a problem that sending, transit, and receiving states all have an interest in eliminating. Because the crime is transnational in nature, there is an incentive for states to cooperate (or coordinate) their efforts to address the problem. By working together, states are likely to be more effective and efficient than they would be on their own, and both receiving states and sending states may be motivated to begin bargaining with each other. First, receiving states have been motivated to cooperate by increasing flows of trafficked and smuggled migrants, facilitated by increasingly transnational criminal networks. Second, sending states have responded to receiving states with concern about the root causes of trafficking and smuggling, and the welfare of their own citizens abroad. Beyond the shared concern that trafficking and smuggling challenge the authority of the state, different states have different ideas about how to best address the problem, largely based on their roles as sending or receiving states. Sending states would like to focus antitrafficking efforts on providing economic opportunities to potential trafficking or smuggling victims, along with easier routes to legal immigration. Receiving states prefer to focus on efforts to keep potential victims in their home states and prosecuting traffickers and smugglers.

These features of the trafficking and smuggling problem lead to several outcomes. First, formal, multilateral cooperative agreements are going to be limited both in their scope and enforcement mechanisms. Since the area in which there is the broadest consensus is the recognition that trafficking and smuggling present a criminal challenge to the authority of the state, formal, multilateral agreements are limited to the policy realm of transnational crime. This is reinforced by the fact that powerful receiving states are primarily concerned with the criminality aspect of trafficking and eliminating unwanted migration flows.

Second, informal cooperative forums allow states to broaden cooperation to include discussions of policy solutions that may not appeal to all states equally (or not at all). Because these cooperative efforts are focused on information exchange and free discussion (often away from the media spotlight), state representatives are free to bring up policies and proposals that may not be supported by all participants. The institutional structures of informal processes provide all states an equal voice in setting the agenda and bringing topics to the table for discussion, which provides traditionally less powerful sending states with a forum to address their concerns. However, the concrete, tangible outcomes that result from these processes almost always reflect the interests of powerful receiving states, which have the resources to implement proposals they support and to kill the ones that they do not.

Third, states will continue to pursue unilateral action to address trafficking and smuggling, since the problem can be addressed unilaterally as well as cooperatively. This allows states to both respond to domestic interests without concern for entangling or long-term international commitments and pursue policy solutions to which other states would not agree.

These three points lead us to a broader conclusion about the state of cooperation on migration-related criminality that is consistent with our observations in the rest of this book. States can and do pursue multilateralism, regionalism, bilateralism, and unilateralism simultaneously, both informally and formally. In this case, the agency charged with administering the multilateral treaties governing antitrafficking and smuggling efforts, UNODC, explicitly encourages and supports these other efforts. Different types of cooperation are better suited to deal with different levels of transactions costs, member surpluses, interest divergence, and state power differentials.

CHAPTER 7

Migrant Rights
The Failure of Multilateral Cooperation

THE WOMAN HAS A NAME: Lahadapurage Daneris Ariyawathie. When she returned home to Sri Lanka from Saudi Arabia after working there as a domestic servant, she needed an operation "to remove dozens of nails and metal objects she said her Saudi employers had hammered into her body after she complained of being overworked" (Human Rights Watch 2010, 10). Although domestic workers, especially those employed in the Gulf States, are at particular risk, migrant workers confront many types of abuse. Some cases are highly publicized, such as the widely reported abuse of migrant construction workers in Qatar preparing for the 2022 World Cup. "Workers described forced labour in 50C heat, employers who retain salaries for several months and passports making it impossible for them to leave and being denied free drinking water. The investigation found sickness is endemic among workers living in overcrowded and insanitary conditions and hunger has been reported" ("Qatar World Cup" 2013).

The issue of rights affects many different types of migrants: workers, self-employed, and family members. In Mexico, "hundreds of thousands of undocumented migrants, including unaccompanied children and families, pass through Mexico each year and many are subjected to grave abuses en route at the hands of organized crime, migration authorities, and security forces. A 2013 report by the Inter-American Commission of Human Rights (IACHR) found that "robberies, extortion, kidnappings and physical and psychological assaults, sexual abuse, murders and disappearances to which [migrants] fall victim . . . have taken a dramatic turn for the worse' in recent years" (Human Rights Watch 2015, 383). In South Africa, "continued incidents of violence against foreign nationals and looting of foreign owned shops in 2014 highlighted the government's inability to address the root causes of xenophobia. In June 2014, bands of local youths attacked Somali shopkeepers in Mamelodi East, Pretoria. Two Somalis were killed and around 100 men, women, and children fled their shops and homes. No one was held accountable for the attacks" (Human Rights Watch 2015, 492).

Moreover, this abuse is not limited to countries of the Global South. The Detention Watch Network investigation of Immigration and Customs Enforcement (ICE) detention facilities in the United States in 2012 revealed poor conditions. "At Pinal County Jail in Arizona complaints regarding sanitation include receiving food on dirty trays, worms found in food, bugs and worms found in the faucets, receiving dirty laundry, and being overcrowded with ten other men in one cell and only one toilet" (Detention Watch Network 2012, 2). Other problems are widespread in ICE detention facilities. At all ten of the facilities reviewed in the report, migrants "reported waiting weeks or months for medical care; inadequate, and in some cases a total absence, of any outdoor recreation time or access to sunlight or fresh air; minimal and inedible food; the use of solitary confinement as punishment; and the extreme remoteness of many of the facilities from any urban area which makes access to legal services nearly impossible" (Detention Watch Network 2012, 3).

Migrants can also lose their lives. Between January and November 2010, Egyptian border guards shot dead at least twenty-eight migrants who attempted to cross the Sinai border into Israel (Human Rights Watch 2010). Between 2000 and 2010, India's Border Security Force killed at least 924 Bangladeshi nationals trying to cross the border between the two countries, according to Odhikar, a Bangladesh human rights monitoring group (Human Rights Watch 2010). Each of these migrants has a name and a family, although most reports of abuse summarize the details and thus lose sight of the human tragedy experienced by each individual migrant.

Why, we ask, do these abuses of migrant rights continue to be so prolific in an age of human rights? In this chapter, we examine the efforts of migrant rights advocates to create international norms that effectively protect migrants and their families. The story is more than a century old, with the earliest mention of workers "in countries other than their own" reflected in the preamble to the ILO, created by the Versailles Peace Treaty after World War I. Pursuant to the establishment of the ILO, membership has become virtually global and three major migrant worker rights conventions have been negotiated: ILO Conventions 66 (1939—withdrawn), 79 (1949), and 143 (1975). When these provided insufficient support for migrant rights, a fourth international convention was negotiated in the United Nations, the International Convention on the Protection of the Rights of All Migrant Workers and Members of Their Families (ICRMW), adopted in 1990. Nonetheless, international cooperation to protect migrants from the abuses described above is nominal: very few countries have actually acceded to these conventions. To explain the absence of widespread international cooperation on migrant rights both before and after World War II, we employ our theoretical framework based on the status quo ante, the preferences of states depending on their position in the migration process, and the power of those states.

Because migratory patterns prior to World War II differed from patterns in the contemporary era, we are able to illuminate more fully the connections between state preferences, power, and international cooperation as well as the role of multilateral institutions as a negotiating arena for migrant rights. In the prewar period, sending states included powerful European states while the receiving states were located primarily in the Americas, states that were less powerful, with the exception of the United States. In this period, sending states were able to incorporate migrant rights into the remit of the ILO. Conventions 66 (1939—withdrawn) and 79 (1949) also reflected European states' concerns for emigrants moving from Europe to the Americas prior to and in the aftermath of World War II. Not surprisingly, this was also supplemented by unilateral action on the behalf of their citizens abroad. In the years following World War II, many sending states transitioned to receiving states and used their power to thwart international cooperation on migrant rights. However, the institutional venues created in the earlier era became the forums that permit sending states in the Global South to employ their growing numerical majority to challenge the status quo, first with Convention 143 in the ILO and then the ICRMW in the UN General Assembly. Receiving states, of course, avoid these international entrapments on their sovereignty by refusing to ratify the treaties.

The ineffectiveness of multilateral forums to promote migrant rights is important to acknowledge. If advocates, among whom we count ourselves, are to be effective, political activity must be carried out at the regional, bilateral, national, or local level.[1] We are not the first scholars or practitioners to observe the absence of international cooperation on migrant rights. However, our argument stands in clear contrast to those of some migrant rights advocates, who seek international forums to pursue their agenda, and of researchers, such as Alexander Betts, who argue that international cooperation is evolving in a "tapestry" of growing norms (Betts 2011). Even in an era of human rights norms, when state interests privilege national sovereignty, international cooperation is not inevitable. Our fear is that, without this corrective to our understanding of international cooperation on migration, resources will be wasted without effectuating much-needed change. This interpretation is confirmed in at least some of the international forums on migration, such as the Global Commission on International Migration. This group's report stated, "National sovereignty in deciding about immigration policy (probably the key determinant of contemporary international migration flows) remains an established principle in international law, subject only to treaty obligations to admit bona fide refugees" ("Report" 2005, 1).

Because of the paucity of international cooperation on migrant rights, we need a better understanding of the determinants of the actual provision of them. Migrants are human beings, men, women, and children, whose rights are enshrined in nine other UN core human rights conventions.[2] In order to understand which states provide migrants with rights, we theorize elsewhere that states with human rights protections and worker protections will better protect voluntary migrants because of their status as humans and as workers, rather than their status as migrants (Money, Lockhart, and Western 2016). This proposition is supported quantitatively using an ILO survey of migrant worker rights.

We begin with an overview of migration patterns prior to World War II, as the identity of sending and receiving states has changed over the past century. We follow with a summary of the international status quo on migrant rights both prior and subsequent to World War II. We then elaborate state preferences for migrant rights, distinguishing between sending and receiving states. Employing these understandings, we trace the history of efforts to create multilateral treaties to protect migrant rights. We then present a quantitative analysis of ICRMW ratifications that supports our contentions that receiving states fail to ratify multilateral migrant rights treaties.

We follow by discussing other multilateral forums—both the UN-sponsored High Level Dialogue and the now annual Conferences on Migration and Development as well as the IOM. These last types of forums illustrate how policy entrepreneurs can enter the decision-making arena. We describe how the IOM, based on its funding structure, provides enhanced incentives for policy entrepreneurs to propose ideas that are implemented whereas the advocacy-based groups that participate in the annual conferences confront a different incentive structure that reduces the likelihood that their ideas will be implemented by states. We briefly review efforts at the regional and bilateral levels to protect migrant rights before comparing our analysis with alternative explanations.

THE STATUS QUO ANTE AND STATE PREFERENCES

Migration Patterns Pre– and Post–World War II. We begin our analysis of international cooperation on migrant rights in the early twentieth century. Because migration patterns have changed significantly over the past century and because our description of migration patterns in chapter 1 focuses primarily on the post–World War II period, it is useful to present a very brief overview of the distinctive migration patterns in the first half of the twentieth century. There are three major patterns to note.[3] The first, and most important for our analysis, is the flow from most European countries to the Americas and Oceania (Australia and New Zealand), as well as other parts of the globe. Until shortly after World War II, most European countries experienced net outmigration, a pattern that continued on the European periphery even after the war. Thus, most European states were sending states in the first half of the twentieth century. A second important migration flow was the movement of labor, through indentured servitude as well as other channels, between regions within colonial empires. Origin states were primarily in Asia and receiving states were East and South Africa and the Caribbean, as well as destination states within Asia.

Finally, there were migratory flows within Europe from the peripheral states such as Ireland, Poland, Italy, and Spain, to early industrializers in Europe: the United Kingdom, Germany, Belgium, and France. Despite the influx of workers from the periphery to the industrial heartland of the European continent, virtually all European countries had net emigration balances (Mitchell 2003). France was the exception due to low fertility rates beginning in the mid-nineteenth century and to population losses in the Franco-Prussian War and World War I (Castles, de Haas, and Miller 2014).[4] The highest levels of outmigration were experienced prior to World War I. Nonetheless, the main image of migration in the century prior to World War II is one of Europeans moving around the globe and European states as sending states—the opposite image of migratory flows after World War II—with France as the primary European exception.

This pattern of international migration contrasts with the patterns of international migration that emerged shortly after World War II, described in chapter 1. As noted above, the early postwar period in Europe was characterized by "overpopulation" and large floating populations displaced by the war—at least thirty million individuals in all (Castles, de Haas, and Miller 2014). However, once reconstruction efforts took hold, underpinned by Marshall Plan funds starting in 1948, most European countries shifted from sending to receiving countries and their preferences changed as a result. Of course, some "traditional receiving states," such as the United States, Canada, Australia, and New Zealand, remained receiving states during the entire time frame while other American states that had been receiving states prior to World War II became sending states or were simply drawn into international migration flows more fully than previously. These migration patterns define the preferences of states that are important for determining whether or not the status quo will be preferred.

The Status Quo Ante before 1945.   What protections were offered to migrants resident in foreign countries prior to World War II? The picture is not as clear as the norm for admissions, which was clearly governed by national sovereignty. In this era, the rights of citizens were not always well established, the rights of foreign residents even less so. Although customary international law did offer basic protections to foreign residents, we argue that legal ambiguities allowed states to privilege national sovereignty over migrant rights. We begin by presenting the case for international customary and treaty law as a bulwark of migrant rights and point out where states have employed international ambiguity to privilege national sovereignty over migrant rights.

Chetail (2014, 61), in a recent survey of customary international law applicable to migrants, describes the development of minimum standards for the treatment of aliens based on the "law of state responsibility." The underlying legal principle arises from the idea that "territorial sovereignty . . . involves the exclusive right to display the activities of a State. This right has as corollary a duty: the obligation to protect within the territory the rights . . . each State may claim for its nationals in foreign territory." That is, because each state has sovereignty over its citizens, it also has the responsibility to protect its citizens abroad; in turn, this implies the duty of the destination state to protect aliens on its national territory.

The international minimum standards for treatment of aliens were not clearly defined but developed in international case law to include "the right to life and respect for physical integrity, the right to recognition as a person before the law, freedom of conscience, prohibition of arbitrary detention, the right to a fair trial in civil and criminal matters, and the right to property" (Chetail 2014, 64). These rights are generally viewed as civil rights, and states were gradually adopting these civil rights for their citizens and, hence, for aliens on their territory. Nonetheless, customary international law retained the "traditional *summa divisio* (the principal division) based on the distinction between citizens and non-citizens" (65). Thus, the status quo at the turn of the twentieth century was national sovereignty over migrant rights with a minimum standard of protection.

The Status Quo Ante after 1945. It is not until after World War II that the status quo for migrant rights changed with the advent of the human rights movement. This advancement was not viewed as a specific enhancement of migrant rights per se but rather aimed at improving the rights that states offered their residents, citizen and noncitizen, as human beings. Migrant rights expanded only as a by-product of the expansion of human rights. As the American Convention on Human Rights (OAS 1969, 69) puts it, "the essential rights of man are not derived from one's being a national of a certain state, but are based on the attributes of the human personality." This change was initiated in the 1948 Universal Declaration of Human Rights by the United Nations. Article 2 of the declaration states that "everyone is entitled to all the rights and freedoms set forth in this Declaration, without distinction of any kind, such as race, color, sex, language, religion, political or other opinion, *national or social origin*, property, birth or other status" (United Nations 1948, emphasis added). However, this declaration is largely aspirational, and it is the widely ratified International Covenant on Civil and Political Rights (ICCPR) in 1966 that begins to provide a wider array of rights for migrants, based on their status as human beings rather than as migrants. Article 2 of the ICCPR contains the nondiscrimination clause that prevents discrimination based on national origin using language identical to the Universal Declaration (Plender 2007, 21–22). The covenant protects the civil rights covered in the minimum international standards listed above including protection from "cruel, inhuman, or degrading treatment or punishment." These human rights agreements expanded the protections available to migrants by defining specific protection responsibilities of states to their residents, whether national or foreign.

The ICCPR and other human rights treaties do not guarantee equal treatment across all areas of the law. Although Chetail (2014, 65) states that "human rights law asserts equality of treatment between citizens and non-citizens in accordance with the national standard," there are some clearly demarcated distinctions between citizens and noncitizens. For example, the right to political participation outlined in Article 25 is reserved specifically for citizens, while Article 13 protects the right of legally resident aliens to have expulsion orders reviewed. Moreover, there are often distinctions between the rights available to legally resident aliens and aliens without permission to reside (illegal or undocumented migrants). Chetail (2014, 70, emphasis added) concludes that, despite nondiscrimination clauses, "*a differential treatment is still permissible* provided that the criteria for such differentiation are 'reasonable and objective,' so that the exact implication for non-citizens is still difficult to grasp with certainty." As a result, many experts view national sovereignty rather than international law as the critical determinant of migrant rights both before and after World War II.[5] Roger Böhning (1988, 133), for example, argues that "the doctrine of sovereignty considers the treatment of foreign nationals—their entry, stay, activities, and expulsion—as falling within the reserved domain of domestic jurisdiction. In this view, every State is free to admit a foreigner or to refuse him entry and to place any limitation or condition on his stay and economic, social, political, cultural, or other activities." Both Torpey (2000) and Salter (2003), in their assessments of the international passport regime, also consider migrant rights to be governed by national sovereignty. As even Chetail (2014, 71–72) acknowledges, customary international law remains difficult to implement at the state level and countries "still have to learn to collaborate on an issue that has been traditionally regarded as a core component of their sovereignty."[6]

Sending State Preferences. We now turn to state preferences vis-à-vis the status quo. Outside of the imperative of ensuring state territorial security, the interests of states in the international system are often opaque. Fortunately, there is a reasonable consensus on the interests of sending and receiving states related to migrant rights. States from which migrants emigrate generally seek to expand the protections of migrants in the country of employment (Lonnroth 1991; Böhning 1988). As Lonnroth (1991, 732) puts it, in describing the interests of the G77 states in the UN convention negotiations,[7] these states wanted "to promote the interests of their citizens living and working in industrialized countries." As noted above, the international law principle of state responsibility acknowledges the state's interest in protecting its citizens abroad.[8] A contemporary example of a sending state's efforts to protect the rights of its emigrants in multilateral, regional, and bilateral forums is the Philippines (OECD 2004). It has been an active proponent of migrant rights in various forums (see below on bilateral agreements). Other states actually have clauses in their constitutions that require them to protect their citizens abroad (Böhning 1988).

An early example of a sending state actively petitioning for the rights of its citizens abroad is Italy (Cometti 1958; Del Boca and Venturini 2003; Vecoli 1995). Emigration from the Italian Peninsula started in earnest after the unification of Italy in 1861. Between 1861 and 1976 more than twenty-six million Italians emigrated, about half to other European countries and most of the remainder to the Americas. The new Italian state issued circulars controlling emigration in 1868, 1873, and 1876 and passed the first emigration legislation in 1888, an attempt to protect prospective emigrants from the wiles of recruitment agencies. Italian efforts extended to the creation of the General Commissariat for Emigration in 1901 under the Ministry of Foreign Affairs.

The preference for and effort to protect their citizens is not the sole interest of sending states. Sending states also want to ensure the continuation of revenues generated by migration in the form of remittances and hence to retain an outlet for their emigrants (Cholewinski, de Guchteneire, and Pécoud 2009). Remittances are not just a modern by-product of emigration. In the Italian case, for example, Cinel (1991, emphasis added) describes numerous laws "introduced to control and protect emigration and *emigrants' remittances*" between 1869 and 1925. Remittances from Italian emigration have been estimated at 5 percent of the Italian national product at the height of emigration between 1906 and 1914, when more than twenty individuals of every thousand residents left Italian shores each year (Cometti 1958; Del Boca and Venturini 2003). Such was the importance of remittances to Italy that the central operative clause of the 1904 French-Italian bilateral migration treaty was to establish public and private mechanisms for monetary transfers between Italy and France (Lowe 1918). Remittances are so significant that sending states do not want receiving states to close the doors to their migrants. Sending states want workers to be treated well but hesitate to demand such guarantees if receiving states would then bar their workers from immigrating.

Receiving State Preferences. In contrast, migrant-receiving states do not want to be constrained by international standards regarding migrant rights. The interests of migrant-receiving states are nicely summarized by Lonnroth (1991) in speaking of the group of "Western and industrial nations" participating in the UN convention negotiations during the 1980s. According to Lonnroth (1991, 722), these states placed an "emphasis on the right of each state to determine the criteria for admission and for regularization," as well as on "the obligations of the migrant workers to comply with the laws and regulations of the state of employment." Finally, "issues of costs to the state due to an inflow of migrant workers were of special interest."

This interest does not necessarily suggest that receiving states want fewer migrants. Rather, they want to be able to determine the number and type of migrants that enter at any point in time. Depending on the demand for migrants, states have been willing to offer significant levels of benefits or have tried to limit the benefits that migrant workers receive (Ruhs 2013). However, receiving states want the freedom to choose which rights to offer to which group of migrants. States want to retain sovereignty over whether to offer to any migrant or group of migrants the right to vote, the right to access the social system, the freedom to move from one job to another, and so on. This variation is evident both geographically and temporally.

The change in the status quo after World War II with the adoption of the Universal Declaration of Human Rights and, more particularly, the ICCPR, increased the number of rights that states were required to offer a nonnational population. However, this new status quo depends on each state's adoption of the various human rights covenants and by the recognition that many of the proposed goals remain aspirations.[9]

International Cooperation on Migrant Rights. This analysis of the status quo and state preferences on migrant rights provides the basis on which to derive several hypotheses, based on our theoretical discussion outlined in chapter 2. Because our analysis spans an entire century, it is important to reiterate that the identity and the power of sending and receiving states have changed over time. Prior to World War II, the receiving countries were located primarily in the Americas and were not particularly powerful. The United States was clearly catapulted to great power status through its participation in World War I when it sat at the Paris Peace Conference as one of the five major powers. Other American states, although some were relatively wealthy, were not considered world powers. On the other hand, many European states were sending states and were major powers. The preferences of sending and receiving states remain as laid out above. However, because of the differences in power, the anticipated outcomes are different. Where sending states are powerful, if they prefer the status quo, the status quo will be retained. Where sending states are powerful and prefer a change in the status quo, the status quo is likely to change.

Prior to World War II, powerful sending states desired greater protections for their emigrants. We thus anticipate they will negotiate an agreement to change the status quo. Weak receiving states will resist these negotiations and will attempt to extract concessions from the sending states. Subsequent to World War II, powerful receiving states desired to retain sovereignty over migrant rights. We thus anticipate that they will resist international negotiations. However, we anticipate that weak sending states will employ existing international institutions to express their preferences for migrant protections. Negotiations post–World War II will follow the route of least resistance, the usage of existing international organizations to press for change, whether the institutions are bilateral, regional, or multilateral. In the contemporary era, given the status quo that privileges national sovereignty, multilateral migrant rights treaties are anticipated only when (less powerful) sending states compose a sufficient majority to adopt treaties without the support of receiving states. And, when adopted, we predict that receiving states will refuse to ratify.

To conclude, from an interstate perspective, sending and receiving states have different interests associated with the level of migrant rights to be provided. Receiving states are interested in retaining their sovereignty over migrant rights; on the other hand, sending states want to protect their migrants' rights through international agreements. The outcome depends on the status quo ante and the power of sending and receiving states. Where the status quo privileges receiving (sending) states, and receiving (sending) states are powerful, the status quo is likely to be maintained. Where receiving (sending) states prefer an alternative to the status quo and are powerful, the status quo is likely to change. When sending (receiving) states have sufficient institutional power in particular international forums, such as the ILO or the UN General Assembly, they may be able to force receiving (sending) states to the bargaining table. But sending (receiving) states are insufficiently powerful to ensure that receiving (sending) states adhere to any agreements that are negotiated.

In the following sections, we describe the efforts to protect migrant rights in the international arena. We begin with the ILO, which originated in the Treaty of Versailles. We examine four separate periods: the negotiation of the charter for the ILO at the Paris conference, Convention 66 (1939), Convention 97 (1949), and Convention 143 (1975). We then describe a fifth period: the efforts of sending states to change the venue of migrant protection to the United Nations, where sending states have a numerical majority in the General Assembly. Wealthy Western receiving states actively participated in the negotiations and helped shape the convention but no receiving state has yet become party to it.

We provide a quantitative analysis that examines the conditions under which states accede to the ICRMW. We examine other contemporary global forums on migration to help ensure that we are not overlooking other types of international cooperation on migrant rights. We also explore the degree of regional and bilateral cooperation on migrant rights, which provides additional evidence that the status of sending and receiving states is crucial to understanding the level of treaty commitment whereas migrant rights are determined primarily by national human rights protections and domestic labor legislation. We also describe the IOM, which creates a different incentive structure for states to co-operate. Both the qualitative and quantitative evidence provide support for our hypotheses regarding the lack of international cooperation on migrant rights.

THE HISTORY OF INTERNATIONAL COOPERATION ON MIGRANT WORKER RIGHTS

Migrant rights have been on the international agenda for more than a century and were one of the earliest issues on the human rights agenda; they were prominent well before the human rights catastrophes of World War II placed human rights on the global agenda. The issue arose in part with the rise of industrialization and the efforts of workers, as well as some more enlightened employers, to improve the conditions of the working classes. There was an early recognition that international competitiveness depended on the costs of doing business, which included workers' wages and benefits. Employers would be forced to limit wages and benefits to those of their international competitors. Hence there were proposals for international legislation on working conditions during the nineteenth century, but it not until 1901 that the International Association of Labor Legislation was established, committed to propagating labor standards for all countries (Shotwell 1934; ILO 1951; Johnston 1970; ILO 2009; Rodgers et al. 2009).

Migrant rights were part and parcel of this effort. Although migration for employment has never been limited to Western Europe, these states were in the forefront of attempting to establish international labor legislation as these were the first nations to industrialize and to develop working-class movements that placed migrant labor on the agenda. National labor unions sought to prevent employers from undercutting local wages and benefits by hiring workers from other countries. So the rights of migrants to equal wages and benefits as national workers became part of the legislative program. This was championed not only by labor unions but by states that were predominantly countries of emigration, such as Italy (Böhning n.d.). Refugee rights, per se, were bundled with worker rights because refugees (in the modern definition of the term) who crossed borders also had to support themselves in their country of residence.

The International Association for Labor Legislation was the first to produce multilateral agreements on labor standards, although the initial treaties did not address migrant rights. The organization was based in Switzerland and, although private, was supported by the Swiss state. The organization members met to discuss the scope of labor standards and to draft proposed treaties. The Swiss government then invited diplomats from the countries that were represented in the organization.[10] Two international treaties were negotiated in this fashion in 1906, one regulating night work for women, a second on the use of white phosphorus in the manufacture of matches (a health hazard for workers in the industry) (Delevigne 1934). Meetings in 1912 and 1913 produced a much more ambitious agenda, including foreign worker access to insurance, but the intervening war led to the collapse of the organization.

Period 1: Migrant Protections in the ILO and the Charter of Workers' Rights. The preamble to the ILO includes a demand for the improvement in the global conditions of workers including "the protection of the interests of workers when employed in countries other than their own" (Versailles Treaty 1919, Part 13). Article 427 of the treaty, commonly known as the Charter of Workers' Rights, includes nine principles that govern workers' conditions. Principle 8 reads, "The standard set by law in each country with respect to the conditions of labor should have due regard to the equitable economic treatment of all workers lawfully resident therein" (Versailles Treaty 1919, Article 427).[11] Although the word "migrant" is not employed in the treaty language, these two phrases represent the first international recognition of migrant workers' rights. What were the conditions that proved propitious to the adoption of this multilateral treaty? An examination of the commission participants, their position in the migration system, and the institutional rules governing decision making provide a clear answer. Sending states formed a majority of the participants in the commission and were able to sustain a two-thirds majority to ensure that migrant workers were included in the remit of the newly formed ILO and that equal treatment would be provided to foreign workers who were legally resident.

World War I served as an exogenous shock that brought the victorious countries together with the purpose of addressing international labor standards, including those of migrant workers. The negotiators at the Paris Conference subsequent to the war received a specific mandate to develop an international organization that would "improve working and living conditions all over the world" (ILO 1951, 6). This mandate developed out of the perception of world leaders that the avoidance of war required that people the world over must be "free from want." A second impetus for the mandate was the Bolshevik Revolution in Russia that raised the issue of labor rights and labor power in other industrialized countries. The negotiations produced two worker-related documents contained in Part 13 of the treaty. The first established an international organization to oversee labor standards—what became the ILO. The second was a charter on worker rights.

The states party to the negotiations were the United Kingdom, the United States, Cuba, France, Belgium, Czechoslovakia, Italy, Poland, and Japan, nine states altogether (Shotwell 1934). The five "major powers," the United Kingdom, the United States, France, Italy, and Japan, each received two votes. The other countries represented at the table were chosen to represent the "minor powers" at the peace conference; of these, Belgium was allocated two votes, the remainder one each. This list is unsurprising given that these states were all part of the victorious Entente Alliance during the war; the United States was an associated power and Cuba declared war against Germany one day after the US declaration, although it did not participate in the actual conflict. Nonetheless, these states represented different positions in terms of international migration. The historical statistics do not provide as clear a picture as we would like to identify states as sending or receiving in 1919.[12] The United States and Cuba, in the New World, were clearly receiving states. In Europe, France underwent its demographic transition earlier than most other states and was importing labor from neighboring European countries by the end of the nineteenth century. However, the remaining states were clearly or marginally sending states (Mitchell 2003). The United Kingdom was a sending state until several decades after World War II. Japan was likely a state in transition from sending to receiving, as its industrialization process proceeded and as it became a great power. Belgium's early industrial revolution in the south (Wallonia) drew in workers from the north (Flanders), but Flemish workers also emigrated to surrounding states. Czechoslovakia, Italy, and Poland were all sending states in the early part of the twentieth century. So the balance between sending and receiving states in the negotiations for the ILO was close. The clear superiority of sending states over receiving states was achieved through the allocation of delegates (Shotwell 1934).[13]

The international status quo, as noted above, provided primarily civil protections for nationals residing in foreign countries, which suggests that sending states would petition for a more extensive set of rights to be acknowledged by receiving states. As is the case in many international negotiations, providing the working draft is a mechanism employed to shape the outcome of the negotiations. The UK delegation provided the earliest complete draft, and this became the discussion document (Rodgers et al. 2009). This draft incorporated migrant workers in the preamble, "the protection of the interests of workers when employed in countries other than their own" (Versailles Treaty 1919). There are no minutes of the negotiations sessions, but Edward Phelan (1934) participated in the negotiations for the United States and provides a detailed description of the debate over each of the articles the UK delegation proposed. The central disputes concerned each state's delegation to the newly founded international organization: the final agreement provides for two government representatives, one employer representative, and one worker representative, although some states sought to have an even representation and others sought to exclude government representatives altogether. The other central dispute concerned whether the conventions, requiring a two-thirds majority, would be binding on all member states or whether states could decide whether or not to ratify the conventions. The latter position won out. There appears to have been no debate over the inclusion of workers "employed in countries other than their own."

The second component of the deliberations was the charter of workers' rights. The British delegation believed that a peace treaty was not the appropriate place for such a charter but was overruled by the other delegates. The Italian delegation made the formal proposal for the charter, and all delegations submitted petitions. The British, despite their initial skepticism, submitted petitions as well, to demonstrate their support, given the backing they had received during the initial negotiations. Nineteen "principles" emerged from this process; these were ordered by level of support and submitted to a two-thirds majority approval process.[14] Nine principles received the required support, including Principle 8: "The Principle that in all matters concerning the rights of workpeople, working conditions, and social insurance, foreign workmen and their families should be treated on the same footing as the nationals of the country in which they reside, and that they may not be subjected as such to any special taxation" (Phelan 1934, 187). Thus migrant rights joined a list that included equal pay for equal work for men and women, the eight-hour day, the living wage, the right of association, weekly rest, child labor, workplace inspections, and labor as a human attribute.

Not surprisingly, the Italian delegation was active in the negotiations in an effort to include migrant workers within the remit of the newly constructed ILO. This is consistent with its position as a sending country and with its domestic legislation and national emigration agency (see above); the lead Italian delegate was Baron Mayor des Planches, the Italian commissioner-general for emigration. The Italian delegation proposed three additional principles associated with migrant workers but was unable to marshal sufficient support for these proposals (Phelan 1934).[15] Given the British hesitance toward a Charter of Worker Rights in the first place and efforts by most states to keep the list to a minimum, it is not surprising that the Italian delegation withdrew these proposals before a vote was taken.

The French delegation appears to present a position at odds with its status as a receiving state. It allied with the Italian delegation to demand equal treatment for migrant workers. This can be explained in part by the personal position of members of the French delegation to the negotiations. The delegation included Leon Jouhaux, the head of the communist Confédération Générale du Travail. As the head of the largest French trade union, Jouhaux represented the demands of labor organizations that sought to establish standards that would prevent migrant workers in France, a receiving state, from undercutting the wages and benefits of native workers. France was also concerned about its ability to recruit sufficient immigrant labor to supplement its workforce, devastated by the war. This was a second reason for supporting equal rights for migrant workers—to facilitate the recruitment of foreign labor (Shotwell 1934).[16]

Organizational Structure and Decision-Making Rules. The Versailles Treaty created the organizational structure of the ILO. It is composed of three principal bodies: the General Conference, the Governing Body, and the International Labor Office. The General Conference meets regularly—every year since World War II—and is the ultimate governing body of the ILO. Each member state is represented by four delegates: two representing the government, one representing workers, and one representing employers. Each member of the delegation can cast his or her vote independently, thus providing a tripartite structure of representation that weights government representation at 50 percent, and workers and employers at 25 percent each. The ILO is the only UN body that has this tripartite representation.

The Governing Body is the executive branch of the ILO with a total of sixteen members: eight elected from the conference at large and eight representing the eight states deemed to be most industrialized. The conference legislates through conventions, recommendations, and resolutions supported by a supermajority of two-thirds of the delegates. These organizational rules are significant for two reasons. First, the tripartite representation that includes representatives of labor from both sending and receiving countries provides a forum and potential for a sending and receiving state alliance, as labor representatives generally support equal rights for migrant workers. That said, these organizational rules are also significant because they set the bar for the type of coalition that must come together to create a convention. A two-thirds majority is a significant hurdle to overcome, even if sending states become a numerical majority and labor representatives support migrant worker rights, given the potential opposition from employers as well as receiving states.

The second operational aspect that is important for understanding international cooperation on migrant rights is that the ILO was associated with the League of Nations, membership in which automatically enrolled that state in the ILO; this remained true in the United Nations as well. Thus, as the League of Nations grew, the ILO grew apace. Table 7.1 shows the membership through 1970. As can be seen, the balance between sending and receiving states was constantly changing.

Period 2: ILO Convention 66 (1939). This convention is subtitled "Convention Concerning the Recruitment, Placing and Conditions of Labor of Migrants for Employment." It sought to regulate recruitment agencies, both public and private, and to provide migrant workers with minimum rights of employment,

Table 7.1
ILO Membership

Year	Countries	Number of members
1919: Founding members	Argentina, Australia, Belgium, Bolivia, Brazil, Canada, Chile, China, Colombia, Cuba, Czechoslovakia, Denmark, El Salvador, France, Greece, Guatemala, Haiti, Honduras, India, Iran, Italy, Japan, Liberia, Netherlands, New Zealand, Nicaragua, Norway, Panama, Paraguay, Peru, Poland, Portugal, Romania, South Africa, Spain, Sweden, Switzerland, Thailand, United Kingdom, Uruguay, Venezuela, Yugoslavia	42
1919: First meeting	Austria,* Germany*	44
1920	Albania, Bulgaria, Costa Rica, Finland, Luxembourg	49
1921	Estonia, Latvia, Lithuania	52
1922	Hungary	53
1923	Ethiopia, Ireland	55
1924	Dominican Republic	56
1931	Mexico	57
1932	Iraq, Turkey	59
1934	Afghanistan, Ecuador, Soviet Union, United States	63
1936	Egypt	64
Withdrawals: 1935 until 1958	Austria, Costa Rica, El Salvador, Germany, Guatemala, Honduras, Italy, Japan, Nicaragua, Paraguay, Romania, Soviet Union (expelled from League of Nations), Spain	51
1940	Estonia, Latvia, and Lithuania annexed by the Soviet Union	48
1945	Iceland	49
1947	Pakistan, Syria	51
1948	Burma (Myanmar), Ceylon (Sri Lanka), Lebanon, Philippines	55
1949	Israel	56
1950	Indonesia, Vietnam*	58
1952	Libya	59
	Readmission of all withdrawals by 1956	72
1954	Beylorussia, Ukraine	74
1956	Jordan, Morocco, Sudan, Tunisia	78
1957	Ghana, Malaysia	80
1959	Guinea	81
1960	Cameroon, Central African Republic, Chad, Congo (Brazzaville), Congo (Kinshasa), Côte d'Ivoire, Cyprus, Dahomey, Gabon, Madagascar, Mali, Nigeria, Senegal, Somalia, Togo, Upper Volta	97

(continued)

Table 7.1
(*continued*)

Year	Countries	Number of members
1961	Kuwait, Mauritania, Niger, Sierra Leone	101
1962	Algeria, Jamaica, Rwanda, Tanzania	105
1963	Trinidad and Tobago, Uganda	107
1964	Kenya, Laos, Zambia	110
1965	Malawi, Malta, Singapore, Yemen	114
1966	Guyana, Lesotho, Nepal	117
1967	Barbados	118
1968	Mongolia	119
1969	Cambodia, Mauritius, South Yemen	122
Withdrawals	South Africa (1966), Albania (1967)	120

*Austria and Germany were not considered founding members but joined the ILO in 1919 and attended the first meeting of the ILO that year. Vietnam was a member 1950–76 and 1980–85, before rejoining in 1992.
Source: Johnston (1970).

including work contracts in workers' native language providing detailed information about the conditions of employment. It also required states party to the convention "to provide foreigners treatment no less favourable than that which it applied to its own nationals" (ILO 1939, Article 10).[17] Why was this convention signed twenty years after the first ILO meeting?

Between 1919 and 1939, the ILO was actively engaged in issues involving migrant workers. Once the Versailles Treaty was signed and ratified, the ILO opened for business immediately, as the peace treaty made provisions for the first session of the ILO to convene in October 1919. Few conventions dealing with migrant workers were adopted. A list of the conventions that deal in any way with migrant workers and the number of parties to the conventions are provided in Table 7.2. All of the treaties listed, with the exception of Conventions 66, 97, and 143, establish standards for national workers but include a clause that requires states to provide reciprocity of national treatment for migrant workers. Although we have listed these conventions in Table 7.2, in order to provide the most complete picture of migrant rights negotiated within the ILO, these reciprocal guarantees are of little importance as they grant national treatment only to migrants from member states that have also signed the treaty, and thus are not a straightforward grant of migrant rights. If only sending states sign these agreements, then migrants will not be covered.

The ILO began with a flurry of activity and, in 1920, established an Emigration

Table 7.2
ILO Conventions on Migrant Workers

Convention	Title of convention	Date adopted	Entry into force	Ratifications
C2*	Unemployment	11/28/1919	7/14/1921	54 (3 denounced)
C19*	Equality of Treatment (Accident Compensation)	6/5/1925	8/9/1926	121
C21	Inspection of Emigrants	6/5/1926	12/29/1927	26 (2 conditional; 5 denounced)
C48* (shelved—revised by C157)	Maintenance of Migrant Pension Rights	6/22/1935	8/10/1938	8 (4 denounced)
C66 (withdrawn)	Migration for Employment	6/28/1939		
C97 (revised)	Migration for Employment	7/1/1949	1/22/1952	49
C118*	Equality of Treatment (Social Security)	6/28/1962	4/25/1964	37 (1 denounced)
C143	Migrant Workers (Supplementary)	6/24/1975	9/12/1978	23
C157*	Maintenance of Social Security Rights	6/21/1982	9/11/1986	4

The wording in the conventions is as follows: "Each Member of the International Labour Organization which ratifies this Convention undertakes to grant to the nationals of any other Member which shall have ratified the Convention . . . the same treatment . . . as it grants its own nationals."

*Conventions based on reciprocity.

Commission and convened conferences on migration in 1924 and 1928 (ILO 1951). But the few treaties addressing migrant rights were of nominal import. The absence of activity on migrant rights can be attributed to the balance between sending and receiving states in the ILO and the requirement for a two-thirds majority to adopt a convention. The Commission on International Labor Legislation that negotiated Part 13 of the Versailles Treaty comprised nine states, the majority of which, in terms of voting power, were sending states. In contrast, the first meeting of the ILO comprised forty-four states with tripartite representation. Table 7.1 provides for a running tab on ILO membership. Until well after World War II, much of the territory around the globe was part of imperial systems, so the membership in the ILO was small—only fifty-six members up through 1949. Membership was fairly evenly divided between receiving states, primarily in the Americas, supplemented by the "traditional settler states" of Australia and New Zealand, and the sending states of Europe and Asia (China and India). Moreover, the tripartite representation of countries meant that sending countries' votes did not uniformly support migrant rights. Since sending states were powerful, they could employ their power and resources to help persuade receiving states to adopt migrant rights. However, they could also change the status quo through unilateral action, and this appears to be the least costly method of achieving the desired results. Chetail (2014) notes, for example, that the minimum standard of treatment was contested by Western countries that wanted their nationals to be treated according to standards of "civilized society"; the states used lack of such treatment as an excuse to intervene in the politics of many Latin American countries. The effectiveness of unilateral action is also emphasized by Torpey (2000, 22):

> The safety and security of the [passport] bearer were assured, or at least improved, by the special legal standing that Europeans enjoyed in many colonies. Europeans, rather than being subject to the laws of the Ottoman Empire (to use a famous example), were subject to European laws, European courts, at lighter sentences for like crimes. It was the military and economic might of the colonial powers that stood behind every lone traveler.

The balance of the ILO membership slowly shifted during the 1930s to favor sending states. Convention 66, though, responded to the needs of receiving states in Latin America that continued to rely on European migration to develop their economies and resented the prohibitions placed on emigration from Germany, Italy, and other Central European countries during the 1930s as these countries prepared for war (Rodgers et al. 2009). The convention predominantly focused on recruitment (see chapter 4) and established regulations governing labor migration, including recruitment, placement, and conditions of labor (Rodgers et al. 2009, 77; ILO 1939). Note that receiving states were important actors in placing migrant rights on the agenda, but only at a time when those states were facing labor market shortages (Rodgers et al. 2009). However, the convention was shelved without a single ratification.

Period 3: ILO Convention 97 (1949). Convention 97 incorporated and extended all the migrant protections spelled out in Convention 66. However, this convention relegates the regulation of recruitment agencies to appendices on which reservations could be placed. So this convention focuses centrally on providing migrant workers with conditions of employment identical to those of the native workforce, including family allowances and social security. Convention 66 made access to these conditions subject to reciprocity, while Convention 97 has no such stipulation. Moreover, several European countries, for the first time, signed and ratified the convention. Why does the picture change in the early post–World War II period?

The impetus for a new convention on migrant rights was no longer the recruitment efforts of Latin American countries but the concern with "surplus populations" in Europe. The war dislocated millions of people, broke up multinational empires (generating minority populations in many countries), and swallowed up the Baltic states, thus generating a new impetus for emigration. In the post–World War II period, European states were confronted with these "surplus populations" that consisted of displaced persons from the war, refugees, stateless populations, and, in many countries, a significant unemployed population (Ducasse-Rogier 2001). States such as Belgium and France, which had been receiving states in the earlier part of the twentieth century, began to experience significant outflows even as they continued to recruit migrants. For example, between 1945 and 1949, Belgium received 174,100 immigrants but sent 186,700 emigrants abroad (Mitchell 2003). The United Kingdom was implicated as well as it began negotiating independence of its many colonial possessions. Between 1945 and 1949, the United Kingdom received 250,400 immigrants but sent more than twice as many abroad: 590,000 (Mitchell 2003). Counting all European countries as countries of emigration, as well as the transition of states of the Americas from receiving to sending states as global inequality worsened, sending states now had a majority in the ILO. Of the fifty-nine member states of the ILO in 1949, thirty-nine (66 percent) could be counted as sending states, only twenty (34 percent) as receiving states.[18]

Even as the war proceeded across the globe, the ILO General Conference met in Philadelphia in 1944.[19] Given the history of the ILO, arising out of World War I, the member states reiterated the objective of the ILO, which was to bring peace. The major product of this meeting was the Philadelphia Declaration, which again incorporated migrant workers as part of the ILO remit. Although the declaration is nonbinding, Article 3 states, "The Conference recognizes the solemn obligation of the ILO to further among the nations of the world programmes which will achieve . . . the provision . . . of facilities for training and the transfer of labour, including migration for employment and settlement." This again implicated the "great powers" that were worried about their "surplus populations" (Ducasse-Rogier 2001).

The mandate of the ILO's Permanent Migration Committee was renewed in February 1940, so the committee was in place at the end of the war, at which time it undertook an assessment of migratory movements. The ILO developed a model agreement for bilateral cooperation for migration and worked to revise the 1939 Convention on Migrant Workers. This culminated in the adoption in 1949 of Convention 97, which provides standards for the organization of migration and equality of treatment, thus far only recognized in the Treaty of Versailles.[20]

As noted earlier, this convention is not well ratified. By 1956, only twelve of the seventy-eight member states had ratified (15 percent), although a number of European states did ratify the agreement—virtually all when they were sending rather than receiving states. These same states have subsequently refused to sign international agreements protecting migrant rights. At the time of ratification, Belgium (1953), Italy (1952), the Netherlands (1952), and the United Kingdom (1951) were net emigration states (Mitchell 2003). Portugal (1978) and Spain (1967) continued to be countries of emigration at the time of their signing. Only five migrant-receiving countries signed the convention: France, Israel, New Zealand, and Uruguay in the early 1950s and the Federal Republic of Germany in the late 1950s (Böhning n.d.; ILO 1949).[21] And, of these states, both France and the Federal Republic of Germany were experiencing large outflows of migrants at the time the convention was negotiated. Israel falls into the pattern common for newly created states in the international system. In order to achieve the international dimensions of statehood, new states often sign on to a wide array of existing international agreements (Beato 1994).

Tracing the membership of the ILO in terms of the balance between sending and receiving states provides a clear picture of when migrant rights will rise on the agenda and result in a convention. The unusual tripartite representation and the two-thirds majority required to adopt a convention placed the bar very high so that the balance between sending and receiving states for much of the early history of the ILO prevented migrant rights from rising. That balance began to change as the membership of the ILO expanded, but sending states did not achieve the critical mass necessary to address migrant rights. Directly after World War II, most European countries were still countries of emigration and the displaced populations from the war and initial high unemployment heightened interest in the possibilities for emigration and hence the need for protection of European citizens abroad. By 1949, new admissions favoring sending countries created a two-thirds majority of sending countries. Thus, a migrant rights treaty was drafted and adopted. Although powerful sending countries ratified the agreement, receiving countries, favoring national sovereignty, failed to support it. Moreover, because powerful sending countries rapidly transitioned to receiving states, they had little incentive to squander resources on persuading receiving states to ratify. Thus, the convention remains a poorly ratified treaty.

Period 4: ILO Convention 143 (1975). Convention 143 comprises two parts: the first deals with undocumented migration and efforts to curtail these flows (Migrations in Abusive Conditions), the second with the treatment of migrant workers in the host state (Promotion of Equality of Opportunity and Treatment of Migrant Workers) (ILO 1975). The rights extended to migrants in Convention 143 extend beyond the workplace to the families of migrant workers, well beyond the guarantees included in Convention 97. This convention reflects the reversal of migration patterns between 1950 and 1975.

Virtually all states classified as countries of emigration in Europe became countries of immigration while the Americas, save the United States and Canada, became states of emigration, as internal and global inequality grew. Independence movements around the globe created new, impoverished nations whose citizens sought better lives abroad. These factors shifted the identity and the number of sending states. As postwar reconstruction in Europe and Japan proceeded, unemployment shrank, "surplus populations" diminished, and many European countries turned to migrants to fill labor market shortages, first from Europe and then from farther afield (Kindleberger 1967). European countries that had experienced "surplus populations" became states of immigration. And as they reached farther and farther afield for migrants, the number of countries engaged in labor migration increased. As a result, the issue of migrant workers again rose on the agenda of the ILO. Unsurprisingly, the initial impetus for a new convention was to provide better treatment and working conditions for migrant workers at the behest of migrant-sending countries. And the balance of power in the ILO was changing to the advantage of this new group of migrant-sending states. The wave of new states that gained independence in the two decades after World War II and joined the United Nations provided for a sending state majority in the ILO, even as some states in the Global South remained or became receiving states (ILO 2009).[22]

In 1971, the General Conference passed a resolution asking that migrant worker rights be added to the agenda, to ensure equality of treatment in law and in practice for all social and labor issues. In 1972, the vulnerability of migrant workers was publicized through the Mont Blanc tunnel incident, in which a group of workers suffocated in the back of a van when it was stuck in the tunnel.[23] The Mont Blanc incident also raised the visibility of smuggling/trafficking of migrant workers. After the economic crisis of 1973–74, followed by slower economic growth and rising unemployment in Europe, ILO member states in Europe began closing the doors to migration, which pushed migrant workers into the hands of smugglers/traffickers and shifted the balance of migration flows from legal, documented migrants to illegal, undocumented migrants. As a result, member states in Europe pushed for a new migrant workers convention to deal with clandestine migration, an effort that was opposed by countries of emigration. The result was a compromise of sorts incorporating both the issue of illegal migration and the issue of migrant rights. In part, the supermajority that supported the convention was generated by a coalition that included sending states that supported the second part of the treaty and receiving states that privileged the first part. To help ensure ratification by member states, the convention provided that a ratifying state may exclude either Part 1 or Part 2 of the convention. In any case, the convention is poorly ratified, with only twenty-three countries—all countries of emigration—signing on. Thus, yet again, even though sending states were able to find a supermajority in the ILO to create a treaty providing for multilateral cooperation on migrant rights, receiving states (and most other states) have refused to be bound by it.

The failure of the ILO treaty to address the concerns of sending countries regarding protections they desired for undocumented workers and the poor ratification rate led to an effort to move the decision-making arena on migrant rights from the ILO to the UN General Assembly. In this institution, sending states were in a majority and were not hampered by the tripartite representation that characterized the ILO.[24] This change in venue is detailed below.

Most recently, experts at the ILO drafted a Multilateral Framework on Labor Migration. This contains nonbinding principles and guidelines for a "rights-based approach to labor migration" and provides governments with a series of best practices. In March 2006, the Governing Body agreed that the framework should be published and disseminated. So the efforts of the ILO to provide standards governing labor migration have continued for almost one hundred years—from 1919 to 2016. Given the majority of European sending states that negotiated the ILO and the Charter of Workers Rights in the Versailles Treaty, the issue of migrant rights was present from the beginning, yet the results have been meager. All migrant-related conventions are poorly ratified, and the most recent efforts consist of a "framework" of best practices rather than any binding agreements.[25]

Efforts to Become Operational (the Birth of the IOM). The ILO also failed in its efforts to become a major actor in the international migration arena, a path that is distinctive from the UNHCR, which has become an operational organization tasked with identifying and protecting refugees globally. This is yet another instance in which migrant worker rights have failed to become implanted in the multilateral system.

In the aftermath of World War II, the ILO determined that manpower and training were arenas to which the ILO could contribute (ILO 1951). There were three perceived parts to the problem—the national manpower programs, meant to fit workers in jobs within the nation; vocational training, equipping workers with the appropriate skills to do the jobs; and finally "manpower had to be redistributed internationally" (ILO 1951, 67). A modest operational capacity was developed to help move migrants, in particular from Germany and Italy to Latin American countries in the early post–World War II period (Johnston 1970, 117).

David Morse, the (American) ILO director-general beginning in June 1948, had bigger ambitions. He elaborated an operational program to provide transportation for migrants. The temporary International Refugee Organization was scheduled for dismantlement, and the ILO proposed to help resolve the problem of "surplus populations in Europe" by taking over the operational capabilities of the dismantled organization. Morse called a conference of interested parties in Naples in October 1951. Twenty-seven countries participated, as did the UN and the five international organizations that were members of the technical working group on migration. Morse proposed a Migration Administration, to carry out "an operating migration programme . . . to effect a solution of current European migration problems" (quoted in Karatani 2005, 533). Morse estimated that 1.7 million persons would emigrate from Europe to other continents over a period of five years and would need international assistance. He also proposed a plan for a migration aid fund to help migrants pay for their passage from Europe with a loan or a grant. However, his entrepreneurship was met with strong opposition from both the United States and the United Kingdom, even though the ILO director was American.

As Karatani (2005, 536) describes it, just as the Naples Conference was called, the US House of Representatives was in the process of authorizing funds to help solve the "surplus population problem" in Europe. However, in light of the growing conflict between the United States and the Soviet Union, the House attached language to the financial provisions to move refugees and migrants: the funds could not be made available to any organization "whose members included communist, communist-dominated or communist-controlled country." The ILO had member states that were coming under communist control in Central Europe—Czechoslovakia, among others. Therefore, the United States could not support an operational role for the ILO. The United States was seconded in its opposition by Australia, which preferred bilateral negotiations, as well as by Canada and the United Kingdom. "Without US support, the ILO knew it had to abandon its plans" (Karatani 2005, 536). The US "sabotage" of the ILO's plans is confirmed by Rodgers et al. (2009, 79).

The problem of "surplus populations" in Europe, however, remained on the agenda. The United States convened a meeting in November 1951, only a month after the Naples Conference. The plans looked remarkably similar to those proposed by the ILO. Yet this time, the United States provided both political and financial support (ten million dollars); as a result, the states attending the conference created the Provisional Intergovernmental Committee for the Movement of Migrants from Europe (PICMME). PICMME's mandate was short—one year. It was to take over the resources released by the now defunct International Refugee Organization, which consisted of personnel expert in international transport, ships, and an annual budget of thirty-four million dollars. The mandate was to move both labor migrants and refugees from Europe to destinations outside of Europe. In contrast to the program proposed by the ILO, the intergovernmental composition and limited mandate of the PICMME would not threaten other countries' sovereign immigration policies. The director named to take over this interim organization was American. When its mandate was extended, it adopted the name Intergovernmental Committee for European Migration (ICEM). This is the organization that ultimately adopted the name of International Organization for Migration (IOM), now a central player on issues of international migration in the contemporary era. The trajectory of the IOM is described below.

US opposition to the ILO plan to gain operational capacity meant that the ILO remains an organization that primarily promotes worker-related standards. When Morse's efforts failed, the organization decided to use its energy toward providing technical assistance to developing countries, in addition to standards setting. Difficulties in convention ratification also led the organization to promote recommendations rather than conventions; recommendations set standards that are voluntary rather than binding on the states that ratify the conventions.

While the ILO remains a prominent player in setting international labor standards, and the standards it sets for all workers apply to migrants as workers, it has been unable to play a central role in migrant worker rights.[26] The organization did not develop an operational capacity to facilitate labor migration—that was handed over to PICMME/ICEM in 1952. And emigration states have chosen to move the forum for migrant rights to the United Nations.

Period 5: The United Nations International Convention on the Protection of the Rights of All Migrant Workers and Members of Their Families (ICRMW). The ICRMW expands the rights of both documented and undocumented workers beyond the workplace. Although the rights of documented workers exceed those of undocumented workers, the convention incorporates virtually all the rights included in the nine other core human rights treaties into a single document dealing with foreign residents (Cholewinski 1997; Nafziger and Bartel 1991; Niessen and Taran 1991).

The story of the shift in migrant protection from the ILO to the UN General Assembly is well known and comes directly out of unhappiness with Convention 143 (Böhning 1991).[27] Both sending and receiving countries were unhappy about some aspects of Convention 143, but the impetus for change came from the developing world. "A range of developing emigration countries was unhappy with the interdiction of clandestine migration and illegal employment as formulated in Part I of Convention No. 143" (Böhning 1991, 705). Receiving states, in contrast, preferred to retain the ILO as the primary venue on worker rights. Sweden, in particular, proposed to await further developments at the ILO, an amendment supported by many receiving states in the 1976 General Conference.

This was a period in the international economic system when the balance of power appeared to shift in favor of developing nations that supplied raw materials to wealthy nations—"commodity power." The era commenced with the 1973 quadrupling of oil prices and the rising prominence of the Organization of the Petroleum Exporting Countries.[28] In 1979, the international system experienced another doubling of the price of oil. This commodity power generated demands of the UN General Assembly for a New International Economic Order in 1975. This attitude is also reflected in the policies of Mexico and Morocco regarding migration. Both states had significant populations of undocumented migrants in the United States and France, respectively, and were unhappy about the ban on undocumented migration and illegal employment contained in Part 1 of Convention 143. They led the charge to change the venue for negotiations on migration from the ILO to the UN General Assembly. The General Assembly was viewed as a more favorable environment for several reasons. The UN convention allows for ratification with reservations, whereas ILO conventions do not, which promised a better ratification record than reflected in Convention 143.[29] According to Böhning (1991, 704), developing countries also wanted to avoid the ILO because "1. The ILO would not propose anything that contradicted No. 143, which promised to close off remittances from undocumented workers; 2. The UN General Assembly had an automatic developing country majority which the ILO, with its tripartite representation, did not; 3. The ILO gave prominence to independent trade unions, which many developing countries did not like." According to Lonnroth (1991, 732), these states also wanted to "to achieve a moral condemnation of some of the states of employment."

Central to our argument, we focus on the automatic sending country majority in the General Assembly, which meant that sending states would be able to endorse any negotiated convention without the support of receiving states and therefore would not have to compromise with developed nations on the text of the convention. In terms of our analysis, this is not a developing country coalition per se. Some states in the Global South have become receiving states, including the Gulf oil states starting in the 1970s and some East Asian newly industrializing countries beginning in the 1980s. Nonetheless, since the early 1950s, the vast majority of sending states are located in the Global South, and once they gained independence, they outnumbered receiving states. Böhning (n.d.) points to another reason to move negotiations from the ILO to the UN General Assembly that is consistent with our hypotheses: many (authoritarian) sending states sought to exclude independent trade unions from the negotiations, which would have been present in ILO forums. While trade unions are often a source of domestic support for migrant rights, unions would be categorically opposed to undocumented migration as a threat to wages and working conditions of both native and documented foreign workers. Developing country emphasis on the rights of undocumented migrants undermined the coalitional potential with domestic trade unions in receiving states.

Taking up the issue in the UN General Assembly was not a done deal. The emphasis was on spelling out the basic rights of migrant workers who are un- documented or in an irregular situation, and developing nations argued that these basic rights lie primarily in the fields of civil and political rights or eco- nomic, social, and cultural rights rather than strictly labor rights, as is the case of the ILO. Morocco and Mexico worked for several years before obtaining a majority in the General Assembly to support Resolution 34/172, which was adopted in December 1979 and established a working group to elaborate a new UN convention on the rights of migrant workers.

The General Assembly working group on migrant workers was formed in October 1980. The Mexican ambassador to the United Nations was initially elected to chair the working group, a position he retained throughout the decade-long negotiations. The initial working draft was submitted by Mexico and Morocco, reflecting their leadership role and the priority they gave the issue. They were supported by the G77, including states with large emigrant pop- ulations. However, receiving countries in the working group were not pleased with the initial draft, which they viewed as condoning illegal migration and employment. Given that they could not stop the working group from moving forward, a coalition of countries from the Northern Mediterranean and Scandi- navian governments with social democratic parties worked to provide an alter- native draft.[30] This coalition came to be known as the MESCA group, and theirs became the working draft. While attentive to the fundamental human rights of migrants, regardless of their status in the host state, these states had for a "key objective . . . to discourage employers from seeking and hiring workers who are undocumented or in an irregular situation" (Böhning 1991, 702). Although it set the parameters of the convention, the MESCA group asked the ILO for as- sistance in drafting the counterproposal to the Mexican-Moroccan draft. Thus, even in this new venue, receiving states were not powerless in shaping the text of the convention.

The actual contours of the convention reflected many different influences (Lonnroth 1991). The three prominent groups participating in the negotiations were the G77 group, the MESCA delegations, and other developed countries— including the United States and Germany. The drafting of the UN convention proceeded without the participation of employers and workers, who would have been included had the venue remained in the ILO. The General Assembly finally adopted ICRMW in 1990, after a full decade of negotiations. However, Böhning (1988, 135) points out that the extension of rights achieved in ICRMW is nominal.

As of 2012, no major recipient state has signed or ratified the convention, whereas forty-six countries of emigration have become party to the conven- tion and an additional seventeen states have signed the convention. Adherence to the convention has not produced much in terms of additional protection on the ground for migrant workers, documented or undocumented.[31] In light of the poor ratification and nominal oversight of the states party to it, it would be difficult to call the convention a success.

This overview of the history of multilateral cooperation on migrant rights is consistent with our hypotheses. The interests of sending states and receiving states are opposed. When the status quo is preferred by powerful states, it is likely to remain unchanged. Where powerful states prefer a change in the status quo, they have the influence and resources to modify the status quo. When less powerful states prefer a change in the status quo, their ability to negotiate a multilateral treaty relies on their institutional power to achieve a majority. However, their meager power is insufficient to bring receiving states on board, so that these agreements remain poorly ratified. Over the nearly hundred-year history of formal multilateral institutions, few migrant rights conventions have been negotiated, despite an institutional context that acknowledged the significance of migrant rights. And very few receiving states have signed onto the agreements once negotiated.[32] Most wealthy states that signed onto Convention 97 were sending states at the time of their ratification, even though their status has changed since then. To further evaluate our theoretical argument, we turn now to our quantitative evidence.

DETERMINANTS OF THE ICRMW RATIFICATION

To provide a more systematic look at "sending" and "receiving" states in terms of support for international cooperation on migrant rights, we have analyzed the determinants of state adherence to the UN convention.[33] Following our theory, in this period, receiving states prefer the status quo of national sovereignty; sending states are able to negotiate a treaty improving migrant rights because of their institutional power in the UN General Assembly. It follows that receiving states are unlikely to ratify the convention. However, as noted above, the migrant rights treaties are not well ratified by either sending or receiving states. So we must take into account the characteristics of both sending and receiving states in evaluating the determinants of UN convention ratification. We follow the qualitative analyses in Cholewinski, de Guchteneire, and Pécoud (2009) to evaluate alternative and complementary hypotheses regarding ICRMW ratification as well as the broader human rights literature on treaty ratification. Our model is a split population model and divides the sample into three groups that we believe reflect the prospects for treaty ratification: those states that are likely never to ratify the agreement, those that might ratify the agreement, and those that actually have ratified the agreement. Our unit of analysis is country-year.

In order to distinguish between sending and receiving states we employ net migration flows and migrant stocks. We can think of migration flows and migrant stocks as sovereignty costs associated with ratifying the international treaty protecting migrant rights. As noted below, sovereignty costs are associated with relinquishing control over an activity that has previously been carried out inside the state to an international forum. We believe that sovereignty costs associated with migration rise with the flow of migrants. Delegating decisions over the treatment of migrants to an international treaty is zero if the state has no migrants. As the number of migrants rises, the costs to the state rise. Annual net migration is defined as migrant inflows minus outflows. These data come from the World Development Indicators dataset and are measured in thousands of migrants. The data are imputed because they are measured only every five years at times. Annual migrant stocks are operationalized as the percentage of foreign born in a state's population. These data also come from the World Development Indicators dataset. Sending state interests are operationalized in terms of remittance inflow. Our theory is consistent with the idea that states dependent on remittance flows will be less likely to ratify the treaty; this is so because sending states are fearful that receiving states are less likely to recruit migrants from states that expect significantly better treatment of their migrants, hence cutting off the remittance flows. These data come from the World Bank.

A number of the authors in the Cholewinski, de Guchteneire, and Pécoud volume (2009) suggest that, of the sending states, only those capable of implementing the convention requirements would consider ratification. We have measured government capacity in three ways. The first measure is the International Country Risk Guide (ICRG). These data are an index of several different measurements, namely, government stability, socioeconomic conditions, investment profile, internal conflict, external conflict, corruption, military in politics, religious tensions, law and order, ethnic tensions, democratic accountability, and bureaucratic quality. High scores indicate less risk and thus greater government effectiveness. This variable has a theoretical range from 0 to 100, but in our sample ranges from 7 to 74. The benefit of this indicator is that we have yearly data across most of our sample. It also takes into account a wide variety of country characteristics.[34]

Our second measure is government effectiveness. These data are part of the Worldwide Governance Indicators dataset. This indicator measures the quality of public services and civil services and the degree to which these services are separated from political pressures. It also measures the creation and implementation of policies and the credibility of governments to commit to policies. These data come from a wide variety of sources including expert sources.[35] The data start in 1996 so are imputed for several years. Finally, we employ logged GDP per capita. These data come from the World Bank. It is argued that this measurement is highly correlated with other characteristics like bureaucratic accountability and government effectiveness. These data cover most of our sample (1990–2011).[36]

We also incorporate hypotheses generated by the human rights research agenda that encompasses both constructivist and rationalist explanations of treaty ratification. The constructivist literature hypothesizes the diffusion of norms in the international system. This hypothesis can be captured, albeit imperfectly, through quantitative analysis. To measure the spread of norms, two variables have been employed. The first variable is world commitment, which we measure in accordance with Simmons (2002). A state's signature is weighted as 1 and a state's ratification is weighted as 2. This is then averaged worldwide. This measurement has a theoretical range of 0 to 3. In our sample, the range is 0 to 0.63, with a mean of 0.25. We also include regional commitment, which is measured in a similar way, but takes into account the region in which a state is located, as defined by the World Bank. This measurement has a theoretical range of 0 to 3. In our sample, the range is 0 to 1.34, with a mean of 0.21.

The rationalist literature focuses on state preferences for human rights, usually operationalized as regime type. The literature indicates that democratic regimes are more likely to ratify human rights treaties than are autocratic regimes; transitional democracies are believed to "lock in" human rights through treaty ratification. To separate established democracies from transitional democracies and autocracies, two variables are used in the analysis in accordance with Epstein et al. (2006). Established democracies are those that score 8 or greater. Emerging democracies are states with polity scores between 0 and 8. Autocracies are those regimes with a polity score of 0 or less. For the purposes of model identification, autocracies are omitted from the model. These data are based on the Polity IV data set. Of the states, 38.6 percent are established democracies, 22.6 percent are emerging democracies, and 38.8 percent are autocracies. In addition, or alternatively, the actual level of human rights is used to evaluate the preferences of states. Therefore, we include the human rights in the country with the idea that current protection of human rights conditions should be consistent with treaty ratification.

Our results are reported in Tables 7.3 and 7.4. Our findings are consistent with the notion that receiving states are the least likely to sign migrant rights treaties. For both treaty signature and treaty ratification, the net migration variable is negatively signed and statistically significant in four of the six models. That is, states that have net outflows of migrants are more likely to sign the treaty. Remittance inflows are positively signed and statistically significant (two of three) for signature ratification but negatively signed and statistically significant (one of three) in the ratification model. The treaty signature results are inconsistent with our hypothesis about sending states' dependence on remittance flows. We discuss these inconsistencies below.

Table 7.3
Estimation Results: Migrant Rights Convention (Signature)

Variable	Model 1	Model 2	Model 3
Equation 1: Hazard			
Global commitment level	−6.209	2.920	1.852
	(3.76)	(4.91)	(3.53)
Regional commitment level	8.788**	7.011[†]	4.704[†]
	(2.34)	(2.25)	(1.82)
Established democracy	−0.586	4.631*	0.446
	(0.73)	(1.76)	(0.73)
Emerging democracy	−0.724	4.090*	−0.652
	(0.73)	(1.76)	(0.73)
Net migration	−0.003**	−0.004	−0.002*
	(0.00)	(0.00)	(0.00)
Foreign-born stocks	−0.023	0.275	0.123
	(0.06)	(0.17)	(0.21)
ICRG	−0.095**		
	(0.04)		
Government effectiveness		−5.74	
		(1.61)	
Log (GDP per capita)			−1.444**
			(0.48)
Remittance inflows	0.000*	−0.000	0.001**
	(0.00)	(0.00)	(0.00)
Human rights	0.248	0.109	0.035
	(0.19)	(0.33)	(0.21)
Intercept	−1.660	−13.923**	4.26
	(1.21)	(3.82)	(2.76)
Equation 2: Cure_p			
Intercept	0.809**	1.314**	1.168
	(0.32)	(0.33)	(0.33)

[†]$p < .1$; *$p < .05$; **$p < .01$.

Table 7.4

Estimation Results: Migrant Rights Convention (Ratification)

Variable	Model 4	Model 5	Model 6
Equation 1: Hazard			
Global commitment level	2.211	−4.272[†]	1.400
	(3.19)	(2.21)	(3.03)
Regional commitment level	4.351*	3.390[†]	2.840[†]
	(1.78)	(1.20)	(1.47)
Established democracy	−1.700[†]	−0.480	−0.404
	(0.93)	(0.82)	(0.78)
Emerging democracy	−0.309	0.182	−0.300
	(0.64)	(0.57)	(0.61)
Net migration	−0.001	0.000	−0.001[†]
	(0.00)	(0.00)	(0.00)
Foreign-born stocks	−0.111	−0.065	−0.100
	(0.09)	(0.06)	(0.80)
ICRG	−0.003		
	(0.03)		
Government effectiveness		0.102	
		(0.46)	
Log (GDP per capita)			−0.63[†]
			(0.35)
Remittance inflows	−0.000	−0.000	−0.626[†]
	(0.00)	(0.00)	(0.35)
Human rights	−0.108	−0.500	−0.950
	(0.14)	(0.14)	(0.13)
Intercept	−2.613	−3.158	1.071
	(1.01)	(0.89)	(2.29)
Equation 2: Cure_p			
Intercept	0.611*	13.590[**]	0.365
	(0.275)	(0.892)	(0.32)

[†]$p < .1$; *$p < .05$; **$p < .01$.

The hypotheses that suggest that state capacity is important for treaty signature appear to be wrong. The ICRG is statistically significant for treaty signature but in the wrong direction—the lower the government capacity, the more likely the state is to sign the treaty. The government effectiveness indicator is not statistically significant. And the GDP per capita variable in both treaty signature and ratification models is statistically significant but in the wrong direction if we use this as an indicator of bureaucratic capacity—poorer (and therefore less capable) governments are more likely to sign the treaty. These findings suggest that barriers to ratification are not associated with lack of state capacity.

The variables that attempt to capture the spread of norms in the international system are significant at the regional level (but not at the global level) for both treaty signature and treaty ratification, providing an indication of regional diffusion: countries whose neighbors sign (ratify) the convention are also more likely to sign the convention. It is not clear whether this is normative behavior or strategic behavior. Simmons (2009) argues that following the path of a state's neighbors in treaty ratification is a method of camouflage. However, an earlier article (Elkins, Guzman, and Simmons 2006) suggests an alternate strategic reason—competition from neighbors. This finding may explain why the sign on the remittance variable is opposite to that anticipated. Emigration states fear competition from other emigration states; this competition is mitigated when neighbors sign the treaty as well.

There is little evidence that democratic states or states that abide by human rights feel compelled to sign and ratify the migrant rights treaty. Of the twelve variables that evaluate the role of democracy, only three are statistically significant, and for treaty ratification, the signs are negative rather than positive. The human rights variable is never statistically significant. These findings suggest that the models proffered to explain human rights treaty ratification do not fit well with migrant rights, as we suggest in our exploration of alternative theories below. Although our results are not as clear as we would like, there is substantial evidence that receiving states are unlikely to sign migrant rights treaties as it infringes on national sovereignty, generating sovereignty costs. However, this does not mean that all states disregard migrant rights: earlier research indicates that states that respect human rights and those with strong labor movements better protect migrants that those with poor human rights records and weak labor movements (Money, Lockhart, and Western 2016). But they do so because migrants are human beings and workers rather than their migrant status.

OTHER INTERNATIONAL FORUMS ON MIGRATION

Thus far, we have focused on formal organizations and treaty commitments on migrant rights. However, the salience of migration has led to the creation of a number of additional international forums. We do not want to overlook the possibility that there are other venues for international cooperation on migration. In fact, many researchers and activists who promote migrant rights point to these alternative venues as the place where cooperation can now take place. The question for us is whether any of these forums provide evidence of cooperation on issues of migrant rights. We examine the history of each international venue in turn.

One of the earliest dialogues is the United Nations Global Commission on International Migration, which was encouraged by then–UN secretary-general Kofi Annan. The commission was convened in December 2003 with nineteen commissioners and tasked to "provide the framework for the formulation of a coherent, comprehensive and global response to the issue of international migration" ("Report" 2005). The commission was assisted by a secretariat and a group of thirty-two "core states." In October 2005, the commission presented its report to Annan. The report served to structure debate in the UN General Assembly in the fall of 2006 on the issue of international migration. It predicted increased global migration based on perceived economic benefits of migration to both receiving and sending countries, as well as the persisting income differentials and the distinctive demographic configurations between migrants' places of origin and destination. However, the report did not recommend the establishment of a new WTO-like international organization within the UN system with responsibility for international migration. National sovereignty was recognized as the central organizing principle of international migration in the foreseeable future. As noted in our introduction, that report states, "National sovereignty in deciding about immigration policy (probably the key determinant of contemporary international migration flows) remains an established principle in international law, subject only to treaty obligations to admit bona fide refugees" ("Report" 2005, 787).

The Global Commission on International Migration was followed by the convening of the High Level Dialogue on International Migration held within the auspices of the UN General Assembly in 2006. However, the absence of consensus on a way to move forward propelled the creation of the now annual Global Forum on Migration and Development (GFMD), extracted from the United Nations setting so that states could discuss issues of mutual concern without committing themselves to binding agreements. That is, receiving states refused to discuss migration issues unless they were guaranteed in advance that no treaties or binding conventions would be negotiated. The GFMD is hosted annually by a different state, rotating between a developed and a developing country. The characteristic feature of these forums is nonbinding dialogue. Moreover, although migrant rights are on the agenda, the central issues addressed in the forums have to do with how to harness migration to the developmental goals of poor states. A second High Level Dialogue was convened in 2013 and endorsed the continuation of the state-led GFMD processes.[37] So these high-profile forums have remained "talking shops" where diplomats, researchers, and activists can discuss migration-related issues. These have not been forums that have produced multilateral governance on migrant rights.[38]

The final multilateral organization that might serve as the locus for cooperative activity on migrant rights is the IOM.[39] As noted above, the IOM was born through US auspices to overtake the ILO's efforts to build an operational capacity to facilitate migration. Initially, it was called the Provisional Intergovernmental Committee for the Movement of Migrants from Europe (PICMME). In 1953, the name was changed to the Intergovernmental Committee for European Migration (ICEM). It retained that title until 1980, when the governing board proposed to acknowledge the global vocation of the organization and changed the name to Intergovernmental Committee for Migration. It was not until 1989–90 that the organization adopted the name that is now well known in the international migration community, the International Organization for Migration. At the same time, the organization changed its bylaws.

Reflecting the initial provisional nature of the organization and its limited remit regarding European "surplus populations," the membership in the organization was consequentially small. However, its budget, administrative staff, and state membership have expanded exponentially since the early 1990s. The structure of this organization is unusual in that less than 10 percent of its funding supports the core administration of the organization (Ducasse-Rogier 2001). That means that more than 90 percent of its funding comes directly from the member states for specific projects. Many projects are generated directly by member state requests. The remainder are based on staff proposals that states agree to fund. The staff therefore has an incentive to propose projects that meet the interests of the client states.

The IOM is an understudied international organization, but given the central role it plays in both voluntary and forced migration, it has been receiving attention—and that attention has usually been negative (Andrijasevic and Walters 2010; Ashutosh and Mountz 2011; Human Rights Watch 2003). In one instance, stakeholders complained that the IOM was tasked with returning internally displaced persons in Darfur but was not tasked with protection of asylum seekers, refugees, or the forcibly displaced (Morris 2005). The International Council for Voluntary Organizations asked, "Is IOM an agency that will do anything as long as there's money with which to do it?" (Morris 2005, 43; Thomas and Schenkenberg van Mierop 2004).

In essence, this is an agency for hire rather than a multilateral institution that binds member states. That said, the IOM staff are migration experts, with both academic and field training in virtually all aspects of migration, from control to the various dimensions of integration. Professional standards, as well as personal choice, suggest that the IOM staff would strongly support migrant rights in all aspects of their work.[40] Although their incentive structure privileges state interests, as states are the clients who ultimately pay the bills and their salaries, projects can be structured to help ensure migrant rights are protected, *if* the project also meets state interests. Ultimately, the protection of migrant rights may result from IOM interventions but only when it is a by-product of projects that seek to meet state interests.

Most recently, the IOM has become a related organization within the UN system (IOM 2016). However, its funding structure remains in place, so its incentives to respond to state interests remain intact. We anticipate that IOM interventions will protect migrant rights only when the staff can design programs to protect migrant rights that are consistent with their clients' interests.

REGIONAL COOPERATION ON MIGRANT RIGHTS

If multilateral cooperation at the level of the international system is not productive, perhaps regional cooperation is a method for improving migrant rights. However, if we look at the record here, it appears less than promising. Deacon and coauthors (2011) provide the only comparative evaluation of the role of regional organizations in developing migrant rights protections. They conclude that the density of regional economic transactions is not a prelude to greater cooperation on migrant rights, reporting "there is little evidence of a positive correlation between intra-regional trade intensity and progress in the area of regional labour and migrant workers' rights." Moreover, migration itself does not trigger regional cooperation on migrant rights. That is, "there is no clear evidence of a positive correlation between the share of intra-regional migration and regional coordination on policies on labour/migrant worker rights" (358).

When examining regional organizations, the authors report the greatest degree of protection within the EU, but only for citizens of member states. The EU is distinctive in its adoption of the "four freedoms" (see chapter 5). In implementing these, the EU has ensured equal treatment of member state citizens in the workplace and, in the Treaty of Maastricht (1993), created a European citizenship and a right of residence in other member states.[41] For "third country nationals," the picture is less rosy. According to a recent report by the OHCHR (2011, 13): "This failure to agree on a rights-based framework for labour migration in the EU is a demonstration of the approach that has dominated the development of EU migration legislation. Firstly, EU institutions have promoted rights-based legislation in the field of migration that Member States refused to adopt; secondly, Member States have favoured a security- and economy-based approach to migration that has systematically sidelined the rights-based approach." So even in the region where organizational ties are most densely knit, the picture on regional cooperation on migrant rights is mixed at best.

Elsewhere, even though regional organizations exist, they are not employed to coordinate action on migrant rights (IOM 2007). In the NAFTA, between Canada, the United States, and Mexico, the labor side agreement "only commits parties to enforce domestic legislation." In Latin America, the Andean Labor Advisory Council and Mercosur's Tripartite Social-Labor Commission have "delivered few practical achievements." The same is true for African regional associations such as the South African Development Community, the East African Trade Union Council, and the Economic Community of West African States (IOM 2007).

The picture in Asia is even dimmer. Asia represents both a source of migrants to other areas of the globe and at least five million intraregional migrants. Tess Bacalla (2012a, 2012b) provides an overview of the lack of progress on regional protection of migrant worker rights within ASEAN. Although ASEAN adopted a regional declaration to protect migrant workers in ASEAN states in 2007, the Cebu Declaration is nonbinding. And efforts to create a binding instrument have been blocked by Malaysia and Thailand, the primary destination countries in ASEAN, along with Singapore.

In conclusion, regional cooperation on migrant rights exists only among EU member states and for member state citizens only.[42] Regional cooperation and coordination on migrant rights appears little more fruitful than at the global multilateral level.

BILATERAL COOPERATION ON MIGRANT RIGHTS

As suggested by our theoretical framework, bilateral cooperation is the most likely form of cooperation on migration among states. The question then arises about how migrant-sending states might extract better guarantees for their citizens from the receiving states given the imbalance in power and wealth that favors receiving states in the contemporary period. Our theoretical frame suggests that this will happen only when powerful states find the status quo costly. The most likely scenario, then, is for the grant of workers' rights when receiving states experience a labor shortage. Empirically we find this pattern is infrequent.

Although BLAs were not unheard of before World War II, they became more common in Europe between 1950 and 1970, when the demand for labor was strong (see chapter 4). The European agreements usually included workplace rights, as spelled out in the ILO "Model Agreement on Temporary and Permanent Migration for Employment," which was annexed to ILO Recommendation 86, adopted in conjunction with ILO Convention 97 in 1949. Article 17 spells out the recommended workplace protections, focusing on equality of treatment with nationals. Most of these agreements, though, are no longer in effect. As noted in chapter 4, subsequent BLAs, concluded by many labor-importing countries in the Middle East and Asia, have often failed to include basic worker protections. Even where labor protections are provided, these agreements are limited to the workplace and therefore do not include a broader array of human rights protections. Although the ILO has expressed optimism that bilateral agreements are being signed, a recent review of BLAs in practice indicates that "so far bilateral labor agreements have concerned only a very small share of total bilateral labor migration flows between the countries involved, their implementation has caused quite a lot of frustration in countries of origin, and they have problems of sustainability and continuity over time" (Martin 2011). This is not a ringing endorsement.

A closer look at one country confirms the minimal amounts of migrant protections offered by bilateral agreements. The Philippines has an explicit labor emigration policy as a component of its development program since 1974 (Go 2004). In 2012, it had nearly 10.5 million citizens living overseas in more than 180 countries, or approximately 11 percent of its population (Philippines, Commission on Filipinos Overseas 2012). The treatment of Filipino overseas workers has been a domestic policy concern, and the Philippines has an active policy of attempting to negotiate bilateral agreements with countries in which its citizens reside (Go 2004). As a result, it is the developing country with the greatest number of bilateral agreements on labor issues and the protections it has forged for its workers through bilateral agreements represent the most extensive rights protections of any country in the Global South.

Table 7.5 provides an overview of all the agreements the Philippines has signed. There are agreements with only twenty-one countries (12 percent of all countries of destination), and this number overstates the importance of several of the agreements, such as one with the United States dating from 1968, dealing with US military hiring of Filipinos in Southeast Asia and the Pacific as a result of the US involvement in the Vietnam War. Two are signed with labor exporting countries, Laos and Indonesia. And several cover only one dimension of the migration stream, health care professionals (United Kingdom, Norway, Bahrain, and Japan). The agreement with Japan is signed by a private service provider rather than a government agency. Almost all of the agreements are MOUs rather than MOAs. This means that they are not legally binding documents. Finally, as column 5 in the table illustrates, the rights that are protected are minor. Often there is an acknowledgment of a goal to protect migrant workers residing in the host country but no means of enforcing those protections. Of the twenty-one countries, only three offer equality with country nationals in the labor market (Iraq, Bahrain, and Jordan).[43] Table 7.6 does show that the Philippines has been able to extend the reach of its bilateral agreements from covering a maximum

Table 7.5

Philippines Bilateral Memoranda of Understanding

Country	Date	Type of agreement	Contents	Worker rights	Restrictive components	Length of agreement
Bahrain	2007	MOA	Ethical recruitment of medical personnel; recruitment practices	Equality of pay and other employment conditions		Indefinite
Canada: Alberta	2008	MOU	Recruitment practices	Affirmation of "principles set forth in international labour conventions"		Two years
Canada: British Columbia	2008	MOU	Recruitment practices	Philippines government monitor in Toronto		Two years
Canada: Manitoba	2008 2010	MOU	Recruitment practices	Affirmation of "principles set forth in international labour conventions"		Indefinite
Canada: Saskatchewan	2006	MOU	Recruitment practices	Philippine government monitors in Toronto		Two years with automatic renewal
Commonwealth of the Northern Mariana Islands	1994	MOU	Recruitment practices	Observance of applicable labor and employment laws	Requires Filipino workers to go through POEA	Indefinite
Commonwealth of the Northern Mariana Islands	2000	MOU	Recruitment practices			One year with automatic renewal
Indonesia		MOU	Recruitment practices	Goal of worker protection		Five years with automatic renewal
Iraq	1982	MOA	Recruitment procedures	Equality of treatment		Three years with automatic renewal

Country	Year	Agreement type	Topic	Worker protection	Details	Duration
Japan; agreement with private service provider	2009	MOU	Health care recruitment	Contract required	Requires Filipino workers to go through POEA; Philippine agreement to help prevent illegal stay	Three years with automatic renewal
Jordan	1981	MOU		Goal of worker protection		
Jordan	1988	Agreement on manpower	Recruitment procedures	Contract required; equality of treatment		Three years with automatic renewal
Jordan	2010		Recruitment procedures	Goal of worker protection; contract required		Three years with automatic renewal
Jordan	2012	Principles of recruitment	Not available			
Korea	2004	MOU	Recruitment procedures	Contract required	Maximum stay of three years; Philippine agreement to help prevent illegal stay	Two years
Korea	2005	MOA	Recruitment procedures	Contract required; goal of worker protection	Workers charged fees; maximum stay; recruitment dependent on reduction of undocumented workers	Two years
Korea	2006	MOU	Same as 2005			
Korea	2009	MOU	Labor and manpower development			Five years
Korea	2009	MOU	Recruitment procedures— supersedes all other agreements	Goal of worker protection	Cooperation to prevent runaways and undocumented migrants	Two years

(continued)

Table 7.5
(*continued*)

Country	Date	Type of agreement	Contents	Worker rights	Restrictive components	Length of agreement
Kuwait	1997	MOU	Labor and manpower development	Contract required; conforms to national laws		Four years with automatic renewal
Kuwait	1997	MOU	Bilateral consultations		Annual; not public	Four years with automatic renewal
Lao People's Democratic Republic	2005	MOU	Technical cooperation	Capacity building		Indefinite
Libya	1979	Agenda for cooperation	Manpower development	Equality with third-country nationals		
Libya	2006	MOU	Recruitment of medical professionals and construction			Five years with automatic renewal
New Zealand	2008	MOA	Labor cooperation	Definitions of decent work		
Norway	2001	MOA	Recruitment of health professionals	Standard employment contract		12/31/2003; can be renewed
Papua New Guinea	1979	MOU	Recruitment of noncitizen contract employees in state service	Goal of worker protection		Indefinite
Qatar	2008	MOA	Recruitment procedures			Three years with automatic renewal
Qatar	2008	Additional protocol	Model contract	Contract required		

Country	Year	Type	Subject	Notes	Duration
Spain	2006	MOU	Health care hiring; pilot program	Equality of treatment	Indefinite
Switzerland	2002	MOA	Exchange of professional trainees	Temporary permits; maximum of eighteen months; annual quota of fifty	Indefinite
Taiwan	1999	MOU	Special hiring facility		One year
Taiwan	2001	MOU	Special hiring facility	Goal of worker protection	Two years
Taiwan	2003	MOU	Renewal	Adoption of prescribed employment contract	
United Arab Emirates	2007	MOU	Recruitment procedures	Goal of worker protection; labor contract required	Five years; may be renewed
United Kingdom	2002	MOU	Recruitment of health professionals	Sample employment contract	Three years with automatic renewal
United Kingdom	2003	MOU	Recruitment of health professionals		Indefinite
United States	1968		Recruitment by US military in the Pacific and South East Asia	Provides terms of employment (outside of United States)	Indefinite

Source: Philippines Overseas Employment Administration (n.d.).

Table 7.6
Philippines MOUs and Coverage of Filipino Overseas Workers

Country	2000 migrant stock	Percentage of total overseas workers	2012 migrant stock	Percentage of total overseas workers
Bahrain	25,061	0.3	66,491	0.6
Canada	310,494	4.2	852,401	8.1
Commonwealth of the Northern Mariana Islands	20,579	0.2	9,004	0.08
Indonesia	n/a	n/a	12,603	0.1
Iraq	n/a	n/a	2,275	0.02
Japan	209,626	2.8	243,136	2.3
Jordan	n/a	n/a	31,224	0.3
Korea	27,033	0.3	68,911	0.6
Kuwait	50,890	0.6	213,638	2.6
Lao People's Democratic Republic	n/a		1,070	0.01
Libya	n/a	n/a	2,724	0.02
New Zealand	16,040	0.2	37,116	0.3
Norway	n/a		23,376	0.2
Papua New Guinea	6,063	0.08%	21,888	0.2
Qatar	33,013	0.4	200,016	1.9
Spain	41,092	0.5	33,274	0.3
Switzerland	16,406	0.2	20,072	0.2
Taiwan	121,079	1.6	84,953	0.8
United Arab Emirates	124,134	1.6	931,562	8.8
United Kingdom	53,663	0.7	218,777	2.0
US overseas military employees	n/a	n/a	n/a	n/a
Total covered	1,055,173	14.2	3,074,511	29.3
Total Filipino overseas workers	7,383,122		10,489,628	

Source: Philippines Overseas Employment Administration (n.d.).

of 14 percent of its overseas worker population to 29 percent from 2000 to 2012. But again, these agreements are not legally binding in international law, and many provide no specific protections. Moreover, some actually require the Philippines to police its citizens to reduce the number of undocumented migrants, and tie future hiring to the management of undocumented migrants.

Just as sending countries were unable to extract migrant rights concessions from receiving countries in multilateral forums, the case of the Philippines demonstrates that sending countries have been only slightly more successful in bilateral forums in extracting migrant rights protections. We deal more fully with BLAs in chapter 3 on labor recruitment where the quid pro quo of access to workers has played a small role in generating leverage to extract migrant rights protections.

ALTERNATIVE EXPLANATIONS

In this section, we juxtapose our explanation with the extant literature on migrant rights. This literature is mainly legal and historical. The legal dimension analyzes the migrant rights conventions and the overlap and substantive differences between migrant rights and other human rights conventions (see, among others, Cholewinski 1997; Cholewinski, de Guchteneire, and Pécoud 2009; Nafziger and Bartel 1991; Chetail 2014). The historical dimension presents the evolution of migrant rights through the negotiation of international conventions beginning with the creation of the ILO in 1919 through the 1990 approval of the ICRMW (see, among others, ILO n.d.-c, 1951; Böhning 1988, 1991, n.d.; Hasenau 1988, 1991; Hune 1985; Lonnroth 1991; and Varlez 1929a, 1929b). There is little empirical quantitative work evaluating the actual state of migrant rights cross-nationally (but for specific countries and regions, see Edelenbos 2009; Human Rights Watch 2010; Mattila 2000; Piper 2004; Ruhs 2012; and Daway 2010). This research illuminates the trajectory of migrant rights but, unfortunately, does little to elucidate the determinants of migrant rights.[44]

However, if we examine the human rights literature more broadly, we find a well-developed theoretical landscape from which we can draw. Broadly speaking, there are two schools of research: the constructivist school that privileges process tracing and case studies (for prominent examples, see Risse, Ropp, and Sikkink 1999, 2013), and the rational choice approach that privileges large-N quantitative analysis (for prominent examples, see Hathaway 2002; Hafner-Burton and Tsutsui 2005; Hafner-Burton and Ron 2009; Simmons 2009). In the past decade, these two schools have become more interested in their complementarity rather than their competition, but each school nonetheless privileges specific theoretical determinants of human rights.

The constructivist school speaks to the role of norms and ideas that are spread primarily through socialization. One of the most well-developed models is the "spiral model" of human rights treaty adoption and compliance (Risse, Ropp, and Sikkink 1999). The initial model was developed to explain the "power of human rights" in authoritarian regimes through the pathway of repression, denial, tactical concessions, prescriptive status, and rule consistent behavior. Transnational networks are crucial actors, setting off a process of elite concessions and the growth of domestic opposition that ultimately leads to the widespread adoption of human rights. Initially the causal mechanism was theorized to work through socialization: instrumental adaptation, argumentation, and habitualization, with an emphasis on elite behavior, although this research also includes attention to the "normative empowerment of domestic advocacy groups." More recent revisions have acknowledged both rational and normative processes that include coercion, changing incentives, persuasion and discourses, and capacity building (see Risse, Ropp, and Sikkink 2013), although this school continues to emphasize the significance of the "logic of appropriateness" while not denying the "logic of consequences."

The rationalist school is most fully developed in Beth Simmons's 2009 work, *Mobilizing for Human Rights*. Her complex theory elaborates different processes for *commitment* to and *compliance* with human rights treaties. For commitment, or treaty ratification, she posits that states pursue their interests in the international system and commit to human rights treaties because these are close to the state's ideal point: "rationally expressive" ratification. She also explains "false negatives," states that adopt human rights protections but that cannot commit to multilateral treaties because of domestic institutions that constrain decision makers in various ways; and "false positives," states that regularly abuse human rights but sign on to the treaty because they believe the initial benefits outweigh the potential costs. Compliance, on the other hand, focuses on domestic politics and the role of treaty commitment in shifting domestic politics through three channels: agenda setting, litigation, and domestic political mobilization.

The rationalist school has refined its theoretical reach to account for variations among regime types: established democracies commit to human rights treaties because of rationally expressive preferences, newly democratized states to create credible commitments, and autocratic states to camouflage their behavior. When these types of states differ in their actual behavior, researchers point to the role of domestic institutions and the actual state of human rights protections. Emulation of neighbors is also cited as a determinant of ratification.[45]

Both constructivist and rationalist theories have significant empirical support and are often complementary. However, the migrant rights treaties are rarely, if ever, incorporated into the empirical analysis, even though the ICRMW is considered one of the ten core human rights conventions. This is an important oversight because the ILO conventions and the ICRMW have had little of the success seen in the other areas, especially in terms of ratification, which is a highly visible sign of commitment. We have evaluated the hypotheses generated by this literature in our quantitative analysis of the ICRMW treaty and have found them mostly lacking in explanatory power. Those states that have privileged human rights—established democratic states—are exactly those that have failed to commit themselves to these migrant rights treaties. The most robust empirical finding from this literature as applied to the ICRMW is the role of regional ratification, which shapes the likelihood of state ratification. So we do not discard this literature entirely, only point out that the logic of international cooperation on migrant rights is dominated by different processes than international cooperation on human rights. Moreover, as noted above, there is little systematic evidence about the actual status of migrant worker rights around the globe—even though there are numerous tales of migrant worker abuse, as noted in the introduction.

We conclude that the extant research either fails to address clearly the determinants of migrant rights conventions and the actual treatment of migrants in the host states or generates theoretical propositions that fail to explain either the timing of the treaties or the ratification rates. Our approach is most closely associated with an alternative vocabulary that has been employed to describe receiving states' lack of treaty ratification. Goodliffe and Hawkins (2006), as well as Wong (2015), adopt the term "sovereignty costs" to indicate the conditions under which states will ratify international treaties. Sovereignty costs are a way of conceptualizing the costs that are generated by states' adherence to an international agreement. In the words of Simmons and Danner (2010, 235), sovereignty costs are "the costs that a state incurs by delegating a function ordinarily performed domestically to an international institution over which it has little, if any, control."[46] For migrant rights, Wong (2015) operationalizes sovereignty costs as the number of immigrants. Hence receiving states confront higher sovereignty costs than do sending states and are therefore more reluctant to ratify migrant rights treaties. We believe our framework is consistent with this framework but that by incorporating the status quo, state preferences, and various forms of power, our theory is better at explaining *when* migrant rights treaties will be negotiated as well as *which* states will ratify these treaties. The sovereignty costs literature explains only which states will ratify treaties when they are negotiated. It does not explain the conditions under which treaties will actually be negotiated. So our theory provides greater leverage in explaining international cooperation on migrant rights. To reiterate, in the contemporary era, we hypothesize that, because powerful receiving states prefer the status quo ante, migrant rights treaties will be negotiated only when sending states find a majority in an international institution to force the drafting of an international treaty. Moreover, if a migrant rights treaty is negotiated in the contemporary era, receiving states are unlikely to ratify the treaty.[47]

There is a considerable wealth of case studies that focus on specific migrant groups in specific countries and their efforts to mobilize for migrant rights (Money and Taylor 2016). We believe that these form the raw data for more systematic theorizing about the domestic politics of migrant rights—by including the variety of political actors that mobilize for and against migrant rights and the institutional structure of politics that shapes the political power of these groups. We believe the research we present elsewhere on the domestic determinants of migrant rights, in which we privilege the level of human rights and the power of workers' organizations, is a step forward in systematizing our knowledge of the determinants of migrant rights at the level of the nation-state (Money, Lockhart, and Western 2016). We stand ready to develop a more sophisticated understanding of the political processes that shape migrant rights at the local, state, and national levels.

CONCLUSIONS

Migrant rights is an important issue in the international system. We have explored the explanatory power of both constructivist and rational accounts of human rights treaty *ratification* and *compliance* as they apply to migrant rights treaty negotiations, ratification, and compliance. We have discounted both frameworks in the migrant rights arena and presented an account of state preferences. The analysis is divided into two periods, 1900 to 1950 and 1950 to present. This periodization is required because patterns of migration have shifted. In the early period, sending states were the major European powers and receiving states were the less powerful ones in the New World. In the latter period, patterns are substantially reversed; the wealthier and more stable states, including those in Europe, are now receiving states while sending states are poorer and less wealthy. Our findings reflect the variation in the power of sending states in their ability to overturn the status quo, which provides few protections for migrant workers. In the early period, powerful sending states were able to create an international institution whose remit included migrant rights. In the latter period, weaker sending states have employed existing institutional structures to negotiate migrant rights treaties but have been unable to persuade powerful receiving states to ratify these treaties. The actual state of migrant rights protections, however, is not closely linked with international cooperation on migration. As we report elsewhere, domestic political forces appear to play a much more important role (Money, Lockhart, and Western 2016). Although no state perfectly protects migrant rights, our argument and evidence suggest that efforts to protect migrants must be aimed at the national and local levels, and that energies expended at the international level are wasted, if not counterproductive.

Our analysis of migrant rights also contributes to the literature on human rights. In this case, we find that states that have traditionally supported human rights in the international system and have led the way in generating treaties and international norms protecting human rights have shunned international commitments. This exception should lead to theoretical revisions to the human rights literature on both treaty ratification and treaty compliance dimensions. First, we recommend that human rights scholars pay greater attention to the difference between political mobilization for citizen rights and political mobilization for noncitizen rights both internationally and, more importantly, domestically. Second, human rights scholars may want to differentiate between rights granted based on a status that cannot be changed (women, children, the disabled, for example) and rights granted based on choice, as is the case with migrants. This, of course, raises the issue of the distinction between forced and voluntary migration, and we acknowledge that a bright line between these two categories is likely to be elusive. Nonetheless, it is distinction worth considering for both theoretical and normative purposes.

Finally, we point to an important empirical reality. The human rights literature suggests that states that support human rights and have high levels of compliance are, and should be, important actors in the international system in the effort to socialize states that do not protect human rights. The absence of these actors pushing for global compliance on migrant rights is another reason that we are skeptical of international cooperation on migrant rights and privilege the domestic political arena for political action.

CHAPTER 8

Theoretical and Policy Lessons

IN FEBRUARY 2014, after twelve migrants from sub-Saharan Africa died trying to swim to Spain from Morocco, Spain's deputy prime minister called for greater international cooperation on migration (Agencia EFE 2014). Five months later, US president Barack Obama made a similar plea for cooperation with Central American sending and transit countries after reports of unaccompanied children traveling from Central America to the United States gained widespread media coverage (Deutsche Welle 2014). Yet, despite much discussion about international cooperation on migration over many, many years, migration policy remains remarkably underinstitutionalized at the international level. In comparison with other economic flows, such as goods, services, and capital, the movement of labor remains largely the prerogative of individual states. The central questions of our research were thus theoretical: Why does international cooperation on migration issues remain so limited? Under what conditions will it arise?

At the same time, there is little consensus about what international cooperation on migration actually involves and what the existing scope of cooperation includes. Our second set of questions was thus empirical. World leaders may be publicly calling for more "cooperation," but what does this mean? What does cooperation on migration look like? Where is it happening already? And combining our empirical assessment and our theoretical expectations, where might we see it in the future? The first challenge to answering these questions lies in the definitions of both "migration" and "cooperation." Crossing international borders can include involuntary and forced migration, which is associated with the refugee and asylum regime, as well as short-term travel for business or pleasure. We limited our study to a third type of migration: voluntary, permanent migration. This involves migrants who voluntarily seek long-term settlement in another country, often for economic motivations. However, as the examples throughout this book demonstrate, the reality of migration is much messier than the legal distinctions allow. The current "migration crisis" in Europe involves a mix of all types of migrants, with a mixture of motivations. Those traveling to Europe include those seeking protection from civil wars in their home countries who were already admitted as refugees in a neighboring country but found that refuge to be unacceptable and have the resources to move onward. They have been joined by economic migrants, complicating the response of host countries. In some cases, the people moving across borders have both legally qualified rights to asylum as well as economic motivations; even when they do not, there is no doubt that war and conflict have exacerbated the economic distress of potential migrants in many sending states. The contemporary refugee regime sorts migrants into "forced" and "voluntary" categories regardless of the mix of motivations, so the scope of "voluntary" migration accounts for the overwhelming majority of individuals living outside their country of origin, whether these are IT specialists, care workers, agricultural laborers, the unemployed, children, or other family members. Nonetheless, we recognize that the voluntary migration regime is intrinsically linked to the refugee and travel regimes. We think that our theoretical and empirical insights may have some applicability to the refugee regime, less so for the travel regime, and we briefly explore those possibilities later in this chapter. Fully developed applications, however, deserve their own books.

While we defined "migration" in a more restrictive manner, our definition of "cooperation" was purposely more expansive. In game theory, cooperation most commonly is viewed as the solution to problems of collective action and public goods provision, where actors share an interest in providing a public good (or preventing a public bad), but no actor wants to incur the costs of providing the good, knowing that other actors might benefit without paying the cost. To overcome this problem, actors engage in cooperative behavior to prevent one side from "cheating" by not contributing while still consuming the good. Cooperation on collective action problems often results in similar types of solutions: formal, institutionalized agreements with strong enforcement mechanisms to prevent cheating by any party. This makes identifying this type of cooperation out in the world fairly straightforward. As we argued, however, voluntary migration presents few problems of collective action. Thus, we loosened our definition of cooperation to include any instances where states negotiate in international forums to address issues related to migration.

In expanding our definition of cooperation beyond the provision of public goods, we were confronted with a large number of issues and a dizzying array of cooperative responses related to migration at the international, regional, and bilateral levels. These responses involve numerous organizations, from the IOM to the ILO, the EU, and the UN Office on Drugs and Crime. The results of these cooperative activities range from international conventions to bilateral treaties and periodic talking shops that do not seem to accomplish much in material terms. Our second empirical challenge, then, was to provide an accounting of all of this activity while making sense of it through a single theoretical framework.

The argument of our book has rested on five fundamental claims. First, post–World War II migration has been primarily unidirectional, from poorer, less stable countries to wealthier, more stable ones. But each country's migration profile is unique, so externalities (both positive and negative) tend to be bilateral. Thus, when international cooperation does emerge, it also tends to be bilateral. Where economies are similar and flows are reciprocal, regional agreements may emerge, but this is a less common condition. Second, the distribution of power within the international system and the status quo ante can explain the paucity of cooperation on migration. Within the contemporary international system, migrant-receiving states are privileged for two reasons: (1) states have sovereignty over admission, but not exit; and (2) sending states tend to be poorer and less powerful. As long as receiving states are satisfied with the status quo of unilateral action, cooperation is unlikely to emerge. The cost of the status quo, however, is subject to exogenous shocks, which leads to our third claim: when these shocks (migration crises, domestic pressures, and so on) raise the costs of the status quo for powerful receiving states, they may seek cooperative solutions. This does not mean that sending states are completely passive. Our fourth claim is that sending states also may initiate cooperation, or take the lead in shaping it, within institutional contexts that privilege numerical majorities. Because sending states outnumber receiving states, sending states may use majoritarian institutions to agitate for changes to the status quo that would serve their interests. Such negotiations are unlikely to get far without the support of receiving states, however, and any resulting agreements will likely be poorly ratified and unenforced.

Our fifth claim situates migration cooperation within the broader phenomenon of international cooperation. While we commonly think of international cooperation as leading to more openness (for example, through the dismantlement of trade barriers), this is frequently not the case when it comes to migration cooperation. Some of the most extensive and formalized arrangements do not facilitate but rather restrict migration or the movement of people. Readmission agreements, for example, facilitate the return of unwanted migrants, and the Palermo Protocols combat trafficking and smuggling; both instances of cooperation seek to reduce flows, not expand them. This sets migration cooperation apart from other types of international cooperation on economic flows, such as trade or finance.

These five claims are undergirded by our broader theoretical approach, which seeks to explain the diversity of cooperative activities in migration through a bargaining framework. We take the position that states are the central actors in the international system, and their interests are fundamental in explaining the form and substance of cooperative outcomes. Their preferences may be shaped by complex domestic forces and filtered through unique institutional structures, although we do not fully explore the roots of these differences. Nevertheless, we argue that these state interests drive international outcomes, and in migration, state preferences depend largely on "market conditions," or the state's position as primarily a migrant-sending or migrant-receiving state. As we noted in our second premise, these market conditions also correlate with state power; migrant-receiving states tend to be more powerful, while sending states are less powerful, at least in the contemporary era.

Our bargaining framework began with the status quo ante. When all states are satisfied with the status quo ante, there is no incentive for cooperation, and all will continue to pursue unilateral action. When this equilibrium is disturbed, or when at least one state is dissatisfied with the status quo, cooperation may emerge. We suggested that there are two mechanisms that may trigger negotiations. First, exogenous events may raise the cost of the status quo for receiving states, prompting them to initiate bargaining with sending states as a way to reduce these new costs. Second, sending states that are dissatisfied with the status quo may find an international forum where they can get their concerns on the agenda and initiate negotiations. Because most states in the international system are sending states, their interests are privileged within institutions based on state membership and majoritarian rules. This institutional power can even lead to international treaties, although we argue that these will be poorly ratified and enforced if powerful receiving states do not support them. States do not have to share interests for cooperation to succeed; the bargaining framework explicitly allows for quid pro quo agreements facilitated by side payments. Powerful receiving states are likely to have more resources to facilitate these types of agreements, so we do expect that cooperation is more likely when powerful states desire a change in the status quo. Sending states have an additional advantage beyond their numerical majority, however; these states can also leverage their cooperation to extract concessions from receiving states if they have better outside options than receiving states. If sending states continue to prefer the status quo, receiving states must induce them to cooperate.

This basic bargaining framework generated five main hypotheses:

H_{1a} Where migration flows are unidirectional and unique and regime support costs exceed negotiation transaction costs, international agreements on migration will be bilateral. (Claim 1)

H_{1b} Where migration flows are reciprocal, freedom of movement agreements may be negotiated. (Exception to Claim 1)

H_2 When powerful states prefer the status quo ante, international cooperation is less likely to occur. (Claim 2)

H_{3a} When less powerful states act as a coalition and find a forum that provides institutional power, bargaining is more likely to occur. (Claim 4)

H$_{3b}$ When an agreement is negotiated without the support of powerful states, those states are unlikely to ratify any negotiated treaty. (Claim 4)

H$_4$ When the costs of the status quo ante rise, receiving states are more likely to initiate international negotiations. (Claim 3)

H$_5$ When the sending state has a better outside option than the receiving state, the sending state will be able to extract concessions from the receiving state. (Claim 3)

We evaluated these hypotheses across what we consider to be the four main issue areas within the realm of voluntary migration: labor recruitment and freedom of movement, migration control, criminality, and migrant rights. Across all four issues, we found a distinct mix of cooperative efforts, which have achieved varying degrees of success, at the bilateral, regional, and multilateral levels. In almost every case, these efforts coexist alongside unilateral action.

In some issue areas, bilateralism seems to dominate (for example, in the cases of labor recruitment and migration control), while in others, we saw multilateral treaties (as in the case of trafficking and smuggling). In every case, our bargaining framework has been useful in explaining this diversity of outcomes. While the bargaining is simplest with just two parties (State A and State B), the logic of the model applies to multiple actor negotiations as well. In some cases, a negotiated win set includes only two states, resulting in a bilateral agreement. In other cases, a negotiated win set may include many states, resulting in a multilateral agreement. In the sections that follow, we review these findings across our four issue areas.

CONTROLLING IMMIGRATION: MIGRANT CRISES AS A KEY DRIVER OF COOPERATION

In chapter 3, we examined the challenge of restricting migration flows, in particular, interior immigration control, as border controls are a component part of the travel regime. We argued that sending, receiving, and transit states generally have clearly disparate preferences. Transit and sending states generally do not want to accept their citizens who have found employment in receiving states even though they may be there without proper documentation. Receiving states, on the other hand, prefer to return unwanted and undocumented migrants. There are no public goods or coordination problems to solve, so states must rely on quid pro quo bargaining if they are to reach any agreement. We found that, as expected, the necessary conditions under which cooperation on restricting migrant flows will emerge are indeed rare.

We find, in accordance with Hypothesis 1a, that the most extensive, formalized cooperation has taken the form of bilateral readmission agreements, and most of these have been concluded with European states. In support of Hypothesis 4, cooperation on migration control is largely driven by the demands of powerful receiving states, reacting to rising costs in retaining the status quo. As the costs of unwanted migration grow and the ability of receiving states to control immigration unilaterally declines, receiving states are more likely to seek cooperation with sending and transit states. Over the past sixty years, European states have increasingly sacrificed sovereignty over migration control for the sake of greater economic and political unity, most significantly with the Schengen Agreement, which created a common external border and freedom of movement within the Schengen Area. These changes to the status quo made European states more likely than other receiving states to pursue cooperation on control with sending states, as they are less able to control immigration unilaterally. Even within Europe, however, we found variation in the number of readmission agreements concluded by receiving states. This variation can be explained by variation in the costs generated by the status quo, unique to each state. We found that increases in immigration from a particular sending state, economic downturns, and an increase in electoral support for right-wing parties are all associated with an increase in the number of readmission agreements concluded by receiving states. Each of these factors indicates an increase in the costs of unwanted immigration, which then makes the side payments needed to induce cooperation from sending and transit states worthwhile for receiving states.

As expected, we found that regional cooperation on migration control is less common. While there are some EU-wide agreements, these have been much harder to conclude and are fewer in number, even though the EU gained the competency to negotiate such agreements in 1999. The preference for bilateralism is driven by the fact that different European states receive immigrants from different sending states. The EU has less to offer in terms of side payments, since one of the main inducements for signing is the promise of visa-free travel, which remains the prerogative of individual member states. This makes it more difficult for the EU to conclude agreements. The major hurdle, however, is the fact that European states have used bilateral readmission agreements as a way to reassert sovereignty over migration enforcement, which they lost by agreeing to free movement in the Schengen Agreement. Relinquishing the tool to the EU undermines its usefulness for individual states.

The current migration crisis in Europe is a specific illustration of what happens when there are rising costs associated with the status quo. Consistent with our fifth hypothesis, sending states may be able to extract more concessions from receiving states when changes to the status quo ante provide sending states with better outside options than receiving states. We found that sending and transit states affected by the crisis are now demanding more compensation from receiving states, even if they have preexisting readmission agreements with individual European states. Turkey, for example, negotiated better compensation from the EU in exchange for a readmission agreement, even as it failed to fulfill its obligations under its preexisting agreement with Greece. This is also an example of our claim that cooperation on migration often leads to reduced, rather than enhanced, migratory flows.

Outside of readmission agreements, we identified RCPs as the most common cooperative forum for addressing issues of migration control. There are several of these informal processes involving different groups of states around the world. The institutional structure of RCPs means that the costs of participation are quite low, discussions within the processes are generally confidential or at least low-profile, the agenda is completely open, and decisions or recommendations are not binding on participants. Since each state has an equal position within the institutional structure, we find that sending states are able to get their interests on the agenda. For example, the Forum for Dialogue in the Western Mediterranean's Malta Declaration section titled "Migration and Development" explicitly links migration control to resolving the root causes of irregular migration, specifically, the lack of economic development in sending states. This reflected the interests of sending states, but the declaration made no concrete commitments nor demanded specific action from receiving states. This supported our third set of hypotheses (3a and 3b), which stated that bargaining is more likely to occur when less powerful states act as a coalition and find a forum that provides institutional power (in this case, the RCP), with the caveat that an agreement is unlikely to be ratified or enforced without the support of powerful states. In the case of the Malta Declaration, there were no commitments that even had to be ratified, just a general acknowledgment of the link between development and unwanted immigration.

Last, cooperation on migration control illustrated our fifth premise: some of the most extensive and formalized cooperative arrangements do not facilitate migration but instead restrict it. Readmission agreements are formal international treaties, and their number continues to grow. While the side payments that receiving states might offer sending states could facilitate migration (through, for example, visa-free travel and expanded legal immigration), the restrictions on migration far outweigh the corresponding expansions.

LABOR RECRUITMENT: MARKET FORCES
AND MARKET FAILURES

In chapter 4, we examined interstate cooperation to facilitate labor recruitment. Labor recruitment has been dominated by unilateral action, as sending and receiving state interests often align. Powerful receiving states usually have been able to meet their labor needs domestically or by simply relaxing immigration controls unilaterally and allowing labor market mechanisms to match immigrant labor with employers. Only under rare circumstances in which market mechanisms have failed have receiving states been motivated to conclude labor recruitment agreements. In this case, sending states may be able to extract greater protections for their migrants or greater labor market access.

Supporting Hypothesis 1a, we found that virtually all labor recruitment agreements have been bilateral, and almost never regional or multilateral. As predicted by Hypothesis 2, even bilateral agreements are rare; as long as powerful receiving states are satisfied with the unilateral status quo, cooperation is unlikely to occur. Receiving states will pursue cooperation with sending states only when there is both unmet labor demand *and* a failure of the market to meet this demand. Market failures are the result of informational asymmetries and adjustment costs. Although these costs are never zero, dense migrant networks, cheap transportation, and geographic proximity can reduce them, again making labor markets function better and international agreements less likely.

We first examined multilateral and regional efforts to facilitate labor mobility and, as expected, found little cooperative behavior. The only multilateral agreement that addresses labor mobility is the GATS Mode 4, but its effect has been very limited. It is designed to facilitate not migration but rather limited, short-term travel to allow for trade in services. Second, its institutional design demands consensus decision making, which means that sending states cannot use it as a forum for advancing their own labor mobility interests.

We next surveyed twenty-eight REOs for evidence of labor mobility agreements and found very few. We distinguished among three types of cooperation: (1) free movement (à la the EU), (2) temporary movement to facilitate trade and investment (à la the GATS Mode 4), and (3) facilitated entry and temporary stay but no access to the labor market (à la APEC) (IOM 2007).[1] Of the twenty-eight organizations surveyed, we found that only four have implemented freedom of movement (the EU, EEA, GCC, and OECS). We discussed these four cases more fully in chapter 5, but the unique factors that they shared included reciprocal movement and low levels of mobility. We found that a number of other regional agreements have mobility provisions that have not been implemented, even when member states already have bilateral agreements in place.

Last, we examined the most common form of labor mobility cooperation: BLAs. We divided these agreements into first-wave agreements, concluded in the period after World War II and into the 1960s, and second-wave agreements, concluded in the 1970s and later. We also discussed the possibility of a new third wave of agreements. In both the first and second waves, labor markets experienced an exogenous shock that motivated some states to pursue BLAs. During the first wave, this was postwar economic growth in Europe coupled with severe labor shortages. We examined the cases of France (which concluded BLAs) and the United Kingdom (which did not), and found support for our argument that states pursue agreements only when the market fails to provide for unmet labor demand. Immediately after World War II, France relaxed restrictions that it had implemented during the Great Depression. A new immigration bureaucracy was created to manage the recruitment and screening of immigrant labor, and it did so in part through BLAs. This effectively reduced information asymmetries by providing workers abroad with information about job opportunities and reduced adjustment costs through free visas, transportation, skills tests, medical exams, and even housing upon arrival. The United Kingdom, on the other hand, had no need to pursue BLAs even after establishing a government-led committee (the Foreign Labor Committee) to oversee recruitment. Unlike France, the United Kingdom already had well-established migrant networks due to Irish, colonial, and Commonwealth migration, which mitigated informational asymmetries and adjustment costs. During World War II, both the government and private employers relied on the Irish, Commonwealth citizens, and colonial subjects to support the war effort. After the war, these groups were well positioned to fill unmet labor market needs without the need for BLAs.

The second wave of BLAs originated in more diverse locales. Oil wealth in the Gulf States fueled unmet labor demand there, leading to BLAs with Asian source countries. Likewise, economic growth in Southeast Asia created unmet labor demand that was exacerbated by new opportunities for citizens from East Asia in the Gulf states, motivating a need for BLAs there. And in Europe, the fall of the Soviet Bloc led to a new wave of BLAs between Western European receiving states and sending states in Central and Eastern Europe. We argued that the third wave of BLAs, if it exists, is composed of agreements that are less about facilitating migration than rewarding sending states for successfully controlling unwanted migration. The most recent agreements, then, are motivated not by market failures—neither informational asymmetries nor adjustment costs—but rather by a need for control. The motivating logic for them is then quite different; these BLAs are side payments made to sending states for cooperation on migration control, which we addressed in chapter 3.

In summary, the evidence we presented in chapter 4 supported our fifth claim: while international cooperation in other issue areas often leads to more openness, the opposite is generally true in migration. Labor recruitment and mobility is one exception to this general trend but, of all the migration issues covered in this book, this is the one on which we see the least cooperation.

FREEDOM OF MOVEMENT: HISTORICAL ANTECEDENTS
AND CONTEMPORARY PRACTICES

The first claim on which the argument of our book has rested is that post–World War II migration has been primarily unilateral, from poorer, less stable countries to wealthier, more stable ones, and that each country's migration profile is unique. However, there are exceptions to the rule, and these exceptions have had profound effects that could not be overlooked in a survey of migration cooperation. In chapter 5, we examined these exceptions. The most notable example is the EU and the institutional iterations that preceded it, along with the TTTA between Australia and New Zealand. However, two regional organizations in the Global South also fit our theoretical propositions.

Following Hypothesis 1b, the most basic difference between freedom of movement and labor recruitment is that the migratory flows are not unidirectional, and thus involve states that cannot be easily categorized as either sending or receiving states in relation to each other. Instead, states in these regions had a long history of reciprocal movement, which enhanced economic efficiency by allowing labor flows to respond to changes in demand. This was facilitated by similar standards of living and levels of social service provision between neighboring states, oftentimes coupled with a common language and culture. The earliest models of free movement agreements, such as the Nordic Common Labor Market and the Benelux Economic Union, exemplified these characteristics.

Once we accounted for this fundamental anomaly in the European and Trans-Tasman cases, the expectations of our argument were useful. In all the cases in which cooperation on free movement occurred, we identified exogenous shocks that changed the status quo of unilateral action. These included labor market shortages, regional economic integration, and, in the case of Australia and New Zealand, a change in the migration policy of the former colonial power, the United Kingdom. The institutional response of creating a free movement zone instead of more restrictive bilateral labor mobility agreements depended on the involved states' level of familiarity with each other and their certainty that flows would remain reciprocal over the long term. Only rarely have both been high enough that states have chosen to sacrifice sovereignty over cross-border migration for the sake of economic efficiency.

The EU's most recent accessions in 2004 and subsequently, however, do not fit with the patterns seen earlier. In the 1990s, the EU received a wave of applications for accession following the collapse of communism from states that clearly did not share the same standard of living as the current member states. The EU was constrained to either offering membership, with all of its benefits including freedom of movement, or excluding the applicants altogether at great political and economic cost. Even long transition periods for completing accession did not ensure that new members would achieve the similar standard of living and level of migratory reciprocity that earlier members had achieved. The decision to admit the new members despite this uncertainty was due to the institutional constraints imposed by the EU's governing documents; if the old members could have excluded the new members from free movement without weakening the union more broadly, they likely would have.

The Trans-Tasman migration had been characterized by reciprocity since Australia and New Zealand were first colonized by the British, but there was little need of codification until the United Kingdom abolished most of the migration privileges for Commonwealth citizens in 1971. The agreement, however, was informal and nonbinding, which meant that it did not constrain either state from making a change if circumstances shifted, and this is exactly what happened. In 2001, Australia unilaterally amended the agreement to restrict the ability of New Zealanders to become permanent residents and access social welfare benefits. This change was not only a response to increasingly unilateral flows from New Zealand, as opposed to the historically reciprocal ones, but also a response to demographic changes within these flows, which included more nonnative New Zealanders who had immigrated to New Zealand from third countries. These changes were fueled by diverging levels of employment and economic prosperity. Absent institutional constraints, the agreement faltered as the conditions that we argued are necessary for freedom of movement disappeared.

We discovered two organizations in the Global South that also met the required conditions: GCC and OECS. We outlined the evolution of freedom of movement in the GCC states and found patterns similar to the European and Trans-Tasman cases. The GCC oil states experienced high demand for labor starting in the late 1970s due to development projects fueled by rising oil revenues. Similar levels of wealth and welfare, language, and culture were also present. Once freedom of movement was in place, however, as in our other cases, mobility remained low—the incentives to move were not large. The GCC is interesting, too, because of the exclusion of the seventh Arabian peninsula state, Yemen. Consistent with our theory, this exclusion is ascribed to wealth disparities in a country that lacks the oil deposits of its neighbors.

In summary, all five cases of freedom of movement that we documented substantiated Hypothesis 1b; where flows tend toward reciprocity, freedom of movement becomes possible. However, institutional histories may lead to continuity even when conditions change. But the conditions under which freedom of movement is likely to occur are exceedingly rare, and we argue that we are unlikely to see it emerge elsewhere, if these conditions do not exist.

CRIMINALITY IN MIGRATION: SUCCESSFUL
MULTILATERAL COOPERATION

In chapter 6, we examined problems of criminality, specifically responses to human trafficking and smuggling. We argued that states have a common interest in reducing crime and maintaining the rule of law, which is reflected in a century-long history of multilateral treaties that are well ratified. Nonetheless, the changing structure and volume of trafficking and smuggling raised the costs of the status quo and brought both sending and receiving states to the negotiating table, as anticipated by Hypothesis 4. The multifaceted nature of the trafficking and smuggling problem actually tapped into a variety of state interests. In some cases, these interests aligned; in other cases, these interests were opposed, changing the amount of bargaining space.

The issue of criminality was one of the few areas where we documented formal, well-ratified, multilateral agreements: the two Palermo Protocols on Trafficking and Smuggling to the Convention Against Transnational Organized Crime. This outcome, however, does not contradict our first claim that flows tend to come from poorer, less stable countries to wealthier, more stable ones, and that these flows tend to create unique bilateral migration profiles, leading to bilateral cooperation. Even though trafficking and smuggling flows also create unique bilateral profiles, receiving states chose to negotiate multilaterally because the side payments needed to induce cooperation from sending states were low and the efficiency benefits of multilateralism were relatively high. Because trafficking and smuggling are associated with criminality that challenges the state, we argued that sending states share an interest with receiving states in curtailing both; receiving states did not need to buy the support of sending states.

Primarily reflecting the concerns of receiving states, the Palermo Protocols have little to say about the exact responsibilities that these states have to victims of trafficking and smuggling. However, as predicted by our third set of hypotheses (H3a and H3b), sending states have used other forums, where they institutionally have more power, to bring up the issue as well. Human trafficking and smuggling are a top priority in the informal RCPs, which structurally provide all participating states with an equal voice. But RCPs are only forums, and the objectives and action plans that they generate are nonbinding. These efforts have resulted in few concrete actions, and the projects that have been implemented are largely related to the criminality aspect of trafficking and smuggling as well, not the human rights of victims or socioeconomic conditions in sending states that generate the supply of trafficked and smuggled individuals. Parts of the RCP action plans that do not enjoy strong support from powerful receiving states simply are not implemented.

Once again, evidence from the issue area of trafficking and smuggling supports our fifth claim that increased cooperation does not facilitate migration. Instead, cooperation is specifically designed to curtail migration facilitated by traffickers and smugglers. Interestingly, the policies that do the most to protect victims' rights and to allow them to remain in destination countries have been implemented unilaterally, not cooperatively. Free from concerns about sovereignty and international precedent, some receiving states have implemented victim-friendly policies in response to domestic political pressure, even as they have avoided making the same commitments internationally.

MIGRANT RIGHTS AND THE FAILURE OF MULTILATERAL COOPERATION

In chapter 7, we examined the protection of migrant rights. We argued that the preferences of sending, receiving, and transit states are disparate. While sending states would like to ensure greater protections for their citizens who migrate abroad, transit and receiving states would like to minimize their international obligations toward these migrants. But sending states also want more open migration, allowing greater access for their citizens. This gives sending states little leverage in pushing for greater migrant rights protection, and access is often prioritized over rights. International conventions on migrant rights have largely stalled or been ineffective, including the ICRMW and various ILO conventions. We argued that the most effective strategy for ensuring migrant rights is to pursue national policies; human rights and labor rights advocates can pressure states to make unilateral, domestic changes in migrant rights protection.

Multilateral cooperation on migrant rights has largely failed, although states have attempted to conclude agreements at least since the Treaty of Versailles. Based on Hypotheses 3a and 3b, we were unsurprised by these failures, since we expected powerful receiving states to oppose such agreements. The more puzzling question was why there were repeated efforts at all; in addition to the ICRMW, the ILO included migrant rights in its original remit, and it explicitly attempted to address migrant rights in subsequent conventions (Conventions 66 in 1939, 97 in 1949, and 143 in 1975). The answer, we found, was consistent with our claims and hypotheses. First, during the pre–World War II period, most migrants were from powerful European states, headed toward traditional settler states like Australia, Canada, and the United States, Latin American countries, and elsewhere around the globe. Since the original ILO membership was small and dominated by these powerful states, they were able to ensure that migrant rights were in the original remit. At the same time, powerful sending states were also able to act unilaterally in advocating for migrant rights.

It was only later, in the post–World War II period, that European states' interests changed as they transitioned into receiving states. As poorer and less stable sending states obtained independence and began to outnumber powerful receiving states, they used their institutional power within the ILO to put migrant rights on the agenda and introduce multilateral treaties. As we predicted in our third set of hypotheses (3a and 3b), however, even though these sending states may succeed in drafting agreements, the agreements do not enjoy widespread ratification. Without the support of receiving states, they are not implemented. More recently, sending states moved the discussion of migrant rights to the UN General Assembly, where the institutional decision-making rules are more favorable than the ILO's rules. Despite widespread support from sending states, the ICRMW remains unenforced after failing to garner support from powerful receiving states. Not only did the treaty negotiations last a long ten years, it took an additional thirteen years to get the twenty ratifications necessary for the treaty to enter into force; and no receiving states in North America, Western Europe, or the Middle East have ratified it.

In many ways, our story of cooperation on migrant rights was one about the *absence* of cooperation. This does not mean that migrant rights cannot be protected; it just means that international cooperation may not be the most effective route. States may act unilaterally to protect migrant rights in response to domestic pressure, and they have, although they often do so under the banner of human rights or labor rights.

THEORETICAL APPLICATIONS FOR THE REFUGEE AND TRAVEL REGIMES

At the beginning of this book, we explicitly limited our study to the voluntary, or economic, migration regime, and we excluded the refugee and travel regimes. While these other two regimes perhaps deserve their own full-length book treatment, we do think that our theoretical framework may apply to the refugee regime, if not the travel regime. Because the travel regime largely involves reciprocal flows, we see our theoretical framework as less applicable.

In the current refugee regime, the status quo is the 1951 Refugee Convention. At the time the convention was drafted and ratified, refugee flows looked very different than they do today. In the aftermath of World Wars I and II, most refugees were European. European states were also politically powerful, and they used this power to create a binding international agreement, obligating states to the principle of non-refoulement of any individual outside of his or her country of origin whose life or rights might be threatened because of race, religion, nationality, membership in a particular social group, or political opinion. The Refugee Convention also served a political purpose in the context of the Cold War, beyond dealing with the pragmatic concerns about European refugees.

It prioritized the values of the Universal Declaration of Human Rights and its emphasis on individualism and political freedoms, thus elevating these rights above social rights prioritized by the communist states, such as access to food, health care, and education (Innes 2015; Hathaway 1991). This further cemented liberal ideology in the new postwar international institutions. At first, the convention applied only to European refugees generated prior to 1951, reflecting its post–World War II origins. It was expanded in the 1967 Protocol to include refugees from all countries, before and after 1951. During the same time period, though, UN member states rejected an alternative agreement, the Declaration on Territorial Asylum, which would have required not just non-refoulement but also admission, and not just territorial asylum but also diplomatic asylum (meaning that asylum seekers would only have to present themselves at an embassy, not physically travel to the country in which the wish to seek asylum) (Innes 2015). With these limitations inherent to the Refugee Convention firmly in place, the expansions in the 1967 Protocol did not threaten the politically powerful states. In fact, they protected them from the new refugee flows generated by anticolonial struggles in Africa and elsewhere during the 1960s.[2] This history is consistent with Hypotheses 1b and 4 in that, in the immediate post–World War II period, refugee flows were regional and reciprocal within the region. Later, in the 1960s, anticolonial wars produced new flows that were also regional and reciprocal within the region. In both cases, this led to multilateral efforts to address refugees.

As patterns of refugee flows have changed, so have the interests of states party to the 1951 Refugee Convention and the 1967 Protocol, particularly those of poorer, less powerful states. The vast majority of refugees today end up in poor, weak states, while wealthy, powerful states manage to accept comparatively few, well-vetted refugees. These poorer recipient states, which may face waves of refugees from war-torn neighbors, may very well prefer to modify their obligations under that status quo 1951 Refugee Convention, but they lack the political power in the international arena to do so. The recent "migration" or refugee crisis in Europe does little to change the fundamental calculus of powerful states when it comes to the refugee regime. Instead of seeking to dismantle the current regime, they look for ways to minimize their obligations by offshoring migrants and refugees to less powerful transit countries or poorer destination countries. The best that less powerful destination countries can hope for, then, is to extract more financial and political support from powerful states to continue to abide by and fulfill their responsibilities under the current refugee regime, either through the UNHCR or directly from other states. This supports Hypothesis 4: exogenous shocks may raise the cost of the status quo, but in this case, they do so for the receiving states least able to challenge it, and they pit them in opposition to powerful receiving states well served by the refugee regime. Hypotheses 3a and 3b also apply, with some minor modifications. In its original formulation, we claimed that sending states, which outnumber receiving states, could use majoritarian international institutions to initiate the cooperation to change the status quo. But less powerful receiving states are the only ones really motivated to challenge the status quo, as they face a coalition of powerful receiving states that oppose any new obligations and sending states that fear a rollback of existing obligations, making them ambivalent toward change, at best. The recent UN New York Declaration for Refugees and Migrants is yet one more attempt to change the status quo by less powerful states, although, for refugee flows, they are on the receiving end of the equation (see discussion below).

We leave a truly unified analysis of cooperation on voluntary migration and refugees for the future, but this brief exploration of our theory's applicability to the refugee regime is promising. The patterns of movement associated with the travel regime suggest that our model would not fit the travel regime well.

CONTRIBUTION TO THE INTERNATIONAL COOPERATION LITERATURE

There is a broad and deep theoretical literature addressing international cooperation and when it might occur.[3] Empirically evaluating theories of international cooperation, however, remains very challenging. The temptation to find cases of international cooperation and then work backward in an attempt to explain why it occurred is strong, but this method relies on selecting on the dependent variable (Geddes 1991). By looking at only cases where cooperation has occurred, one has no way of knowing if the factors that seem to explain it are unique to cooperative outcomes or if they are just as likely to lead to noncooperative outcomes. Certainly, scholars have attempted to address this. Humphreys (2001), for example, uses bargaining theory to explain cooperation in forest management by looking at failed attempts at intergovernmental negotiations and successful attempts. But, even here, international negotiations occur in every case; there is no examination of instances where states did not initiate negotiations at all, just an explanation of why they failed.

Our research strategy has offered something unusual: an examination of the null cases, where nothing happened at all. We did this by surveying an entire issue area and identifying all the possible ways that states might cooperate, whether they ever initiate efforts or not. This ensured that we did not select on the dependent variable of cooperation. We did not just look at where states have attempted to negotiate; we looked at the empty space too, where the status quo of unilateral action continues. Empirically, we also took a broad view of potential cooperative activities and examined informal as well as formal interstate activities. If we had defined cooperation as the presence of a multilateral treaty, this book would have been quite short. By taking a broader view, we can see that there is a lot of international activity surrounding migration policy, and this activity is explainable and predictable. Furthermore, we did not view the dependent variable of cooperation as hierarchical, with formal, multilateral cooperation as the pinnacle of cooperation, and other cooperative activity as just an interim step along the way. Instead, we identified these other types of cooperation as rational solutions to particular policy challenges and endpoints themselves. This method of broadly surveying an entire issue area and broadly conceiving of all the types of cooperative interaction that might occur can be applied to many other international issues. This would complement existing empirical work that more narrowly defines both cooperative outcomes and where to look for them.

Our research suggests that the agenda on international cooperation might profitably expand in several ways. First, as noted in chapter 1, the research on "lateralisms," or international regime membership size, remains underdeveloped. There is, indeed, some knowledge connecting the scope of the market externality or domain of the public good to the size of membership. We have adopted what we believe is a useful framework for analyzing the type of international agreement that is likely to arise: bilateral, regional, or multilateral (Thompson and Verdier 2014). This framework juxtaposes the transaction costs of negotiating many treaties with the costs of regime maintenance engendered by the "membership surplus," the benefits that arise for many states when the regime is structured to attract the state with the highest compliance cost. However, to this we have added the patterns of migration that create unique state migration profiles, to predict the circumstances under which bilateralism should dominate. An attention to patterns of flows may be useful in understanding the evolution of cooperation in other arenas of international economic interactions. For example, when FDI was concentrated among wealthy Western democracies, reciprocal flows generated informal cooperation and voluntary guidelines. When investment began to be directed to countries of the Global South and was nonreciprocal, we saw the rise of bilateral investment treaties. Attention to changing patterns of FDI could have alerted scholars to the potential for this phenomenon, rather than capturing the phenomenon after it was already widespread (Elkins, Guzman, and Simmons 2006).

Second, our research suggests that the institutionalization of the international system that has become more prominent in the post–World War II period will serve to beget yet more international agreements. These institutions provide forums with specific decision rules for changing the status quo. Depending on the size of the coalition unhappy with the status quo and the decision rule in effect, treaties may well emerge that seek to change the status quo. This is true in multilateral forums such as the UN General Assembly and the ILO, as our research has illustrated. It is also true in regional forums, where sending states have attempted to open the doors to their neighbors' more vibrant labor markets. However, this leads us to our third point, that international treaties are binding only on those states that ratify them. At least in the arena of international migration, the negotiation of treaties does not necessarily portend cooperation, if the states that are necessary to put the regime into effect are absent (Western 2015). We are not ignorant of the possibility that these treaties may be one method of creating new international norms to which states might adhere in the future. However, the other possibility is that the treaties remain paper tigers. More attention to the rise of poorly ratified treaties is in order, as is research on the impact of these treaties on state behavior.

Finally, we reiterate what has been previously acknowledged, that although international cooperation often has a positive connotation, it does not necessarily lead to greater openness to international flows or to greater market efficiency. It is always important to remember the distinction between a positive research agenda and a normative value system. By better understanding the causal relationships underpinning state interaction in the international system, we hope that activists are better equipped to achieve their normative goals. We turn to the potential policy lessons below.

POLICY LESSONS?

In 2011, the Transatlantic Council on Migration published a book titled *Improving the Governance of International Migration*, stating that "most actors agree that greater international cooperation on migration is needed." The book then went on to explore the key steps to building a more cooperative system of governance and the goals that could be achieved (Transatlantic Council on Migration 2011). In 2013, the OECD's David Khoudour (head of the Migration and Skills Unit) wrote that "the phenomenon of migration today requires an international cooperation framework that views migrants not only through a security lens, but as key players in countries' economic and social development" (Khoudour 2013, 2). Even the pope has chimed in, releasing a statement in time for the World Day for Migrants and Refugees in 2014 calling for "greater international cooperation to improve conditions for the world's rising number of migrants" (Rocca 2013).

We support many of the goals that proponents of greater international cooperation seek to achieve. Like Khoudour, we agree that policymakers should consider the relationship between migrants and economic and social development. Like Pope Francis, we certainly support improving conditions and living standards for the millions of migrants who leave their homes in search of better lives. But the findings of this book challenge the assumption that more international cooperation is the best way of achieving these goals or, in some cases, that it is even possible.

Advocates of international cooperation sometimes assume that cooperation in one venue or on one issue can (and will) grow deeper and broader. We strongly disagree with this assumption. States are strategic, and they will pursue cooperation when it serves their interests. We do not mean that cooperation cannot be lasting or self-reinforcing—it can. But pursuing international cooperation can also be costly for states; it may involve some forfeiture of sovereignty, a transfer of resources to another state, compromise, and a loss of unilateral authority. States calculate the ratio of costs and benefits to cooperation, and they act accordingly. There may be some role for trust building and establishing a working relationship in advancing future cooperation, since this can lower the costs of cooperation, but these features will not outweigh material interests.

International cooperation does have a role in migration policy, as we have seen in our examination of the Palermo Protocols and European readmission agreements, for example. There are few instances, however, of successful cooperation on facilitating migrant flows and protecting migrant rights. Advocates that care about these issues can take some lessons from our book.

First, state interests are multidimensional, and each migration issue or problem may tap into a variety of interests, such as concern for human rights, demand for immigrant labor, and the protection of national security. Migration policy advocates should tap into the interests that appeal to states and link these to their particular policy goals. This certainly worked for antitrafficking activists, who successfully linked trafficking with national security.

Second, migration policy advocates should abandon the push for international cooperation (particularly formal cooperation) when it is likely to be unsuccessful, based on an evaluation of state interests. Instead, they should focus on domestic law, where they may have a far greater chance of success by removing the hurdle of national sovereignty and aligning themselves with powerful domestic interests groups. We see this, for example, in the case of trafficking, where advocates for trafficking victims were effective in influencing US law by forming an unusual coalition between some feminist groups and evangelical Christians. Around the world, migrant advocates have succeeded in getting legislation passed to protect migrant rights by aligning themselves with labor unions. And last, advocates for greater access for migrants have achieved some success by aligning themselves with the employers that demand migrant labor.

On 19 September 2016, the UN General Assembly adopted the New York Declaration for Refugees and Migrants by consensus (UN 2016a, 2016b). It commits member states to protect the human rights of all refugees and migrants and sets in motion two international negotiations. The first, a Global Compact on Refugees, focuses on developing guidelines to address "large movements" of refugees; the second addresses a Global Compact for Safe, Orderly, and Regular Migration, both to be concluded by 2018. We will not comment extensively on either agreement and are particularly cautious about making any predictions about the potential for a Global Compact on Refugees. However, our research does speak directly to the prospects for a Global Compact for Safe, Orderly, and Regular Migration. We find it unsurprising that the United Nations has adopted the New York Declaration unanimously. We have hypothesized that sending states (and poor countries that host large numbers of refugees) can take advantage of majoritarian international institutions to challenge the status quo and attempt to project their preferences onto the international stage. Receiving states, especially European receiving states, may also be amenable to international negotiations because of the high costs associated with the European "migrant crisis." However, the declaration itself does not change the status quo of national sovereignty over entry, exit, and the treatment of migrants, as presented in our text. In fact, the commitment to protecting migrant rights refers to demonstrating "full respect for international law and human rights law, and where applicable, international refugee law and international humanitarian law" (UN 2016b, 2). The only mention made of the ICRMW and the ILO conventions discussed in chapter 7 is to invite states that have not ratified the treaties to do so.

The New York Declaration initiates interstate negotiations on voluntary migration. Again, our theory predicts that this is not an unusual event. However, we do venture a prediction on the outcome of the negotiations. There is no doubt that both sending and receiving states will bargain hard over the contents of any treaty. If sending states are able to dominate the discussions, we suggest a global compact that reflects their preferences but that receiving states will not ratify. If, however, receiving states dominate the negotiations, the content is likely to reflect receiving state preferences for control and readmission, although sending states may be able to extract concessions on small numbers of regular admissions or other side payments. The third possible outcome would be prolonged negotiations that may or may not result in an agreement. We suggest the first and the third outcomes are more likely as the second would create regime maintenance costs for receiving states that likely would exceed the cost of negotiating a series of bilateral agreements that reflect each receiving state's unique migration profile. Thus, despite the euphoria of the international organizations and the NGOs involved in the successful conclusion of the New York Declaration, we remain pessimistic about the prospects for changing the underlying emphasis on national sovereignty.

This book has provided a theoretical framework for understanding the scope and potential of international cooperation on migration. We have surveyed a broad range of activities at the international, regional, and national levels, covering everything from formal treaties to informal discussion forums. We hope this provides useful guidance for those working to make life better for both those who seek to migrate and those living in the societies that receive them, as well as those remaining at home.

NOTES

Chapter 1. Migration Patterns and the Prevalence of Bilateralism

1. These positions echo a broader debate in international relations about the possibilities for cooperation in the international system. The scholarly research on international cooperation is usually divided into three groups. Realists claim that international institutions are epiphenomenal, reflecting the interests of the powerful state(s) in the international system. The realists are countered by the school of neoliberal institutionalists who point out problems of collective action that prevent states from maximizing their utility (Koremenos, Lipson, and Snidal 2001). From this perspective, international cooperation provides mechanisms to achieve Pareto optimal solutions. Constructivists have emphasized the importance of nonstate actors and ideas as central to global governance.

2. Alexander Betts (2014) uses the term "survival migration" to encompass a broader notion of "forced" migration where human lives are at risk.

3. We argue that voluntary flows incorporate virtually all of the other categories of migrants enumerated by other scholars and that we do not need a more refined classification of migrants to understand the possibilities of cooperation. This classification stands in contrast to that employed in Betts's (2011) edited volume, which disaggregates flows into specific types, such as low-skilled migration, high-skilled migration, family reunification, "life-style" migration, and so on.

4. There is a large literature on the rise of "radical right," "extreme right," or populist parties, concentrated on but not limited to Europe, whose central political platform is opposition to immigration. See, for example, Kitschelt (1997), Merkl and Weinberg (1997), and Betz and Immerfall (1998).

5. Nestlé is the best known of the infant formula manufacturers that marketed their products in the developing world to the detriment of infant health. As a response to their practices, Nestlé was the subject of a global consumer boycott, and the World Health Organization adopted the "International Code of Marketing Breast-Milk Substitutes" in 1981 (Krasny 2012).

6. A cynical observer might explain this emphasis by theorizing that wealthy, Western democracies primarily experience the dislocation produced from migration, whereas developing countries have long experienced the dislocation produced by other international economic flows. The focus on migration, it follows, is generated by Western-centric research rather than by the actual levels of dislocation generated by distinctive economic flows.

7. The World Trade Organization began, of course, as the General Agreement on Tariffs and Trade in 1947. The OECD Guidelines for Multinational Enterprises were first published in 1976; the 2011 edition is the fifth update of the guidelines, which cover about 85 percent of all foreign direct investment flows.

8. For example, Gratton and Merchant (2013) document US efforts both to encourage voluntary return and to deport Mexicans (and Mexican Americans) during the 1930s Great Depression.

9. The number of "core" human rights varies with the source and the date of the statement.

The United Nations Office of the High Commissioner for Human Rights defines the following as "core" human rights treaties: ICERD 1965 (International Convention on the Elimination of all forms of Racial Discrimination); ICCPR 1966 (Covenant on Civil and Political Rights); ICESCR 1966 (Covenant on Economic, Social and Cultural Rights); CEDAW 1979 (Convention on the Elimination of All Forms of Discrimination Against Women); CAT 1984 (Convention against Torture and Other Cruel, Inhuman, or Degrading Treatment or Punishment); CRC 1989 (Convention on the Rights of the Child); ICRMW 1990 (International Convention on the Protection of the Rights of All Migrant Workers and Members of Their Families); CPED 2006 (International Convention for the Protection of All Persons from Enforced Disappearance); CRPD 2006 (Convention on the Rights of Persons with Disabilities); and OP-CAT 2002 (Optional Protocol to the CAT).

10. It is probably more accurate to say that migrants receive a bundle of rights upon entry, as the bundle of rights varies across states. Not all states have ratified and implemented the "core" UN human rights treaties, and many states offer migrants rights additional to those included in the core treaties.

11. Thompson and Verdier (2014) coin the term "lateralism" to denote the variation in the types of international cooperation, such as bilateralism, regionalism, and multilateralism. Koremenos, Lipson, and Snidal (2001) refer more generically to membership size.

12. Some states are also labeled as "transit states," those that serve as a conduit between sending and receiving states. We acknowledge this distinction but argue that transit states can still be classified as either sending or receiving based on their net migration flow. See the "Market Conditions and State Preferences" section of chapter 2 for a more detailed justification.

13. Hatton (2007) refers to the absence of reciprocity and Sykes (2013) refers to the "one-way problem."

14. Of all migrants, 60 percent move within the Global North or within the Global South.

15. The UNDP divides states into "developed" (Human Development Index of .9 and above) and "developing" (Human Development Index below .9). This is similar to the distinction between the Global North and the Global South (UNDP 2009).

16. For France, these are the top "third country national" stocks, that is, foreign-born residents from non-EU member states.

17. The changing pattern of foreign direct investment is reflected in the rise of bilateral investment treaties that connect developed to developing states; see Elkins, Guzman, and Simmons (2006).

18. For all countries except the United States, see Observatory of Economic Complexity, http://atlas.media.mit.edu/en/profile/country/ (accessed 28 December 2015). For the United States, see United States, Department of Commerce, Census Bureau, Economic Indicators Division, http://www.trade.gov/mas/ian/build/groups/public/@tg_ian/documents/webcontent/tg_ian_003364.pdf (accessed 28 December 2015).

19. Of course, the presence of the EU and, in particular, the Schengen Agreement stretches the locus of potential migration within the member states. Throughout the text we deal with the EU as a unique case. However, even here, because of migrant networks, the stocks as well as the flows are country-specific.

20. Koremenos, Lipson, and Snidal (2001) provide three conjectures regarding membership in institutional design: membership becomes more restrictive with the severity of the enforcement problem and with uncertainty about preferences, and membership becomes less restrictive with severity of the distribution problem.

21. For example, the original ECOWAS agreement provided for freedom of movement to

be implemented over a 15-year period, from 1975 to 1990. However, only the first provision, for visa-free travel for less than ninety days, has been implemented (UNDP 2009).

Chapter 2. A Bargaining Framework for Understanding Cooperation

1. The new terminology for corporate rules governing the international behavior of firms is "shared values."

2. Nonstate actors include, but are not limited to, domestic and international nongovernmental organizations (NGOs) as well as "policy entrepreneurs." Intergovernmental organizations (IGOs), by definition, are creations of governments.

3. Eytan Meyers (2004) provides a nice summary of the theoretical literature. For a more recent overview, see Money (2010). Also see Messina and Lahav (2005) for a compendium of many of the central theoretical research articles on immigration policy.

4. The vocabulary for these two types of states includes the dichotomies of sending/receiving, source/host, and origin/destination. We employ these terms interchangeably to provide some variation in vocabulary.

5. The international trade literature looks to the abundance and scarcity of factors of production relative to other states in the international system and labels some countries as labor abundant and capital scarce (with a comparative advantage in labor-intensive production) and other countries as capital abundant and labor scarce (with a comparative advantage in capital-intensive production). These classifications are uncontroversial (Odell 2000).

6. Here we do not elaborate the determinants of migrant flows in the international system. See Castles, de Haas, and Miller (2014, chap. 2) for an overview of the literature.

7. See chapter 7 for details.

8. The game theoretic literature makes reference to discount rates of the parties to the negotiations. A low discount rate reflects the patience of the state—the state has the capacity to endure the status quo for a long time. A high discount rate reflects the impatience of the state—the state needs a deal immediately. States with low discount rates have greater bargaining power than those with high discount rates.

9. We recognize the framework that Betts (2011) provides for his edited volume that identifies private goods, "club goods," and public goods as a means of organizing and explaining the types of cooperation or governance that arise. Our contribution differs in significant ways from his useful effort by incorporating migration patterns, the status quo, the bargaining framework, and the role of institutional structures in shaping international cooperation on voluntary migration. Our volume also organizes evidence that supports the hypotheses we propose, rather than the descriptive edited volume.

Chapter 3. Controlling Immigration

1. To understand the distinctions and protection responsibilities regarding asylum seekers in first asylum countries and in safe third countries, see European Commission (2016): "1) First country of asylum (Article 35 of the Asylum Procedures Directive): Where the person has been already recognized as a refugee in that country or otherwise enjoys sufficient protection there; 2) safe third country (Article 38 of the Asylum Procedures Directive): where the person has not already received protection in the third country but the third country

can guarantee effective access to protection of the readmitted person." Also see Money and Western (forthcoming) regarding the quality (or lack thereof) of refuge.

2. To be granted refugee status, individuals are required to demonstrate persecution based on "race, religion, nationality, membership of a particular social group, or political opinion" (United Nations General Assembly 1951, 14). "Subsidiary protection" may be provided based on the presence of indiscriminant violence that threatens death. For example, the European Union (2004), via EU Directive 2004/83/EC, provides that subsidiary protection may be granted when there are "substantial grounds" that the person faces "a real risk of suffering serious harm." Article 15 of the directive defines serious harm as "(a) death penalty or execution; or (b) torture or inhuman or degrading treatment or punishment of an applicant in the country of origin; or (c) serious and individual threat to a civilian's life or person by reason of indiscriminate violence in situations of international or internal armed conflict" (EU 2004, 3, 8).

3. Because of the Syrian Civil War, Germany waived both national and European regulations regarding safe country criteria and the responsibility for asylum determination for most of 2015 for Syrians. Moreover, all asylum claimants reaching the German border had their cases adjudicated, but most claimants met with failure. See Eurostat (2016c).

4. In the first quarter of 2016, the acceptance rate for Afghan asylum seekers was 21 percent; 25 percent received subsidiary protection, 7 percent received humanitarian protection, and 47 percent were rejected (Eurostat 2016c).

5. Of course, not all states abide by the human rights conventions. There are periodic reports of mass expulsions from Gulf oil states, African states, and Asian states, among others.

6. Here we exclude the costs to the deported immigrant; but see Ellermann (2008) for the costs to the deportee.

7. In fact, investing state resources in control may be more costly than allowing a completely unfettered flow of undocumented immigrants (Myers and Papageorgiou 2000).

8. See, for example, various Eurobarometer polls.

9. Wong (2012) also suggests that receiving states are unlikely to negotiate agreements with states that are likely to defect from the agreement, either because they do not care about their reputations in the international system or because they lack the capacity to implement the agreement. This is operationalized by Wong as regime type, civil war, fragile states, and human rights abuses.

10. Free movement between Australia and New Zealand has been in place longer, but it was under the auspices of the British Empire rather than via agreement between the two states. We describe in chapter 5 how Australia and New Zealand formalized this informal arrangement in 1973. However, that arrangement places virtually no restrictions on residence and therefore does not generate an undocumented population.

11. The Schengen Agreement was controversial when it was first drafted in 1985, and only five countries originally signed on: France, Germany, Belgium, Luxembourg, and the Netherlands. In addition, the agreement did not take effect until ten years later, in 1995. In the years since, however, the Schengen Area has gradually grown to include twenty-five countries, including every member of the European Union except the United Kingdom and Ireland (Romania, Bulgaria, and Cyprus are not yet members of Schengen, but they are set to become members in the future; Norway, Lichtenstein, and Switzerland are Schengen members even though they are not EU members).

12. This phenomenon was documented in depth in a special issue of *International Organization* in 2000 titled "Legalization and World Politics" (Goldstein et al. 2000).

13. This is consistent with Betts's 2006 claim that increasing migration caused states to sign bilateral readmission agreements. However, we model the costs that states incur that change

their best alternative to negotiated agreement as well as the signatories to the agreements, which illuminates the fact that European states signed readmission agreements whereas other receiving states failed to do so.

14. Moreover, bilateral readmission agreements are treaties that are usually ratified by legislatures and can produce political debate that prevents ratification even after the treaty is negotiated and signed. Ellermann (2008) documents a case of a readmission agreement that was rejected by a local parliament.

15. A 1991 report to the European Council from the ministers responsible for immigration suggested that increasing cooperation on a wide range of economic, social, financial, and political issues, as well as assistance for addressing the root causes of migration, should be conditional on readmission agreements (Coleman 2009).

16. This text is common to a number of European Community readmission agreements, including ones with Albania, Hong Kong, Macao, and Sri Lanka (Coleman 2009).

17. Statistics from the IGC (see 2002 against 2006) are not consistent but do support the dramatic rise in readmission agreements after 1990.

18. EU-wide readmission agreements are addressed in the "Regional Cooperation" section.

19. This is described as "self-limited sovereignty" by Christian Joppke (1998).

20. The exclusion of France from the analysis is particularly noteworthy, especially because it has concluded a large number of readmission agreements. Cross-nationally comparable migrant flow data are available, however, only for the post-1994 period, which would severely truncate the analysis. Thus, we exclude those data.

21. Data on government welfare expenditures come from the OECD. Data on population and total migrant stock come from the World Bank; since migrant stock data are available only in five-year intervals, data points for intervening years are interpolated.

22. The growth rate of real GDP per capita data come from Heston, Summers, and Aten (2009); the unemployment rate data come from the ILO (2010).

23. There is some difficulty in comparing data among destination countries because the data are reported differently. Some countries (Finland, Italy, Spain, and Sweden) report only the combined inflow of foreigners and citizens of the destination country from a particular country. Citizen inflows, however, are not truly immigrants, since they are already citizens of the destination country. Other countries (Belgium and the Netherlands) report only data on foreign flows, not citizen flows. Our solution is to use the data on the combined citizen and foreign inflows wherever possible and the foreign inflow figures for Belgium and the Netherlands. While the data do not represent the exact same concept, the correlation between foreign inflows and foreign and citizen inflows is about 90 percent.

24. We tried numerous alternative measures of welfare costs, including welfare expenditures per capita, welfare expenditures as a percentage of GDP, welfare expenditures interacted with migrant stock, welfare expenditures interacted with migrant flows, and various other specifications. None of the alternatives delivered significant results, and most were not in the expected direction.

25. See, for example, Christina Boswell's (2011) work on societal steering and control narratives.

26. Thanks to Luis Guarnizo, a colleague at the University of California, Davis, for pointing out this possible interpretation.

27. We also tested our data using the Weibull model, which allows for the effect of independent variables to vary over time. However, this model presents another problem; it assumes that the effect of the variables is either increasing or decreasing monotonically over time, which is an equally unrealistic assumption (Box-Steffensmeier and Jones 2004). Nevertheless,

in this case the substantive results from the Weibull model are very similar to those of the Cox model. We display the Cox results because the model has the fewest restrictions.

28. GDP growth is statistically insignificant but requires the time-variant correction (which is also statistically insignificant). In the case of GDP growth, the inflection in the direction of the relationship is at about t = 9, or nine years after the beginning of our analysis. GDP growth has a negative, albeit insignificant, effect on the probability of signing agreements at the beginning of our analysis and then, by 1989, the effect changes direction. This means that somewhere around 1989, higher economic growth no longer reduces the likelihood that a receiving country will sign a readmission agreement; in fact, high growth rates begin to make it *more* likely that a country will sign an agreement. We suspect that this time-variant effect might be due to the broader patterns in the business cycle that our particular time frame captures. Between 1984 and 1993, the average annual GDP growth rate (per capita) in our sample of receiving countries dropped from 3.5 percent to –1.4 percent. By 1995, the average growth rate had recovered, rising to 3.4 percent. Since these economic trends affected all of the receiving states in our sample, our results might be skewed. A larger sample, over a longer period of time, might provide more robust, significant results.

29. There is also a large literature on their implications for refugee and asylum policy (Collinson 1996; Lavenex 1998; Achermann and Gattiker 1995).

30. Betts (2006) implies that states are motivated by their logistical inability to unilaterally prevent migrants from crossing their borders. For example, in the early 1990s, approximately one to two hundred thousand undocumented migrants were arriving each year to Europe from Northern African countries, and sixty-five thousand of these were sub-Saharan Africans in transit. This, argues Betts, was the impetus for the proliferation of readmission agreements between European and North African states. Our argument is consistent with this observation but is generic to all states and provides additional reasons for the impetus to sign agreements.

31. Cassarino (2010) gives the example of France signing many readmission agreements with Latin American countries and Spain's inability to do so, given the salience of Latin American migration to Spain.

32. See, for example, Odell (2000).

33. For third country nationals with whom Turkey had a readmission agreement, the provisions of readmission took effect immediately. However, Turkey had few readmission agreements other than with European countries. Moreover, individual readmission agreements negotiated between individual EU member states and Turkey remained in force.

34. There is a discrepancy between the EU–Turkey Joint Action Plan, which mentions 4.2 billion euros, and the EU–Turkey Statement, which indicates a prior commitment of 3 billion euros, to which the agreement offers an additional 3 billion euros. These are both official documents of the European Union (European Commission 2015, 2016).

Chapter 4. Labor Recruitment

1. We are unaware of any regional recruitment agreements, although REOs do have BLAs among member states (see below).

2. Normally, freedom of movement is abridged in some way. For example, the EU, the best known case of freedom of movement, allows workers to look for jobs for a maximum of six months; in the absence of employment at that point, they are required to return home (Money and Geddes 2011).

3. *Nishimura Ekiu v. United States*, 142 U.S. 651 (1982), citing an 1892 US Supreme Court decision.

4. The Philippines is an early example of a state that consciously adopted emigration as a development strategy in the mid-1970s (O'Neil 2004).

5. Population loss through emigration can also be seen as a signal to governments that their citizens disapprove of their governance: citizens are voting with their feet. Albert Hirschman (1970) makes this point in his book *Exit, Voice, and Loyalty*, and many authoritarian regimes spent the Cold War period policing their borders to prevent citizens from emigrating. This is also reflected in the views of many sending states that see their emigrants as deserters, with Mexico as a prominent example in the nineteenth century and throughout much of the twentieth (FitzGerald 2008).

6. Issues of state interests in the brain drain are inconclusive. States may have an interest in retaining highly skilled individuals, whose educational costs the government may have provided. However, they also have the countervailing interests listed below.

7. For a contrary opinion, see Hatton (2007). According to Hatton, sending countries "do not on the whole place any value on seeing more of their citizens emigrate. According to the UN's periodic survey, only 5 percent of developing country governments in 2001 thought that the level of emigration from their country was too low" (Hatton 2007, xx).

8. For sending state preferences regarding the treatment of their emigrants abroad, see chapter 7.

9. State responses and unmet demand for labor have varied over time and have included slavery and indentured servitude, industry recruitment, and state-led recruitment. Here, however, we focus on the post–World War II period only.

10. There are also personal costs associated with migration.

11. In chapter 7, we examine the efforts by sending states to extract rights not only for their documented expatriates but also for their undocumented expatriates. If undocumented migrants obtain access to the same rights as documented migrants, this would serve as a method of expanding access to receiving country labor markets.

12. Negotiations in the communications and financial services sectors continued past 1994 and were ultimately concluded in 1996 and 1997, respectively. These sector-specific negotiations led to broader commitments in these two economic sectors.

13. There are some WTO negotiating coalitions that cross the developed/developing state divide, such as the Cairns Group, agricultural exporters that include Australia, Canada, and New Zealand as well as sixteen countries that are considered to fall in the developing category (Cairns Group n.d.).

14. However, there may be other state preferences that are projected through regional institutions onto the international stage as well. Margheritis (2013) argues that South American countries, led by Argentina, sought to project a human rights approach to migration through labor mobility agreements in Mercosur, in part to shame states from the Global North into treating their emigrants more fairly.

15. Excluded from this list are REOs that have since been absorbed in the European Union: the Benelux Union (Belgium, the Netherlands, and Luxembourg) and the Nordic Union (Denmark, Finland, Iceland, Sweden, and Norway). The Trans-Tasman Travel Arrangement between Australia and New Zealand is another example of freedom of movement. Each of these is described in detail in chapter 5.

16. The three criteria used are (1) "ratification of free movement protocol," (2) "proportion of REC member countries whose nationals do not require a visa for entry," and (3) "propor-

tion of REC member countries whose nationals are issued with a visa on arrival" (UNECA 2016, 44).

17. This is acknowledged in the IOM/World Bank/WTO (2004) survey that suggests that there are multiple reasons why sending and receiving states negotiate BLAs: migrant receiving countries sign bilateral agreements to combat irregular migration, to respond to labor market needs of temporary or permanent nature, to promote economic links with sending countries. Migrant-sending countries sign these agreements to relieve labor surpluses, protect the rights of their nationals abroad, limit the effects of brain drain by ensuring the return of their nationals.

18. Margaret Peters (2013) does have a working paper in which she gathered and analyzed some four hundred agreements that had been deposited in the United Nations Treaty Collection (https://treaties.un.org/).

19. This discussion draws on Money (1999) and references listed therein (CES 1964, 1969; Minces 1973; Tapinos 1975; Wihtol de Wenden 1988; Noiriel 1988; Weil 1991; Lequin 1992). In English, Freeman (1979) provides the earliest systematic overview; also see Hollifield (1992, 1994), Silverman (1992), the chapter on France in Hammar (1985), and SOPEMI annual reports (various years).

20. France also had special provisions for Algerians before and after Algerian independence in 1961 and for Africans from prior French colonies. Black Africans, however, did not arrive in France in large numbers, and both privileged groups were ultimately folded into the standard immigration control regime (Miller and Martin 1982; Money 1999).

21. Most treaties were valid for one or two years but in practice were renewed automatically.

22. We can locate no other references to this agreement in the large British immigration literature, other than the 2004 OECD report. Paul's (1997) detailed account of British recruitment schemes in the early post–World War II period makes no mention of this or any other BLAs.

23. See Money (1999). The classic chronicle of British immigration legislation is by Ian Macdonald (1972, 1983), continued by Macdonald and Blake (1991). Also see Fransman (1982) and Grant and Martin (1982). Layton-Henry (1992) provides a good overview of immigration control in Britain, and Layton-Henry (1994) is the source for the most recent legislation.

24. Ireland became a republic on 18 April 1949 as a result of the Irish Republic of Ireland Act 1948. It was no longer a member of the British Commonwealth as of that date.

25. The Italian government indicated a 1947 bilateral guest worker agreement with the United Kingdom, but this is not acknowledged by the British government (Paul 1997).

26. See chapter 5 on freedom of movement for a detailed description of the policies of individual member states in light of the seven-year transition period.

27. See Sykes (2013) for a detailed explanation of the various externalities. Sykes also acknowledges "important nonpecuniary externalities," "welfare migration," and the potential for congestion of public facilities. He also notes the potential for "migration diversion" generated by bilateral or regional rather than multilateral agreements.

Chapter 5. Freedom of Movement

1. The backlash against Polish immigration was implicated as one of the factors leading to the successful Brexit referendum (Sudarshan 2016).

2. Our statistics suggest that approximately 6.8 million citizens of the EU 15 live in another EU country as of 2013. See Table 5.7.

3. Iceland and Norway are incorporated into the free movement zone, even though they

are not members of the European Union. The Agreement on the European Economic Area between the European Union and the European Free Trade Association went into force on 1 January 1994. The remaining members of EFTA are Iceland, Lichtenstein, and Norway. The EEA provides the "four freedoms" for EFTA members on a reciprocal basis with the EU member states.

4. OECS is the other regional organization in the Global South that has recently created freedom of movement. However, this regional agreement is so new that we have been unable to gather sufficient evidence to analyze this case here. See the "Regional Cooperation" section in chapter 4 for an analysis of other regional organizations.

5. Brexit is the moniker for British exit from the European Union, as the result of a referendum called in June 2016.

6. In Stephen Krasner's (1976) "modified neo-realist" argument about hegemony and the structure of the international economic system, he too refers to the stickiness of institutions in retaining policies that would otherwise be considered dysfunctional from a national interest perspective.

7. This is a right guaranteed in the United Nations Declaration on Human Rights (1948), although not every state provides its citizens this right.

8. Current regulations state: "Jobseekers cannot be expelled if they prove that they are continuing to seek employment and have a genuine chance of finding a job" (European Commission, Employment, Social Affairs and Inclusion 2016). Of course, this implies that they can be expelled if they are not looking for work or do not have a genuine chance of finding a job.

9. New Zealand and Australia continue to maintain complete freedom of movement and residence, but Australia has revoked the right of New Zealanders to any state benefits unless they are vetted through the points system applicable to all potential immigrants. See the section on the TTTA below.

10. The creation of a common passport zone that requires member states to control entry of third country nationals at external borders but allows all who enter to travel freely is the subject of the travel regime and will not be addressed in this book. This does not detract from the explanation of freedom of movement, as this is not conditional on a common passport zone.

11. Thanks to Eiko Thielemann for highlighting this dimension of policy to us.

12. Here, we follow economists' definition of full employment to include the friction of job placement, so that full employment does not coincide with no unemployment.

13. This convention required that residents in another country should have "equal status" to social benefits as the citizens of that country (Wendt 1981, 217). The convention did not grant new rights to Nordic migrants; it merely codified twelve earlier bilateral (and multi-country) agreements.

14. Finland joined the Northern Council in 1955, subsequent to Soviet troop withdrawal from Finnish territory. However, it participated in the drafting of the Nordic Common Labor Market agreement.

15. This section draws on Lange (1954), Mouritzen (1995), Padelford (1957), Salvesen (1956), Tunander (2007), and Wendt (1981).

16. Populations in 1951 are as follows: Sweden (6,960,000), Denmark (4,252,000), Finland (4,017,000), Norway (3,242,000), and Iceland (142,000). Data from http://population pyramid.net.

17. Iceland entered the common passport zone in 1966.

18. Iceland ultimately joined the Nordic Common Labor Market in 1982 (Fischer and Straubhaar 1995).

19. See Wendt (1981) for a discussion of labor market cooperation for the medical professions.

20. Examining the Nordic Common Labor Market in 1995, forty years after it was adopted, Fischer and Straubhaar (1995, 207) conclude: "If labour is legally free to move, this makes people (especially in border areas) more mobile internationally but it does not in itself induce mass migration from one country to another. People's social and cultural ties to their local environment are an important obstacle to migration which has been commonly underestimated from the perspective of theoretical economics." They also attribute the lack of migration in the Nordic area to "the development of systems of social security and welfare [which] allows for immobility even under conditions of long term unemployment" (209).

21. The population of Sweden in 1976 was approximately 7,986,000 (http://populationpyramid.net/sweden/1976/).

22. The ratio between Denmark and Finland was greater at .60, but Finland did not join until later.

23. Denmark joined the EEC in 1973. This required a supplementary protocol that voided Denmark's inspection requirements for the Nordic Passport Union for EEC citizens but also required Denmark to take back undesirable foreigners (Wendt 1981, 189).

24. Unemployment statistics for Iceland are unavailable.

25. Our chapter does not describe BLEU, established in 1921, as this agreement did not include freedom of movement, although, as noted below, there was a 1926 bilateral agreement facilitating labor movement via unlimited access to work permits. BLEU originated in the aftermath of World War I. In the nineteenth century, Luxembourg and Alsace-Lorraine were part of the German Zollverein. After World War I, Alsace-Lorraine became French territory and Luxembourg looked to create an economic union with Belgium or France. A treaty was negotiated with Belgium in 1921 creating an economic union, including the use of the Belgian franc in Luxembourg (Meade, Liesner, and Wells 1962, 57).

26. Nationals of member states have been EU citizens since the Maastricht Treaty in 1992. In this analysis, we focus on mobility of citizens of member states rather than of third country nationals.

27. With the Brexit vote in June 2016, the United Kingdom decided to withdraw from the European Union, although the exact date of withdrawal is as yet unknown.

28. The 2004 and 2007 accessions did have seven-year transition periods, but economic convergence was insufficient to deter one-way flows. See the discussion below.

29. The agreement between Belgium and Italy is rather infamous as Belgium repaid Italy two hundred kilograms in coal per Italian working in the coal mines. This situation continued until the Marcinelle mine disaster in 1956, in which 136 Italians were killed (about half of the casualties) and Italy began paying more attention to the conditions of its citizens in the Belgian coal mines (Money 1999).

30. Bok (1955, 6) puts the number at 300,000 of 1.4 million workers, or 21.4 percent.

31. According to Bok (1955, 54), "Labor mobility is further hampered by the unwillingness of most European workers to leave their native locality. The effects of this reluctance to move were strikingly apparent in the efforts to transplant some 5,000 French miners who were scheduled to be laid off in the process of modernizing Cevennes mines. As provided in the Treaty, the High Authority and the French government agreed in 1953 to share the expenses of moving and readapting the workers and jobs were arranged for them in Lorraine. Despite this assistance the resistance both of the workers and of the whole community is very stubborn. . . . As a result, by the beginning of 1955 only 258 of the 5,000 had volunteered to leave and even

this meager number could not be transferred immediately because of the housing shortage in Lorraine."

32. Spaak was foreign minister in the Belgian government from 1939 to 1945, prime minister from 1945 to 1950, and foreign minister again from 1954 to 1957. Beyen was foreign minister in the Dutch government from 1952 to 1956. Harryvan (2009) argues that Beyen was important in the EEC negotiations because he championed "horizontal integration" as opposed to the "vertical" or sectoral integration proposed by Spaak and Monnet. However, both ideas included freedom of movement for labor.

33. Our analysis is confirmed by Henderson (1962, 137), who reports, "[Paul-Henri Spaak] pointed out that the experience gained by those who founded the Dutch-Belgian-Luxembourg customs union influenced the Common Market negotiations and this was 'to be seen in the similarities between the setting up of the present European Community and the creation of Benelux.'"

34. Unemployment statistics for Luxembourg are unavailable.

35. We omit Luxembourg from the comparison.

36. All three "southern" accessions were controversial on a number of dimensions, in particular agriculture and fisheries. However, free movement of Spanish and Portuguese workers in the EEC was also a difficult issue to resolve. See Dinan (1999, 104–9).

37. Unemployment statistics for Portugal are unavailable.

38. The 2004 directive also deals with important welfare and social security issues, and provides for the transferability of social and welfare entitlements (Eichenhofer 1997).

39. See various issues of the *Economist* to follow the role of intra-EU migration in the Brexit campaign, such as "Brexit Brief: Immigration. Let Them Not Come" (12 April 2016).

40. This privilege was employed by the white settler population rather than the indigenous populations.

41. This official confirmation was necessary as the United Kingdom modified its definitions of citizenship in the 1971 Immigration Act that affected Australians and New Zealanders. See the Origins of the Trans-Tasman Travel Arrangement section below.

42. New Zealand and Australia did begin talks in the early 1990s about creating a common border for customs and immigration purposes, but they came to a grinding halt over the issue of short-term entry. Australia has a universal visa program for entry, whereas New Zealand admits 80 percent of short-term visitors under visa waiver programs (Bedford, Ho, and Lidgard 2000). With neither side willing to modify its short-term entry program, it seems clear that the countries' divergent views on migration and movement will prevent the establishment of a common border.

43. Both Australia and New Zealand are countries of immigrants; since 1945 alone, 6 million people have migrated to Australia, and approximately 2.5 million people have migrated to New Zealand (Castles and Vasta 2004; Pool and Bedford 1997).

44. Although New Zealand is free to restrict benefits to Australians residing in New Zealand, it has not yet chosen to do so.

45. In 1990, Australia had a population of 17,096,000, while New Zealand's population numbered 3,397,000.

46. This seemingly dramatic shift in immigrant demographics prompted a political backlash in New Zealand. Immigration issues became a hot-button issue in the 1996 election, when the New Zealand First party coined its "Asian Invasion" slogan (Bedford 2003).

47. Until changes in 2005, immigrants needed to reside in New Zealand as permanent residents for only three years before applying for citizenship (New Zealand Department of

Internal Affairs n.d.). New Zealand's naturalization requirements were relatively easy and did not differ dramatically from Australia's, but it was easier to achieve the first step of permanent residency in New Zealand than in Australia (see www.citizenship.gov.au).

48. Ibrahim (2010, 124) provides a note of caution, pointing to "the weak translation of these legislations and policies into effective execution."

49. Statistics are poor. The Gulf Cooperation Council reports 22,000 GCC nationals working in member states in 2004 and 35,000 in 2013 (GCC 2014). All of these statistics indicate a minute portion of the population moving among the GCC states as a result of freedom of movement.

50. The closest is by Willem Maas (2006), but his subject is European citizenship rather than mobility per se. Mobility rights, in his account, are the first grants of citizenship rights.

51. There is a much wider array of theories that have been developed to elucidate various dimensions of integration in Europe. See, for example, Nelson and Stubb (2003) and Wiener and Diez (2004). The three briefly presented here are representative of major paradigms in international relations.

52. Another label for this school is liberal intergovernmentalism.

53. As noted above, our argument could be framed as a neorealist argument along the lines of Krasner (1976), who also notes institutional stickiness.

54. The secondary sources on the origins of freedom of movement in the OECS provide insufficient information for an additional case study.

Chapter 6. Criminality in Migration

1. Another way to distinguish between the issues of undocumented migration discussed in chapter 3 and criminality discussed in this chapter is to draw the distinction between "victimless crime" and crime that creates victims. Alternatively, we can think about the distinction between civil and criminal penalties.

2. There is a third protocol to the Convention Against Transnational Organized Crime: the Protocol Against the Illicit Manufacturing and Trafficking in Firearms, Their Parts, and Components and Ammunition.

3. We deal specifically with issues of migrant rights in chapter 7.

4. This is the concept, discussed in previous chapters, proposed by Thompson and Verdier (2014).

5. In October 1997, in an independent initiative, Italy submitted a draft of the Multilateral Convention to Combat Illegal Migration by Sea to the Legal Committee of the International Maritime Organization (IMO) that also addressed smuggling. The committee shelved the proposal because the delegates thought the IMO was not the appropriate venue to address the issue. From then on, the UN Commission on Crime Prevention and Criminal Justice was the undisputed venue for addressing human smuggling, and the Austrian proposal was the foundation for the discussion (International Council on Human Rights Policy 2010).

6. The states that took longer to sign, ratify, or accede to the Trafficking Protocol were Australia, Cambodia, the Czech Republic, the Dominican Republic, and São Tomé and Príncipe.

7. The states that never signed, ratified, or acceded to the Smuggling Protocol were Afghanistan, Chad, China, Colombia, Gabon, Jordan, Malaysia, Micronesia, Qatar, Saint Lucia, Singapore, Sudan, the UAE, Vietnam, and Zimbabwe.

8. A United Nations Special Rapporteur was appointed in 2004 to monitor the protocol on trafficking, and that position has been periodically renewed. She may take individual

complaints and may visit countries to examine and report on their state of compliance. She makes annual reports to the United Nations Human Rights Council, although they do not systematically evaluate the state of compliance with the protocol. States are not required to report on their activities, and there are no sanctions associated with failure to comply ("Special Rapporteur" 2014).

9. In 2007, several international agencies interested in trafficking launched UN.GIFT (Global Initiative to Fight Human Trafficking), an interagency information hub to coordinate the activities of ILO, IOM, the Organization for Security and Cooperation in Europe, UNICEF, UNODC, and OHCHR and to promote the participation of civil society and business. It was initially funded by the United Arab Emirates.

10. One of the three actions for implementation is to "promote the celebration of regional meetings between migration authorities, ministries of foreign affairs and other governmental organizations on human rights and NGOs interested in the defense of human rights of migrants." It is not clear how "celebrating meetings" would have any effect on human rights, nor why such celebrations need to be "promoted."

11. These agreements are between Benin and Nigeria, Nigeria and Italy, Mali and Côte d'Ivoire, Greece and Albania, Laos and Thailand, the United Kingdom and the United States, and Cambodia and Vietnam.

12. The agreements were between Turkey and Hungary ("Security Agreement" 2014), Haiti and the Bahamas, and the United States and Mexico (the 2004 US-Mexico Action Plan for Cooperation and Border Security).

13. See TVPA 2000 Section 108 (a) for a description of the minimum standards and Section 110 (d)(1) for a description of the prescribed sanctions.

14. The TVPA includes a separate definition of "sex trafficking," which does not include a force or coercion element and thus includes consensual migrant prostitution in the definition. But the enforcement of the TVPA is limited to "severe forms of trafficking in persons," which must include force, fraud, or coercion (Chuang 2006).

Chapter 7. Migrant Rights

This chapter builds on an earlier analysis; see Money, Lockhart, and Western (2016).

1. This is consistent with the argument made by Martin and Abimourched (2009).

2. See chapter 1, note 9, for the list of "core" human rights conventions.

3. This brief overview is drawn from Castles, de Haas, and Miller (2014).

4. In World War I alone, France lost 1.4 million people, with an additional 1.5 million permanently handicapped (Castles, de Haas, and Miller 2014).

5. The one protection that appears to be more widely adopted by wealthy Western democracies is the right provided in Article 13 of the ICCPR, which requires individual judicial review of expulsion (deportation) decisions. As a result, mass expulsions that were common in the pre–World War II period in wealthy Western states have given way to the "individualization" of deportation. This principle is not widely adhered to in other regions of the world; mass expulsions of migrants are not uncommon in African or Gulf oil states (Castles, de Haas, and Miller 2014).

6. Chetail (2014, 71) ultimately points out that although migrant rights are established in customary international law and in treaty law, there remains the significant problem of actual implementation of these rights: "More generally, international migration law is facing two major difficulties. Its first challenge remains its implementation at the state level. . . . The

other key challenge of international migration law operates at the inter-state level. . . . [States] still have to learn to collaborate on an issue that has been traditionally regarded as a core component of their sovereignty." If states do not implement customary international law and have difficulties in cooperating internationally, it is difficult to place great weight on this dimension of customary international law, by Chetail's own criteria of customary international law (see chapter 2).

7. G77 is a group of developing nations within the United Nations General Assembly originally organized in 1964. The membership has since expanded, although the name of the group has been retained.

8. The consensus is not absolute. See, for example, David FitzGerald (2008), who describes Mexico's attitude toward its emigrants, ranging from deserters of the national project to indifference and to actively promoting emigrant interests. Also see Shain and Barth (2003) on diasporas as possible threats to sending country governments.

9. An example is Article 25(1) of the UN Universal Declaration of Human Rights, which proclaims that "everyone has the right to a standard of living adequate for the health and well-being of himself and of his family, including food, clothing, housing and medical care and necessary social services, and the right to security in the event of unemployment, sickness, disability, widowhood, old age, or other lack of livelihood in circumstances beyond his control."

10. Most European countries had branches of the International Association for Labor Legislation, as did the United States and Canada (Delevigne 1934).

11. See below for the original wording (Phelan 1934, 187).

12. We employ B. R. Mitchell's *International Historical Statistics* (2003) to confirm the position of sending and receiving states.

13. Sending countries and (votes): United Kingdom (2), Japan (2), Italy (2), Belgium (2), Czechoslovakia (1), Poland (1). Receiving countries and (votes): United States (2), France (2), Cuba (1). Sending countries had ten votes; receiving countries had five votes.

14. Sadly, there is no record of delegation votes on these principles (Phelan 1934).

15. These are as follows: "10. The principle of freedom of migration subject to the consent of the Governments and trade unions of the countries directly concerned. . . . 18. The principle that any State shall have the right to send special officials to assist in any way and to protect its own emigrant workpeople, and that any State to which they have migrated shall be obliged to admit such officials and to assist them in the performance of their duties. 19. The principle that reciprocity of action should be established between voluntary organisations recognized by their Government for the purpose of assistance and protection of workpeople."

16. Our interpretation differs from that of Böhning (as quoted in Rodgers et al. 2009, 75). But see Phelan (1934, 195).

17. In contrast to Convention 97, this convention allowed/required reciprocity on the treatment of foreigners.

18. The classification is close but may be inexact. Receiving states in 1949 include Argentina, Australia, Bolivia, Brazil, Canada, Chile, Colombia, Costa Rica, Cuba, Dominican Republic, Ecuador, El Salvador, Guatemala, Haiti, Honduras, Liberia, Mexico, New Zealand, Nicaragua, Panama, Paraguay, Peru, South Africa, the Soviet Union, the United States, Uruguay, and Venezuela. All other states are considered sending states in 1949. Data, where available, are taken from Mitchell (2003).

19. The ILO continued to function during the war, as it was based in Switzerland, a neutral country.

20. Annex I deals with recruitment by private agencies; Annex II covers government-

sponsored arrangements for group transfers; and Annex III provides for exemption from customs duties on workers' possessions.

21. Böhning (n.d., 15) notes that the United Kingdom declared Convention 97 to be applicable to its colonial territory of Hong Kong.

22. Recall that joining the UN provides automatic membership in the ILO unless the state actively opts out of membership (ILO 2009). As of 2016, ILO membership numbers 187.

23. Some of the constructivist literature emphasizes a "catalyzing event" as an important determinant of the rise of a particular dimension of human rights on the international agenda. While it is probably true that, in retrospect, researchers can point to an important event that received significant publicity shortly prior to mobilization efforts for human rights, there are many "catalyzing events" that do not generate mobilization.

24. See Böhning (n.d., 21) for a detailed analysis of government votes.

25. Böhning (1988, 134) does make the point that ILO standards apply to workers generally and therefore also to migrant workers, irrespective of the fact that the general standards have been complemented by specific standards that protect only migrant workers. If migrant workers are viewed as workers, the ILO conventions provide standards for their treatment without having separate migration conventions.

26. But see ILO (1999) for the periodic follow-up on migrant rights

27. There is a large secondary literature on various aspects of this convention. Our discussion draws on Böhning (1988, 1991, n.d.), Cholewinski (1997), Cholewinski, de Guchteneire, and Pécoud (2009), Edelenbos (2009), Hasenau (1988, 1991), Hune (1985), Lonnroth (1991), Mattila (2000), Nafziger and Bartel (1991), Niessen and Taran (1991), and Taran (2000).

28. OPEC was initially created in 1960; however, its ability to systematically affect the global price of oil did not take hold until the early 1970s. When the demand for oil began to outstrip supply, the OPEC cartel's power increased.

29. The issue is not clear-cut though; because of problems of ratification of migration conventions in the ILO, the 1949 treaty provided for three annexes that can be excluded by states during the ratification process. And, as noted above, the 1975 convention has two parts that can be ratified separately.

30. These countries included Greece, Italy, Portugal, and Spain and Finland, Norway, and Sweden. At the time, the Northern Mediterranean countries were still known as countries of emigration, although the demographics began to change during the 1980s so, ultimately, these countries became net countries of immigration by the time the agreement was finally concluded. According to Lonnroth (1991), the interests of this group were to make the document as useful as possible, once the process could not be stopped. Interestingly, Lonnroth also points out that these states had an "interest in making international legal system function effectively" and that the Convention could serve as an "umbrella for bilateral and regional agreements."

31. See Edelenbos (2009) for an overview of the operational components of the convention.

32. See our concluding chapter that includes the most recent multilateral negotiations stemming from the New York Declaration for Refugees and Migrants that initiated negotiations on the Global Compact for Safe, Orderly and Regular Migration.

33. We thank Tom Wong for sharing his analysis of the convention ratification with us. We employ a different model specification and include different variables, so our analysis differs from his in a number of areas.

34. A criticism of ICRG is that the coding rules are not transparent.

35. Criticisms of these data include that it is difficult to determine how the indices were created and that the data do not cover a significant amount of time.

36. The problem with this indicator is that we are largely relying on the correlation of this variable with other variables.

37. See Martin (2015) for a recent overview of these developments.

38. We do not claim that global forums are ineffective in promoting development, only that global forums are ineffective in promoting migrant rights.

39. Most of the evidence in this section of the report comes from Ducasse-Rogier (2001), who has gathered information about the IOM from its archives. This remains the only systematic history of the organization to date.

40. See literature on bureaucratic interests, including Carpenter (2001) and Barnett and Finnemore (1999).

41. This is not an unlimited right of residence. Citizens of other member states must be self-supporting and have access to health insurance.

42. The EU has adopted directives on family reunification, on long-term resident status, on students, and on researchers. So the picture for third country nationals is mixed rather than a complete failure to protect migrant rights at the EU level.

43. The Spanish/Philippines agreement has a press announcement attached, indicating that Filipino workers are treated equally to Spanish workers under Spanish law, but this was not part of the MOU itself. Moreover, the announcement was for the Spanish domestic audience, to reassure Spanish workers that Filipino workers would not undercut domestic wages or working conditions.

44. The Cholewinski, de Guchteneire, and Pécoud volume (2009, chap. 1) does examine the barriers to ratification of the ICRMW and cites "low awareness and misperceptions," "lack of capacity and resources," and "legal and political obstacles."

45. The literature is not fully captured by the cited authors. In particular, the rationalist school includes important contributions by, among others, Hathaway (2002, 2007) and Hafner-Burton and coauthors (Hafner-Burton and Tsutsui 2005; Hafner-Burton and Ron 2009). For a recent overview of the literature on human rights, see Hafner-Burton (2012).

46. Simmons and Danner (2010, 235), citing Bradley and Kelley (2008, 19), also note that "sovereignty costs are higher for subjects that have traditionally been regulated by the state, such as criminal law and punishment." Migration has also been traditionally regulated by the state and hence has high sovereignty costs.

47. Recall that our hypotheses are different for the pre–World War II period because of distinctive migration patterns and distributions of power.

Chapter 8. Theoretical and Policy Lessons

1. APEC is the Asia-Pacific Economic Cooperation. It was established in 1989 to promote greater economic interdependence among the twenty-one member states. They "work towards the realization of free and open trade and investment in the Asia-Pacific" (APEC n.d.).

2. See Okello (2014) for a brief history of the refugee regime's development in Africa and the subsequent 1969 Organisation of African Unity Convention on Refugees.

3. See Keohane (1984), Oye (1985), and Fearon (1998), among many others.

REFERENCES

Achermann, Alberto, and Mario Gattiker. 1995. "Safe Third Countries: European Developments." *International Journal of Refugee Law* 7 (1): 19–38.

Acosta, Diego. 2016. "Free Movement in South America: The Emergence of an Alternative Model?" Migration Policy Institute. http://www.migrationpolicy.org/article/free-movement-south-america-emergence-alternative-model.

Acosta Arcarazo, Diego, and Luisa Feline Freier. 2015. "Turning the Immigration Policy Paradox Upside Down? Populist Liberalism and Discursive Gaps in South America." *International Migration Review* 49 (3): 659–96.

Acosta Arcarazo, Diego, and Andrew Geddes. 2014. "Transnational Diffusion or Different Models? Regional Approaches to Migration Governance in the European Union and Mercosur." *European Journal of Migration and Law* 16:19–44.

Adamson, Fiona. 2006. "Crossing Borders: International Migration and National Security." *International Security* 31 (1): 165–99.

Adepoju, Aderanti, Femke van Noorloos, and Annelies Zoomers. 2010. "Europe's Migration Agreements with Migrant-Sending Countries in the Global South: A Critical Review." *International Migration* 48 (3): 42–75.

African Union. 2006. "The Migration Policy Framework for Africa." Addis Ababa: African Union.

Agencia EFE. 2014. "Spain Urges International Cooperation on Immigration." 14 February. http://latino.foxnews.com/latino/news/2014/02/14/spain-urges-international-cooperation-on-immigration/.

Alderson, Arthur S., and François Nielsen. 1999. "Income Inequality, Development, and Dependence: A Reconsideration." *American Sociological Review* 64 (4): 606–31.

al-Muqdad, Omar. 2015. "The Journey to Europe: One Syrian Refugee's Story." *New Arab*, 18 March. https://www.alaraby.co.uk/english/features/2015/3/18/the-journey-to-europe-one-syrian-refugees-story.

"Amendement de l'arrangement entre le gouvernement de la République du Burundi, le gouvernement de la République Démocratique de Congo et le gouvernement de la République du Rwanda à la libre circulation de leurs ressortissants au sein de la CEPGL, signé à Bujumbura le 7 décembre 1980." 1980. Nairobi: IOM Regional Office.

Amnesty International. 2014. "The Human Cost of Fortress Europe: Human Rights Violations Against Migrants and Refugees at Europe's Borders." London: Amnesty International. www.amnesty.eu/content/assets/Reports/EUR_050012014_Fortress_Europe_complete_web_EN.pdf.

Andrijasevic, Rutvica, and William Walters. 2010. "The International Organization for Migration and the International Government of Borders." *Environment and Planning D: Society and Space* 28:977–99.

"Anwebeabkommen (Recruitment Agreements)." n.d. Migration and Integration, Goethe Institute. www.goethe.de/lhr/prj/daz/glo/gla/en8496073.htm.

APEC (Asia-Pacific Economic Cooperation). n.d. "Scope of Work." http://www.apec.org.

Aronowitz, Alexis. 2001. "Smuggling and Trafficking in Human Beings: The Phenomenon, the Markets That Drive It, and the Organizations That Promote It." *European Journal on Criminal Policy and Research* 9 (2): 163–95.

Ashutosh, Ishan, and Alison Mountz. 2011. "Migration Management for the Benefit of Whom? Interrogating the Work of the International Organization for Migration." *Citizenship Studies* 15 (1): 21–38.

Australia Department of Immigration and Citizenship. 2005. "Population Flows: Immigration Aspects 2004–2005 Edition." Canberra: Department of Immigration and Citizenship. http://www.immi.gov.au/media/publications/statistics/popflows2004-5/index.htm.

Axelrod, Robert. 1985. *The Evolution of Cooperation.* New York: Basic Books.

Babar, Zahra R. 2011. "Free Mobility within the Gulf Cooperation Council." Doha, Qatar: Center for International and Regional Studies, Georgetown University School of Foreign Service in Qatar.

Bacalla, Tess. 2012a. "ASEAN Locks Horns on Migrant Workers' Rights." *Reporting ASEAN.* http://www.aseannews.net/asean-locks-horns-on-migrant-workers-rights/.

———. 2012b. "Intra-ASEAN Labor Migration: It Ain't All Bad." http://verafiles.org/intra -asean-labor-migration-it-aint-all-bad/.

Baquero-Herrera, Mauricio. 2005. "Open Regionalism in Latin America: An Appraisal." *Law and Business Review of the Americas* 11 (2): 139–83.

Barnett, Michael N., and Martha Finnemore. 1999. "The Politics, Power, and Pathologies of International Organizations." *International Organization* 53 (4): 699–732.

BBC. 2008. "Brasil Tem 600 Mill Imigrantes Ilegais, Diz Entidade." *Globo.com*, 27 March. http://g1.globo.com/Noticias/Brasil/0,,MUL365307-5598,00.html.

Beato, Andrew M. 1994. "Newly Independent and Separating States' Succession to Treaties." *American University International Law Review* 9 (2): 525–58.

Bedford, Richard. 2003. "New Zealand: The Politicization of Immigration." *Migration Information Source.* http://www.migrationpolicy.org/article/new-zealand-politicization-immigration.

Bedford, Richard, Elsie Ho, and Jacqueline Lidgard. 2000. "International Migration in New Zealand: Context, Components, and Policy Issues." Population Studies Centre Discussion Paper 37, University of Waikato.

Beine, Michel, Frédéric Docquier, and Hillel Rapoport. 2008. "Brain Drain and Human Capital Formation in Developing Countries: Winners and Losers." *Economic Journal* 118 (528): 631–52.

Bennett, William J., and Charles W. Colson. 2000. "The Clintons Shrug at Sex Trafficking." *Wall Street Journal*, 10 January.

Bennhold, Katrin. 2015. "Migrants in Germany Fleeing Poverty Find Only a Ticket Home." *New York Times*, 28 September. http://www.nytimes.com/2015/09/29/world/europe /germany-migrants-refugees.html.

Benvenisti, Eyal. 2006. "'Coalitions of the Willing' and the Evolution of Informal International Law." Tel Aviv University Law Faculty Papers 31, Tel Aviv University.

Betts, Alexander. 2006. "Towards a Mediterranean Solution? Implications for the Region of Origin." *International Journal of Refugee Law* 18 (3–4): 652–76.

———, ed. 2011. *Global Migration Governance.* Oxford: Oxford University Press.

———. 2014. *Survival Migration: Failed Governance and the Crisis of Displacement.* Ithaca, NY: Cornell University Press.

Betts, Katherine. 2003. "Immigration Policy under the Howard Government." *Australian Journal of Social Issues* 38 (2): 169–92.

Betz, Hans-Georg, and Stefan Immerfall. 1998. *The New Politics of the Right: Neo-populist Parties and Movements in Established Democracies*. New York: St. Martin's.

Betz, Timm, and Cali Mortenson Ellis. 2009. "Stay at Home Migrants? The Strategic Effects of Readmission Treaties on International Migration." Paper presented at the annual meeting for the American Political Science Association, Toronto, 3–6 September.

Bhatnagar, Pradip, and Chris Manning. 2005. "Regional Arrangements for Mode 4 in the Services Trade: Lessons from the ASEAN Experience." *World Trade Review* 4 (2): 171–99.

Birrell, Bob, and Virginia Rapson. 2001. "New Zealanders in Australia: The End of an Era?" *People and Place* 9 (1): 2–15.

Biswaro, Joram Mukama. 2011. *The Quest for Regional Integration in Africa, Latin America, and Beyond in the Twenty First Century: Experience, Progress and Prospects*. Brasília: Fundação Alexandre de Gusmáo.

Bobeva, Daniela, and Jean-Pierre Garson. 2004. "Overview of Bilateral Agreements and Other Forms of Labour Recruitment." In *Migration for Employment: Bilateral Agreements at a Crossroads*. Paris: OECD.

Böhning, Roger. 1988. "The Protection of Migrant Workers and International Labor Standards." *International Migration* 26 (2): 133–46.

———. 1991. "The ILO and the New UN Convention on Migrant Workers: The Past and Future." *International Migration Review* 25 (4): 698–709.

———. n.d. "A Brief Account of the ILO and Policies on International Migration." Geneva: ILO. http://www.ilo.org/public/english/century/information_resources/download/bohning.pdf.

Bok, Derek Curtis. 1955. *The First Three Years of the Schuman Plan*. Princeton Studies in International Finance 5. Princeton, NJ: International Finances Section, Department of Economics and Sociology, Princeton University.

Bond, Eric W., and Tain-Jy Chen. 1987. "The Welfare Effects of Illegal Immigration." *Journal of International Economics* 23:315–28.

Boswell, Christina. 2011. "Migration Control and Narratives of Steering." *British Journal of Politics and International Relations* (13): 112–25.

Bouteillet-Paquet, Daphné. 2003. "Passing the Buck: A Critical Analysis of the Readmission Policy Implemented by the European Union and Its Member States." *European Journal of Migration and Law* 5:359–77.

———. 2011. "Smuggling of Migrants: A Global Review and Annotated Bibliography of Recent Publications." New York: United Nations Office on Drugs and Crime.

Box-Steffensmeier, Janet M., and Bradford S. Jones. 2004. *Event History Modeling: A Guide for Social Scientists*. New York: Cambridge University Press.

Bruch, Elizabeth. 2004. "Models Wanted: The Search for an Effective Response to Human Trafficking." *Stanford Journal of International Law* 40 (1): 1–46.

Brücker, Herbert, Gil S. Epstein, Barry McCormick, Gilles Saint-Paul, Alessandra Venturini, and Klaus Zimmermann. 2001. "Managing Migration in the European Welfare State." Fondazione Rodolfo Debenedetti. http://www.frdb.org/upload/file/paper1_23jun01.pdf.

Bueno de Mesquita, Bruce, and Alastair Smith. 2012. "Domestic Explanations of International Relations." *Annual Review of Political Science* 15:161–81.

Bueno de Mesquita, Bruce, Alistair Smith, Randolph M. Siverson, and James D. Morrow. 2004. *The Logic of Political Survival*. Cambridge, MA: MIT Press.

Cairns Group. n.d. "Member States." http://cairnsgroup.org/Pages/map/index.aspx.

"Caribbean Migrants Fly 6,000 Miles to Turkey in Bid to Enter Europe Illegally." 2016. *Daily Express*, 17 May. https://www.express.co.uk/news/world/670907/Caribbean-migrants-fly-6-000-MILES-to-Turkey-in-bid-to-enter-Europe-illegally.

CARICOM. 2016. "CARICOM Single Market and Economy (CSME): Overview." http://caricom.org/work-areas/overview/caricom-single-market-economy.

Carpenter, Daniel P. 2001. *The Forging of Bureaucratic Autonomy*. Princeton, NJ: Princeton University Press.

Cassarino, Jean-Pierre. 2007. "Informalizing Readmission Agreements in the EU Neighborhood." *International Spectator: Italian Journal of International Affairs* 42 (2): 179–96.

———. 2010. "Dealing with Unbalanced Reciprocities: Cooperation on Readmission and Implications." In *Unbalanced Reciprocities: Cooperation on Readmission in the Euro-Mediterranean Area*, edited by Jean-Pierre Cassarino. Washington, DC: Middle East Institute. http://www.mei.edu/sites/default/files/publications/ReadmissionWeb.pdf.

———. 2014. "Inventory of Agreements Linked to Readmission." www.jeanpierrecassarino.com/datasets/ra.

Castles, Stephen. 2004. "The Factors That Make and Unmake Migration Policies." *International Migration Review* 38 (3): 852–84.

Castles, Stephen, Hein de Haas, and Mark J. Miller. 2014. *The Age of Migration: International Population Movements in the Modern World*. 5th ed. New York: Guilford.

Castles, Stephen, and Ellie Vasta. 2004. "Australia: New Conflicts and Old Dilemmas." In *Controlling Immigration: A Global Perspective*, 2nd ed., edited by Wayne A. Cornelius, Takeyuki Tsuda, Philip L. Martin, and James F. Hollifield, 141–73. Palo Alto, CA: Stanford University Press.

CCPCJ (Commission on Crime Prevention and Criminal Justice). 1997. "Report of the Secretary General: Measures to Prevent Trafficking in Children." Doc. E/CN.15/1997/12.

"Cémac: La Libre Circulation des personnes de A à Z." 2013. *Le Gabon Émergent*, 13 November. http://www.gabonemergent.org/2013/11/c%C3%A9mac-la-libre-circulation-des-personnes-de-a-%C3%A0-z-o.html.

CEPGL. 1976. Convention Establishing the Economic Community of the Great Lakes Countries, 20 September, U.N.T.S. 1092 (16748). https://treaties.un.org/Pages/showDetails.aspx?objid=08000002800f81f4&clang=_en.

"CEPGL (Economic Community of the Great Lakes Region)." 2014. http://en.reingex.com/CEPGL-Africa.html.

Cerna, Lucie. 2009. "The Varieties of High-Skilled Immigration Policies: Coalitions and Policy Outputs in Advanced Industrial Countries." *Journal of European Public Policy* 16 (1): 144–61.

Cernadas, Pablo Cerianai. 2013. "Migration, Citizenship, and Free Movement in South America: A Rights-Based Analysis of Regional Initiatives." Paper presented at the UNRISD Conference, Geneva.

CES (Conseil Économique et Social). 1964. *Problèmes posés par l'immigration des travailleurs africains in France*. No. 15. Paris: Journal Officiel de la République Française.

———. 1969. *Le problème des travailleurs étrangers*. No. 7. Paris: Journal Officiel de la République Française.

Chanda, Rupa. 2002. "GATS and Its Implications for Developing Countries: Key Issues and Concerns." DESA Discussion Paper 25, United Nations Economic and Social Affairs.

Charter of the Gulf Cooperation Council. 1981. https://www.files.ethz.ch/isn/125347/1426_GCC.pdf.

Checkel, Jeffrey T. 2001. "Social Construction and European Integration." In *The Social Con-

struction of Europe, edited by Thomas Christiansen, Knud Erik Jörgensen, and Antje Wiener, 50–64. London: Sage.

Chetail, Vincent. 2014. "The Transnational Movement of Persons under General International Law: Mapping the Customary Law Foundations of International Migration Law." In *Research Handbook on International Law and Migration*, edited by Vincent Chetail and Céline Bauloz, 1–72. Cheltenham: Edward Elgar Publishing.

Chick, Kristen. 2015. "Thousands Flee Economic Despair in Kosovo for EU Countries, Welcome or Not." *Los Angeles Times*, 15 February. http://www.latimes.com/world/europe/la-fg-kosovo-refugees-20150215-story.html.

Choi, Changkyu. 2006. "Does Foreign Direct Investment Affect Domestic Income Inequality?" *Applied Economic Letters* 12 (12): 811–14.

Cholewinski, Ryszard. 1997. *Migrant Workers in International Human Rights Law: Their Protection in Countries of Employment.* Oxford: Clarendon.

Cholewinski, Ryszard, Paul de Guchteneire, and Antoine Pécoud, eds. 2009. *Migration and Human Rights: The United Nations Convention on Migrant Workers' Rights.* Cambridge: Cambridge University Press.

Chuang, Janie. 2006. "The United States as Global Sheriff: Using Unilateral Sanctions to Combat Human Trafficking." *Michigan Journal of International Law* 27 (2): 437–94.

Cinel, Dino. 1991. *The National Integration of Italian Return Migration: 1870–1929.* Cambridge: Cambridge University Press.

Coase, Ronald. 1960. "The Problem of Social Cost." *Journal of Law and Economics* 3:1–44.

Coleman, Nils. 2009. *European Readmission Policy.* Boston: Martinus Nijhoff.

Collins, Simon. 2006. "Why Settlers Just Won't Settle Down." *New Zealand Herald*, 23 March. http://www.nzherald.co.nz/nz/news/article.cfm?c_id=1&objectid=10373943.

Collinson, Sarah. 1996. "'Safe Third Countries' and 'Readmission': The Development of an Asylum 'Buffer Zone' in Europe." *Transactions of the Institute of British Geographers* 21 (1): 76–90.

COMESA (Common Market for Eastern and Southern Africa). 2016. "Zambia, Zimbabwe Takes Lead in Moving COMESA Free Movement Agenda Forward." www.comesa.int.

Cometti, Elizabeth. 1958. "Trends in Italian Emigration." *Western Political Quarterly* 11 (4): 820–34.

Constant, Amelie F., and Bienvenue N. Tien. 2011. *Germany's Immigration Policy and Labor Shortages.* EZA Research Report 41. http://www.iza.org/en/webcontent/publications/reports/report_pdfs/iza_report_41.pdf.

Cornia, Giovanni Andrea. 2011. "Economic Integration, Inequality, and Growth: Latin America versus the European Economies in Transition." DESA Working Paper 101.

Cronjé, J. B. 2013. "An Assessment of Labour Mobility in SADC, COMESA and EAC and Prospects for the Tripartite FTA." Tralac. https://www.tralac.org/discussions/article/5339-an-assessment-of-labour-mobility-in-sadc-comesa-and-eac-and-prospects-for-the-tripartite-fta.html.

———. 2014. "The Admission of Foreign Legal Practitioners in South Africa: A GATS Perspective." In *Monitoring Regional Integration in Southern Africa: Yearbook 2013*, edited by André du Pisani, 78–104. Stellenbosch, South Africa: Trade Law Center.

"Cuban Migrants: The Last Wave." 2016. *Economist*, 14 January.

Cunningham, Erin. 2016. "Europe Wants to Deport Afghan Migrants, but Kabul Is Reluctant to Accept Them." *Washington Post*, 19 March. https://www.washingtonpost.com/world/asia_pacific/europe-wants-to-deport-afghan-migrants-but-kabul-is-reluctant-to-accept-them/2016/03/17/8b2d9e6a-e54e-11e5-a9ce-681055c7a05f_story.html.

Das, Kasturi. 2006. "GATS Negotiations and India: Evolution and State of Play." Centad (Centre for Trade and Development) Working Paper 7.

Daway, Patricia R. P. Salvador. 2010. "Migrant Workers' Rights and Status under International Law: The Asian Experience." *Journal of East Asia and International Law* 2:263–92.

Dawson, Laura Ritchie. 2012. "Labor Mobility and the WTO: The Limits of GATS Mode 4." *International Migration* 51 (1): 1–23.

Deacon, Bob, Philippe De Lombaerde, Maria Cristina Macovei, and Sonya Schröder. 2011. "Globalization and the Emerging Regional Governance of Labor Rights." *International Journal of Manpower* 32 (3): 334–65.

Declaración Conjunta Tuxtla II. 1996. Signed at the Reunión de Jefes de Estados y de Gobierno de Centroamérica y México Tuxtla II, San Jose, Costa Rica, on 16 February. http://www.sica.int/busqueda/busqueda_archivo.aspx?Archivo=decl_1097_1_27052005.pdf.

De Giorgi, Giacomo, and Michelle Pellizzari. 2006. "Welfare Migration in Europe and the Cost of a Harmonised Social Assistance." Institute for the Study of Labor Discussion Paper 2094. http://repec.iza.org/dp2094.pdf.

de Haas, Hein. 2008. "Migration and Development. A Theoretical Perspective." Working Paper 9, International Migration Institute, Oxford University.

Del Boca, Daniela, and Alessandra Venturini. 2003. "Italian Migration." IZA Discussion Paper 938. http://papers.ssrn.com/sol3/papers.cfm?abstract_id=475021.

Delevigne, Sir Malcolm. 1934. "The Pre-war History of International Labor Legislation." In Shotwell, *Origins of the International Labor Organization*, 19–54.

DeStefano, Anthony. 2007. *The War on Human Trafficking: U.S. Policy Assessed.* New Brunswick, NJ: Rutgers University Press.

Detention Watch Network. 2012. "Expose and Close: Executive Summary." https://www.detentionwatchnetwork.org/pressroom/reports/2012/expose-and-close.

Deutsche Welle. 2014. "Obama Wants Cooperation from Central America over Immigrants." 26 July. http://www.dw.de/obama-wants-cooperation-from-central-america-over-immigrants/a-17810047.

———. 2016. "Gabriel: German Coalition Reaches Deal on New Asylum Laws." 28 January. http://www.dw.com/en/gabriel-german-coalition-reaches-deal-on-new-asylum-laws/a-19010271.

DICE Database. 2006. "Bilateral Labor Agreements, 2004." Munich: Ifo Institute.

Dicken, Peter. 2011. *Global Shift: Mapping the Changing Contours of the World Economy.* New York: Guilford.

Diebold, William, Jr. 1959. *The Schuman Plan: A Study in Economic Cooperation 1950–1959.* New York: Praeger.

Dinan, Desmond. 1999. *Ever Closer Union: An Introduction to European Integration.* 2nd ed. Boulder, CO: Lynne Rienner.

Ditmore, Melissa, and Marjan Wijers. 2003. "The Negotiations on the UN Protocol on Trafficking in Persons." *Nemesis* 4:79–88.

Djajić, Slobodan. 1987. "Illegal Aliens, Unemployment, and Immigration Policy." *Journal of Development Economics* 25:235–49.

Doomernik, Jeroen, and Michael Jandl. 2008. *Modes of Migration Regulation and Control in Europe.* Amsterdam: Amsterdam University Press.

Doomernik, Jeroen, and David Kyle. 2004. "Introduction." *Journal of International Migration and Integration* 5 (3): 265–72.

Doyle, Michael. 2013. "Farmers Want Obama to Back off Immigration Workplace Enforcement." McClatchy Washington Bureau, 5 September. http://www.mcclatchydc.com/2013/09/05/201303/farmers-want-obama-to-back-off.html.

Drake, William J., and Kalypso Nicolaïdis. 1992. "Ideas, Interests, and Institutionalization: Trade in Services and the Uruguay Round." *International Organization* 46 (1): 37–100.

"A Dream of Schengen." 2017. *Economist*, 10–16 June, 49.

Ducasse-Rogier, Marianne. 2001. *The International Organization for Migration 1951–2001.* Geneva: International Organization for Migration.

Duerden, Martin. 2009. "What Are Hazard Ratios?" Hayward Medical Communications. http://www.medicine.ox.ac.uk/bandolier/painres/download/whatis/What_are_haz_ratios.pdf.

EAC (Eastern African Community). 2015. "EAC Employers, Unionists Urge Free Movement of Labor." Trademark East Africa. https://www.trademarkea.com/news/eac-employers-unionists-urge-free-movement-of-labour.

ECCAS (Treaty Establishing the Economic Community of Central African States). 18 October 1983. http://www.wipo.int/wipolex/en/other_treaties/details.jsp?treaty_id=297.

Economic Forum of the Western Mediterranean. 2013. "5 + 5 Dialogue: Chronology of the Main Meetings (2002–2013)." http://westmediterraneanforum.org/wp-content/uploads/2013/09/131017_chronology5+51.pdf.

Edelenbos, Carla. 2009. "Committee on Migrant Workers and Implementation of the ICRMW." In Cholewinski, de Guchteneire, and Pécoud, *Migration and Human Rights*, 100–121.

Eichenhofer, Eberhard. 1997. *The Social Security of Migrants in the European Union of Tomorrow.* Osnabrück: Universitätsversalg.

Elkins, Zachery, A. T. Guzman, and Beth A. Simmons. 2006. "Competing for Capital: The Diffusion of Bilateral Investment Treaties 1960–2000." *International Organization* 60 (4): 811–46.

Ellermann, Antje. 2008. "The Limits of Unilateral Migration Control." *Government and Opposition* 43 (2): 168–89.

———. 2009. *States against Migrants: Deportation in Germany and the United States.* Cambridge: Cambridge University Press.

Epstein, David L., Robert Bates, Jack Goldstone, Ida Kristensen, and Sharyn O'Halloran. 2006. "Democratic Transitions." *American Journal of Political Science* 50 (3): 551–69.

Equality Now. 2014. "Survivor Stories: Real Stories. Real Change. Real Solutions." http://www.equalitynow.org/sites/default/files/Survivor_Stories.pdf.

Erlanger, Steven, and Allison Smale. 2015. "Europe's Halting Response to Migrant Crisis Draws Criticism as Toll Mounts." *New York Times*, 28 August. https://www.nytimes.com/2015/08/29/world/europe/europe-migrant-refugee-crisis.html?_r=0.

European Commission. 2005. "Readmission Agreements." Press Release Database, Memo 05/351 (5 October). http://europa.eu/rapid/press-release_MEMO-05-351_en.htm.

———. 2011. "Communication from the Commission to the European Parliament and the Council: Evaluation of EU Readmission Agreements." Brussels: COM (2011) 0076 final (23 February). http://eur-lex.europa.eu/legal-content/en/ALL/?uri=CELEX%3A52011DC0076.

———. 2012. "Proposal for a Council Decision Concerning the Conclusion of the Agreement between the European Union and the Republic of Turkey on the Readmission of Persons Residing without Authorization." Brussels: COM (2012) 239 final (22 June). http://eur-lex.europa.eu/legal-content/EN/TXT/?qid=1502821503673&uri=CELEX:52012PC0239.

———. 2014. "Statement of Commissioner Malmström on the Entry into Force of the Re-admission Agreement between Turkey and the EU." Press Release Database (1 October). http://europa.eu/rapid/press-release_STATEMENT-14-285_en.htm.

———. 2015. "EU–Turkey Joint Action Plan." Press Release Database (15 October). http://europa.eu/rapid/press-release_MEMO-15-5860_en.htm.

———. 2016. "Factsheet on the EU–Turkey Statement." Press Release Database (19 March). http://europa.eu/rapid/press-release_MEMO-16-963_en.htm.

European Commission, Employment, Social Affairs and Inclusion. 2016. "The Right to Look for a Job." http://ec.europa.eu/social/main.jsp?catId=459&langId=en.

"European Migrant Crisis." 2016. Wikipedia. https://en.wikipedia.org/wiki/European _migrant_crisis.

European Union. 1968. "Regulation (EEC) No 1612/68 of the Council of 15 October 1968 on Freedom of Movement for Workers within the Community." *Official Journal of the European Union* L257:2–12. http://eur-lex.europa.eu/LexUriServ/LexUriServ.do?uri=CELEX :31968R1612:EN:HTML.

———. 1996. "Council Recommendation of 30 November 1994 Concerning a Specimen Bi-lateral Readmission Agreement between a Member State and a Third Country." *Official Journal of the European Union* C274:20–24. http://eur-lex.europa.eu/legal-content/EN /TXT/?uri=CELEX:31996Y0919(07).

———. 2004. Council Directive 2004/83/EC. *Official Journal of the European Union* L304:12–23. http://eur-lex.europa.eu/legal-content/en/TXT/?uri=CELEX:32004L0083.

———. 2009. "The Schengen Area and Cooperation." Accessed 15 August 2017. http://eur-lex .europa.eu/legal-content/EN/TXT/HTML/?uri=LEGISSUM:l33020&from=DA.

———. 2010a. "European Union Citizenship, a Wide Set of Rights and Obligations." http://ec .europa.eu/justice/policies/citizenship/policies_citizenship_intro_en.htm.

———. 2010b. "Right of Union Citizens and Their Family Members to Move and Reside Freely within the Territory of the Member States." http://europa.eu/legislation_summaries /internal_market/living_and_working_in_the_internal_market/l33152_en.htm.

———. 2013. "Agreement between the European Union and the Republic of Turkey on the Readmission of Persons Residing without Authorization." *Official Journal of the European Union* 57 (L134): 3. http://eur-lex.europa.eu/legal-content/EN/TXT/?uri=CELEX :22014A0507(01).

Eurostat. 2016a. Asylum and Managed Migration Database (migr_asydcfsta; migr_asydcfina). http://ec.europa.eu/eurostat/web/asylum-and-managed-migration/data/database.

———. 2016b. "EU Member States Granted Protection to More Than 330,000 Asylum Seekers in 2015." http://ec.europa.eu/eurostat/documents/2995521/7233417/3-20042016-AP-EN .pdf/34c4f5af-eb93-4ecd-984c-577a5271c8c5.

———. 2016c. "First Instance Decisions in the EU-28 by Outcome, Selected Citizenships, 2nd Quarter 2016." http://ec.europa.eu/eurostat/statistics-explained/index.php/File:First _instance_decisions_in_the_EU-28_by_outcome,_selected_citizenships,_2nd_quarter _2016.png.

"Exoplanets: Planets Come in Different Species." 2017. *Economist*, 22 June.

Eyck, F. Gunther. 1954. "Benelux in the Balance." *Political Science Quarterly* 69 (1): 56–91.

Fabi, Randy. 2013. "WTO Overcomes Last Minute Hitch to Reach Its First Global Trade Deal." Reuters, 7 December. http://www.reuters.com/article/2013/12/07/us-trade-wto -idUSBRE9B505220131207.

Fearon, James D. 1998. "Bargaining, Enforcement, and International Cooperation." *International Organization* 52 (2): 269–305.

Finckenauer, James O., and Jennifer Schrock. n.d. "Human Trafficking: A Growing Criminal Market in the US." Washington, DC: National Institute of Justice International Center. https://www.ncjrs.gov/pdffiles1/nij/218462.pdf.

Finnemore, Martha, and Kathryn Sikkink. 1998. "International Norm Dynamics and Political Change." *International Organization* 52:887–912.

Fischer, Peter A., and Thomas Straubhaar. 1995. *Migration and Economic Integration in the Nordic Common Labor Market.* Copenhagen: Nordic Council of Ministers.

FitzGerald, David. 2008. *A Nation of Emigrants: How Mexico Manages Its Migration.* Berkeley: University of California Press.

Fitzpatrick, Joan. 2003. "Trafficking as a Human Rights Violation: The Complex Intersection of Legal Frameworks for Conceptualizing and Combatting Trafficking." *Michigan Journal of International Law* 24 (4): 1143–68.

"14,000 CARICOM Skills Certificates Issued, Says CARICOM Secretary General." 2014. *Kaieteur News,* 11 November. http://www.kaieteurnewsonline.com/2014/11/11/14000-caricom -skills-certificates-issued-says-caricom-secretary-general/.

Fransman, Laurie. 1982. *British Nationality Law and the 1981 Act.* London: Fourmat.

"Free Movement of Persons." 2014. OECS.org.

Freeman, Gary P. 1979. *Immigrant Labor and Racial Conflict in Industrial Societies: The French and British Experience, 1945–1975.* Princeton, NJ: Princeton University Press.

———. 1994. "Can Liberal States Control Unwanted Migration?" *Annals of the American Academy of Political and Social Science* 534:17–30.

Gabriel Pérez, Luis, Connie Núñez Vélez, David Felipe Domínguez, Omar Hernández Hussein, and Santiago Uribe Saenz. 2013. "Enabling Labor Mobility: CAN Decision 545: Andean Labor Migration Instrument." https://www.lexology.com/library/detail.aspx?g =c2ed1fdf-5c52-4507-b568-coecc3do786d.

Gallagher, Anne. 2001. "Human Rights and the New UN Protocols on Trafficking and Migrant Smuggling: A Preliminary Analysis." *Human Rights Quarterly* 23 (4): 975–1004.

Gamlen, Alan, and Katharine Marsh, eds. 2011. *Migration and Global Governance.* Glos, UK: Edward Elgar.

GATS (General Agreement on Trade in Services). 2016. "Sectoral Classification List (W/120)." United Nations Trade Statistics. http://unstats.un.org/unsd/tradekb/Knowledgebase /Sectoral-Classification-List-W120.

Gatsi Tazo, Eric-Adol. 2009. "La Condition juridique des étrangers en zone CEMAC." https:// www.memoireonline.com/11/12/6517/La-condition-juridique-des-etrangers-en-zone -CEMAC-Contribution-au-diagnostic-de-lintegration.html.

Gay, François, and Paul Wagret. 1970. *Le Bénélux.* Paris: Presses Universitaires de France.

Geddes, Andrew, and Christina Boswell. 2011. *Migration and Mobility in the European Union.* New York: Palgrave Macmillan.

Geddes, Barbara. 1991. "How the Cases You Choose Affect the Answers You Get: Selection Bias in Comparative Politics." *Political Analysis* 2:131–50.

Ghosh, Bimal, ed. 2000. *Managing Migration: Time for a New International Regime?* Oxford: Oxford University Press.

Ghosh, Palash. 2012. "India's 'Mexican' Problem: Illegal Immigration from Bangladesh." *International Business Times,* 6 February. http://www.ibtimes.com/indias-mexican-problem -illegal-immigration-bangladesh-213993.

Go, Stella P. 2004. "Fighting for the Rights of Migrant Workers: The Case of the Philippines." In *Migration for Employment: Bilateral Agreements at a Crossroads.* Paris: OECD. http:// www.adbi.org/files/2011.01.18.cpp.sess2.2.go.asian.labor.migration.pdf.

Goldstein, Judith, Miles Kahler, Robert O. Keohane, and Anne-Marie Slaughter. 2000. "Introduction: Legalization and World Politics." *International Organization* 54 (3): 385–89.

Goodliffe, Jay, and Darren G. Hawkins. 2006. "Explaining Commitment: States and the Convention against Torture." *Journal of Politics* 68 (2): 358–71.

Grant, Lawrence, and Ian Martin. 1982. *Immigration Law and Practice.* London: Cobden Trust.

Gratton, Brian, and Emily Merchant. 2013. "Immigration, Repatriation, and Deportation: The Mexican-Origin Population in the United States, 1920–1950." *International Migration Review* 47 (4): 944–75.

Grimwade, Nigel. 2013. "Theory of Economic Integration: A Review." In *The New Palgrave Dictionary of Economics,* edited by Steven N. Durlauf and Lawrence E. Blume. http://www.dictionaryofeconomics.com/article?id=pde2013_E000336.

Guiraudon, Virginie, and Gallya Lahav. 2000. "A Reappraisal of the State Sovereignty Debate: The Case of Migration Control." *Comparative Political Studies* 33 (2): 163–95.

Gulati, Girish J. 2012. "Explaining Support for Anti–Human Trafficking Legislation in the United States Congress." Paper presented at the annual meeting of the American Political Science Association, New Orleans, 30 August–2 September.

Gulf Cooperation Council. 2016. "Starting Point and Goals." Accessed 10 August 2016. www.gcc-sg.org/en-us/AboutGCC/Pages/StartingPointsAndGoals.aspx.

Gulf Cooperation Council, Secretariat General. 2014. "The Process and Achievements." Riyadh, Saudi Arabia: GCC Division of Information Affairs.

Haas, Ernst B. 1958. *The Uniting of Europe: Political, Social, and Economic Forces 1950–1957.* Palo Alto, CA: Stanford University Press.

Hafner-Burton, Emilie M. 2012. "International Regimes for Human Rights." *American Review of Political Science* 15:265–86.

Hafner-Burton, Emilie M., and James Ron. 2009. "Seeing Double: Human Rights Impact through Qualitative and Quantitative Eyes." *World Politics* 6 (2): 360–401.

Hafner-Burton, Emilie M., and Kiyoteru Tsutsui. 2005. "Human Rights in a Globalizing World: The Paradox of Empty Promises." *American Journal of Sociology* 110 (5): 1373–1411.

Haftel, Yoram. 2012. *Regional Economic Institutions and Conflict Mitigation: Design, Implementation, and the Promise of Peace.* Ann Arbor: University of Michigan Press.

Haggard, Stephan. 1990. *Pathways from the Periphery: The Politics of Growth in Newly Industrializing Countries.* Ithaca, NY: Cornell University Press.

Hailbronner, Kay. 1997. "Readmission Agreements and the Obligations on States under Public International Law to Readmit Their Own and Foreign Nationals." *Zeitschrift für ausländisches öffentliches Recht und Völkerrecht* 57:1–49.

Hainmueller, Jens, and Michael J. Hiscox. 2007. "Educated Preferences: Explaining Attitudes toward Immigration in Europe." *International Organization* 61 (2): 399–442.

Hainmueller, Jens, and Daniel J. Hopkins. 2014. "Public Attitudes toward Immigration." *Annual Review of Political Science* 17:225–49.

Hamilton, Bob, and John Whalley. 1984. "Efficiency and Distributional Implications of Legal Restrictions on Labour Mobility." *Journal of Development Economics* 14:61–75.

Hammar, Tomas. 1985. *European Immigration Policy.* Cambridge: Cambridge University Press.

Hansen, Randall, Jobst Koehler, and Jeannette Money, eds. 2011. *Migration, Nation States, and International Cooperation.* New York: Routledge.

Hanson, Gordon, Kenneth F. Scheve, and Matthew J. Slaughter. 2007. "Public Finance and Individual Preferences over Globalization Strategies." *Economics and Politics* 19 (1): 1–33.

Hanson, Gordon H., and Antonio Spilimbergo. 2001. "Political Economy, Sectoral Shocks, and Border Enforcement." *Canadian Journal of Economics* 34 (3): 612–38.

Hargreaves, Steve. 2013. "I Was a Modern-Day Slave in America." *CNN Money*, November 25. http://money.cnn.com/2013/11/21/news/economy/human-trafficking-slave/.

Harryvan, Anjo G. 2009. *In Pursuit of Influence: The Netherlands' European Policy during the Formative Years of the European Union, 1952–1973.* Brussels: P.I.E. Peter Lang.

Hasenau, Michael. 1988. "Setting Norms in the United Nations System: The Draft Convention on the Protection of the Rights of All Migrant Workers and Their Families in Relation to ILO in Standards on Migrant Workers." *International Migration* 26 (2): 133–57.

———. 1991. "ILO Standards on Migrant Workers: The Fundamentals of the UN Convention and Their Genesis." *International Migration Review* 25 (4): 687–97.

Hathaway, James C. 1991. "Reconceiving Refugee Law as Human Rights Protection." *Journal of Refugee Studies* 4 (2): 113–31.

Hathaway, Oona. 2002. "Do Human Rights Treaties Make a Difference?" *Yale Law Journal* 111 (8): 1935–2042.

———. 2007. "Why Do Countries Commit to Human Rights Treaties." *Journal of Conflict Resolution* 51 (4): 588–621.

Hatton, Timothy J. 2007. "Should We Have a WTO for International Migration?" *Economic Policy* 22 (50): 339–83.

Hatton, Timothy J., and Jeffrey G. Williamson. 2003a. "Demographic and Economic Pressure on Emigration out of Africa." *Scandinavian Journal of Economics* 105 (3): 465–86.

———. 2003b. "What Fundamentals Drive World Migration?" Discussion Paper 2003/23, World Institute for Development Economics Research.

Held, David, and Anthony McGrew, eds. 2002. *Governing Globalization: Power, Authority, and Global Governance.* London: Wiley-Blackwell.

Henderson, W. O. 1962. *The Genesis of the Common Market.* Chicago: Quandrangle Books.

Herm, Anne. 2008. "Recent Migration Trends." Eurostat Statistics in Focus 98/2008. Brussels: EU. http://epp.eurostat.ec.europa.eu/portal/page/portal/eurostat/home/.

Hermele, Kenneth. 2015. *The Migration and Development Nexus: Looking for a Triple Win.* Sweden: Forum Syd. www.forumsyd.org/PageFiles/5762/Migrationsrapport.pdf.

Heston, Alan, Robert Summers, and Bettina Aten. 2009. "Penn World Tables Version 6.3." Philadelphia: Center for International Comparisons of Production, Income and Prices, University of Pennsylvania.

Hirschman, Albert O. 1970. *Exit, Voice, and Loyalty: Responses to Decline in Firms, Organizations, and States.* Cambridge, MA: Harvard University Press.

Hoadley, Stephen. 2003. "Immigration Policy: A Steady Convergence." *New Zealand International Review* 28 (1): 17–20.

Hollifield, James. 1992. *Immigrants, Markets, and States: The Political Economy of Postwar Europe.* Cambridge, MA: Harvard University Press.

———. 1994. "Immigration and Republicanism in France: The Hidden Consensus." In *Controlling Immigration: A Global Perspective*, edited by Wayne A. Cornelius, Philip L. Martin, and James F. Hollifield, 143–76. Stanford, CA: Stanford University Press.

———. 2000. "Migration and the 'New' International Order: The Missing Regime." In Ghosh, *Managing Migration, 75–109.*

Horizon Brazil. n.d. "Mercosur Residence Agreement." http://www.horizonvistosbrasil.com .br/en/documentation-foreigners/mercosur-residence-agreement/.

Hufbauer, Gary, and Sherry Stephenson. 2007. "Services Trade: Past Liberalization and Future Challenges." *Journal of International Economic Law* 10 (3): 605–30.

Human Rights Watch. 2003. "The International Organization for Migration (IOM) and Human Rights Protection in the Field: Current Concerns." https://www.hrw.org/legacy /backgrounder/migrants/iom-submission-1103.pdf.

———. 2010. "Human Rights Watch Work on Abuses against Migrants in 2010." http://www .hrw.org/print/reports/2010/12/12/rights-line.

———. 2015. "World Report: Events of 2014." https://www.hrw.org/world-report/2015.

Humphreys, David. 2001. "Forest Negotiations at the United Nations: Explaining Cooperation and Discord." *Forest Policy and Economics* 3:125–35.

Hune, Shirley. 1985. "Drafting an International Convention on the Protection of the Rights of All Migrant Workers and Their Families." *International Migration Review* 19 (3): 570–615.

Ibrahim, Badr El Din A. 2010. "Intra-national Labour Mobility among the Arab Gulf Co-operation Council States in the Context of the Financial Crisis and the Gulf Monetary Union." In *Intra-regional Labour Mobility in the Arab World*, 117–44. Geneva: International Organization for Migration.

Ibriga, Luc Marius, and Kassem Salam Sourwema. 2014. "Guide de la libre circulation des personnes et des biens en Afrique de l'ouest." Ouagadougou: Laboratoire Citoyennetés.

ICMPD (International Center for Migration Policy Development). 2012. "History." http:// www.icmpd.org/History.1686.0.html.

IGC (Intergovernmental Consultations on Migration, Asylum and Refugees). 2002. "IGC Report on Readmission Agreements." http://www.baliprocess.net/files/ReturnsProject/IGC %20Report%20on%20Readmission%20Agreements%20Jan%202002.pdf.

———. 2006. "IGC Report on Readmission Agreements." Geneva: IGC.

———. 2009. "Overview of the Intergovernmental Consultations on Migration, Asylum and Refugees (IGC)." Presentation at the Global Meeting of Chairs and Secretariats of Regional Consultative Processes on Migration (RCPs), Bangkok, 4–5 June. http://www.iom.int /jahia/webdav/shared/shared/mainsite/microsites/rcps/rcp_bkk/igc_pres_rcp_bkk.pdf.

ILO (International Labor Organization). n.d.-a. "Multilateral, Bilateral Agreements and MOUs on Labor Migration." www.ilo.org/migrant/areas/multlateral-bilatera-agreements /leng—en/index.htm.

———. n.d.-b. "Ratification by Convention." http://www.ilo.org/dyn/normlex/en/f?p=1000 :12001:::NO:::.

———. n.d.-c. "Origins and History." http://www.ilo.org/global/about-the-ilo/history /lang—en/index.htm.

———. 1939. "c66 Migration for Employment Convention (Withdrawn)." http://www.ilo.org /ilolex/cgi-lex/convde.pl?C066.

———. 1949. "c97 Migration for Employment Convention (Revised)." http://www.ilo.org /ilolex/cgi-lex/convde.pl?C097.

———. 1951. *Lasting Peace the I.L.O. Way*. Geneva: ILO.

———. 1975. "C143 Migrant Workers (Supplementary Provisions)." http://www.ilo.org/dyn /normlex/en/f?p=NORMLEXPUB:12100:0::NO::P12100_INSTRUMENT_ID:312288.

———. 1999. "Migrant Workers. Summary of Reports on Conventions Nos. 97 and 143 and Recommendations Nos. 86 and 151." http://www.ilo.org/public/english/standards/relm /ilc/ilc87/r3-1b4.htm.

———. 2004. *ILO Migration Survey 2003: Country Summaries*. Geneva: ILO.

———. 2005. "A Global Alliance against Forced Labour: Global Report on Forced Labour 2005." http://www.ilo.org/global/publications/books/WCMS_081882/lang—en /index.htm.

———. 2009. *The ILO and the Quest for Social Justice, 1919–2009*. Geneva: ILO.

———. 2010. "Unemployment, Total" (Data file). http://www.ilo.org/ilcstat.

———. 2015. "Joint Labor Migration Program for Africa." http://www.ilo.org/addisababa/media-centre/video/WCMS_402365/lang—en/index.htm.

Imson, Manuel. 2013. "Labor Migration in Asia." Geneva: International Labor Organization. http://www.ilo.org/wcmsp5/groups/public/---asia/---ro-bangkok/---ilo-jakarta/documents/presentation/wcms_214655.pdf.

Inglis, Christine. 2004. "Australia's Continuing Transformation." *Migration Information Source.* Accessed 26 October 2014. http://www.migrationpolicy.org/article/australias-continuing-transformation.

Innes, Alexandra. 2015. *Migration, Citizenship, and the Challenge for Security.* New York: Palgrave Macmillan.

International Council on Human Rights Policy. 2010. "Irregular Migration, Migrant Smuggling and Human Rights: Towards Coherence." http://www.ichrp.org/files/reports/56/122_report_en.pdf.

IOM (International Organization for Migration). 2007. "Free Movement of Persons in Regional Integration Processes: Supplemental Materials." Prepared for the International Dialogue on Migration Intersessional Workshop on Free Movement of Persons in Regional Integration Processes in Geneva, 18–19 June. https://www.iom.int/jahia/webdav/site/myjahiasite/shared/shared/mainsite/microsites/IDM/workshops/free_movement_of_persons_18190607/idm2007_handouts.pdf

———. 2011. "Bilateral Labor Agreements in Practice: Issues and Challenges." http://www.academia.edu/2067682/_2011_Bilateral_Labour_Agreements_in_Practice_Issues_and_Challenges.

———. 2016. "IOM Becomes a Related Organization to the UN." 25 July. www.iom.int/news/iom-becomes-related-oranization-un.

IOM/World Bank/WTO. 2004. "Background Paper." Presented at the Trade and Migration Seminar, Geneva, 4–5 October. http://www.iom.int/jahia/webdav/site/myjahiasite/shared/shared/mainsite/microsites/IDM/workshops/Trade_2004_04051004/seminar%20docs/background.pdf.

Jachimowicz, Maia. 2006. "Argentina: A New Era of Migration and Migration Policy." *Migration Information Source.* http://www.migrationinformation.org/USfocus/display.cfm?ID=374.

Jamaica Information Service. 2010. "CARICOM Committed to Free Movement of Labor—PM Skerrit." 5 July. http://jis.gov.jm/caricom-committed-to-free-movement-of-labour-pm-skerrit.

Johnston, G. A. 1970. *The International Labor Organization: Its Work for Social and Economic Progress.* London: Europa Publications.

Joppke, Christian. 1998. "Why Liberal States Accept Unwanted Immigration." *World Politics* 50 (2): 266–93.

Jupp, James. 2002. *From White Australia to Woomera.* New York: Cambridge University Press.

Jurje, Flavia, and Sandra Lavenex. 2015. "ASEAN Economic Community: What Model for Labor Mobility?" Working Paper 2015/02, NCCR Trade Regulation.

Kabamba, Bob. 2003–4. "Frontières en Afrique centrale: Gage de souveraineté." *Fédéralisme Régionale* 4. http://popups.ulg.ac.be/1374-3864/index.php?id=294.

Kapiszewski, Andrzej. 2004. "Arab Labor Migration to the GCC States." In *Arab Migration in the Globalized World.* Geneva: IOM, 115–33.

Karatani, Rieko. 2005. "How History Separated Refugee and Migrant Regimes: In Search of Their Institutional Origins." *International Journal of Refugee Law* 17 (3): 517–41.

Kaur, Amarjit. 2010. "Labor Migration in Southeast Asia: Migration Policies, Labour Exploitation and Regulation." *Journal of the Asia Pacific Economy* 15 (1): 6–19.

Keesing's Report. 1975. *The European Communities: Establishment and Growth*. New York: Charles Scribner's Sons.

Keohane, Robert O. 1984. *After Hegemony: Cooperation and Discord in the World Political Economy*. Princeton, NJ: Princeton University Press.

Khoo, Siew-Ean. 2002. "Immigration Issues in Australia." *Journal of Population Research* Special Edition: 67–78.

Khoudour, David. 2013. "Migration, Inequality, and Development: Why International Cooperation Is Needed." *World Post*, 19 December. https://www.huffingtonpost.com/oecd/migration-inequality-and-_b_4453898.html.

Kindleberger, Charles P. 1967. *Europe's Postwar Growth: The Role of Labor Supply*. Cambridge, MA: Harvard University Press.

Kirişci, Kemal. 2014. "Will the Readmission Agreement Bring the EU and Turkey Together or Pull Them Apart?" Centre for European Policy Studies. https://www.ceps.eu/publications/will-readmission-agreement-bring-eu-and-turkey-together-or-pull-them-apart.

Kitimbo, Adrian. 2014. "Is It Time for Open Borders in Southern Africa?" Johannesburg: Brenthurst Foundation.

Kitschelt, Herbert. 1997. *The Radical Right in Western Europe*. Ann Arbor: University of Michigan Press.

Koehler, Jobst. 2011. "What Government Networks Do in the Field of Migration: An Analysis of Selected Regional Consultative Processes." In Kunz, Lavenex, and Panizzon, *Multilayered Migration Governance*, 67–94.

Koelbl, Susanne. 2015. "The Next Wave: Afghans Flee to Europe in Droves." *Spiegel Online*, 30 October. http://www.spiegel.de/international/world/crisis-in-aghanistan-leads-wave-of-migrants-to-head-to-europe-a-1059919.html.

Koremenos, Barbara, Charles Lipson, and Duncan Snidal. 2001. "The Rational Design of International Institutions." *International Organization* 55 (4): 761–99.

Koslowski, Rey, ed. 2011a. *Global Mobility Regimes*. New York: Palgrave Macmillan.

———. 2011b. "US Immigration Reform: Plenty of Ideas; Little Action." Paper presented at the Center for Migration Studies Conference on US Immigration Reform, New York, 3 March. http://cmsny.org/wp-content/uploads/2016/02/koslowski_-_us_immigration_reform._plenty_of_ideas__little_action.pdf.

Krasner, Stephen D. 1976. "State Power and the Structure of International Trade." *World Politics* 28 (3): 317–47.

Krasny, Jill. 2012. "Every Parent Should Know the Scandalous History of Infant Formula." *Business Insider*, 12 June. http://www.businessinsider.com/nestles-infant-formula-scandal-2012-6/#e-bad-publicity-sparked-a-global-boycott-of-nestl-11.

Kunz, Rahel, Sandra Lavenex, and Marion Panizzon, eds. 2011. *Multilayered Migration Governance: The Promise of Partnership*. London: Routledge.

Laczko, Frank. 2003. "Europe Attracts More Migrants from China." *Migration Information Source*. http://www.migrationinformation.org/Feature/display.cfm?ID=144.

Lake, David A. 2009. "Open Economy Politics: A Critical Review." *Review of International Organizations* 4 (3): 219–44.

Lange, Halvard. 1954. "Scandinavian Co-operation in International Affairs." *International Affairs* 30 (3): 285–93.

Lavenex, Sandra. 1998. "'Passing the Buck': European Union Refugee Policies towards Central and Eastern Europe." *Journal of Refugee Studies* 11 (2): 126–45.

Lavenex, Sandra, and Emek M. Uçarer, eds. 2002. *Migration and the Externalities of European Integration.* Lanham, MD: Lexington Books.

Layton-Henry, Zig. 1992. *The Politics of Immigration.* Oxford: Blackwell.

———. 1994. "Britain: The Would-Be Zero Immigration Country." In *Controlling Immigration: A Global Perspective,* edited by Wayne A. Cornelius, Philip L. Martin. and James F. Hollifield, 273–96. Stanford, CA: Stanford University Press.

Leblang, David. 2010. "Familiarity Breeds Investment: Diaspora Networks and International Investment." *American Political Science Review* 104 (3): 584–600.

Lequin, Yves, ed. 1992. *Histoire des étrangers et de l'immigration en France.* Paris: Larousse.

"Letter from Carlo Sforza to Paolo Emilio Taviani (Rome, 10 June 1950)." 1950. Virtual Knowledge Center on Europe. https://www.cvce.eu/en/obj/letter_from_carlo_sforza_to_paolo _emilio_taviani_rome_10_june_1950-en-88eddd98-6a04-4ed6-afb9-adafa779f0b9.html.

Licht, Amanda A. 2011. "Change Comes with Time: Substantive Interpretation of Nonproportional Hazards in Event History Analysis." *Political Analysis* 19 (2): 227–43.

Lindley, Anna. 2011. "Remittances." In Betts, *Global Migration Governance,* 242–65.

Lipson, Charles. 1991. "Why Are Some International Agreements Informal?" *International Organization* 45 (4): 495–538.

Lloyd, Paulette, and Beth A. Simmons. 2012. "Framing and Transnational Legal Organization: The Case of Human Trafficking." Paper presented at the annual meeting for the International Studies Association, San Diego, 1–4 April.

Lloyd, Paulette, Beth A. Simmons, and Brandon Stewart. 2012. "The Global Diffusion of Law: Transnational Crime and the Case of Human Trafficking." Unpublished manuscript, Indiana University, Department of Sociology.

Lockhart, Sarah P., and Jeannette Money. 2011. "The Trans-Tasman Travel Arrangement." In Hansen, Koehler, and Money, *Migration, Nation States, and International Cooperation,* 44–74.

Lonnroth, Juhani. 1991. "The International Convention on the Rights of All Migrant Workers and Members of Their Families in the Context of International Migration Policies: An Analysis of Ten Years of Negotiation." *International Migration Review* 25 (4): 710–36.

Lowe, Bouteixe Ellsworth. 1918. "International Aspects of the Labor Problem." PhD diss., Columbia University. https://archive.org/details/internationalaso1lowegoog.

Lubbers, Marcel, Mérove Gijsberts, and Peer Scheepers. 2002. "Extreme Right-Wing Voting in Western Europe." *European Journal of Political Research* 41 (3): 345–78.

Maas, Willem. 2003. "Creating European Citizens: The Genesis of European Rights." Paper prepared for the European Union Studies Association Biennial Conference, Nashville, 27–29 March.

———. 2006. *Creating European Citizens.* Lanham, MD: Rowman & Littlefield.

Macdonald, Ian A. 1972. *The New Immigration Law.* London: Butterworths.

———. 1983. *Immigration Law and Practice in the United Kingdom.* London: Butterworths.

Macdonald, Ian A., and Nicholas Blake. 1991. *Immigration Law and Practice in the United Kingdom.* London: Butterworths.

MacKellar, Michael, and Thomas Gill. 1976. "Trans-Tasman Travel." Press release, 20 February.

Maguid, Alicia. 2007. "Migration Policies and Socioeconomic Boundaries in the South American Cone." In *Migration without Borders: Essays on the Free Movement of People,* edited by Antoine Pécoud and Paul de Guchteneire, 259–78. New York: UNESCO.

Manuh, Takyiwaa. 2016. "Intra-African Migration." Paper prepared for the Migration Symposium and Asylum Symposium, Geneva, 10–11 October.

Margheritis, Ana. 2013. "Piecemeal Regional Integration in the Post-neoliberal Era: Negotiating Migration Policies within Mercosur." *Review of International Political Economy* 20 (3): 541–75.

Martin, Ivan. 2011. "Bilateral Labor Agreements in Practice: Issues and Challenges." Geneva: IOM. www.academia.edu/2067682/_2011_Bilateral_Labour_Agreements_in_Practice _Issues_and_Challenges.

Martin, Philip. 2004. "Policy Responses to Unauthorized or Irregular Workers." *Intereconomics* 39 (1): 18–20.

Martin, Susan. 2015. "International Migration and Global Governance." *Global Summitry* 1 (1): 64–83.

Martin, Susan, and Rola Abimourched. 2009. "Migrant Rights: International Law and National Action." *International Migration* 47 (5): 118–36.

Masci, David. 2004. "Human Trafficking and Slavery." *CQ Researcher*, 26 March, 273–96.

Mashayekhi, Mina. n.d. "GATS 2000 Negotiations. Options for Developing Countries." *Third World Network*. http://www.twnside.org.sg/title/mina.htm.

Massey, Douglas. 1987. *Return to Aztlan: The Social Process of International Migration from Western Mexico*. Berkeley: University of California Press.

Massey, Douglas S., and Zai Liang. 1989. "The Long-Term Consequences of a Temporary Worker Program: The US Bracero Experience." *Population Research and Policy Review* 8:199–226.

Mattar, Mohamed. 2013. "Transnational Legal Responses to Illegal Trade in Human Beings." *SAIS Review of International Affairs* 33 (1): 137–59.

Mattila, Heikki S. 2000. "Protection of Migrants' Human Rights: Principles and Practice." *International Migration* 38 (6): 53–71.

Mattoo, Aaditya, and Antonia Carzaniga, eds. 2003. *Moving People to Deliver Services*. Washington, DC: World Bank.

Mayda, Anna Maria. 2006. "Who Is against Immigration: A Cross-Country Investigation of Individual Attitudes towards Immigrants." *Review of Economics and Statistics* 88 (3): 510–30.

McKibben, Heather Elko. 2015. *State Strategies in International Bargaining: Play by the Rules or Change Them?* New York: Cambridge University Press.

McReynolds, MaryAnne. 2008. "The Trafficking Victims Protection Act: Has the Legislation Fallen Short of Its Goals?" *Policy Perspectives* 15:33–56.

Meade, James E., Hans H. Liesner, and Sidney J. Wells. 1962. *Case Studies in European Economic Union: The Mechanics of Integration*. London: Oxford University Press.

Mecham, Michael. 2003. "Mercosur: A Failing Development Project?" *International Affairs* 79 (2): 369–87.

"Meeting of Dutch, Belgian, and Luxembourg Officials Held on 7 June 1950 at the Belgian Ministry of Foreign Affairs with a View to Preparing for the Negotiations on the Creation of an International Coal and Steel Pool." 1950. Virtual Knowledge Center on Europe. https://www.cvce.eu/content/publication/2003/10/30/93f5ef2a-0dfc-46e4-9c45 -1051da6ec167/publishable_en.pdf

Merkl, Peter H., and Leonard Weinberg, eds. 1997. *The Revival of Right-Wing Extremism in the Nineties*. London: Frank Cass.

Messina, Anthony M., and Gallya Lahav. 2005. *The Migration Reader: Exploring Politics and Policies*. Boulder, CO: Lynne Rienner.

Meyer, Angela. 2015. "Preventing Conflict in Central Africa: ECCAS Caught between Ambitions, Challenges, and Reality." Central Africa Report 3, Institute for Security Studies. www.issafrica.org.

Meyers, Eytan. 2004. *International Immigration Policy: A Theoretical and Comparative Analysis*. New York: Palgrave Macmillan.

Migration Policy Institute. 2012. *Migration Information Source*. http://www.migrationpolicy.org/programs/migration-information-source.

Miko, Francis T. 2004. "Trafficking in Women and Children: The US and International Response." 26 March. Washington, DC: Congressional Research Service.

Miller, Mark J., and Philip L. Martin. 1982. *Administering Foreign-Worker Programs: Lessons from Europe*. Lexington, MA: Lexington Books.

Minces, Juliette. 1973. *Les Travailleurs étrangers en France*. Paris: Seuil.

Ministry of Foreign Affairs of Turkey. 2007. "Chair's Summary." Joint Conference of UNODC and the Budapest Process with the Organisation of the Black Sea Economic Cooperation (BSEC) on Trafficking in Human Beings in the Black Sea Region, 9–10 October, Istanbul. https://www.iom.int/jahia/webdav/shared/shared/mainsite/microsites/rcps/budapest-process/2007_WG_Meeting_Joint_Conference_Conclusion_Remarks.pdf.

MIREM (Migration de Retour au Maghreb). 2009. "Robert Schuman Center for Advanced Studies, European University Institute." http://rsc.eui.eu/RDP/research-projects/mirem/.

Mitchell, Brian R. 2003. *International Historical Statistics: Europe 1750–2000*. 5th ed. New York: Palgrave Macmillan.

Moch, Leslie Page. 1995. "Moving European: Historical Migration Practices in Europe." In *Cambridge Survey of World Migration*, edited by Robin Cohen, 126–30. Cambridge: Cambridge University Press.

Money, Jeannette. 1999. *Fences and Neighbors: The Political Geography of Immigration Control*. Ithaca, NY: Cornell University Press.

———. 2010. "Comparative Immigration Policy." In *The International Studies Encyclopedia*, edited by Robert Allen Denemark and Renée Marlin-Bennett. Chichester: Wiley-Blackwell. http://www.oxfordreference.com/view/10.1093/acref/9780191842665.001.0001/acref-9780191842665

Money, Jeannette, and Andrew Geddes. 2011. "Mobility within the European Union." In Hansen, Koehler, and Money, *Migration, Nation States, and International Cooperation*, 31–43.

Money, Jeannette, Sarah Lockhart, and Shaina Western. 2016. "Why Migrant Rights Are Different Than Human Rights." In *Elgar Handbook on Migration and Social Policy*, edited by Gary Freeman and Nikola Mirilovic, 399–418. Cheltenham, UK: Edward Elgar.

Money, Jeannette, and Kristina Victor. 2015. "The 1965 Immigration Act: The Demographic and Political Transformation of Mexicans and Mexican Americans in U.S. Border Communities." In *The Immigration and Nationality Act of 1965: Legislating a New America*, edited by Gabriel J. Chin and Rose Cuison Villazor, 315–47. Cambridge: Cambridge University Press.

Money, Jeannette, and Shaina Western. Forthcoming. "The Fates of Survival Migrants: The Quality of Refuge." In *The Paradox of Human Rights in a Globalizing World*, edited by Heather Smith-Cannoy. Philadelphia: Temple University Press.

Money, Jeannette, and Timothy W. Taylor. 2016. "Voluntary International Migration." In *Oxford Bibliographies in International Relations*, edited by Patrick James. http://www.oxfordbibliographies.com/view/document/obo-9780199743292/obo-9780199743292-0167.xml?rskey=wLERCv&result=1&q=international+voluntary+migration#firstMatch.

Moravcsik, Andrew. 1998. *The Choice for Europe: Social Purpose and State Power*. Ithaca, NY: Cornell University Press.

Morcom, Corin, and Andreas Schloenhardt. 2011. "All about Sex?! The Evolution of Trafficking in Persons in International Law." Human Trafficking Working Group, University of Queensland. http://www.law.uq.edu.au/documents/humantraffic/international-law/Evolution-of-Int-Law-relating-to-Trafficking-in-Persons.pdf.

Morehouse, Christal, and Michael Blomfield. 2011. "Irregular Migration in Europe." Migration Policy Institute. https://www.migrationpolicy.org/pubs/TCMirregularmigration.pdf.

Morris, Tim. 2005. "Speaker's Corner: IOM: Trespassing on Others' Humanitarian Space?" *Forced Migration Review* 22:43.

Mouritzen, Hans. 1995. "The Nordic Model as a Foreign Policy Instrument: Its Rise and Fall." *Journal of Peace Research* 32 (1): 9–21.

Myers, Gordon M., and Yorgos Y. Papageorgiou. 2000. "Immigration Control and the Welfare State." *Journal of Public Economics* 75 (2): 183–207.

Nafziger, James A. R., and Barry C. Bartel. 1991. "The Migrant Workers Convention: Its Place in Human Rights Law." *International Migration Review* 25 (4): 771–99.

Nash, Jay Robert. 1976. *Darkest Hours: A Narrative Encyclopedia of Worldwide Disasters from Ancient Times to the Present.* Lanham, MD: M. Evans.

Nassar, Heba. 2010. "Intra-regional Labour Mobility in the Arab World: An Overview." In *Intra-regional Labour Mobility in the Arab World*, 9–41. Geneva: International Organization for Migration.

Nelson, Brent F., and Alexander Stubb. 2003. *The European Union: Readings on the Theory and Practice of European Integration.* 3rd ed. Boulder, CO: Lynne Rienner.

New Zealand Department of Internal Affairs. n.d. "Requirements for New Zealand Citizenship." Wellington: Department of Internal Affairs. http://www.dia.govt.nz.

New Zealand Department of Labor. 2005. "Migration Trends 2004/2005." Wellington: Department of Labor.

New Zealand Immigration Service. n.d. "Research and Statistics." https://www.immigration.govt.nz/about-us/research-and-statistics.

New Zealand Ministry for Culture and Heritage. 2005. "Immigration Regulation." Wellington: Ministry for Culture and Heritage. http://www.teara.govt.nz.

Ng, Eric C. Y., and John Whalley. 2008. "Visas and Work Permits: Possible Global Negotiating Initiatives." *Review of International Organizations* 3:259–85.

Nielson, Daniel L., and Michael J. Tierney. 2003. "Delegation to International Organizations: Agency Theory and World Bank Environmental Reform." *International Organization* 57 (2): 241–76.

Nielson, Julia, and Daria Taglioni. n.d. "A Quick Guide to the GATS and Mode 4." Paris: OECD, Trade Directorate.

Niessen, Jan, and Patrick A. Taran. 1991. "Using the New Migrant Workers' Rights Convention." *International Migration Review* 25 (4): 859–65.

Noiriel, Gérard. 1988. *Le Creuset français: Histoire de l'immigration, XIXe–XXe siècle.* Paris: Seuil.

OAS (Organization of American States). 1969. *American Convention on Human Rights.* U.N.T.S. 1144 (17955). https://treaties.un.org/pages/showdetails.aspx?objid=0800000280of10e1.

Odell, John S. 2000. *Negotiating the World Economy.* Ithaca, NY: Cornell University Press.

———, ed. 2006. *Negotiating Trade: Developing Countries in the WTO and NAFTA.* Cambridge: Cambridge University Press.

OECD (Organisation for Economic Co-operation and Development). 2004. *Migration for Employment: Bilateral Agreements at a Crossroads.* Paris: OECD.

———. 2011. *OECD Guidelines for Multinational Enterprises.* Paris: OECD.

———. 2015. *International Migration Outlook 2015.* Paris: OECD. http://www.oecd-ilibrary

.org/social-issues-migration-health/international-migration-outlook-2015_migr_outlook -2015-en.

OECS (Organisation of Eastern Caribbean States). 2010. "Treaty of Basseterre (Revised)." http://www.govt.lc/treaty-of-Basseterre.

Ogalo, Victor. 2012. "Achievements and Challenges of Implementation of the EAC Common Market Protocol in Kenya: Case of Free Movement of Labor." http://www.fes-kenya.org /media/activities/EAC Common Market.

OHCHR (Office of the High Commissioner for Human Rights). 2002. "Principles and Guidelines on Human Rights and Human Trafficking." http://www.ohchr.org/Documents /Publications/Traffickingen.pdf.

———. 2011. "Rights of Migrant Workers in Europe." http://europe.ohchr.org/Documents /Publications/Migrant_Workers.pdf.

Okello, J. O. Moses. 2014. "The 1969 OAU Convention and the Continuing Challenge for the African Union." *Forced Migration Review* 48:70–73.

O'Neil, Kevin. 2004. "Labor Export as Government Policy. The Case of the Philippines." Migration Policy Institute. http://www.migrationpolicy.org/article/labor-export-government -policy-case-philippines.

Orchard, Cynthia, and Andrew Miller. 2014. "Protection in Europe for Refugees from Syria." Forced Migration Policy Briefing 10, Refugee Studies Centre. https://www.rsc.ox.ac.uk /files/publications/policy-briefing-series/pb10-protection-europe-refugees-syria-2014.pdf.

Ostrand, Nicole. 2015. "The Syrian Refugee Crisis: A Comparison of Responses by Germany, Sweden, the United Kingdom, and the United States." *Journal on Migration and Human Security* 3 (3): 255–79.

Ostry, Sylvia. 2000. "The Uruguay Round North-South Grand Bargain: Implications for Future Negotiations." The Political Economics of International Trade Law Working Paper, University of Minnesota.

Ott, Stephanie. 2015. "Baffling Kosovo Mass Exodus Exposes Domestic Hardships." *Al Jazeera,* 13 March. http://www.aljazeera.com/indepth/features/2015/03/baffling-kosovo-mass -exodus-exposes-domestic-hardships-150308120251939.html.

Outshoorn, Joyce, ed. 2004. *The Politics of Prostitution: Women's Movements, Democratic States, and the Globalisation of Sex Commerce.* Cambridge: Cambridge University Press.

Oye, Kenneth. 1985. "Explaining Cooperation under Anarchy: Hypotheses and Strategies." *World Politics* 38 (1): 1–24.

Padelford, Norman J. 1957. "Regional Cooperation in Scandinavia." *International Organization* 11 (4): 597–614.

Panizzon, Marion. 2012. "Readmission Agreements of EU Member States: A Case for EU Subsidiarity or Dualism?" *Refugee Survey Quarterly* 31 (4): 101–23.

Paoletti, Emanuela. 2011. "Power Relations and International Migration: The Case of Italy and Libya." *Political Studies* 59:269–89.

Paul, Kathleen. 1997. *Whitewashing Britain: Race and Citizenship in the Postwar Era.* Ithaca, NY: Cornell University Press.

Pécoud, Antoine, and Paul de Guchteneire, eds. 2007. *Migration without Borders: Essays on the Free Movement of People.* New York: Berghahn Books.

Peters, Margaret E. 2013. "Immigration, Delegation, and International Law." Working paper, Department of Political Science, University of California, Los Angeles.

Pew Research Center. 2013a. "Immigration: Key Data Points from Pew Research." Accessed 3 November 2014. http://www.pewresearch.org/key-data-points/immigration-tip-sheet -on-u-s-public-opinion/.

———. 2013b. "Population Decline of Unauthorized Immigrants Stalls, May Have Reversed." http://www.pewhispanic.org/2013/09/23/population-decline-of-unauthorized-immigrants-stalls-may-have-reversed/.

Phelan, Edward J. 1934. "The Commission on International Labor Legislation." In Shotwell, *Origins of the International Labor Organization*, 127–98.

Philippines Commission on Filipinos Overseas. 2012. "Stock Estimates of Overseas Filipinos 2012." www.cfo.gov.ph/downleads/statistics.html.

Philippines Overseas Employment Administration. n.d. "Bilateral Labor Agreements." www.poea.gov.ph/lmi_kiosk/labor_agreements.htm.

Piore, Michael J. 1979. *Birds of Passage: Migrant Labor and Industrial Societies*. Cambridge: Cambridge University Press.

Piper, Nicola. 2004. "Rights of Foreign Workers and the Politics of Migration in South-East and East Asia." *International Migration* 43 (5): 71–97.

Plender, Richard. 2007. *Basic Documents on International Migration Law*. Leiden: Martinus Nijhoff.

Pollack, Mark A. 1997. "Delegation, Agency, and Agenda Setting in the European Community." *International Organization* 51 (1): 99–134.

Pool, Ian, and Richard Bedford. 1997. "Population Change and the Role of Immigration." In *Proceedings of the Population Conference, 12–14 November*, 62–117. Wellington: New Zealand Immigration Service.

Putnam, Robert D. 1988. "Diplomacy and Domestic Politics. The Logic of Two-Level Games." *International Organization* 42 (3): 427–60.

"Qatar World Cup Migrant Workers Dead." 2013. *Guardian*, 26 September. Accessed 13 June 2016. http://www.theguardian.com/global-development/2013/sep/26/qatar-world-cup-migrant-workers-dead.

Rahman, Md Mizanur. 2012. "Bangladeshi Labour Migration to the Gulf States: Patterns of Recruitment and Processes." *Canadian Journal of Development Studies/Revue canadienne d'études du développement* 33 (2): 214–30.

Randazzo, Marianna. 2014. "No Dogs, No Italians: Remembering the Marcinelle Tragedy." *L'ideamagazine*. www.lideamagazine.com/dogs-italian/.

Ratha, Dilip. 2005. *Remittances: Development Impact and Future Prospects*. Washington, DC: World Bank.

RCM (Regional Conference on Migration). 2009a. "Historical Plan of Action." http://www.rcmvs.org/plan_accion.htm.

———. 2009b. "Plan of Action." http://www.rcmvs.org/plan_accion.htm.

"Report of the Heads of Delegation to the Minsters of Foreign Affairs." 1956. Brussels: Secretariat.

"Report on the Global Commission on International Migration." 2005. *Population and Development Review* 31 (4): 787–98.

Risse, Thomas, Stephen C. Ropp, and Kathryn Sikkink, eds. 1999. *The Power of Human Rights: International Norms and Domestic Change*. New York: Cambridge University Press.

———, eds. 2013. *The Persistent Power of Human Rights: From Commitment to Compliance*. New York: Cambridge University Press.

Robertson, W. 1956. "Benelux and Problems of Economic Integration." *Oxford Economic Papers New Series* 8 (1): 35–50.

Rocca, Francis X. 2013. "As Migration Rises Worldwide, Pope Calls for International Cooperation." *Catholic News Service*, 24 September. http://www.catholicnews.com/data/stories/cns/1304029.htm.

Rodgers, Gerry, Eddy Lee, Lee Swepston, and Jasmien Van Daele. 2009. *The International Labor Organization and the Quest for Social Justice, 1919–2009*. Ithaca, NY: ILR Press.

Rodrik, Dani. 2002. "Feasible Globalizations." Working Paper 9129, National Bureau of Economic Research. http://www.nber.org/papers/w9129.

Roig, Annabelle, and Thomas Huddleston. 2007. "EC Readmission Agreements: A Reevaluation of the Political Impasse." *European Journal of Migration and Law* 9:363–87.

Rubia, Kathleen. 2011. "The Inter-regional Mobility Aspects of the Proposed Tripartite Free Trade Area." In *Monitoring Regional Integration in Southern Africa: Yearbook 2010*, 46–59. Stellenbosch, South Africa: Trade Law Center for Southern Africa, Konrad-Adenauer Stiftung.

Rudolph, Christopher. 2003. "Security and the Political Economy of International Migration." *American Political Science Review* 97 (4): 603–20.

Ruhs, Martin. 2012. "The Human Rights of Migrant Workers: Why Do So Few Countries Care?" *American Behavioral Scientist* 56:1277–93.

———. 2013. *The Price of Rights: Regulating International Labor Migration*. Princeton, NJ: Princeton University Press.

Ruhs, Martin, and Ha-Joon Chang. 2004. "The Ethics of Labor Immigration Policy." *International Organization* 58 (1): 69–102.

Saadi, Redouane. 2005. "Migration Dynamics and Dialogue in the Western Mediterranean." In *World Migration Report 2005*, 75–81. Geneva: International Organization for Migration.

Sáez, Sebastián, ed. 2013. *Let Workers Move: Using Bilateral Labor Agreements to Increase Trade in Services*. Washington, DC: World Bank. https://openknowledge.worldbank.org/handle/10986/15800.

Salter, Mark B. 2003. *Rights of Passage: The Passport in International Relations*. Boulder, CO: Lynne Rienner.

Salvesen, Kaare. 1956. "Cooperation in Social Affairs between the Northern Countries of Europe." *International Labour Review* 73:334–57.

Sampson, Gary P. 2003. "The Closer Economic Relations Agreement between Australia and New Zealand." In *Regionalism, Multilateralism, and Economic Integration*, edited by Gary P. Sampson and Stephen Woolcock, 202–23. New York: United Nations University.

Sandholtz, Wayne, and Alec Stone Sweet. 1998. *European Integration and Supranational Governance*. New York: Oxford.

Santos, Fernanda. 2014. "US and Arizona Yield on Immigration." *New York Times*, 30 May. http://www.nytimes.com/2014/05/31/us/us-and-arizona-yield-on-immigration.html.

Sassen, Saskia. 1996. *Losing Control?* New York: Columbia University Press.

Schenk, Caress. 2015. "Labor Migration in the Eurasian Union: Will Freedom of Movement Trump Domestic Controls?" PONARS Eurasia Policy Memo 378.

Schloenhardt, Andreas. 2009. "United Nations Protocol to Prevent, Suppress and Punish Trafficking in Persons, Especially Women and Children." Brisbane, Australia: Human Trafficking Working Group at the University of Queensland.

Schuman, Robert. 1950. "Speech of 9 May 1950." http://users.belgacombusiness.net/schuman/9May1950.htm.

Scoop Independent News. 2008. "Cablegate: Qatar's Bilateral Labor Agreements." http://www.scoop.co.nz/stories/WL0802/S00570/cablegate-qatars-bilateral-labor-agreements-all-pomp-and.htm.

"Security Agreement with Hungary Focuses on Trafficking and Terrorism." 2014. *Journal of Turkish Weekly*, 23 September. www.turkishweekly.net/news/164444/security-agreement-with-hungary-focuses-on-trafficking-terrorism.html.

Shain, Yossi, and Aharon Barth. 2003. "Diasporas and International Relations Theory." *International Organization* 57 (3): 449–78.

Shalal, Andrea. 2016. "Turkey Will Accept Delay in EU Visa Liberalization to Year-End." Reuters, 4 September. http://www.reuters.com/article/us-europe-migrants-eu-turkey -idUSKCN11A050.

Shelley, Louise. 2010. *Human Trafficking: A Global Perspective*. New York: Cambridge University Press.

Shenon, Philip. 2000. "Feminist Coalition Protests US Stance on Sex Trafficking Treaty." *New York Times*, 13 January.

Sherman, Amy. 2013. "Obama Holds Record for Cracking Down on Employers Who Hire Undocumented Workers, Says Wasserman Schultz." *PolitiFact Florida*, 3 July. http://www .politifact.com/florida/statements/2013/jul/03/debbie-wasserm.

Sherwood, Harriet. 2014. "Ten Years On and Poles Are Glad to Call Britain Home." *Guardian*, 26 April. http://www.theguardian.com/uk-news/2014/apr/26/polish-immigration-britain -cities-elections.

Shotwell, James T., ed. 1934. *The Origins of the International Labor Organization*. New York: Columbia University Press.

Silverman, Maxim. 1992. *Deconstructing the Nation: Immigration, Racism, and Citizenship in Modern France*. London: Routledge.

Simmons, Beth A. 2002. "Capacity, Commitment and Compliance: International Institutions and Territorial Disputes." *Journal of Conflict Resolution* 46 (4): 829–56.

———. 2009. *Mobilizing for Human Rights: International Law in Domestic Politics*. New York: Cambridge University Press.

Simmons, Beth A., and Allison Danner. 2010. "Credible Commitments and the International Criminal Court." *International Organization* 64 (2): 225–56.

Simmons, Beth A., Frank Dobbin, and Geoffrey Garrett. 2006. "Introduction: The International Diffusion of Liberalism." *International Organization* 60 (4): 781–810.

Sölner, Fritz. 1999. "A Note on the Political Economy of Immigration." *Public Choice* 100:245–51.

Sommo Pende, Achille. 2010. "L'Intégration sous-regional en CEMAC à l'épreuve de la liberté de circulation des biens et des personnes." Master's thesis, Université Catholique d'Afrique Central, Mémoire Online, http://www.memoireonline.com/08/10/3812/m_Lintegration -sous-regionale-en-CEMAC—lepreuve-de-la-liberte-de-circulation-des-biens-eto.html.

SOPEMI (Système d'observation permanente des migrations internationales). Various years. "Trends in International Migration." Paris: Organisation for Economic Co-operation and Development.

Spaak, Paul-Henri. 1956. "Brussels Report on the General Common Market." Brussels: Information Service of the High Authority of the European Coal and Steel Community.

"Special Rapporteur on Trafficking in Persons, Especially in Women and Children." 2014. http://www.ohchr.org/EN/Issues/Trafficking/Pages/TraffickingIndex.aspx.

Staring, Richard. 2004. "Facilitating the Arrival of Illegal Immigrants in the Netherlands: Irregular Chain Migration versus Smuggling Chains." *Journal of International Migration and Integration* 5 (3): 273–94.

Statewatch. 2012. "From Tunis in 2003 to Malta in 2012: The First 5 + 5 Dialogue Summit since the Arab Uprising Focuses on Immigration and Security." http://database.statewatch.org /article.asp?aid=31893.

Statistics New Zealand. n.d. "Labour Market." https://www.stats.govt.nz/topics/labour -market.

Stephenson, Sherry, and Gary Hufbauer. 2011. "Labor Mobility." In *Preferential Trade Agree-*

ments: Policies for Development, edited by Jean-Pierre Chauffour and Jean-Christophe Maur, 275–306. New York: IBRD and World Bank.

Stewart, James, Darlene Clark, and Paul F. Clark. 2007. "Migration and Recruitment of Healthcare Professionals: Causes, Consequences, and Policy Responses." Focus Migration Policy Brief 7 (1). http://focus-migration.hwwi.de/The-Migration-and-Re.2496.0.html?&L=1

Stoeker, Sally. 2000. "The Rise in Human Trafficking and the Role of Organized Crime." *Demokratizatsiya* 8 (1): 129–44.

Stolz, Barbara. 2005. "Educating Policymakers and Setting the Criminal Justice Policymaking Agenda: Interest Groups and the 'Victims of Trafficking and Violence Act of 2000.'" *Criminal Justice* 5 (4): 407–30.

———. 2007. "Interpreting the US Human Trafficking Debate through the Lens of Symbolic Politics." *Law and Policy* 29:311–38.

"Study: Many Benefit from Caricom Free Movement." 2011. *Jamaica Observer*, 5 July. http://jamaicaobserver.com/Study:-many-benefit-from-Caricom-free-movement.

Sudarshan, Rohit. 2016. "Understanding the Brexit Vote: The Impact of Polish Immigrants on Euroscepticism." Humanity in Action. http://www.humanityinaction.org/knowledgebase/772-understanding-the-brexit-vote-the-impact-of-polish-immigrants-on-euroscepticism.

Sykes, Alan O. 2013. "International Cooperation on Migration: Theory and Practice." *University of Chicago Law Review* 80 (1): 315–40.

Tapinos, Georges. 1975. *Immigration étrangère en France*. Paris: Presses Universitaires de France.

Taran, Patrick A. 2000. "Human Rights of Migrants: Challenges of the New Decade." *International Migration* 38 (6): 7–51.

Temprano Arroyo, Heliodor. 2002. "Latin America's Integration Process in Light of the European Union's Experience." Economic Paper 173, European Commission, Directorate-General for Economic and Financial Affairs.

Thomas, Manisha, and Ed Schenkenberg van Mierop. 2004. "IOM, Darfur and the Meaning of Undermining (MoU)." *ICVA (International Council of Voluntary Organizations) Talk Back* 6 (1): 1–6.

Thompson, Alexander, and Daniel Verdier. 2014. "Multilateralism, Bilateralism, and Regime Design." *International Studies Quarterly* 58:15–28.

Thouez, Colleen, and Frédérique Channac. 2006. "Shaping International Migration Policy: The Role of Regional Consultative Processes." *West European Politics* 29 (2): 370–87.

Tino, Angelo. 2016. "Marcinelle Mine Disaster Revisited by a Crisis-Shaken Europe." Equal Times, 8 August. https://www.equaltimes.org/marcinelle-mine-disaster-revisited?lang=en#.WZ7snLHMyRs.

Torpey, John. 2000. *The Invention of the Passport: Surveillance, Citizenship, and the State*. New York: Cambridge University Press.

Traité instituant l'Union economique Benelux. 1958. www.wipo.int/edocs/lexdocs/treaties/fr/beu/trt_beu.pdf.

Tralac (Trade Law Centre). 2016. "SADC Legal Texts and Policy Documents." https://www.tralac.org/resources/by-region/sadc.html.

Transatlantic Council on Migration. 2011. *Improving the Governance of International Migration*. Washington, DC: Verlag Bertelsmann Stiftung and Migration Policy Institute.

Traynor, Ian. 2015. "Confusion as Germany Announces Curbs on Syrian Refugees." *Guardian*, 6 November. https://www.theguardian.com/world/2015/nov/06/germany-imposes-surprise-curbs-on-syrian-refugees.

Treaty Constituting the European Coal and Steel Community. 1951. Luxembourg: Publishing Services of the European Communities. http://www.cvce.eu/en/obj/treaty_establishing _the_european_coal_and_steel_community_paris_18_april_1951-en-11a21305-941e-49d7 -a171-ed5be548cd58.html.

Treaty Establishing the European Economic Community. 1957. Luxembourg: Publishing Services of the European Communities. http://www.cvce.eu/en/obj/treaty_establishing_the _european_economic_community_rome_25_march_1957-en-cca6ba28-0bf3-4ce6-8a76 -6b0b3252696e.html.

Treaty of Rome. 1957. http://www.eurotreaties.com/rometreaty.pdf.

Trevena, Paulina. 2009. "'New' Polish Migration to the UK: A Synthesis of Existing Evidence." Working Paper 3, ESRC Centre for Population Change. http://www.cpc.ac.uk/publications /cpc_working_papers/pdf/2009_WP3_New_Polish_Migration_to_the_UK_Trevena.pdf.

Tunander, Ola. 2007. "Nordic Cooperation." Ministry of Foreign Affairs, Norway. Accessed 12 October 2010. http://odin.dep.no/odin/engelsk/norway/foreign/032005-990418/dok -bn.html.

UNCTAD (United Nations Commission on Trade and Development). 2014. "World Investment Report." http://unctad.org/en/PublicationChapters/wir2014ch1_en.pdf.

UNDP (United Nations Development Programme). 1990. "Human Development Report." New York: United Nations. http://hdr.undp.org/en/reports/global/hdr1990.

———. 2009. "Human Development Report." New York: United Nations. http://hdr.undp.org /en/content/human-development-report-2009.

UNECA (United Nations Economic Commission for Africa). 2010. "Assessing Regional Integration in Africa IV." Addis Ababa: UNECA. http://siteresources.worldbank.org /INTAFRREGINICOO/Resources/1587517-1271810608103/UNECA-4th-Africa-RI -Assessment-May2010.pdf.

———. 2016. Africa Regional Integration Index Report 2016. New York: United Nations. http:// www.uneca.org/publications/africa-regional-integration-index-report-2016.

UNHCR (United Nations High Commissioner for Refugees). 2015. "Global Report 2014." www .unhcr.org/gr14/index.xml.

UNICEF. 2014. "Child Protection Information Sheet: Trafficking." Accessed 23 September 2014. www.unicef.org/people/files/Trafficking.pdf.

United Nations. 2016a. "Addressing Large Movements of Refugees and Migrants." http:// refugeesmigrants.un.org.

———. 2016b. "New York Declaration for Refugees and Migrants. Document A/71/L.1." http:// documents-dds-ny.un.org.

United Nations, Department of Economics and Social Affairs, Population Division. 2005. "International Migration Flows to and from Selected Countries: The 2005 Revision."

———. 2013. "International Migrant Stock by Destination and Origin." http://www.un.org/en /development/desa/population/migration/data/estimates2/estimatesorigin.shtml.

United Nations General Assembly. 1948. Universal Declaration of Human Rights. 10 December. http://www.un.org/en/universal-declaration-human-rights/.

———. 1951. Convention Relating to the Status of Refugees. 28 July. United Nations Treaty Series 189:137. http://www.refworld.org/docid/3be01b964.html.

United Nations Office of the High Commissioner for Human Rights. 2014. The Core Human Rights Instruments and Their Monitoring Bodies. http://www.ohchr.org/EN /ProfessionalInterest/Pages/CoreInstruments.aspx.

UNODC (United Nations Office of Drugs and Crime). 2006. "Toolkit to Combat Trafficking in Persons." https://www.unodc.org/pdf/Trafficking_toolkit_Oct06.pdf

———. 2008. "Toolkit to Combat Trafficking in Persons." Accessed 6 June 2016. https://www
.unodc.org/unodc/en/human-trafficking/2008/electronic-toolkit/electronic-toolkit-to
-combat-trafficking-in-persons---index.html.

———. 2009. "Anti–Human Trafficking Manual for Criminal Justice Practitioners. Module 6."
http://www.unodc.org/documents/human-trafficking/TIP_module6_Ebook.pdf.

———. 2010. "Toolkit to Combat Smuggling of Migrants." Accessed 6 June 2016. https://
www.unodc.org/unodc/en/human-trafficking/migrant-smuggling/toolkit-to-combat
-smuggling-of-migrants.html#Overview%20of%20Toolkit.

———. 2014. "UN.GIFT (Global Initiative to Fight Human Trafficking)." http://www.ungift.org.

US Department of Health and Human Services. 2003. "Trafficking Victims Protection Act of
2000 Fact Sheet." http://archive.acf.hhs.gov/trafficking/about/TVFA_2000.pdf.

US Department of Justice. 2004a. "Assessment of US Government Activities to Combat
Trafficking in Persons." Accessed 2 December 2013. http://www.justice.gov/archive/ag
/annualreports/tr2004/us_assessment_2004.pdf.

———. 2004b. "Report to Congress from Attorney General John Ashcroft on US Government Efforts to Combat Trafficking in Persons in Fiscal Year 2003." http://www.justice.gov
/archive/ag/annualreports/tr2003/050104agreporttocongresstvpravo.pdf.

US Department of State. 2006. "Fact Sheet: Distinctions between Human Smuggling and
Human Trafficking 2006." http://www.state.gov/m/ds/hstcenter/90434.htm.

———. 2007. "Trafficking in Persons Report." http://www.state.gov/j/tip/rls/tiprpt/2007/.

van Oudenaren, John. 2005. *Uniting Europe: An Introduction to the European Union*. 2nd ed.
Lanham, MD: Rowman & Littlefield.

Varlez, Louis. 1929a. "General Principles of an International Convention on the Conditions
and Contracts of Employment of Foreign Workers: I." *International Labor Review* 19 (3):
317–37.

———. 1929b. "Migration Problems and the Havana Conference of 1928." *International Labor
Review* 19 (1): 1–19.

Vecoli, Rudolph J. 1995. "The Italian Diaspora 1876–1976." In *Cambridge Survey of World
Migration*, edited by Robin Cohen, 114–22. Cambridge: Cambridge University Press.

Verdier, Daniel. 2008. "Multilateralism, Bilateralism, and Exclusion in the Nuclear Proliferation Regime." *International Organization* 62 (3): 439–76.

Versailles Treaty. 1919. "Part XIII: Articles 405–427." Accessed 15 June 2016. http://avalon.law
.yale.edu/imt/partxiii.asp.

Von Koppenfels, Amanda Klekowski. 2001. "Informal but Effective Regional Consultative
Processes as a Tool in Managing Migration." *International Migration* 39 (6): 61–84.

Wallace, Helen. 2004. "An Institutional Anatomy and Five Policy Models." In *Policy-Making in
the European Union*, 5th ed., edited by Helen Wallace, William Wallace, and Mark Pollack,
49–92. Oxford: Oxford University Press.

Ward, David, and Jane Young. 2000. "New Zealand Immigration to Australia." Canberra,
Australia: Department of Immigration and Multicultural Affairs.

Watson, Noel, Denis Leander-Watson, and Miranda Allbrook. 2007. "Pilot Study to Assess the
Likely Impact of the Free Movement of Labor in the CSME on the OECS Labor Market."
Jamaica: A-Z Information Jamaica Limited.

Webbie, Wendy Chateau. 2015. "Four Years on since the Implementation of the Free Movement of OECS Nationals." www.oecs.org/media-center/press-releases/economic union.

Weil, Patrick. 1991. *La France et ses étrangers: L'Aventure d'une politique de l'immigration de
1938 à nos jours*. Paris: Gallimard.

Weir, Fred. 2013. "Russia Needs Immigrants, but Can It Accept Them?" *Christian Science*

Monitor, 27 October. http://www.csmonitor.com/World/Europe/2013/1027/Russia-needs-immigrants-but-can-it-accept-them.

Weisman, Jonathan. 2007. "Immigration Bill Dies in Senate." *Washington Post*, 29 June, A01.

Wendt, Frantz. 1981. *Cooperation in the Nordic Countries: Achievements and Obstacles*. Stockholm, Sweden: Nordic Council by Almqvist and Wiksell International.

Western, Shaina. 2015. "Hollow Commitments: An Analysis of Treaty Negotiations and Ratification Rate." PhD diss., University of California, Davis.

Wickramasekara, Piyasiri. 2015. "Bilateral Agreements and Memoranda of Understanding on Migration of Low Skilled Workers: A Review." Geneva: International Labor Office.

Wiener, Antje, and Thomas Diez. 2004. *European Integration Theory*. Oxford: Oxford University Press.

Wihtol de Wenden, Catherine. 1988. *Les immigrés et la politique*. Paris: Presses de la Fondation Nationale des Sciences Politiques.

Wilders, Geert, Marine Le Pen, Matteo Salvini, and Heinz-Christian Strache. 2015. "Restoring Europe's Borders and Sovereign Nations." *Wall Street Journal*, 15 October.

Winckler, Onn. 1997. "Immigration Policy of the Gulf Cooperation Council (GCC) States." *Middle Eastern Studies* 33 (3): 480–93.

———. 2010. "Labor Migration in the GCC States: Patterns, Scale, and Policies." In *Migration and the Gulf*, 70–86. Washington, DC: Middle East Institute.

Winer, Jonathan M. 1997. "Alien Smuggling: Elements of the Problem and the US Response." *Transnational Organized Crime* 1 (3): 50–58.

Wong, Tom K. 2012. "Bilateral Cooperation in Immigration Control: Why Sending States Commit to Readmission Agreements." Paper presented at the annual meeting of the International Studies Association, San Diego.

———. 2015. *Rights, Deportation, and Detention in the Age of Immigration Control*. Stanford, CA: Stanford University Press.

Woods, N. 2002. "Global Governance and the Role of Institutions." In Held and McGrew, *Governing Globalization*, 25–45.

World Bank. 2011. "World Development Indicators." Washington, DC: World Bank.

Wright, Greg. 2012. "Skilled Worker Shortage to Worsen." Society for Human Resource Management. http://www.shrm.org/hrdisciplines/global/articles/pages/skilled-worker-shortage-worsens.aspx.

WTO (World Trade Organization). 2013a. "Ministerial Decision of 7 December 2013. Operationalization of the Waiver Concerning Preferential Treatment to Services and Service Suppliers of Least-Developed Countries." WT/MIN(13)/43/WT/L/918.

———. 2013b. "WTO Members and Accession Candidates." Geneva: WTO.

Yamada, Miwa. 2012. "Comparative Analysis of Bilateral Memoranda on Anti–Human Trafficking Cooperation between Thailand and Three Neighboring Countries: What Do the Origin and Destination States Agree Upon?" IDE Discussion Paper 349. http://ir.ide.go.jp/dspace/bitstream/2344/1140/1/ARRIDE_Discussion_No.349_yamada.pdf.

Yen, Hope. 2012. "US Sees Sustained Drop in Illegal Entries." *Washington Times*, 6 December.

Zhang, Sheldon X. 2007. *Smuggling and Trafficking in Human Beings: All Roads Lead to America*. Westport, CT: Praeger.

Zimmerman, Klaus F. 2004. "European Labor Mobility: Challenges and Potentials." Discussion Paper of DIW Berlin 460, German Institute for Economic Research.

Zolberg, Aristide. 2006. *A Nation by Design*. Cambridge, MA: Russell Sage Foundation.

INDEX

The letter *f* following a page number denotes a figure. The letter *t* following a page number denotes a table.

www.ingramcontent.com/pod-product-compliance
Lightning Source LLC
Chambersburg PA
CBHW021119270326
41929CB00009B/958